BRITANNIA SECONDARY SCHOOL
1001 COTTON DRIVE
VANCOUVER, B.C.   V5L 3T4

Year	Name of Student	Class
90/91	Christina Chan Rm. 305	1/c

OUR LAND: BUILDING THE WEST

VIVIEN BOWERS
STAN GARROD

General Editor
Peter Massiah

Consultants
Ken Cooper
Sean McKierahan

gage EDUCATIONAL PUBLISHING COMPANY
A DIVISION OF CANADA PUBLISHING CORPORATION
TORONTO ONTARIO CANADA

Copyright © 1987 Gage Educational Publishing Company
A Division of Canada Publishing Corporation
Toronto • Ontario • Canada

Canadian Cataloguing in Publication Data

Bowers, Vivien, 1951 –
    Our land : building the west

For use in grade 10.
Includes index.
ISBN 0-7715-8165-3

1. Canada—History—19th century. 2. Canada, Western—History. 3. British Columbia—History.
4. Canada—Economic conditions. 5. British Columbia—Economic conditions. I. Garrod, Stan. II. Title.

FC170.B69 1987   971   C87-093243-8
F1026.B69 1987

Cover: Born in Victoria in 1871, Emily Carr developed a style of painting uniquely Canadian. This painting, done about 1912 and titled "Sawmills, Vancouver," demonstrates her technique.
(Emily Carr, 1871-1945, "Sawmills, Vancouver" c. 1912, oil on canvas, 36.0 × 45.5 cm, Gift of Dr. & Mrs. Max Stern, Dominion Gallery, Montreal, The McMichael Canadian Collection, 1979.26.2)

ISBN 0-7715-8165-3

Project Editor: Bruce Bartlett
Co-ordinating Editor: Graham Draper
Maps and Diagrams: James Loates *illustrating*
Book Design: Michael van Elsen Design Inc.

3 4 5 6 BP 93 92 91 90 89

Written, Printed, and Bound in Canada.

Acknowledgments

The publisher is grateful to the many individuals and organizations who assisted in the preparation of this book. In particular, the helpful contributions made by the following are acknowledged:

W.J.B. Devitt, CIP Inc.;
Kathie Gibson, B.C. Federation of Agriculture;
Harold Halvorson;
Wayne Shinners, Int. North Pacific Fisheries Commission;
George Sled, Victoria Park Secondary School;
Sylvia van Kirk, University of Toronto.

Illustrations acknowledgments are on page 432.

Contents

Preface

To understand fully groups of people or nations, we must know their past. What events have created this nation? How did the events shape the behavior of the people? Through a knowledge of the past in general and the history of a people specifically, we can begin to understand the present and predict implications of actions now taken. Similarly, to appreciate the forces acting on a society we must know their position in relation to other people, nations and events. Where is a place located in the world? How does the location of a people or nation influence their actions? How will their location limit or invite future developments? Knowing their geography helps us to understand a group of people.

Aspects of history and geography are brought together in schools as social studies, a subject that combines questions about time and place into investigations of societies. Social studies also typically includes topics drawn from the other social sciences: economics, sociology, anthropology, political science, and so on. Viewed as a whole, social studies may seem a bewildering array of topics and techniques without a clear focus. On closer inspection though, it becomes a subject area with tremendous scope for investigation and potential for understanding societies. Throughout *Our Land: Building the West*, a social studies approach has been used to study the past and the present of our own people, the Canadian society.

A central theme of *Our Land: Building the West* is the examination of the factors that have shaped, and continued to shape, Canada and Canadians. As you proceed through the book, you will identify ways in which Canadians have interacted with our physical environment—how it has influenced our behavior and how the actions of Canadians have modified the environment. You will discover that much of Canada's economy has been built on the exploitation of natural resources harvested from our environment.

A second major theme explores Canada's cultural heritage. The social history of this country has been shaped by a cultural diversity that is still ongoing. At times this diversity has led to political pressures that have only been released through confrontation or rebellion.

A third important theme focusses on Canada's role in a changing world. Increasingly, Canada's economic wellbeing is directly tied to the relationships we develop with other countries throughout the world. Our trading partnerships are critical in maintaining international relationships.

Our Land: Building the West has been organized into four units of study. The first two are historic in nature. Unit 1, titled "Action in the East," investigates the political, social and economic forces in eastern Canada following 1800 that led to Confederation in 1867. The five chapters in this unit show that the British colonies in North America were very much influenced by events throughout the world. The second unit, chapters 6 to 10, focusses on developments in western Canada, both before and after Confederation. This unit devotes a substantial portion of its space to the growth of British Columbia, first as separate British colonies and then as a province of the Dominion of Canada.

The third unit of study is strongly economic in character, exploring Canada's development as an industrial nation. You will see how the Canadian economy has evolved over time and how such change has influenced workers in our society. Two chapters, chapters 13 and 14, explore in detail Canada's trading relationship with other parts of the world, the United States and the Pacific Rim.

The final unit is titled "British Columbia Makes a Living." Each of the seven chapters investigates an aspect of British Columbia's economy. The importance of the resource base is shown as are the cultural patterns that result from such an economic foundation. Problems and issues particular to each of B.C.'s major industries show present-day patterns and raise questions about the future. Case studies bring the reader closer to the issues being studied.

As you read through this book you will encounter words in **boldface type**. This signals you that meanings of the terms are expanded in the glossary on pages 424-426. The index on pages 427-431 will be useful to you to find topics in the book. Good luck with your studies.

UNIT 1
ACTION IN THE EAST

Chapter 1

North America to 1815

Have you ever wondered:

- Why Canada has two official languages?
- Why Canada's head of state is a king or queen?
- Why Canada is so much like the United States, but still remains a separate nation?

Some of the answers to these questions can be found in conflicts that took place two hundred years ago and more. This chapter briefly reviews these conflicts and their impact on Canada's history to 1815.

First, you will survey the conflict between Britain and France for control of North America, a struggle which ended with the British conquest of New France in 1760, and led to the Quebec Act of 1774. Next, you will review the conflict between Britain and thirteen of its North American colonies, which resulted in the American Revolution. You will also briefly review the flight of colonists still loyal to Britain from the newly formed United States, examining the impact of the Loyalists on the Quebec colony and the problems that led to the Constitutional Act of 1791. Finally you will review the War of 1812 between the United States and Britain, particularly its impact on Britain's remaining colonies in North America.

As you read this chapter, consider the following key questions:

- How did the British conquest of Quebec affect its colonies to the south?
- Why did thirteen of Britain's North American colonies rebel against the mother country and set up their own country?
- Who were the Loyalists?
- What was the Constitutional Act of 1791?
- What role did the War of 1812 play in shaping Canada's early history?

The British Conquest of New France

Between 1600 and 1760, France and Britain were locked in an ongoing rivalry over Acadia, Newfoundland and Quebec. This rivalry would lead to war, resulting in a British victory that turned most of French-speaking North America into a colony of the British Empire.

War Over North America

A major cause of British-French rivalry was the desire of each nation to control the rich resources of North America. The cod-fishing grounds off Newfoundland and Acadia and the fur trade along the St. Lawrence River were sources of great wealth to the nations that controlled them.

While France and Britain fought over these areas, other Europeans were settling the lands along the Atlantic coast to the south. During the 1600s, the Dutch, Swedes, Danes, and Spanish all established colonies on the east coast of what is today the United States. By 1700, Britain had gained control over all of these colonies, except Florida. Large numbers of British colonists had come to North America and settlement was expanding rapidly.

To the north, much of what is now eastern Canada was still under French control. Unlike the lands to the south, however, New France and Acadia had few colonists by 1700. By the time the French began in earnest to settle the St. Lawrence River Valley, they were greatly outnumbered by the British colonists to the south.

War between Britain and France broke out in the mid-1700s over the resource-rich Ohio River Valley south of the Great Lakes. There, French and British merchants were competing for the Indian fur trade. In 1749, France claimed the Ohio Valley. A chain of French forts was constructed to block British advances into the area. Fighting began between the French and the British in the Ohio Valley in 1754. Then, in 1756, the Seven Years War broke out, locking the British and French empires in armed conflict in Europe, India and North America.

French strategy in the Seven Years War was to seek a decisive victory in Europe, while the British chose to launch an all-out offensive against the French in North America. By 1757, the British had gained control over the Ohio Valley. Weakened by a naval blockade and prolonged siege, the French fortress at Louisbourg fell to the British in 1758.

Although his British forces were victorious, General James Wolfe was mortally wounded on the Plains of Abraham. Study this illustration. Was the artist sympathetic to the British, or not? Explain your answer.

After a two-month siege by British forces, the city of Quebec fell in 1759. There, on the Plains of Abraham, the army of General James Wolfe defeated the French forces led by General Louis-Joseph Montcalm. The French at Montreal, surrounded by British soldiers and artillery, surrendered in September 1760. The conquest of New France was complete. In 1763, the Treaty of Paris ended the Seven Years War. Under the terms of this treaty, New France became part of the British Empire.

1. What was the major cause of rivalry between Britain and France in North America?
2. Where and when did the British complete their conquest of New France?

The Quebec Act

For many people in France, the loss of New France was a blessing. The colony of New France had never become self-supporting, nor had it ever attracted a large number of settlers. French kings and their advisors had usually shown little interest in the colony. For all of its rich resources, it had cost France more than it had returned in fish and furs. A leading French writer of the eighteenth century,

Voltaire, had called it "just a few acres of snow." To the people of France, New France was a distant and isolated wilderness.

New France was, however, a peopled wilderness. By 1750, the settlers of New France and their Indian allies numbered several hundred thousand people, among them some 65 000 of European origin. By this time, most of the settlers and their families had been born in North America and had few ties to France. In their isolation, they had come to think of themselves not so much as French but as *les Canadiens*, the people of Canada. Quebec was their home: in it they had created a distinctive way of life for themselves. As French-speaking Roman Catholics, the Canadiens differed in both language and religion from their British conquerors. Their laws and their customs were unlike those of the British colonists to the south of Canada.

Uncertain about their future, the Canadiens worried about what would happen to their way of life under British rule. The conquest of New France had also created problems for the British. How could they best govern a people so different from themselves?

With the end of the war, British military rule in Quebec was replaced by a civilian government. Control now lay in the hands of a governor appointed by Britain and the members of his council. The Proclamation of 1763, which created the Quebec colony, included a promise that Quebec would receive English laws and an elected Assembly as quickly as possible. The British hoped that these promises would draw English-speaking settlers from the Atlantic Colonies to Quebec. Neither the Canadiens nor the few hundred newly arrived British merchants and officials in the Quebec colony were satisfied with this arrangement.

Protection for the Canadien way of life, including traditional laws and the Roman Catholic religion, was also promised by the Proclamation of 1763. But, this protection was so vague that most Canadiens remained fearful about the future of their culture under British rule.

British colonists were upset because Governor James Murray appeared in no hurry to introduce an elected Assembly. The colonists wanted to be able to elect representatives, make their own laws and shape the culture of the colony. In Britain and its colonies, at this time, Roman Catholics were not allowed to take part in political life. Creation of an elected Assembly would give the small number of British residents control over Quebec. Governor Murray recognized that the introduction of an elected Assembly could create serious conflicts between the Canadiens and the British colonists in Quebec. His refusal to put this aspect of the Proclamation into effect would cost him his job.

By 1767, another factor became important in this issue. Britain was becoming alarmed by the increasing friction between the American colonies to the south and the mother country. Sir Guy Carleton, the British governor of Quebec from 1766 to 1770, feared that this friction might lead to a revolt in the British-American colonies. He realized that, should such a revolt occur, Britain needed to have loyal subjects in Quebec. When Carleton returned to London in 1770, he tried to persuade the British government that the distinctive Quebec way of life had to be retained if the colony was to stay within the British Empire. He claimed that the Canadiens would never be **assimilated**; they would never become English-speaking Protestants. French laws, customs, language and the Roman Catholic religion had to be guaranteed by British law.

Carleton was not acting out of humanistic concern for the Canadiens. He was an aristocratic Protestant and had a very poor understanding of Quebec society. Carleton believed that the *seigneurs* of Quebec were like the landed gentry of Britain and that the priests helped to keep the common people in their proper place. By guaranteeing the power of the *seigneurs* and the clergy, argued Carleton, these leaders would ensure loyalty to Britain from the people of Quebec.

The result of Carleton's forceful arguments was the Quebec Act of 1774. This statute gave a unique status to the Canadiens within the British Empire. It allowed them to retain their language, Roman Catholic religion and their **civil laws**, while providing English **criminal law** for the colony.

The Quebec Act also enlarged the territorial limits of the colony beyond those set out in the Proclamation of 1763 (see map page 9). Lands formerly reserved for Native peoples, including the Ohio Valley, were now to be part of Quebec. The inclusion of the Ohio Valley as part of Quebec would block the westward expansion of the increasingly troublesome colonies, such as Virginia, to the south. Control over the valuable fur trade would now go to the merchants of Quebec City and Montreal. To the east, Labrador was attached to Quebec, giving the colony control over rich fishing and sealing grounds.

The Quebec Act made no provision for an elected Assembly. The colony would continue to be ruled by a governor appointed by the British government. A council of local leaders would advise and assist the governor.

Sir Guy Carleton, like his predecessor, James Murray, grew to see the Canadiens as potential British citizens rather than enemies. He resisted moves that would give English-speaking settlers complete control in the colony.

THE QUEBEC ACT

The following are excerpts from the Quebec Act of 1774, one of the most important documents in Canadian history. It guaranteed the rights of the Canadiens to practice the Roman Catholic faith (referred to as "the Church of Rome"), allowed the continued use of French **civil law** (referred to as "the laws of Canada"), and decreed that English **criminal law**, which was less harsh than that of France, would apply in the Quebec colony.

...it is hereby declared, that his Majesty's subjects, professing the religion of the Church of Rome of and in the...Province of Quebec, may have, hold and enjoy the free exercise of the Church of Rome...and that the clergy of the said Church may hold, receive, and enjoy, their accustomed dues and rights, with respect to such persons only as shall profess the said religion.

And be it further enacted...that all his Majesty's *Canadian* subjects, within the province of Quebec...may also hold and enjoy their properties and possessions, together with all customs and usages relative thereto, and all other civil rights...all matters of controversy, relative to property and civil rights, resort shall be had to the laws of *Canada*, as the rule for the decision of same....

And whereas the certainty and lenity of the criminal law of *England*, and the benefits and advantages resulting from the use of it, have been sensibly felt by the inhabitants, from an experience of more than nine years, during which it has been uniformly administered, that the same shall continue to be administered, and shall be observed as the law of the Province of Quebec.

Again, the failure to create an elected Assembly angered the British population of the colony. But the British government had little choice. An elected Assembly would have meant giving the right to vote both to Quebec's English-speaking Protestant minority and to the French-speaking Catholic majority. The Roman Catholic population of Great Britain at this time did not enjoy the right to vote, so to allow Roman Catholics in Quebec to vote would create problems for the British government at home. Yet to deny Quebec's Roman Catholic population the vote, while giving it to the British minority, would have given a tiny group power over the vast majority.

The Canadiens, particularly the *seigneurs* and the clergy, reacted favorably to the Quebec Act and the safeguards it provided for their traditional way of life. For their part, the English merchants of the colony were pleased by the expansion of Quebec's territory. They saw the potential wealth to be gained from the resources of Labrador and the Ohio Valley.

1. In your own words, explain how and why Guy Carleton's arguments resulted in the Quebec Act of 1774.
2. Summarize the key provisions of the Quebec Act. Why did Carleton insist on these provisions? Which provisions benefited the Canadiens? the British merchants?

The American Revolution and its Consequences

Within a year of the Quebec Act, the American Revolution began. The following is a brief review of the causes and key events of the rebellion which greatly reduced Britain's empire in North America.

The Growing Crisis in the Thirteen Colonies

Separated from Britain by the Atlantic, with long traditions of governing themselves through their own elected assemblies, the thirteen colonies developed their own identity and way of life. This identity strengthened as the colonies grew in population and prosperity through the early years of the eighteenth century. By the 1770s, many of the colonists had come to see themselves more as Americans than as British subjects. Others, however, continued to feel close ties to Britain and loyalty to the mother country. Their loyalties to Britain were soon severely tested.

The British government had been unhappy with the colonists' military effort during the Seven Years War. The British regular army did most of the fighting that brought about the conquest of New France. Few colonists had volunteered to join the fight.

Even more infuriating to the British was the fact that merchants in places such as Boston continued to trade illegally with the French in Canada and Acadia throughout the war, as they had done for half a century or more. The British reaction was to enforce vigorously the Navigation Acts, the first of what the American colonists came to call the "Intolerable Acts." The Navigation Acts required that trade between Britain and the colonies be carried on British ships. The Royal Navy was called in to stop smuggling and illegal trading

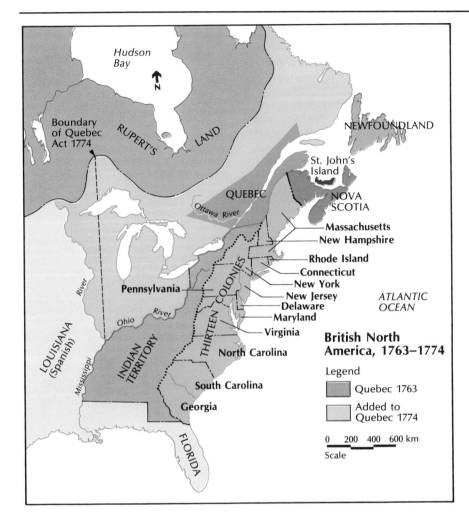

British North America, 1763–1774

Legend

Quebec 1763

Added to Quebec 1774

0   200   400   600 km

Scale

After 1774, Quebec occupied a major part of the continent, limiting the westward expansion of the colonists from the thirteen colonies.

by colonial merchants. The Admiralty Court of the Navy tried and convicted the colonial smugglers without the trial-by-jury procedure to which the colonists were accustomed. The colonists argued that Britain not only was deliberately restricting colonial trade, but also was denying them the basic right of trial-by-jury.

Britain also took steps to meet the growing costs of defending the North American colonies. The first was the Stamp Act of 1765. Stamps now had to be affixed to legal documents and newspapers to certify that a tax had been paid. It was the first tax to be levied directly by Parliament on the North American colonies. Angry colonial opposition to this second "Intolerable Act" led to its repeal a year later.

The Quartering Act of 1765, another "Intolerable Act," further angered the colonists. It required them to use their homes to provide room and board for British soldiers. In 1767, Britain imposed yet another "Intolerable Act," the Townshend Acts (so named for the cabinet minister who had sponsored them). This required colonists to pay duties on tea, glass, paints and paper imported from Britain. Colonial leaders reacted by urging a boycott of British goods. Parts of the Townshend Acts were then repealed, but the import tax on tea remained.

This illustration of "The Boston Massacre" was drawn by Paul Revere, the American revolutionary, from reports of the incident. How did Revere portray the British in the picture?

The colonists' opposition to the Stamp Act and Townshend Acts stemmed from their frustration at being taxed by a government in which they had no representation. At a New York meeting to protest the Stamp Act, colonial leaders coined the slogan, "taxation without representation is tyranny." In Boston in 1770, a clash with British troops resulted in the deaths of some colonists during a protest over the Townshend Acts. This event became known as the "Boston Massacre." Three years later, Boston was the site of another major confrontation. As a protest against the tea tax, a band of colonists threw bales of tea from British ships into Boston Harbor. The British government's reaction to the "Boston Tea Party" was swift. It closed Boston Harbor and suspended the Massachusetts Assembly, and in 1774, introduced a new Quartering Act which saw British troops housed in Boston homes.

The Quebec Act, passed the year after the "Boston Tea Party," was the final "Intolerable Act." Colonial leaders in Massachusetts, Pennsylvania and Virginia were outraged by it. Three issues in particular upset them: the blockage of westward expansion of the American colonies into the Ohio Valley; the protection given to the Roman Catholic religion; and the failure to provide an elected Assembly for the Quebec colony. These features of the Quebec Act provided more fuel to the already smouldering fire of rebellion in the American colonies.

In October of 1774, the Continental Congress, a meeting of leaders from the thirteen American colonies, was held in Philadelphia. Again, the colonists called for a boycott of British goods. The Congress discussed the formation of a union of British North American colonies. To the north of the thirteen colonies, however, although they were invited, neither Quebec nor Nova Scotia showed much willingness to become part of the proposed union.

Three things made Quebec and Nova Scotia different from the American colonies to the south. First, they had only been British colonies for a short period of time: Quebec since 1763, and Nova Scotia since 1713. Places such as Massachusetts had been British colonies for a century and a half. Second, the leading figures in Quebec and Nova Scotia were, for the most part, not outspokenly rebellious. The kinds of frictions between colonial leaders and the British government that existed in the thirteen colonies were absent in Quebec and Nova Scotia. Finally, isolation played a role. Quebec and Nova Scotia were, to some extent, cut off from the colonies to the south. Centres such as Montreal, Quebec City and Halifax were several days' journey from Boston, New York, and Philadelphia, the important centres to the south.

American resentment became armed rebellion in 1775. The colonists of Massachusetts were the first to take up muskets against the British. Rebels from the other colonies quickly joined them.

The rebels believed that they needed to control Nova Scotia and Quebec in order to deny Britain a base for military operations against the thirteen colonies. At first the rebels hoped these colonies would join their revolution. Three American agents, one of whom was Benjamin Franklin, had visited Quebec in 1774. They returned with a report that Quebec was "seething with sedition." However, the Continental Congress of 1774 had been marked by vehement attacks on the privileges extended to Quebec's Roman Catholic population. These actions overweighed the Congress's appeal to anti-British sentiment among the Canadiens. At the same time, the merchant class in Quebec had not been greatly affected by the

REPUBLICAN GOVERNMENT

The victorious rebels created a new nation, the United States of America, with a republican form of government. A republic has a democratic form of government that takes its authority from the people it governs. The people of a republic elect the head of state, the president, as well as the lawmakers. The Constitution of the United States, adopted in 1783, limited the powers of the American president and the length of time he could hold office.

By contrast, Britain in 1775 was a monarchy. The head of state, the king, was not elected but held the position by right of birth. The British monarch theoretically had absolute powers. However, these powers had been steadily restricted since the signing of the Magna Carta in the thirteenth century. In the eighteenth century, the king ruled through the support he received from the powerful leaders of British society.

"intolerable acts" to which their American counterparts so vehemently objected.

Having failed to persuade Quebec to join their cause, the Americans decided to invade it. Montreal fell to an advancing American army travelling north along Lake Champlain and the Richelieu River. The army then proceeded on to Quebec City. On New Year's Eve, 1775, a second American force from Maine joined them and together the armies attacked the walled city, but failed to break its defences. They then held the city under siege throughout the winter. During the siege, the Americans tried to convince the Canadiens to join the rebellion against their British conquerors. Yet, for the most part, the people of Quebec remained indifferent to both sides in the conflict.

In the spring of 1776 the British brought supplies and reinforcements to Quebec by ship. The American armies, disease-ridden and short of ammunition and food, had to retreat southward from Quebec. As well, most of the American soldiers were farmers who had to return to their land for spring planting. The British forces pursued them, but not vigorously enough. The Americans were able to regroup and resupply their troops. Then, in October of 1777, they inflicted a crushing defeat on the British at Saratoga, halfway between Montreal and New York City. But the Americans realized the difficulty in winning a war fought in Quebec and changed their strategy. They no longer sought to conquer Quebec, but now concentrated on driving the British forces out of the thirteen colonies.

On July 4, 1776, colonial leaders meeting in Philadelphia had issued the "Declaration of Independence." They were now firmly committed to breaking all ties with the mother country and to establishing an independent **republic.**

The American Revolution continued for five years following the Declaration of Independence. After the Battle of Saratoga, the balance swung more and more to the American side. The final defeat for the British came at Yorktown, Virginia, in 1781. There, the defeated General Cornwallis surrendered to the victorious Americans, ending the revolution.

The Treaty of Paris, negotiated by the United States, France and Britain, was signed in 1783, formally ending the war. The French, who had given military aid to the thirteen colonies, were still hopeful of regaining lost lands in North America. They wished to see an independent but weak United States, forced to rely on France for support. The British, realizing they were in no position to fight another costly war to protect Canada, adopted a conciliatory position towards the Americans. In addition to recognizing the independence of the United States, Britain gave up much of the Ohio territory to the new country. The Americans were finally free to pursue their long-thwarted dream of westward expansion.

The American Revolution changed the character of North America. A new nation had been created, greatly shrinking the size and strength of Britain's empire in North America. The response of the Canadiens to the Revolution had shown that Quebec would remain a distinctive community on the North American continent, neither British nor American. Furthermore, the Revolution had created an important new group in North America, the United Empire Loyalists.

1. Give four examples of the "Intolerable Acts" that caused the thirteen colonies to rebel against Britain.
2. How did the system of government in the newly created United States differ from the British system of government?

The Loyalists

Many of the American colonists remained loyal to Britain throughout the rebellion. After the war, Benjamin Franklin, one of the leading figures in the new United States, estimated that only one-third of the colonists had supported the rebels. One-third had stayed loyal to Britain and the other third stayed neutral, waiting to see who won.

Those loyal to Britain were harassed by the rebels, both during and after the war. As a result, many fled the American colonies. During the Revolution, there was a slow but steady movement of Loyalist refugees into Quebec and Nova Scotia. After the war, more than 100 000 colonists still loyal to Britain left the United States. Nearly 60 000 went to Britain or the Caribbean; the rest came north by ship to Nova Scotia or Quebec during the period 1781-1783. Over the next decade, another 10 000 or so would make their way overland into the area between Niagara Falls and Montreal.

The United Empire Loyalists, as these refugees came to call themselves, represented a wide range of people in the American colonies. Among their numbers were wealthy merchants and professionals, tradespeople, pioneer farming families, black slaves and freemen and a nation of Loyalist Iroquois Native people. Most were rewarded for their loyalty with food rations, a little money and, above all, free land.

13

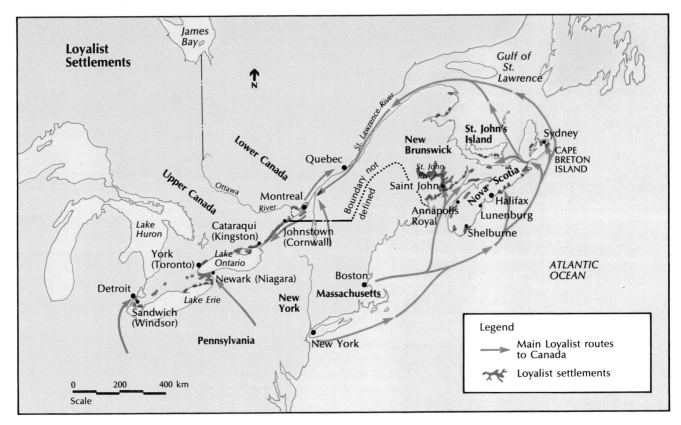

The St. John River Valley attracted many of the Loyalists from the rebellious American colonies. Other Loyalists settled along the coast of present-day Nova Scotia and Prince Edward Island, and along the St. Lawrence River and the lower Great Lakes.

The majority of the Loyalists settled in the Maritimes. Some settled in Nova Scotia, while others began to clear lands on the other side of the Bay of Fundy, along the St. John River. At the mouth of the river, where previously there had been only a fort and some small trading outposts, Loyalists founded the city of Saint John. Small groups of Loyalists received land grants on St. John's Island (now Prince Edward Island) and on Cape Breton Island. Many of the Loyalists had lived in cities such as Boston and New York and found the process of clearing land and building homes and farms very difficult. However, the land was fertile, there were rich stands of timber, and many soon prospered. New industries such as sawmilling were established to serve the greatly increased population of the Maritimes.

Population increase brought with it problems for the British government. The colonists along the north shore of the Bay of Fundy were used to having their own elected assemblies in the colonies from which they had fled. They did not want to be governed from distant and hard-to-reach Halifax. In 1784, Britain created the new colony of New Brunswick with its own elected Assembly. In 1820, Cape Breton would become part of the Nova Scotia colony, while St. John's Island, a separate colony since 1769, was renamed Prince Edward Island in 1799.

Many of the Loyalists who settled in Quebec received land grants in the Eastern Townships south of Montreal. Others were given land along the St. Lawrence and on the shores of the Great Lakes in the western portion of the Quebec colony. Most of the Loyalists who settled in the colony were experienced farmers. By 1790, there were several thousand Loyalist farm families in the western area of the Quebec colony. Towns grew up at Niagara, York (present-day Toronto) and Kingston.

These western Loyalist settlers were chiefly English-speaking Protestants. All were used to living in colonies with elected assemblies, yet the Quebec Act was still the constitution for this largest of Britain's North American colonies. The Loyalists became increasingly frustrated both with the lack of an elected Assembly in Quebec and with the traditional French laws used in the colony to govern land and property. They wanted a system of government that was more like the one they had known in the American colonies.

1. In your own words, explain who the Loyalists were, where they settled, and how they were different from the Canadiens.
2. What problems did the arrival of the Loyalists create for the British government?

The Constitutional Act of 1791

In 1791, Britain split the Quebec colony. The western portion newly settled by the Loyalists became the colony of Upper Canada, covering the southern portion of what is today the province of Ontario. The area east of the Ottawa River, long settled by the Canadiens, became the colony of Lower Canada. The colonies took their names from their location along the St. Lawrence River. Upper Canada was the up-stream colony, while Lower Canada straddled the lower reaches of the river.

In addition to its division of the Quebec colony, the Constitutional Act created elected assemblies for both Upper and Lower

Canada. The power of these assemblies was, however, quite limited. Britain's leaders felt that the legislatures in the thirteen colonies had been too strong. To prevent the same situation from arising in the Canadas, the Constitutional Act gave the colonial governors, appointed by the British, a great deal more power than was held by the elected assemblies.

Just as before 1791, the governor would choose the members of his Executive Council. These members would assist him in ruling the colony. The members of the elected Assembly would vote on matters of taxation for the colony, but most other laws would be made by the governors and their Executive Councils. Even laws passed by the Assembly could be turned down by the governor. The British government could overturn any law passed by a colonial elected Assembly within two years of its passage.

The Roman Catholic religion and the traditional civil laws of the Canadiens, both protected under the Quebec Act, were also made part of the new constitution. At the same time, the Maritime colonies were given governmental systems similar to that set out in the Constitutional Act. In short, the new constitutional framework was intended to prevent rebellion and to bring stability to British North America.

1. Why did the Constitutional Act of 1791 divide the Quebec colony into two? How and why did it limit the powers of the elected assemblies?

The War of 1812-1814

The peace between Britain and the United States, following the American War of Independence, was short-lived. In the summer of 1812, hostilities again broke out, largely as a result of two other conflicts: the Napoleonic Wars in Europe and the so-called "Indian Wars" in the western territories of the United States.

Britain and France had been intermittently at war since the beginning of the French Revolution in 1789. They had been steadily at war since 1803. As the armies of Napoleon, the French Emperor, swept across Europe, Britain found itself relying more and more heavily on naval power to control French ambitions. In the early stages of this war, American traders had done a brisk business with both sides in the European conflict. But as Britain tightened its naval blockade of Europe's Atlantic coast, American trading vessels became subject to British harassment. Britain insisted on stopping and searching American vessels in an attempt to find deserters from its navy. Such British action created great resentment among many Americans.

To the west, the boundaries of the American republic had been greatly expanded by the "Louisiana Purchase." Sold to the United States by Napoleon in 1803, the Louisiana Territory effectively doubled the size of the United States. As American settlers moved west to occupy these new lands, they met armed resistance from groups of Native peoples. Tecumseh, chief of the Shawnees, formed an alliance of these groups to block the settlers. There was some evidence that the British supported these "Indian wars" by supplying Tecumseh and his allies with guns and ammunition.

Angered by this interference by Britain in United States expansion plans, a group of influential members of the United States Congress, known as the "War Hawks," argued strongly for war against Britain. Their ambition was to remove the British influence on the western frontier and to seize the British colonies to the north. In June of 1812, the War Hawks carried a Congressional vote resulting in a declaration of war on Britain. With a United States population of 8 million pitted against a mere half million in British North America, claimed the War Hawks, an American victory would be both quick and easy.

On October 13, 1812, hostile American forces crossed the Niagara River at Queenston. They were met by British and Canadian forces, led by General Isaac Brock, who successfully defended the heights from the invaders.

In fact, there was no victory. The states on the eastern seaboard felt that war with Britain would make an already-difficult situation even worse. These states remained essentially neutral throughout the war, thus removing any real threat to New Brunswick and Nova Scotia. Most of the battles that were fought in 1812 and 1813 were in the St. Lawrence-Great Lakes area, primarily on or near the Niagara Peninsula. The war in effect produced a stalemate. While regular British troops did most of the fighting, volunteer militia units in both the Canadas also played a role. Upper Canadian settlers, many of them recent immigrants from the United States, ignored American appeals to "throw off the British yoke." Instead, they took up arms against their would be "liberators." In Lower Canada, Canadien militia units also took up arms against the invaders. This behavior was in marked contrast to the Canadien indifference during the American Revolution of 1776-1783.

This map shows the major battles of the War of 1812. What role might geography play in the selection of battle sites?

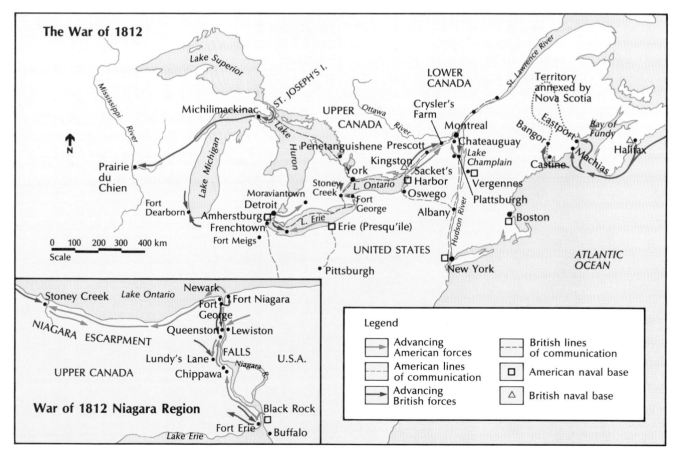

With the temporary end of the Napoleonic Wars in 1814, the British naval blockade was removed from Europe and British troops were freed for action in North America. With both sides weary of war, an armistice was signed on Christmas Eve, 1814.

The war had shown how difficult it was for Britain to defend Canada from American attack. Britain had found the cost of the war very high. As well, the war had pointed up a division between the Canadas. Most Upper Canadians had fought as British subjects, supporting Britain in its war with the Americans. Lower Canadians, on the other hand, had fought as Canadiens protecting their homeland from invasion. Both sides felt justifiable pride after the American invasion had been turned back. But their pride was based on different ideas about Canada. These differences widened the split between the Canadiens and the British in North America.

1. Describe three factors that contributed to the beginning of the War of 1812.
2. Explain why the much larger American forces were not able to take over the Canadas.

Summary

The rivalry between France and Britain for control over North America established two distinctive ways of life there. The French-speaking Canadiens were concentrated along the St. Lawrence River. A second French-speaking group, the Acadians, lived in what are now the Maritime Provinces. British colonies were established along the Atlantic coast of North America from Newfoundland to Georgia.

Following the conquest of New France in 1759-1760, the British decided that the traditional way of life of the Canadiens should be protected in order to ensure their loyalty. Protection for their Roman Catholic religion, their language and their traditional property laws was included in the Quebec Act of 1774.

To the south of Quebec, thirteen of the North American colonies were growing increasingly unhappy with British rule. A series of measures passed by the British government helped to push these colonies into open rebellion in 1775, leading to the American Revolution and the creation of the United States of America. After several years of war, the British were driven from the thirteen colonies.

The flight of the Loyalists from the United States greatly increased the population of the remaining British colonies in North America. It also created a number of problems for French- and English-speaking colonists. The Constitutional Act of 1791 attempted to resolve these problems by dividing the Quebec colony into Lower Canada and Upper Canada. It also provided elected assemblies for the two new colonies, but the power of these assemblies was very limited.

In the early nineteenth century, tensions between Britain and the United States, resulting from the Napoleonic Wars in Europe and the Indian Wars in the American West, led to war in 1812. In this war, the Americans failed in their attempt to conquer Britain's North American colonies. Events both in Britain and in the United States played a significant role in shaping developments in Canada.

REVIEW

Checking Back

1. Write one or two sentences to summarize the significance of each of the following.
   Sir Guy Carleton   Constitutional Act
   Quebec Act   War Hawks
   American Revolution   War of 1812
   United Empire Loyalists

2. (a) In 1770, Sir Guy Carleton claimed that the Canadiens would never be assimilated. Explain, in your own words, what it means for a people to become assimilated.
   (b) Reread this chapter to find three pieces of evidence to support Carleton's position that a guarantee of Canadien rights would ensure Canadien loyalty to the British.

Using Your Knowledge

3. At times, historians try to imagine how Canada would be different if the past could be changed. Write one or two paragraphs describing what Canada would be like today if the British government had decided to change the Quebec Act to meet the demands of the Thirteen Colonies.

4. (a) In your study of the American Revolution, you learned that the Thirteen Colonies sent representatives to Quebec to try and convince the people they should join the rebellion. Write a list of the arguments you think the representatives might have used to persuade the people of Quebec to rebel against British rule.
   (b) What counterarguments might the people of Quebec have offered?

5. (a) People who flee their country in time of war or to escape persecution are often called refugees. Is it correct to call the United Empire Loyalists refugees? Explain your answer.
   (b) How might the experiences of the United Empire Loyalists and those of modern-day refugees be the same? How might they be different?

Chapter 2

The Struggle for Reform in the Canadas, 1815-1840

The Constitutional Act of 1791 had created two colonies, Upper and Lower Canada, out of the old Quebec colony. The colony had been divided in order to preserve the distinctive ways of life of the Loyalists and the Canadiens. As well, the Constitutional Act had included provisions designed to protect those two very different ways of life.

The world was changing very rapidly as the nineteenth century began. The Napoleonic Wars were changing the political map of Europe. The Industrial Revolution was under way in Britain, creating dramatic changes in the lives of ordinary people in the British Isles. The Industrial Revolution also brought greater democracy to Britain in the form of responsible government. The changes brought about by the Industrial Revolution greatly affected Britain's colonies in North America too. Tens of thousands of immigrants arrived in the Canadas as Britain's population grew rapidly during the Industrial Revolution. They brought with them a way of life, religious beliefs and political ideas that differed from those of the Loyalists and the Canadiens.

These changes had not been anticipated when the Constitutional Act was written in 1791. What had been a solution of conflicts between Loyalists and Canadiens now created new conflicts in both Upper and Lower Canada. In both colonies, the structure of government allowed powerful elites to hold a great deal of power without having responsibility to the people through the elected assemblies. In Lower Canada, the protection given the way of life of the Canadien majority created new conflicts with immigrants from Britain.

These conflicts gave rise to demands for political reform in the colonies. The reformers wanted to limit the power of the oligarchies (government by a few powerful people) by making them responsible to elected representatives. The oligarchies used their power to prevent the changes the reformers were demanding. Frustration over their failure to achieve change through peaceful means led some of the reformers in both Upper and Lower Canada to armed rebellion in the years 1837-1838.

In this chapter, you will first look at some of the major social and political events of the first thirty years of the nineteenth century, seeing how events in Britain and the United States shaped developments in Canada. Next, you will examine the political structures of the Canadas during the 1830s; you will see how these structures failed to provide a satisfactory form of government in the Canadas. Finally, you will look at the rebellions of 1837-1838 in the Canadas. As you read the chapter, you will explore these key questions:

- How was the world changing in the early 1800s? How did these changes affect Britain's colonies in North America?
- Who held economic and political power in Upper and Lower Canada at this time?
- What changes did the reformers want to see in the colonies?
- What events led to armed uprisings in the colonies? What happened to those rebellions?

British North America in the Early Nineteenth Century

To a large extent, events in Canada during the early nineteenth century were shaped by changes occurring in Britain and the United States. One of these events was the Industrial Revolution, leading to political changes in Britain which would influence the Canadas. A second event was massive immigration to the Canadas, first from the United States and then from Britain. You will now look in turn at each of these.

The Industrial Revolution and its Political Consequences

After the final defeat of Napoleon in 1815, Britain was much stronger than it had been when it lost its American colonies in the revolution of 1775. During those forty years, the Industrial Revolution had profoundly changed Britain's economy and society.

In 1775, Britain, like all European countries, had been a predominantly agricultural nation. Most people lived in rural areas, making their living through farming or cottage industries. Social and political power rested with the landed **aristocracy.** The aristocracy had its origins in feudal times; its members still owned vast estates which they rented to peasant farmers. Their power was felt through their chamber of Parliament, the House of Lords. The king selected his ministers from the House of Lords.

The economic philosophy of the time was **mercantilism.** The government controlled many aspects of colonial trade and commerce for the benefit of the Crown and those in power. Under mercantilism, the role of Britain's colonies was to provide wealth for the mother country. The vast British Empire created many opportunities for trade. British merchant ships carried goods and raw materials from all parts of the globe to be sold in Europe.

Trade began to create a new class of wealthy and powerful men during the late eighteenth century. Many invested their riches in the new mills and factories created by the Industrial Revolution. Industrialization greatly increased the power of this new **"middle" class** of **capitalists** and merchants. It also brought with it important changes in British society.

Britain's population grew sharply during the Industrial Revolution, rising from 8 million in 1780 to 13 million in 1831. As well, the population distribution changed significantly. Cities grew rapidly in size and importance. Mills and factories drew thousands of workers to the towns, creating crowded slums.

Rural areas also felt the impact of the Industrial Revolution. Agriculture shifted from a self-sufficient way of life to an important business. Ownership of much of Britain's farmland was rapidly concentrated in the hands of a few wealthy families. Agricultural lands, once worked communally by peasant farmers, were "enclosed." Fences now surrounded the small plots and common grazing lands that had been combined into large farms. Enclosure created a large rural population of working poor and tenant farmers. It also forced many rural families off the land. Many left for the cities to seek jobs in the factories. Others came to North America as part of the "Great Migration."

These economic and social changes brought significant changes to British government. Control over Parliament passed gradually from the landed aristocracy to the industrialists, bankers and merchants. These groups wanted to be able to buy raw materials and food cheaply. They wanted unrestricted access for British industrial

Pulled by jobs in the cities, and pushed by the loss of their farms, British workers migrated towards the cities. Slum conditions quickly developed.

products to every part of an expanding world market. By the beginning of the nineteenth century, they had begun to gain control over the British government.

Their rivals, the landed aristocracy, had long used their control over Parliament to protect British agricultural interests. They feared that imports of lower priced grain and other food might reduce their incomes. They limited trade through restrictive laws and a system of **tariffs** designed to add to the Royal treasury.

After the American Revolution, the two rival groups vigorously debated the best way to run the country and its now-reduced empire. This debate led to the emergence of the first true political parties in Britain.

The **Liberals,** or **Whigs,** were champions of the middle class merchants and industrialists. Whig is a Scots Gaelic word meaning "horse thief," and was originally applied to Presbyterian religious dissenters. The Whigs were influenced greatly by the writings of Adam Smith. Smith created an economic philosophy known as *laissez faire. Laissez faire* is a French phrase meaning "let it be" or "leave it alone." Its key feature is the theory that nations become prosperous when individuals are freed from government control over economic activity. Smith's doctrine of *laissez faire* contrasted sharply with the mercantilist doctrine of government control over economic activity.

The **Conservatives** were members of the traditional ruling class based on the landed aristocracy. They strongly resisted political change during the late eighteenth century. They acquired their name because they wanted to "conserve," or protect, the old system of government and econonic power. In their inflexibility, they had helped create the conditions that had led to the American Revolution. They were closely linked with the Church of England [Anglican Church] and with the system of private education in Britain. The Conservatives were opposed to public education and to the granting of widespread religious freedoms. The Conservatives were popularly known as **Tories,** an Irish term meaning "bandits." The word may have its origins in the takeover of Irish lands by the British aristocracy after Cromwell's conquest of Ireland in the mid-seventeenth century.

During the late eighteenth century, much of Europe experienced great economic and political unrest. The French Revolution broke out in 1789; in various forms, it continued until the defeat of Napoleon in 1815. This revolution influenced political thinkers all over the world. Revolutions broke out in Spain, Greece, Russia and Latin America in the 1820s.

In Britain, the Conservative government managed to avoid revolution during the 1820s by passing a series of reform laws. These laws increased free trade and reduced restrictions on the activities of trade unions. They also gave Catholics the right to vote, more than thirty years after Catholics in Lower Canada had gained that right under the terms of the Constitutional Act.

Yet the Whigs and their middle class supporters wanted even greater reforms. The Whigs came to power in the election of 1830, committed to parliamentary reform. In particular, they wanted to give greater power to the middle class and to the industrial towns of Britain. These changes were achieved through passage of the Great Reform Bill of 1832. Under the bill, the number of eligible voters nearly doubled. However, women, workers and the poor were still unable to vote. More representation in the House of Commons was given to the populations of the growing towns and cities, while seats were taken away from the less populated rural areas controlled by the landed gentry.

One reform introduced at this time, **responsible government,** made Britain a more democratic nation. Until the election of the Whigs in 1830, the king had been able to choose his ministers, the heads of government departments, as he wished. He knew the parliamentary majority would support his choice. Close ties between the House of Lords and the Conservatives in the House of Commons assured the Crown of such support. However, the election of a Whig government marked the end of this unity in Parliament.

Under responsible government, ministers of the Crown now had to have the support, or confidence, of the elected Commons. With this change, the power of the Crown was now limited by the elected representatives of the people. The government (the prime minister and his cabinet) could be defeated on a vote of "no confidence" if it acted against the wishes of Parliament. An election would then be called to elect a new government.

Demands for responsible government would almost immediately be heard in British North America, as you will see later in this chapter.

1. What group held power in Britain before the Industrial Revolution? What groups held power after the Industrial Revolution? What reforms did the latter seek?
2. What key reforms did the Liberals introduce into Britain's parliamentary system after their election in 1830? How did they affect the power of the Crown?

Population Changes: "Late Loyalists" and the Great Migration

The Constitutional Act of 1791 had created the two separate colonies of Upper and Lower Canada. It preserved and protected their two very different cultural traditions in order to ensure their loyalty to Britain. However, in the early nineteenth century, immigration would greatly change the character of both colonies in ways that could not have been foreseen in 1791.

The first phase of such immigration was the arrival from the United States of the "late Loyalists" during the period between 1791 and 1812. Some of these immigrants were true Loyalists who had waited to see if they would receive compensation for their losses during the American Revolution. Others were opportunists, drawn north by the promise of cheap land in good locations. The late Loyalists increased Upper Canada's population from 14 000 in 1791 to 90 000 by 1812. Another 10 000 late Loyalists settled in the Eastern Townships of Lower Canada.

A second wave of immigration, roughly the years 1815-1850, came mostly from the British Isles. Thousands of Irish, Scots and English found themselves displaced by changes resulting from the Industrial Revolution and so set out for the new world. Often called the Great Migration, this great wave of new arrivals to British North America would blur, but not wipe out, the Canadien and Loyalist origins of modern Canada.

THE GREAT MIGRATION

Most immigrants who came to Canada during the Great Migration were very poor but they could get cheap transportation to Canada. Passage to Montreal or Quebec by sailing ship in the 1820s was 7 pounds, about two months wages for a farm laborer, meals included. Children travelled for half fare. These immigrants faced extreme hardships, both on board ship and in the colonies to which they travelled. Sicknesses such as cholera were common on board ship: tens of thousands died on their way to North America. The survivors faced great problems as they tried to find work or clear land for pioneer farms.

The following description of the plight of an immigrant family, living in a cave in Upper Canada, was written in 1821:

The mother, who continued to shed tears, told me, that she and her family were Irish immigrants. They had been induced by a series of misfortunes, to set sail for Canada, with the intention of obtaining land, and had, after many difficulties, got thus far in their voyage; but, being now destitute of money, they were unable to procure a lodging, and knew not where to apply for work, assistance, or information. "A husband and these two boys," said the woman, "are all

C.W. JEFFERYS

that now remain to me. My little girl died in the ship and they threw her into the sea. Aye, sure, that was the worst of all," continued she, in an agony of grief. "Poor babe! She had neither prayers nor a wake!"

[Excerpted from John Howison, *Sketches of Upper Canada*, published in 1821.]

The population of British North America doubled between 1815 and 1835. With the rapid growth of population came a period of economic prosperity. Large areas of forest land, traditional hunting grounds for Native peoples, were cleared and pioneer farms established. Growing towns and villages, many of them founded only a few years earlier, became centres of industrial and commercial activity.

The newcomers, whether from the United States or the British Isles, brought with them ways of life different from those of the Canadiens or the original Loyalists. Some brought political ideas that had been influenced by the recent revolutions in the United States and France. Others brought with them the reform-minded ideas of the British Whigs. These political views would soon play a major role in the shaping of colonial government in the Canadas.

Some Scots and Irish settlers brought with them deep feelings of animosity toward the English. They resented the treatment their countrymen had experienced at the hands of English conquerors. In particular, they resented the way in which the British landed gentry had treated peasant farmers, whose lands they had taken over. Religious matters also set these newcomers apart from the early Loyalists. Many of the Irish and Scottish settlers who came to Canada were Roman Catholics. Others were Methodists and Presbyterians, who resented the exclusive privileges extended to the Anglican Church in Upper Canada. Their demands for change would contribute to the new political movements in British North America during the 1820s and 1830s.

1. Explain the terms "late Loyalists" and "Great Migration."
2. Suggest several ways the new waves of immigrants caused problems for the British leaders of the Canadas.

Government and Society in the Canadas
The Structure of Colonial Government

While the Constitutional Act of 1791 had given each of the colonies an elected Legislative Assembly, the real power rested with the governor and his councils. The legislators in the elected Assembly had little control over the actions of the governor who was appointed by the British Government.

An explanation of the organization of parliamentary governments may be useful here. Basically, any parliamentary system of government has three components: the **legislative**, the **executive** and the **judiciary**. The legislative branch of government approves laws, the executive branch sees that these laws are translated into action, and the judiciary ensures that the laws are enforced.

In parliamentary governments, the executive branch drafts most of the laws that come before the legislative branch for approval. The legislators debate these draft laws and then approve them, reject them or pass them in amended form. The executive may also make laws without the approval of the elected legislators if no taxes are involved. Such laws are known as "orders in council."

Under the Constitutional Act of 1791, the executive in Upper and Lower Canada comprised the **governor** and his **Executive Council**. There was a governor general responsible for both Upper and Lower Canada, who represented the British Crown. He resided in Quebec City, capital of Lower Canada. A **lieutenant-governor,** resident in York (Toronto), was appointed to represent the British Crown in Upper Canada. He reported, in theory, to the governor general in Quebec–who was also the lieutenant-governor for Lower Canada. In reality, there were effectively two governors, one for each of the Canadas.

The Constitutional Act called for an Executive Council in each of the Canadas to assist the governor. Members of this council were appointed by the governor for life. They advised and assisted him in the management of public affairs. The Executive Council functioned much like a federal or provincial **cabinet** does today. Each member headed a government department, directed the activities of that department and hired its employees. The fact that the Executive Council was appointed by the governor, not chosen by the elected members of the Legislative Assembly, meant that there was no responsible government in the Canadas. In other words, the Executive Council was not answerable or "responsible" to the Legislative Assembly. The power of the elected Legislative Assembly was further limited by the **Legislative Council.** The Legislative Council formed an upper chamber, similar to the British House of Lords, in the colonial government. Any bill passed by the Assembly had to receive the approval of the Legislative Council before becoming law. The members of this council were also appointed by the governor. Most of the Executive Council would be members of this body also. The governor also had to give his approval to any legislation passed in the colony. Even then, the British government could overturn any law within two years of its passage by the colonial legislators.

Within British parliamentary tradition, laws regarding taxation

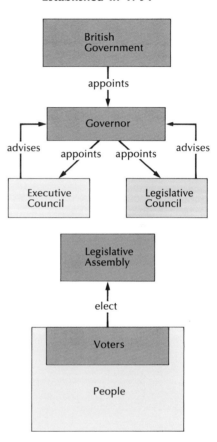

Structure of Government Established in 1791

Who has power under this system of government established by the Constitutional Act of 1791?

must be approved by the elected legislature. The imposition of taxes on the American colonies by the British Parliament without the approval of the colonial legislatures had been one of the causes of the American Revolution.

The Constitutional Act gave each elected Assembly the power to raise money for local purposes. However, the Constitutional Act also called for one-seventh of all public lands in the Canadas to be set aside to cover the expenses of government. Money from the sale or rent of these **Crown Reserves** could be used by the governor and his council to pay government expenses, without approval of the Assembly.

LIFE IN UPPER CANADA

A contemporary observer has left the following description of pioneer life in Upper Canada in 1821:

The majority of its inhabitants were indeed very poor when they commenced their labours, and had a variety of discouraging circumstances to contend with...the peculiarities of the climate, the almost inaccessible situation of their farms, the badness of the roads, and the immense woods...

Diminutive log houses, surrounded by a few acres of cleared land, presented themselves...A profusion of decayed and half-burnt timber lay around, and the serpentine roots of trees, blown down by tempests, stretched into the air, in the most fantastic forms. In different places, piles of burning timber sent forth columns of smoke, which enveloped the forests far and wide. Axes rung [sic] in every thicket, and the ear was occasionally startled by the crashing of trees falling to the ground....

Upper Canada, though destitute of those advantages which high agricultural improvement and a dense population never fail to bestow, is still in many respects, a delightful place of residence...There is a freedom, an independence and a joyousness, connected with the country...

[The country] is delightful to one, who, like me, has [seen] the famishing and healthless poor of a large city; who has visited those alleys where starving human wretchedness takes refuge...Though Upper Canada may be inferior to the old world, in many respects, she still has one superlative advantage over it, which is, a man may travel through her various settlements again and again, and never have his mind agitated, nor his feelings harassed, by the voice of misery, or the murmurs of discontent. Another circumstance tends to make Europeans partial to Canada. They find themselves to be of much more importance there than they would be at home; for the circle of society is so limited, and the number of respectable people in the Province so small....

[Excerpted from John Howison, *Sketches of Upper Canada*, published in 1821.]

Land was also set aside for the Anglican Church under the terms of the Constitutional Act. These lands were known as the **Clergy Reserves.** One-seventh of all public lands were to be set aside for the maintenance of "a Protestant Clergy" in the colonies. Revenue from these lands would be used to pay the costs of churches, schools and other Anglican Church activities in the Canadas. These institutions were intended to play an important part in keeping British traditions alive in Canada.

1. Name the three branches of parliamentary government. In your own words, explain the function of each.
2. Who held real power in the British North American colonies after 1791?
3. What were the Crown Reserves? What was their purpose?
4. What were the Clergy Reserves? Why had they been created by the authors of the Constitutional Act? How might Upper Canadians who were not members of the Church of England feel about the Clergy Reserves?

Upper Canada: The Family Compact, Reformers and Radicals

Social, political and economic power in Upper Canada during the early 1800s lay in the hands of a small group of families which, because of intermarriage among its members, came to be known as the **Family Compact.** It controlled nearly every aspect of public life in Upper Canada. Members of the Family Compact included wealthy landowners, educators and leaders of the Anglican Church. They were closely linked to the lieutenant-governor for Upper Canada, both socially and politically. Nearly all of the Executive Council for the province was drawn from the Family Compact. The oligarchy used its power on the Executive Council to protect its privileged position and to attack its critics. It could veto bills it did not like and even expel its opponents from the Assembly. The Family Compact argued that it was only natural that they should be the leaders of their community. They saw themselves as the superior members of Upper Canadian society, loyal to the Monarchy, pillars of the church and the only ones educated enough to govern properly.

The attitudes of the Family Compact toward public education and other democratic institutions is nicely summed up in the following statement. It was made by a member of the oligarchy

Layout of a Typical Township in Upper and Lower Canada

Legend

Clergy Reserves

Crown Reserves

Road allowance

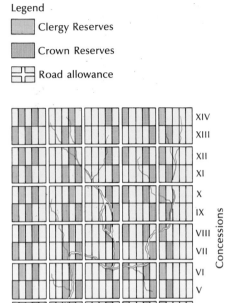

One-seventh of the land of each township in Upper Canada was set aside for Clergy Reserves to support a Protestant clergy. Heated debates over who should benefit from these reserves led Lord Durham to recommend they be eliminated.

John Strachan was both an Anglican minister and an educator. He was rector of York when the town was burned by American troops during the War of 1812. What effect might this experience have had on Strachan's views on political reform?

during debate over a move to bring public school to Upper Canada: "What do you need such schools for? There will always be enough Englishmen to carry out public business. We can leave the Canadians to clean up the bush." The Family Compact had no need for public schools. Their children attended schools such as York's Upper Canada College, run by the Anglican Church. Critics of the Family Compact called the college a "Prepare-a-Tory" school. The Family Compact had a strong ally in the Anglican Church. One of the leading members of the oligarchy was John Strachan, the first Anglican Bishop of Toronto. He strongly supported the Tory cause, and was an outspoken opponent of any reforms. Strachan resisted any changes such as public schooling that might end the Anglican Church's privileged place in the colony.

Through their power on the Executive Council, the Family Compact controlled the sale of Crown lands, including the assignment of the Crown and Clergy Reserves. They also had control over public works projects such as the building of roads, bridges and canals. Its use of this power led the Family Compact into direct conflict with the pioneer farmers of Upper Canada.

Much of the best farmland in the colony was kept for the Crown and Clergy Reserves or sold to members of the Family Compact. They knew that increasing demand for farmland, created by immigration to Upper Canada, would drive up the price of these lands. Many of these lands lay idle, uncleared bush in the midst of struggling pioneer farms. These farmers wanted to buy some of the unused land to increase their capacity to produce food for the growing population of Upper Canada. They were also concerned about the transportation problem created by the idle lands. The uncleared areas blocked road routes, raising the cost of transporting crops to markets. The impact of the Family Compact's control over land grants and road building is shown in the following statement by Robert Gourlay, a spokesman for the grievances of the pioneer farmers.

> These blocks of wild land place the actual settler in an almost hopeless condition; he can hardly expect during his lifetime, to see his neighbourhood contain a population sufficiently dense to support mills, schools, post-offices, places of worship, markets or shops; and, without these, civilization retrogrades.
>
> Roads under these circumstances can neither be opened by the settlers, nor kept in proper repair, even if made by the Government. The inconvenience arising from the want of roads is very

great...I met a settler from the Township of Warwick...returning from the grist mill at Westminster, with flour and bran of thirteen bushels of wheat; he had a yoke of oxen and a horse attached to his waggon, and had been absent nine days, and did not expect to reach home until the following evening...he assured me that he had to unload wholly or in part several times, and after driving his waggon through the swamps, to pick out a road through the woods where the swamps and gulleys were fordable, and to carry his bags on his back and replace them in the waggon [to cover] a distance less than 90 miles [150 kilometres].

[Statement made by Robert Gourlay to Lord Durham following the Rebellion of 1837.]

Gourlay organized meetings of farmers to hear their concerns and to help them present their grievances directly to the British government. In response, the Family Compact used their power on the Executive Council to have Gourlay arrested and expelled from the colony. One of Gourlay's most vehement attackers was Bishop Strachan:

There has been here for a year past a Mr. Gourlay from Fifeshire trying to set us by the ears. He has done a great deal of mischief in the Colony by seditious publications exciting discontent among the people. I saw through him at once and opposed him with my usual vigour upon which the Press groaned with his abuse of me. By this he destroyed much of his influence. A character like Mr. Gourlay in a quiet Colony like this where there is little or no spirit of inquiry and very little knowledge may do much harm...by exciting uneasiness irritation & exciting unreasonable hopes.

[Letter written by John Strachan, December 1, 1818.]

On November 27, 1818, the Family Compact used their control over the Assembly to have passed *An Act to Prevent Certain Meetings in the Province of Upper Canada*. It made the kind of meeting held by Gourlay and the farmers illegal.

Opposition to the Family Compact grew steadily in the 1820s. In the election of 1824, the Tories lost their majority in the Assembly. The victorious **Reformers** were led by Marshall Bidwell, the son of an American immigrant. They set out to make government and society in Upper Canada more democratic.

One of the Reformers' first acts was to pass a bill allowing Methodist ministers to conduct weddings, a power previously

Robert Gourlay arrived in Upper Canada in 1817. He immediately began to gather information on land policy and life in Upper Canada for an immigrant's guide. Gourlay wanted to use the guide to encourage immigrants to settle on his land holdings. The Family Compact opposed Gourlay's activities and cancelled his land grant. Gourlay's criticism of the Family Compact's actions led to two libel trials and, in 1819, his banishment from Upper Canada on charges of sedition. How did the Reformers use Gourlay's banishment to help their cause?

A Methodist minister and educator, Adolphus Egerton Ryerson was also an important member of the reform movement in Upper Canada. Ryerson is best remembered for his demands for government sponsored schools and compulsory education. What benefits would Upper Canada get from such an education system?

reserved for the Anglican Church. Strachan accused the Methodists of wanting to create an American-style republic. Through the influence of the Family Compact on the Executive Council, the bill was thrown out. Two years later, the Family Compact again used its power to veto a bill approved by the Legislative Assembly calling for the sale of the Clergy Reserves. The proceeds of the sale would have been used to finance public education in the colony.

Religious freedom and public education were becoming important issues in Upper Canada. By the early 1820s, Methodists and other Protestant sects clearly outnumbered the Anglicans in the colony, especially among the pioneer farming families. By supporting greater religious freedom, the Reformers gained the backing of the Methodists in Upper Canada, particularly their leader Egerton Ryerson.

Ryerson wanted important changes made in the way Upper Canada was run, changes that would benefit the farmers, small merchants and workers of the colony. He fought for religious freedom and an end to the privileged place of the Anglican Church in colonial society. Above all, he was a passionate advocate of a free public school system paid for out of government revenues. Like most of the Reformers, Ryerson was loyal to the British Crown and British parliamentary traditions. These men wanted only such rights and freedoms as they felt they were entitled to as British subjects.

Some of the Reformers wanted greater changes than those demanded by men like Bidwell and Ryerson. This group, known as **Radicals,** had been influenced by republican ideas from France and the United States. They wanted to see an end to British rule in Canada. Led by men like William Lyon Mackenzie, these men wanted to destroy the power of the Family Compact. They also wanted to ensure that no oligarchy could ever again be established in Canada. To achieve this end, Mackenzie called for the establishment of a republican form of government, responsible only to the people.

Mackenzie was a newspaperman, a member of the Legislative Assembly and the first mayor of Toronto. He used all of these roles to attack the Family Compact and to argue for a new system of government for Canada. His newspaper, the *Colonial Advocate*, was a major weapon in his attacks on the oligarchy. One editorial described the Family Compact in this way:

[It is] the most extraordinary collection of sturdy beggars, parsons, priests, pensioners, army people, navy people, placemen, bank directors and stock and land jobbers ever assembled to act as a paltry screen for a rotten government. They cost the country about 40 000 pounds a year and the good laws by which it might benefit they tomahawk. They don't like to be called a *nuisance*.

Indeed, the members of the Family Compact did not like to be called a nuisance. They were enraged by Mackenzie's attacks on their power and privilege. In 1826, a gang of young Tory thugs, many of them sons of Family Compact leaders, broke into the offices of the *Colonial Advocate* and smashed its printing press. This attack only strengthened Mackenzie's demands for change. Accused of libel by the Family Compact, Mackenzie was expelled from the Assembly four times in 1831. Each time, he was reelected by the voters of York.

Conflict between the Tories and the Reformers came to a head in Upper Canada as a result of the election of 1836. The lieutenant-governor of Upper Canada, Sir Francis Bond Head, had emerged as the true leader of the Conservatives. He used his position to campaign against reform, smearing the Reformers by calling them "Yankee-loving traitors." The lieutenant-governor made the key election issue loyalty to the Crown versus republicanism. Ironically, Bond Head was attacking reform at the same time as the Whig government in Britain was introducing major reforms to the mother country's system of government.

The Conservatives were aided in their efforts by the voting system in the colony. Only white adult male landowners could vote. Women, servants, landless workers and non-white people were unable to take part in the election. To further complicate things, voting was not done in secret as it is today. Votes were cast by a show of hands, with balloting being used only if there was no clear winner. Supporters of each faction would use verbal and even physical intimidation to influence the voters. The Tories, for example, were able to use the Orange Order, Irish Protestants fiercely loyal to the Crown, to provide a little muscle on voting day.

The judges and magistrates were often members of the Family Compact. Many Reformers were arrested, while justice turned a blind eye to the Tory mobs. Sir Francis Bond Head's campaign worked: the election of 1836 resulted in a landslide Conservative victory. Many of the moderate Reformers, including Marshall Bidwell and Robert Baldwin, gave up in despair. The Radicals, led by Mackenzie, began to plot an armed rebellion against the Family Compact-controlled colonial government.

William Lyon Mackenzie used his newspaper, the Colonial Advocate, *to demand reform and the end of the oligarchy created by the Family Compact. Frustrated by his inability to bring about change peacefully, Mackenzie organized an armed rebellion in 1837. Do you believe armed rebellion is sometimes necessary? Explain.*

1. What is sedition? Why would the Family Compact regard Gourlay's efforts to help farmers air their grievances as seditious?
2. What does Strachan's letter (page 33) tell you about his views of the majority of Upper Canadian settlers?
3. How might the farmers of Upper Canada have felt after passage of the act prohibiting their meetings?
4. What problems did pioneer farmers in Upper Canada face because of the Crown lands?
5. Why did Ryerson and the Methodists support the Reformers?
6. How did the system of voting in Upper Canada help the Tories rather than the Reformers?

Lower Canada: The *Château Clique* and The Patriotes

The struggle for reform in Lower Canada, as in Upper Canada, was rooted in conflicts between the elected Legislative Assembly and the powerful oligarchy which controlled the Executive Council. During the early 1830s, the political conflict in Lower Canada was made more complex by the desire of the Canadien majority to protect their culture. The Canadiens felt that their culture was threatened both by the governing oligarchy and by the many English-speaking immigrants who were coming to the colony.

In Lower Canada the conflict was not between Conservatives and Liberals as it was in Britain or Upper Canada. Here, the roots of conflict lay in the history of Quebec and the conquest of that French outpost by the British. As you have learned, both the Quebec Act and the Constitutional Act of 1791 had protected the traditions and culture of French Canada. These traditions found their political expression in the elected Legislative Assembly, which was dominated by the Canadien majority in Lower Canada. The British governor of the colony, however, drew the members of his Executive and Legislative Councils from the British merchant class.

This powerful oligarchy was known as the *Château Clique.* The group took its name from the Château St. Louis, the governor's mansion in Quebec City. Among its members was John Molson, founder of the famous brewing company. The *Château Clique* favored the building of canals to link the factories of Montreal and Quebec to markets in Upper Canada. As well, they actively fought against traditional land and civil laws in the colony. The *Château Clique* wanted the Canadien population to adopt a British way of life. During the 1830s, the *Château Clique* blocked the efforts of reformers to achieve responsible government in the form of an elected Legislative Council.

The British merchant class was angered by what they saw as the blocks that the Canadien-dominated Assembly placed in the way of freer trade and commerce with Upper Canada. Transportation between the Canadas was difficult in the early 1800s. The growing market in Upper Canada was being served by American suppliers, not the industries of Montreal and Quebec. The Executive Council sought funds to build canals and roads to link the colonies. The taxes to pay for these projects had to be approved by the Assembly.

The British in Lower Canada regarded the Canadiens as ignorant and backward people. They could not understand why the Canadiens kept their old ways of farming, fur trading and doing business. The Canadiens' lack of interest in the new agricultural and industrial methods that had resulted from the Industrial Revolution was incomprehensible to the British merchants.

For their part, the Canadiens regarded the British as arrogant conquerors. They resented the power and privileges enjoyed by the members of the *Château Clique* and other British merchants. They feared that the best lands in the colony would go to English-speaking immigrants. The Canadiens were angered by the low opinion many of the British had of their traditional way of life. Above all, they were concerned that this attitude would lead the British to seek assimilation of the Canadiens into the newcomers' way of life. The French writer de Tocqueville, who visited Lower Canada in 1831, noted that the Canadiens "regard with jealousy the daily arrival of newcomers from Europe. They feel that they will end up being absorbed...the English and French merge so little that the latter keep the name Canadiens, the others continuing to call themselves English."

The gap between the two cultures widened as economic conditions worsened in Lower Canada during the 1830s, especially for the ordinary Canadiens. Many of the industrial jobs in the factories and mills of Quebec and Montreal went to British immigrants. When an economic depression began in 1833, unemployment rose in the cities, affecting Canadiens and immigrants alike. In the countryside, the harvest was poor.

Cornelius Krieghoff sensitively recorded the Canadiens' way of life in his paintings. He lived and travelled in Lower Canada throughout the mid-1800s.

The Canadiens saw the immigrants as an economic as well as a cultural threat. That threat was made more ominous by outbreaks of cholera brought to Quebec by the immigrants. One cholera outbreak in 1832 killed more than 3000 residents of Quebec City. That same year, English soldiers killed three Canadiens during an election rally. All of these problems served to increase anti-British feelings in the colony.

Such feelings were only part of the growing struggle for reform in Lower Canada, however. Improved travel and communications had brought the educated young men of the colony into contact with new political ideas then finding expression in the United States and France. Well-educated, trained as doctors, lawyers or scholars, these young Canadiens were unable to play a significant role in government because of the power of the English oligarchy. Their frustrations were rooted both in the cultural division between French and English in Lower Canada and in the undemocratic nature of the colonial government.

The reform movement in Lower Canada combined Canadien nationalism with republican ideas of democratic government. These ideas found eloquent expression in a brilliant young lawyer and spellbinding orator, Louis Joseph Papineau. Under his leadership, the Parti Canadien, which held four-fifths of the seats in the Legislative Assembly, often clashed with the governor and his Council. The Assembly steadfastly refused to approve taxes for building canals and roads. Such taxes, they argued, would place heavy burdens on small farmers while helping the wealthy British merchants.

By 1832, the Reformers in Lower Canada had split into two groups, a moderate wing led by John Neilson and a more radical group led by Papineau. The radical wing took the name Patriotes, reflecting the nationalist spirit of their cause. The Patriotes were able to effectively control the Assembly. After the killings during the 1832 election, they passed a motion of censure against the governor. During the same session, the Patriotes approved a bill calling for an elected Legislative Council in the colony. Such a move would have paved the way for responsible government in Lower Canada.

In 1834, the Assembly went even further in its demands for responsible government. The Patriotes approved a list of ninety-two resolutions outlining the Canadien grievances over the way the colony was governed. They again demanded an elected Legislative Council, and sought all of the powers and privileges enjoyed by members of the British Parliament. With the ninety-two resolutions as their platform, the Patriotes won an overwhelming victory in the election of 1834. A resolution calling for responsible government was again approved by the Assembly in 1836.

In 1837, Britain's colonial secretary, Lord Russell, responded to these demands with ten resolutions of his own. While acknowledging the need for increased popular support for the government, Russell firmly rejected any form of responsible government for the colony. His response strengthened the reformers' demands for greater democracy, not only in Lower Canada but in Upper Canada and Nova Scotia as well. It also served to dangerously widen the gap between the British and Canadiens in Lower Canada.

This portrayal of Louis Joseph Papineau was painted by C.W. Jefferys long after the rebellions of 1837. What is Jefferys trying to say about Papineau? What event do you think has just taken place?

THE BRITISH VIEW OF THE CANADIENS

The following description of the Canadiens was written in the early 1800s and shows the attitude held by many British residents of Lower Canada.

The French Canadiens are an inoffensive, quiet people, possessed of little industry and less ambition....The Habitans [sic] content themselves with following the footsteps of their forefathers. They are satisfied with a little, because a little satisfies their wants. They are quiet and obedient subjects, because they feel the value and benefit of the government under which they live....They are religious from education and habit, more than from principle....They live in happy mediocrity, without a wish or endeavour to better their condition....

The Habitans have almost every resource within their own families...they make their own bread, butter and cheese; their soap, candles and sugar....They build their own houses, barns, stables and ovens. Make their own carts, wheels, ploughs, harrows, and canoes...

A Canadien will seldom or never purchase that which he can make himself; and I am of the opinion that it is this saving spirit of frugality alone, which has induced them to follow the footsteps of their fathers, and which has prevented them from profiting by the modern improvements...and the new implements of agriculture introduced by the English settlers.

[John Lambert, *Travels through Lower Canada, and the United States of America in the years 1806, 1807 and 1808*, London, 1810.]

The reform movement in Lower Canada was much more anti-British in sentiment than its counterpart in Upper Canada. The reformist Canadiens found support from Irish Catholics who had come to Quebec in the Great Migration. Both the Irish and the Canadiens felt oppressed by their Protestant, British rulers. Papineau was joined on Patriote speakers' platforms by men like Edmund O'Callaghan, who wrote in his newspaper, *The Vindicator*, on April 14, 1837: "The British government have decided to make Lower Canada the Ireland of North America. One duty now remains–let them study the history of the American Revolution."

1. What was the name given to the oligarchy in Lower Canada? How did their views of how Lower Canada should be governed differ from those of the Canadiens?
2. What reforms were Papineau and his Patriotes seeking?
3. Why were many Irish immigrants to Lower Canada willing to support the Patriotes?

The Rebellions

Within seven months of O'Callaghan's warnings, armed conflict broke out in Lower Canada between Patriotes and British troops. A month after that, open rebellion occurred in Upper Canada. Although these rebellions were quickly put down, uprisings occurred again in 1838. In this section, you will look at the 1837 rebellions in each of the Canadas, as well as those of 1838.

Lower Canada: 1837

In reaction to Lord Russell's rejection of the Patriotes' appeal for responsible government, a public meeting held at St. Charles on the Richelieu in May of 1837 voted to resist British "oppression." Delegates to the meeting adopted resolutions calling for a boycott of British goods and banks. Other resolutions hinted at the possibility of annexation with the United States or the creation of an independent Canadien nation. Papineau was proclaimed the leader of Canadien resistance to the British.

In the Assembly, the Patriote majority continued to refuse to approve taxes needed by the government. The British governor of the colony responded by announcing that he would use money in the colonial treasury without the approval of the elected Assembly. The Patriotes reacted angrily to this violation of the Constitutional Act of 1791.

Papineau's son and other young Patriotes formed a group holding strongly republican views, calling themselves *Fils de la Liberté*. The name means "sons of liberty," after the name of one of the groups that had started the American Revolution. During the summer and fall of 1837, street clashes between the *Fils de la Liberté* and the Tory Doric Club were common.

In October of 1837, the Patriotes held a mass meeting at St. Charles to plan their resistance to British rule. The mood was one of intense Canadien nationalism combined with a passionate salute to the spirit of the American Revolution.

Speaker after speaker in the angry mood of the meeting called for armed rebellion against the British. Only Papineau argued for moderation. He called on his followers to use the existing political system to achieve the changes they demanded. But his was the lone voice of moderation in the meeting hall, lost among the echoing calls for armed revolt. Wolfred Nelson rebuked Papineau, saying

This flag was carried by patriots during the battle of St. Eustache. The muskellunge was a local symbol, but the **J.-B⁺** *for Jean Baptiste and the branch of a maple tree were symbols of Canadien nationalism. Suggest a reason why these symbols might have been chosen.*

"the time has come to melt down our tin plates and spoons to make bullets." Patriote newspapers jubilantly reported the St. Charles meeting, spreading the call for armed rebellion. But the rebels never even had time to properly plan and organize a rebellion, let alone launch it. The Catholic Church publicly denounced the Patriotes and called on the Canadiens to remain loyal to the British Crown.

The Doric Club responded with more violent attacks on the Patriotes. On November 6, 1837, members of the Doric Club attacked the *Fils de la Liberté* as they left one of their meetings. They then ransacked the offices of the Irish pro-Patriote newspaper, the *Vindicator* and wound up the evening by attacking Papineau's home.

The British governor, fearing an armed uprising was about to begin, proclaimed **martial law.** All political meetings and marches were banned. Ten days after the Doric Club attacks, warrants were issued for the arrest of Papineau and the other Patriote leaders on charges of **treason.**

British troops were sent to arrest the would-be revolutionaries. The British soldiers were trained professionals, well-armed and well-supplied. The Patriotes, on the other hand, were armed with hunting muskets, pitchforks and scythes. Only one in ten had a gun. Ill-equipped and poorly trained, they were also badly led. The orators who inspired them to rebellion were lawyers and writers, not soldiers.

The Patriotes resisted what they viewed as the illegal arrest of their leaders by the British. Pursued by the British troops, the Patriotes had one brief moment of success on November 22, 1837. Barricaded in a stone house in the village of St. Denis, Patriotes led by Wolfred Nelson fought 350 British soldiers to a stand-off. Among the Patriotes at St. Denis was Georges Etienne Cartier, later to be one of the Fathers of Confederation.

The rebels were unable to hold out against the British soldiers. They soon ran short of supplies. They also faced the opposition of the Catholic Church which would not allow them to bury their dead in church cemeteries. The villages of St. Eustache, St. Benoit and St. Charles where rebel leaders and their supporters had sought refuge quickly fell to the British. The Patriotes at St. Denis held out until December 1, 1837, then surrendered to a British force that outnumbered them two to one. Patriote resistance crumbled, and their leaders fled. Many, among them Papineau, escaped to the United States.

Events following the rout of the Patriotes served to widen the gap between the Canadiens and the British in Lower Canada. At St. Eustache, the British found the body of one of their soldiers mutilated by the rebels. In revenge, many homes in the village were sacked and burned by British troops and civilians, members of the Doric Club and Orangemen, who had accompanied them in the pursuit of the Patriotes. Drunken and filled with pride over their easy victories, the Doric Club members and Orangemen drove families out into the snow while the British commanders looked the other way.

Papineau's flight had begun before the first shot was fired. He had never approved of armed rebellion, even when it was forced upon him. Papineau watched from the distance as St. Eustache and St. Denis burned. He lived for many years under a false name in the United States.

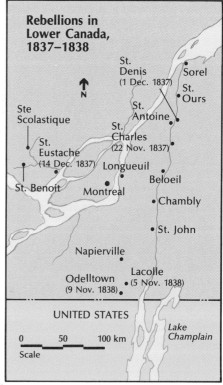

The rebellion in Lower Canada took place in the last months of 1837. How might the environment have affected the outcome of the rebellion?

1. What events triggered the rebellions of 1837 in Lower Canada?

2. In a short paragraph, explain who was to blame for the violence during the rebellions in Lower Canada.

3. How might Canada's history have been different if the Patriotes had won in 1837?

Upper Canada: 1837

News of unrest in Lower Canada reached Upper Canada in October of 1837. In that month, troops stationed in Toronto were sent to Lower Canada to deal with the anticipated rebellion there. William Lyon Mackenzie saw the events in Lower Canada during the fall of 1837 as his chance to launch an armed uprising in Upper Canada. As an ardent admirer of the American Revolution and the republic it had created, Mackenzie felt that a similar revolution was needed in Upper Canada. He shared many of the views of the Patriotes in Lower Canada and communicated frequently with their leaders. In the late summer of 1837, he received a message from the Patriotes, asking him for his support should an uprising start in Lower Canada that year.

Mackenzie saw his chance to seize control of Upper Canada when the British troops stationed at York were sent to Lower Canada in order to suppress the Patriotes. The rebels had been planning for several months. During the summer of 1837, political meetings

A CALL FOR SUPPORT

Mackenzie published the following handbill on November 27, 1837 in an effort to attract support for an armed uprising in Upper Canada:

BRAVE CANADIANS! God has put into the bold and honest hearts of our brethren in Lower Canada to revolt–not against "lawful" but against "unlawful authority". The law says we shall not be taxed without our consent by the voices of the men of our choice, but a wicked and tyrannical government has trampled upon that law–robbed the exchequer–divided the plunder–and declared that, regardless of justice they will continue to roll their splendid carriages, and riot in their palaces, at our expense–that we are poor spiritless, ignorant peasants, who were born to toil for our betters. . . .

CANADIANS! Do you love freedom? I know you do. Do you hate oppression? Who dare deny it? Do you wish. . . .Then buckle on your armour, and put down the villains who oppress and enslave our country. . . .One short hour will deliver our country from the oppressor; and freedom in religion, peace and tranquility, equal laws and an improved country will be the prize. . . .

. . .the prize is a splendid one. A country larger than France or England; natural resources equal to our most boundless wishes–a government of equal laws–religion pure and undefiled–perpetual peace–education to all–millions of acres of lands for revenue–freedom from British tribute–free trade with all the world–but stop–I could never enumerate all the blessings attendant on independence!

Up then, brave Canadians! Get ready your rifles, and make short work of it. . .our enemies in Toronto are in terror and dismay.

were held in many Upper Canadian towns and villages. Rebel militia units were raised. They drilled and held target practice throughout the fall of that year.

Mackenzie came up with a plan of action in November, 1837. His plan for taking over the government of Upper Canada called for a two-pronged attack. One group of rebels would march on Toronto, the other on Hamilton. In Toronto, they would seize 4000 guns from the city hall, arrest Governor Bond Head, and declare their independence from Britain. A convention would then be held to create a republican form of government for Upper Canada.

However, confusion surrounded the start of the ill-fated rebellion. December 7, 1837, had been chosen as the day for the attack to begin. The first rebels arrived at Montgomery's Tavern on Yonge Street, just outside Toronto, on December 4. There, the rebels fought their first skirmish with forces loyal to the government. Colonel Robert Moodie was shot dead as he tried to ride away from Montgomery's Tavern to warn the governor.

When Mackenzie and his rebels began to march down Yonge Street the next day, the element of surprise had been lost. The government had been able to organize a group of armed men led by Colonel Allan Napier McNab to defend the capital of Upper Canada. The British troops were on their way back from Lower Canada. Above all, there was little popular support for the marchers. Fewer than 800 would-be rebels could be assembled for the attack. The march into the city quickly turned into a wild retreat as the rebels were ambushed by Sheriff William Jarvis and a party of fewer than thirty men.

Mackenzie's bold plan ended in humiliating defeat at the Battle of Montgomery's Farm. Colonel McNab and his Loyalist forces chased the rebels across the ploughed fields as they fled. In his flight, Mackenzie dropped a briefcase containing all of his plans for rebellion and the names of those who had taken part in the aborted uprising.

Mackenzie himself escaped, fleeing to the United States. From Rochester, New York, Mackenzie and a party of rebel exiles took over Navy Island in the middle of the Niagara River on December 13, 1837. There, he declared his Provisional Government of Upper Canada. He continued to find little support in either Canada or the United States. A group of Loyalist militia, acting on McNab's orders, burned and sank the *Caroline*, an American vessel being used to supply Mackenzie's rebels on Navy Island, The sinking of the *Caroline* in American waters almost started a war between

LACK OF POPULAR SUPPORT FOR MACKENZIE

Mackenzie had been unable to get widespread support for his rebellion, despite the settlers' many grievances. An Upper Canadian farmer, who had supported Mackenzie's demands for reforms, explained his refusal to join the ill-fated rebellion, saying "I was a Scotch Radical and would have helped Mackenzie all I could–until he drew the sword. That proved to me that he was not constitutional, and I wouldna any such doings."

1. In your own words, explain what the farmer meant by the phrase "he was not constitutional."

Britain and the United States. Some Americans, sympathetic to the rebels, called for an invasion of Canada.

However, the American government did not want a war. In the end, they arrested Mackenzie for breaking American neutrality laws and jailed him for a short time, an experience that dulled his enthusiasm for American institutions.

SUSANNA MOODIE

News of the rebellion spread swiftly, if not accurately, to the pioneer farms of Upper Canada. Susanna Moodie wrote the following description of how she and her family learned of the uprising:

On the 4th of December–that great day of the outbreak...we were met by old Jenny who had a long story to tell us, of which we could make neither head nor tail–how some gentleman had called in our absence, and left a large paper, all about the Queen and the Yankees; that there was war between Canada and the States; that Toronto had been burnt and the governor killed, and I know not what other strange and monstrous statements...

[Reaching our cabin] we found the elucidation of Jenny's marvellous tales: a copy of the Queen's proclamation, calling upon all loyal gentlemen to join in putting down the unnatural rebellion....

[The next day, after her husband had left for Toronto] several poor settlers called at the house...on their way to Peterborough; but they brought with them the most exaggerated accounts. There had been a battle, they said, with the rebels, and the loyalists had been defeated; Toronto was besieged by sixty thousand men, and all the men in the backwoods were ordered to march instantly to the relief of the city....

The honest backwoodsmen, perfectly ignorant of the abuses that had led to the present position of things, regarded the rebels as a set of monsters, for whom no punishment was too severe, and obeyed the call to arms with enthusiasm. The leader of the insurgents must have been astonished at the rapidity with which a large force was collected, as if by magic, to repel his designs.

Susanna Moodie's book Roughing It in the Bush *has become an important source of information on life in Upper Canada. What kinds of information do you think historians would find in early settlers' accounts of life in the Canadas? How reliable do you think these accounts would be?*

1. What were Mackenzie's reasons for calling for rebellion in Upper Canada?
2. Give reasons why Mackenzie found little support in Upper Canada for his rebellion.

The Rebellions of 1838

The rebellions of 1837 in both Lower and Upper Canada were quickly suppressed by the British. Both had failed because they had been unable to attract widespread popular support. The rebellions of 1837 showed that the vast majority in both provinces, despite widespread grievances, were content to use peaceful, constitutional means to achieve political ends.

However, events in 1838 showed that these grievances continued. More battles were fought, and more blood shed, after the rebellions of 1837 than during them. Throughout 1838, a secret guerrilla army carried out a series of attacks along the boundary between Upper and Lower Canada. This secret group was known as the Patriot Hunters and was based in the United States. Its members struck at prominent Tory targets, burning houses and barns, and sometimes murdering their inhabitants.

The Patriot Hunters had as their symbol an eagle flanked by stars. On their membership card was the image of the eagle, clutching the British lion in its talons. Their aim was to invade and capture Canada in order to liberate it from what they saw as British tyranny. The few forays the group made into Upper Canada were crushed by British troops and the militia. Ineffectual as they were, these raids in 1838 renewed fears of another American invasion of Canada.

In Lower Canada, armed uprisings also broke out in 1838. There, a parallel group known as *les Freres Chasseurs*, had been preparing for armed rebellion since the defeat of the Patriotes in 1837. Led by Robert Nelson, a doctor living in Montreal, *les Freres Chasseurs* were better financed and organized than the Patriotes had been in 1837. Nelson's organization had cells of supporters throughout Lower Canada. They also had a more capable military leadership which recognized the need for the insurgents to be well-armed if the rebellion was to succeed.

Les Freres Chasseurs organized a brief and ineffectual uprising in February of 1838. However, a second campaign was attempted in November. This uprising began with the seizure of the strategic seigneury of Beauharnois, thirty kilometres from Montreal. But, a party of Loyalist Caughnawaga natives attacked the rebels and captured them, holding them until British troops arrived.

Meanwhile, Robert Nelson, leader of *les Freres Chasseurs*, was on his way back from the United States with money and arms for the rebels. Loyalist patrols, alerted by the events at Caughnawaga, spotted Nelson and captured the rebel leader. Once again, the rebels, short of arms and ammunition, were doomed to defeat. Again, too, the army and Loyalist volunteers scoured the countryside in search of rebels.

The British revenge on the failed revolutionaries was far more violent than the uprisings themselves. Two of the Upper Canadian rebels, Peter Matthews and Samuel Lount, were hanged in April 1838. Ironically, Lount, who was Mackenzie's lieutenant, had saved the lives of Sheriff William Jarvis' family during the 1837 uprising by keeping his fellow marchers from setting fire to the Jarvis home.

In Lower Canada, martial law was declared and the elected Assembly suspended following the rebellion in 1837. A new governor general, Lord Durham, was sent to the colony to restore order and to solve "the Canadian problem." Durham feared further armed insurrection if he bowed to local Tory demands for harsh punishments for the rebels. Instead of ordering eight rebel leaders hanged, as the British demanded, he had them exiled to the West Indies. The British government overturned his lenient sentences and Durham angrily resigned his post. He returned to Britain where he wrote a report on the rebellions of 1837 that would become a turning point in Canadian history. You will learn more about Lord Durham's report in the next chapter. The British reacted much more harshly to the rebellion of 1838 in Lower Canada. This time there was no Lord Durham to send the rebel leaders into West Indian exile. Martial law was still in effect from the earlier rebellion: 1200 men were rounded up by the army and jailed as suspected rebels. Of their number, 108 were brought before court martial for trial and all but ten were sentenced to death. Twelve *Freres Chasseurs* were actually hanged before the British realized that executions might lead to another uprising. Fifty-eight of the condemned men were transported to the Australian penal colony and the rest set free. Robert Nelson, the rebel leader, managed to escape to the United States. He abandoned his hope of becoming "president of the new republic" and returned to his medical practice.

In Upper Canada, 885 men were arrested for treason in 1838 and jailed. Of these, twenty were hanged publicly. The Tories hoped the hangings would deter any would-be rebels. Ninety-two were transported to penal colonies. Other supporters of Mackenzie fled to the United States to avoid similar fates.

1. What evidence in the text shows the Patriot Hunters were influenced by American revolutionary ideas?
2. Suggest reasons why the British government so severely punished the rebels following the 1838 rebellion. What did the government hope to gain?

Summary

The Industrial Revolution in early nineteenth-century Britain created movements of political reform that would have repercussions in the North American colonies. Thousands of immigrants from England, Scotland and Ireland, many of them displaced by the Industrial Revolution, arrived as part of the Great Migration. These immigrants brought with them new social and political ideas that greatly affected life in the Canadas.

Oligarchies held power in each of the British North American colonies. In Upper Canada, the Family Compact used its power in the Executive and Legislative Councils to prevent reforms that would have aided pioneer farmers. The major issues that caused discontent among the farmers were the idle Crown lands and the role of the Anglican Church. With its vast Clergy Reserves, the Anglican Church was able to block religious freedoms and public schooling.

In Lower Canada, the *Château Clique* attempted to use its power in government to build canals linking the colony to markets in Upper Canada. The Canadien reformers, known as Patriotes, used their power in the Assembly to block these efforts. They feared that the British merchant classes wanted to destroy the traditional Canadien way of life.

At first, reformers in both colonies sought changes through the elected assemblies and appeals to the British Parliament. They appealed for responsible government in the colonies, knowing that this would give the elected representatives of the people control over the government. However, the oligarchies, supported by the British, blocked the reformers' efforts.

In frustration, some of the reformers in both colonies turned to armed rebellion. Some of them called for an end to colonies' ties with Britain and the creation of independent republics. Rebellions occurred in both Canadas in late fall of 1837. The rebellions were poorly organized, badly led and lacked popular support. Both were quickly put down by British troops and civilians loyal to the government. However, unrest and clashes between government troops and rebels continued throughout 1838 as well.

REVIEW

Checking Back

1. Write one or two sentences to summarize the significance of each of the following.

   Great Migration   Late Loyalists
   Great Reform Bill   Oligarchies
   Colonial   Rebellions of
      Government   1837-1838

2. Give one example of an event that took place outside the Canadas, and yet changed the settlers views on how their government should be run.

3. Write one or two sentences to explain how each of the following groups thought that Canada should be governed.

   Tories   Reformers   Radicals

4. Compare the political goals of William Lyon Mackenzie with those of Louis Joseph Papineau.

5. Study the picture of Canadien life found on page 38 and write two facts about life in Lower Canada.

Using Your Knowledge

6. Identify ways the Industrial Revolution changed British economic practices. How did these changes influence the political system?

7. Write an editorial supporting any one of the groups who were fighting for control over the government of Upper Canada.

8. Create a time line to show the steps that led to armed rebellion in Upper Canada. Use your time line as a reference and explain why some reformers felt armed rebellion was the only way to achieve responsible government.

9. Imagine you have the power to change the past. Plan a course of action that would prevent rebellion in Lower Canada.

10. List the steps that were taken by the British to end the rebellions in Upper and Lower Canada. Were the rebel groups treated differently in Upper and Lower Canada? Support your answer with facts.

Chapter 3

Changes in Colonial Government, 1838-1849

Although they had failed in both the Canadas, the rebellions of 1837 and 1838 had alarmed the British government. These events reminded the British of how they had lost thirteen of their North American colonies sixty years earlier. Only six British colonies now remained in eastern North America: Upper Canada, Lower Canada, New Brunswick, Nova Scotia, Prince Edward Island and Newfoundland. Some observers in both Britain and the Canadas noted

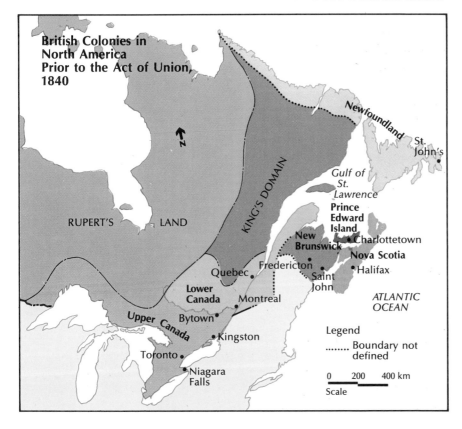

British Colonies in North America Prior to the Act of Union, 1840

After having lost many of their possessions in North America, the British were anxious to keep control of their six remaining colonies. What geographic and cultural characteristics tended to discourage co-operation among the colonies?

similarities between the conditions that had led to the rebellions of 1837-1838 and those that had sparked the American Revolution. Lord Durham was sent to the Canadas as governor general in 1838. It was his responsibility to seek solutions to the problems in Upper and Lower Canada.

In this chapter, you will first look at the solutions set forth by Durham in the famous report which he wrote after his visit to the colonies. Then you will see how two major solutions suggested by Durham–a legislative union of the Canadas and the granting of responsible government to the colonies–were eventually put into practice.

As you read this chapter, these key questions should be kept in mind:

- What did Durham see as real causes of the rebellions of 1837-1838?
- What does "responsible government" mean? Why did Durham recommend it in his report?
- How did the Act of Union affect the relationship among the five colonies?
- How did responsible government come about in Nova Scotia? in the Canadas?

A Solution Sought

Lord Durham's report is one of the most famous and controversial documents in Canadian history. The report attempted to outline a solution to the problems of colonial government. This section will look first at Durham's visit to Canada, then the report itself, and finally at colonial reactions to the report.

Lord Durham in the Colonies

John "Radical Jack" Lambton, the first Earl of Durham, is known to students of Canadian history as Lord Durham. He was a powerful advocate of political reforms in Britain during the 1830s. For example, he urged that voting should be done by secret ballot and that the vote be given to all male taxpayers.

Led by speakers like Durham, critics of the British government accused it of neglecting its North American colonies. They claimed that this neglect had given rise both to the American Revolution of the 1770s and to the rebellions of 1837-1838 in the Canadas. They argued that the British government had neither provided good leadership nor allowed enough democracy for the colonies, thus enabling groups like the Family Compact and the Château Clique to become petty tyrants.

Early in 1838, British Prime Minister Melbourne asked Durham to head a commission of inquiry into the rebellions of 1837-1838, and to make recommendations for the future of the Canadas. Durham was also asked to serve as governor general of both Upper and Lower Canada. Durham's acceptance delighted Melbourne and quieted the critics who were using the "Canadian problem" to harass and embarrass the Melbourne government. On both sides of the Atlantic, people who wanted to see political change in the colonies were pleased by Durham's appointment.

Lord Durham arrived at the port of Quebec City in May 1838 to a warm welcome from the people of Lower Canada. He invited leaders from both Canadas and the Atlantic colonies to meet with him and discuss solutions to the problems of colonial government.

Durham already had in mind one possible solution: the joining of all the colonies into a single legislative union. In other words, Durham wanted to create an elected Assembly which would include representatives from each of the colonies. These legislators would make laws that applied to all of the colonies. Such an assembly would make it impossible for a local oligarchy to control the political life of any individual colony. There would be enough taxpayers in this union to provide the government with the funds needed for such large-scale projects as railway and canal building. Such projects, at this time, were bigger than any individual colony could handle.

Durham discovered, however, that none of the colonies wanted to be part of his proposed legislative union. Each colony feared getting involved with the problems of the others if it had to share a government with them. Durham abandoned the idea of a legislative union of all the colonies. A union of Lower and Upper Canada without the Maritimes, however, would remain part of his proposed solution.

During Durham's visit to Upper Canada, William and Robert Baldwin, leading reformers in the Upper Canada colony, suggested to him the idea of "responsible government" for British North America. This idea was already in practice in Britain itself. Let us take a closer look at what it meant.

In Britain, those people allowed to vote elected the members of the House of Commons. The party getting the largest number of

Lord Durham was an aristocrat, the son-in-law of a former British prime minister. His years in politics had earned him a reputation as a reformer.

members in Parliament would then form a government, headed by the prime minister (usually the leader of the winning party). The prime minister would choose members of his party to be part of his Executive Council, or **cabinet**. This council gave advice to the monarch and was responsible for the day-to-day running of the country. Each cabinet minister headed a department, staffed by civil servants, who carried out the work of the government.

The Baldwins wanted to see a similar system for the government of the colonies. The colonial governor, appointed by the British government, would still act as the chief representative of authority (or head of state) in the colonies. However, this appointed governor would have to choose his Executive Council from the elected members of the Legislative Assembly of the colony. ("Legislative Assembly" was the name used for the body of representatives elected by colonial voters.)

This Executive Council would then give advice to the colonial governor. The governor would have to accept such advice in all domestic matters, those matters which concerned life in the colony itself. For example, if the Executive Council's members wanted to spend tax money to build roads, and had the support of a majority of members in the Assembly, the colonial governor would have to allow this spending, whether he liked the idea or not. If the Baldwins' proposal was accepted, the real power in the colony would no longer rest with the appointed governor, but with the elected Legislative Assembly, whose members sat in the Executive Council.

In such a system, the government is said to be "responsible" to the elected Assembly, who in turn represent the people of the colony. The structure of responsible government is shown on page 55.

In a letter of August 1838 to Lord Durham, Robert Baldwin summed up his case for responsible government:

> I would ask Your Lordship, would the people of England endure any system of Executive Government over which they had less influence than that which at present exists [in the Canadas]? Your Lordship knows they would not. Can you then expect the people of these colonies with their English feelings and English sympathies to be satisfied with less...They can see a reason why their relations with foreign countries should be placed in other hands: but none why their domestic concerns should not be managed upon similar principles to those applied in the administration of the Imperial Government....

Robert Baldwin

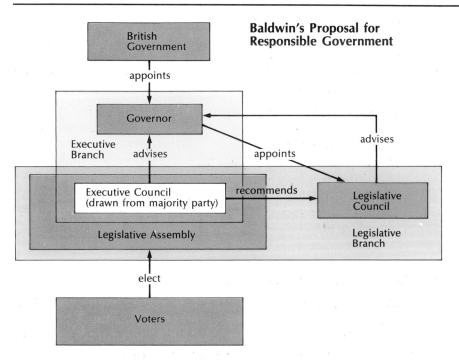

Baldwin's Proposal for Responsible Government

The Baldwins' proposal appealed to Durham for a number of reasons. First, it called for a form of government similar to Britain's, with which he was of course already familiar. Second, the proposal would provide responsible government for local issues. This provision would silence complaints that these issues were under the control of a government outside the colony. But it would still allow the British government to retain power in all other matters such as foreign trade and defence. Finally, the proposal was acceptable to important political leaders in all six of the colonies. For these reasons, Durham was prepared to recommend to the British Parliament that responsible government be extended to all of the British North American colonies except one: Lower Canada. Here, Durham faced a major problem. He feared that, under responsible government, the French-speaking majority of Lower Canada would use its power to block the wishes of the British minority. As you will shortly see, Durham had a very unfavorable opinion of the Canadiens and their way of life. Despite these views he treated the Patriote rebels leniently following their convictions (see Chapter 2, page 48). His leniency towards the rebels aroused great anger both in the British Colonial Office and among the English-speaking population of Lower Canada. As a result of this criticism of his actions, five months after his arrival in the colonies, Durham resigned from the position of governor general and returned to Britain. There, he wrote the report that would shape future British policies regarding its North American colonies. You will now get a closer look at that report.

1. Recall from Chapter 2 the definition of an oligarchy. Why were the ties between government and commercial life so important to the oligarchies in the colonies?
2. Why, in your opinion, might Durham have believed that an elected Assembly governing all of the colonies could end the power and privileges enjoyed by local oligarchies like the Château Clique in Lower Canada and the Family Compact in Upper Canada?

Lord Durham's Report

The following are excerpts from the report prepared by Lord Durham and his staff for the British government. In the report, he deals with four main topics. They are: the causes of conflict in Lower Canada; the causes of conflict in Upper Canada; the proposal for responsible government; and the proposal to unite the two Canadas into a single colony. Here is what Durham had to say about each of these topics:

On the Causes of Conflict in Lower Canada:
Durham felt strongly that the conflict in Lower Canada was a result of the differences of outlook between the Canadien majority and the British minority. He believed that the British commercial and industrial economy, as represented by this minority, was superior to the older agricultural economy of the Canadiens. He felt that the British way of life had to take control in Lower Canada if economic progress was to be achieved there.

> I expected to find a contest between a government and a people: I found two nations warring in the bosom of a single state: I found a struggle, not of principles, but of races [ethnic groups];...[a] deadly animosity...now separates the inhabitants of Lower Canada into the hostile divisions of French and English.
>
> [The English in Lower Canada] complain loudly and bitterly of the whole course pursued by the Imperial government, with respect to the quarrel of the two races...they feel that being a minority, any return to the due course of constitutional govern-

ment would again subject them to a French majority; and to this I am persuaded they would never peaceably submit...

It will be acknowledged by everyone who has observed the progress of Anglo-Saxon [British] colonization in America, that sooner or later the English race was sure to predominate even numerically in Lower Canada...

I entertain no doubts as to the national character which must be given to Lower Canada; it must be that of the British Empire;...it must henceforth be the first and steady purpose of the British government to establish an English population, with English laws and language, in this province and to trust to none but a decidedly English legislature....

1. Why did Durham see the Canadien way of life as an obstacle to British-style progress in the colonies?
2. What problems might have arisen if an attempt had been made to force the Canadiens to adopt an English way of life?

On the Sources of Conflict in Upper Canada:
Durham discovered that the issue of the "Clergy Reserves" was the chief item of conflict in Upper Canada. As you have seen, many leading members of the Tory party were connected with the Anglican Church. Through their influence, the Anglican Church, or "Church of England," as Durham calls it, had come to control much of the province's public lands. These church-controlled lands were known as the "Clergy Reserves."

[In Upper Canada] the question of greatest importance was that of the clergy reserves...the reformers, or opposition, were generally very successful in their appeals against the project of the Tory or official party, which was that of devoting them exclusively to the maintenance of the [Anglican] Church....A still stronger objection to the creation of a Church establishment in this colony is, that not merely are the members of the Church of England a small minority at present; but, [as most] emigrants are not members of the Church of England, the disproportion is likely to increase, instead of disappearing, in the course of time. The mass of British emigrants will be either from the middle classes of Great Britain, or the poorer classes of Ireland; the latter almost exclusively Catholics, and the former in a great proportion either Scotch Presbyterian or English Dissenters [e.g. Baptists]...

It is most important that this question be settled....I know of no mode of doing this but by repealing all provisions in Imperial Acts that relate to the...clergy reserves....

1. What was the Tory position on the Clergy Reserves?
2. What reason does Durham give for recommending an end to the Clergy Reserves?

On Union of the Canadas:
Durham believed that union of the two Canadas would help to solve the political, economic and cultural problems of both colonies. In particular, he saw union as the only way to **assimilate** the Canadiens into a dominant British culture:

> ....I believe that tranquility can only be restored by subjecting the province [Lower Canada] to the vigorous rule of an English majority; and that the only [effective] government would be that formed by a legislative union.
>
> If the population of Upper Canada is rightly estimated at 400 000, the English inhabitants of Lower Canada at 150 000 and the French at 450 000, the union of the two provinces would not only give a clear English majority, but one that would be increased every year by the influence of English emigration; and I have little doubt that the French, when once placed by the legitimate course of events and the working of natural causes, in a minority, would abandon their vain hopes of nationality....

1. In your own words, sum up (a) why Durham felt that the Canadiens should be assimilated by the British and (b) why the Clergy Reserves should be abolished.
2. In your own words, describe responsible government. Explain why Durham saw responsible government as a solution to the problems of the colonies in British North America.
3. What does Durham identify as the sources of the movement toward annexation of the colonies to the United States? How would responsible government help to deal with this problem?
4. Under a republican form of government, the executive branch (president plus cabinet) are separate from the legislative branch. Compare this with the nature of the executive and legislative branches under responsible government. Suggest some advantages and disadvantages to each system.

On Responsible Government:
Durham observed that many colonists envied the economic prosperity and democratic system of government enjoyed in the United States. He noted that some colonial leaders even wanted the colo-

nies to become part of the United States. If the British government failed to grant responsible government to the colonies, Durham argued, their annexation by the United States would be a strong possibility.

> The irritation caused by the late insurrection...induced a large portion of the population to look with envy at the material prosperity of their neighbours in the United States, under a perfectly free and eminently responsible government; and, in despair of obtaining such benefits under their present institutions, to desire the adoption of a republican constitution, or even an incorporation with the American Union....The different parties believe that when the case is once fairly put before the mother country, the desired changes in the policy of their government will be readily granted: they are now tranquil, and I believe loyal; determined to abide the decision of the Home Government, and to defend their property and their country against rebellion and invasion. But I cannot but express my belief that this is the last effort of their almost exhausted patience....and...that the government of the colony should henceforth be carried on in conformity with the views of the majority in the Assembly.

1. Give reasons why it would be tempting for colonists to consider annexation with the United States.

Some people in the Canadas saw annexation with the United States as a solution to economic problems. In 1849, 325 Montreal citizens published the Annexation Manifesto calling for immediate union with the United States. Do you think the cartoonist supported this view?

Reactions to Lord Durham's Report

The immediate reaction to Lord Durham's report was mixed. Tories in Britain and their counterparts in the colonies saw the report as an attack on their privileges and power. Most Canadien leaders were furious over Durham's views of their culture and over his desire to submerse them in a union with Upper Canada.

In general, reform-minded people on both sides of the Atlantic applauded Durham's recommendations. Reformers in all the colonies favorably received his idea for responsible government. The headline of *The Hamilton Journal* of August 2, 1839, read: "Death to the Family Compact and up with the Durham Constitution!" "No document has ever been promulgated in British North America that has given such general satisfaction as this report," wrote Francis Hincks in his newspaper, the Toronto *Examiner*, on June 24, 1839. Hincks then set about organizing hundreds of "Durham meetings" and "Durham Constitutional Clubs" throughout Upper

Canada. At these meetings, flags were waved and songs sung in support of the reformers' cause.

Durham's report was just as enthusiastically received in the Atlantic colonies. On April 11, 1839, Joseph Howe, a vocal reformer, wrote the following editorial in his newspaper, the *Nova Scotian*:

HOW THE CANADIENS SAW THEMSELVES: THE CASE OF ETIENNE PARENT

During the 1830s, many educated young Canadiens had come to believe that the people of Quebec had been better off before the British came. They believed the people of New France had greater control over their religion, language and culture, all of which were now threatened by the British. Many of the Lower Canadian rebels of 1837-1838 had held these beliefs. When Durham's report appeared, these Canadiens became even more resentful of the British.

Other Canadiens felt differently. In his Quebec City newspaper *Le Canadien*, Etienne Parent had not only translated and published Durham's report, but had written a carefully argued analysis of it. He urged that Canadiens focus on the recommendation for responsible government, rather than on Durham's anti-French sentiments. Parent believed that reformers in the two Canadas could use responsible government both to protect the rights of French Canadians and bring about educational, religious and agricultural changes to Lower Canada. He believed that the Canadiens had to take advantage of industrialization and commerce in order to strengthen their culture. His arguments were opposed by the Catholic Church and the traditionalists, but

Etienne Parent

they would influence reformers like Louis-Hippolyte LaFontaine [see page 63] and play a major role in the achievement of responsible government in Canada.

The remedy for the local executives [Executive Councils]...in all the Colonies, has two prime recommendations, being perfectly *simple* and eminently *British*. It is to let the *majority* and not the *minority* govern, and compel every Governor to select his advisors from those who *enjoy the confidence of the people*, and can *command a majority in the popular* [elected legislative] *branch*.

The Family Compact in Upper Canada reacted negatively to Durham's report. They feared the results if both union of the Canadas and responsible government were adopted. R.B. Sullivan, a member of the Family Compact, summed up this negative reaction in 1839:

It is said...the Union...would give a decided [advantage] to the British party in the Legislature.

The proposition for a union of the provinces is...founded on a fallacy—a supposed [agreement] of purpose among the whole British population. But the fact is otherwise. The population of Upper Canada is divided into political parties....American political agitation has infected many of them with republicanism, and with notions of politics inconsistent with colonial dependence... If then this democratic party were to have even partial success in the Upper Canada elections there would be two contending parties amongst the British representation in the United Legislature.

The French Canadians have shown that they are united as a party....they will unquestionably unite themselves with the one of the British parties which will undertake the most for them. The democratic party being the weakest in the British representation will unquestionably undertake anything for the sake of gaining French support....

1. Reread Joseph Howe's quotation. What are the "two prime recommendations" to which he refers?
2. According to R.B. Sullivan, Durham's proposal is "founded on a fallacy." What is a fallacy? Why does Sullivan regard Durham's proposal as being based on a fallacy?
3. What divisions does Sullivan see within the population of Upper Canada? What possible political alliance does he fear? What would be the effect of such an alliance?
4. Which groups in British North America favored Durham's recommendations? Which groups disliked the report? Explain why each group felt as they did.

A Solution Tried

From Lord Durham's Report to the Act of Union

Lord Sydenham was considered one of the ablest administrators sent from Britain to North America. He was experienced both as a politician and as a businessperson. He arrived in Lower Canada in October 1839 and died in September 1841 as a result of a fall from a horse.

The British government of 1839 was not yet ready to grant responsible government to its North American colonies. The colonial secretary, Lord Russell, believed strongly in the principle that a colony was different from a nation. Responsible government was unacceptable to him. With responsible government, the British-appointed governor of a colony would have to follow the advice of an Assembly elected by the colonists. This advice might differ from the advice the British government wished the governor to follow. Russell felt that, in all colonial matters, the wishes of the British government were more important than the desires of the colonists.

As a result of Russell's strong views, the British government rejected Durham's recommendation calling for responsible government. But, it did accept the recommendation calling for union of the two Canadas. A single colony, or province, would be created from Upper and Lower Canada. Upper Canada would be known as Canada West and Lower Canada as Canada East. The new province would assume the debts of each colony as a single debt. There would be one elected Legislative Assembly in which each of the Canadas would have equal representation. This measure was adopted because representation by population would have created a Canadien majority in the Assembly.

Charles Poulett Thompson, soon to be known as Baron Sydenham, arrived in the Canadas as their new governor general. He was charged with the responsibility of gaining approval for the proposed union from both Upper and Lower Canada.

When Sydenham travelled to Lower Canada, the proposed Act of Union was enthusiastically received there by the British minority. For them, the union would serve to put the rebellious Canadiens in their place. It would also encourage English commerce and industry at the expense of the traditional Canadien way of life based on farming and the fur trade. The *Gazette*, a Montreal English newspaper, editorialized that literacy in English, not property, should be the requirement of anyone seeking the right to vote in the united colony.

Faced with such anti-French bigotry, Canadien moderates who had supported Lord Durham's recommendations for responsible government actively opposed the Act of Union. The Catholic Church joined in this opposition.

These concerns were ignored by Sydenham, who then travelled to Toronto to seek the endorsement of the Upper Canadians for the proposed union. Despite the strong objections of the Family Compact, the Tory-dominated Assembly gave the idea overwhelming approval. It had been persuaded to do so by Sydenham's promise of a British loan that would cover the combined debts of the two colonies. Reformers in the Upper Canadian Assembly also supported the proposal. As Sullivan had anticipated, they foresaw the possibility of an alliance with reform-minded Canadien legislators to bring about responsible government. The legislators of Upper Canada did insist on two changes to the proposed Act. First, the capital of the United Province was to be located at Kingston, halfway between Montreal and Toronto. Second, English was to be the only official language of the colony.

The Act of Union was approved by the British Parliament in July 1840. Royal proclamation of the Act followed in February 1841. Apart from creating a single colony, the Act of Union brought little change to the government of the Canadas. The structure of government established under the Constitutional Act of 1791 was maintained. There was still a governor appointed by the British government, his Executive Council and an elected Assembly. Now, however, there would be only one such government for both the Canadas.

No rebellion greeted passage of the Act of Union, despite French-Canadian opposition to it. Rioting broke out in the Canadas during the election of 1841, but as mob violence was a common feature of voting during this period, the riots created few concerns. Instead, reformers in both Canada West and Canada East set out to find ways of working together toward the achievement of responsible government.

Louis-Hippolyte LaFontaine strongly opposed the combining of the debts of Upper and Lower Canada into a single debt. Lower Canada owed almost nothing while Upper Canada owed about £1 000 000, or over £2 for every man, woman and child (approximately one week's wages for an average laborer in 1840).

1. How did the Act of Union change, and not change, the government of the Canadas?
2. Why did some Canadien leaders oppose the Act of Union?

Responsible Government Achieved in the Atlantic Colonies

Responsible government came first in the Atlantic colonies. There had been heated public discussion and angry debates in their Legislative Assemblies, but no violence or rebellion. In the Atlantic colonies, as in the Canadas, the powerful elites had used every means at their disposal in trying to silence their critics.

However, two factors present in the Canadas were missing in the Atlantic colonies. First, there was no bitter political division between the French and English populations. New Brunswick's French-speaking population, while sizable, lacked the political power of the Canadiens in Canada East. Second, there was no large population of recent immigrants from the United States. In the Canadas, the loyalties of these immigrants were questioned, and they were often accused of seeking a republican form of government similar to the American system. Most of the population of the Atlantic colonies had its roots in the Loyalist migrations that followed the American Revolution.

The fight for responsible government in Nova Scotia was led by Joseph Howe, the fiery Halifax newspaperman. In 1836, Howe had been elected to the Nova Scotia Assembly. There, he argued that since responsible government was now the basis of Britain's government it should also be so for the colonies. He insisted that it was the right of the elected Assembly, not the governor, to name the members of the Executive Council.

Howe wrote to Lord Russell to state his case: "We seek nothing less than British subjects are entitled to; we will be content with nothing less." Twice Howe led the Assembly to a vote of "no confidence" in the governor. Each time, the British government chose to recall the governor and appoint a new representative in Nova Scotia.

To satisfy Howe and his followers, the governor appointed him and two other Reformers to the Executive Council in 1840. Yet by 1843 they were refusing to sit on the Executive Council in order to express their lack of confidence in Lord Falkland, the governor of Nova Scotia. The British withdrew Falkland in 1846 and replaced him with Sir John Harvey. Harvey was instructed to act solely as the representative of the British government and to avoid any involvement in local politics.

Like Falkland, Harvey was unable to form an Executive Council in which Howe and his Reformers would work with the Tories. He

In a speech in 1837, Joseph Howe stated "I wish to live and die a British subject, but not a Briton only in the name. Give me–give to my country, the blessed privilege of her [Britain's] Constitution and her laws;. . .Let us be contented with nothing less."

called an election in 1847 to break the deadlock. The Reformers scored a decisive victory, so Harvey called upon them to form his Executive Council. In January 1848, J.B. Uniacke, now the leader of the Reform party, formed an all-Reform Executive Council, drawn from the members of his party sitting in the Assembly. Responsible government had been achieved in Nova Scotia. No force of arms or act of rebellion had been needed. It had been a matter of waiting until the attitudes of the British government coincided with the desires of the colonists and their elected representatives.

The following year, responsible government was extended to New Brunswick. Prince Edward Island received responsible government in 1851, and Newfoundland in 1855.

Responsible Government Achieved in the Canadas

As the first governor of the United Canadas, Sydenham was given two tasks: to bring economic prosperity to the Canadas, and to prevent the introduction of responsible government. Sydenham died in September 1841, from injuries suffered in a fall from his horse. Yet during his short period of office, he did carry out the first of his two tasks. However, he had not been as successful with the second. By the time of his death, the Reformers had managed to make some notable advances toward colonial self-government.

Under pressure from the Reformers, Sydenham ended the practice of lifetime appointments to the Executive Council and invited Reformers from the elected Assembly to form part of the Council. In Upper Canada, he resolved the Clergy Reserves issue by a division of the lands among all the churches, Catholic and Protestant alike. They were to use the revenues from these lands to provide schools. His District Councils Act of 1841 established a system of local government in Canada West. It gave the residents of towns and cities more say in decisions affecting local public works such as road building.

Through these measures, Sydenham hoped to show that he could rule with popular support, thus proving that responsible government was unnecessary. These moves brought Sydenham considerable support in the Assembly, even among some Reformers. But he largely ignored the Canadiens, whom he mistrusted.

The early 1840s saw the Reformers growing in strength. Led by Robert Baldwin in Canada West and LaFontaine in Canada East, they remained convinced that responsible government was needed.

Francis Hincks, Baldwin's chief lieutenant in Canada West, realized what the Family Compact had feared. He saw, as did LaFontaine, that an alliance between the Reformers of Canada West and their Canadien counterparts would form a majority in the Assembly. Hincks moved to Montreal to help Baldwin and LaFontaine forge an alliance of the two Reform groups.

Sydenham's death created an opportunity for the reform alliance to show its strength. His successor, Sir Charles Bagot, also attempted to hold back responsible government. The Tories of Canada West threw their support behind the new governor, but they were a minority in the Assembly. Bagot knew that he needed the backing of representatives from Canada East to have majority support in the Assembly. He needed such support in order to raise money through taxes or to spend tax money on public works.

Therefore, Bagot set out to bring Canadiens into his Council in order to win their support. He invited LaFontaine to join the Executive Council. LaFontaine said he would, as long as Robert Baldwin was also invited. Bagot agreed. Five Reformers replaced five Tory members of the Executive Council. Responsible government had not yet been achieved, however. Though he had made concessions to the Reformers, the governor still dominated the Executive, appointing its members from both parties in the Assembly.

Bagot resigned in 1843 because of ill health. His successor, Sir Charles Metcalfe, was determined to block any further erosion of the governor's power. Over the objections of Baldwin and LaFontaine, whose Reformist alliance formed a majority in the Assembly, Metcalfe appointed his personally-chosen candidates to public office. Angered because they had not been consulted about these appointments, Baldwin, LaFontaine and other Reformers resigned from the council. Their resignations soon forced Metcalfe to call an election.

During the election campaign of 1844, which was more dirty and vicious than normal, Metcalfe branded advocates of responsible government as disloyal to Britain. These accusations, combined with the effective use of bribery and armed gangs of thugs, led to a narrow Tory victory. Metcalfe then appointed all of the members of his Executive Council from the Tory majority in the Assembly.

During Metcalfe's term as governor of the Canadas, major changes were taking place in Britain that would set the stage for the achievement of responsible government in the North American colonies. The era of reformers in Britain, begun in the 1830s, had turned into a quiet political revolution by the mid-1840s. With the end of the old mercantilist system, the colonies were now free to trade as they liked. One of the major obstacles to responsible government had been removed. If Britain no longer controlled the economic life of the colonies, there seemed little reason why it should control their political life either.

As these changes were taking place, Metcalfe retired as governor because of ill health. The Liberal government in Britain named Lord Elgin as his successor in January 1847. Elgin was Durham's son-in-law. Like Durham, Lord Elgin was strongly committed to a more democratic system of government for the colonies. So, too, was the new colonial secretary, Lord Grey, Durham's brother-in-law. Grey instructed Elgin to introduce responsible government as soon as possible.

In the 1848 election in the Canadas, the Reformers won a large majority in the Assembly. Elgin immediately called upon Baldwin and LaFontaine to form a government and to name the members of the Executive Council. Like the prime minister in Britain, they selected these members from their own party in the Assembly. The Executive Council, with the approval of the Assembly, would shape government policy. Responsible government appeared to have been achieved in the Canadas.

The real test of responsible government would come when the colonial government took an action of which the governor disapproved. If the governor overruled the measure, there was no real responsible government. If he granted the act Royal Assent despite his objections, responsible government had been truly achieved.

The first such test came in 1849, with the passage of the Rebellion Losses Bill by the Assembly. This bill provided compensation for persons who had suffered property damage during the rebellion of 1837-1838. Most of the people were Canadiens who had not taken part in the rebellions. However, some of the persons to be compensated were rebels whose property had been destroyed by the British. For this reason, the Tory opposition in the Assembly bitterly opposed the bill. Elgin himself was known not to favor it. Like the Tories, he did not think it right that people who had rebelled against the colonial government a dozen years earlier should now be compensated by the government. The question was whether Elgin would sign the bill into law. Despite threats against his life, he did sign it, on the grounds that responsible government required him to follow the advice of his Executive Council. Responsible government had passed its first test.

THE MONTREAL RIOTS, 1849

Elgin's signing of the Rebellion Losses Bill led to a violent protest and riots by Tories in Montreal. The capital of the Canadas had been moved to Montreal from Kingston in 1844. It was there that Elgin resided and there that he signed the controversial bill. Reverend William Rufus Seaver, a shopkeeper and Congregational minister, was an eyewitness to the riots. He wrote the following account of them in his diary:

> Business is terrible *dull* and nothing is now talked about but a *republican government.* Today the Govn [Governor] came to town on horseback…went home about 3 o'clock…and came again to town attended by his officers and a Guard more than usually numerous. What is this all about? was at once the inquiry….It was rumoured that the Bill indemnifying the Rebellion losses was now to be sanctioned…on the report spreading through town (which it did like wildfire) an immense mob assembled and sourounded [sic] the Parliament house to see what his Excellency [Elgin] intended to

> do–when it was finally announced that he had really given the Royal Sanction to the Bill, then there was *trouble*–as his Excellency left the House for his carriage at the door he was assailed with stones, clubs, & rotten & good eggs by thousands, and he was struck in the face with an egg, his carriage windows broken etc. but by the speed of his horses he was enabled to escape with no injury except to his carriage and his equipage–I stop here for the cry is raised that the *Parliment House* is on fire-fire-fire is the cry–and from my shop door I see the red flames light up the Heavens–I go–more after I see what the row is–

> …about 8 o'clock [in the evening] while Parliament was still sitting a mob (it can be called nothing else tho' composed of some of our most worthy citizens) assembled around the House, and commenced the destruction of the building, by breaking windows etc. Soon the doors were broken open and a stout fellow sprang into the speakers chair with the exclamation, "*I dissolve Parliment.*" This was the Signal–and immediately in the face of the members, and an immense

A second test of responsible government came a decade later. In 1859, the government of the Canadas approved a bill placing a **tariff** of 20 percent on imported goods to raise money for public works. A tariff is a tax or duty paid on products brought into a country. The bill upset British manufacturers who lobbied the Colonial Secretary to stop the tariff. The British government threatened to disallow the bill if the colonial government did not withdraw it. Politely, but firmly, the Canadians refused. In the words of Alexander Galt, a member of the Executive Council:

> Self-government would be utterly annihilated if the views of the Imperial Government were to be preferred to those of the people of Canada. It is therefore the duty of the present government distinctly to affirm the rights of the Canadian legislature to adjust taxation of the people in the way they deem best.

multitude of spectators the Gas Pipes were fired in a dozen places, and the building wraped in flames. . . . All was lost, nothing saved, and the structure now is but a heap of smoking ruins.

1. Why were the Montreal Tories outraged by the signing of the Rebellion Losses Bill?
2. What, in your opinion, might have happened if the Tory rioters had killed or seriously injured Elgin?
3. Compare the actions of the Tory rioters in Montreal to Mackenzie's rebels in Toronto. In your opinion, which is the more serious act of political defiance?

The British Colonial Office backed down. The principle of responsible government had been reaffirmed.

1. In your own words, define responsible government.
2. Compare the achievement of responsible government in Nova Scotia with its achievement in the Canadas.
3. What important test of responsible government occured in 1849? in 1859?

Summary

Already famous as an advocate of political change in Britain, Durham was sent to the North American colonies in order to find some solutions to the problems that had created the rebellions of 1837-1838. Reformers like Robert Baldwin in Upper Canada impressed

Durham with their arguments that the colonies should be given responsible government. Durham found little acceptance for his idea of a legislative union of all the colonies, yet he did continue to favor a union of Upper and Lower Canada.

Durham's report addressed the causes of political unrest in both Upper and Lower Canada. He recommended that the Clergy Reserves, long a source of conflict between the Reformers and the Family Compact in Upper Canada, be abolished. The source of conflict in Lower Canada Durham identified as the irreconcilable differences between the older Canadien way of life and that of the British newcomers. The only solution of this conflict, in Durham's view, was the forced assimilation of the Canadiens into a British way of life. To achieve this, Durham recommended the union of Upper and Lower Canada into a single colony in which British values and institutions would prevail. Durham also addressed the on-going conflict between reformers and Tory oligarchies in all of the British North American colonies. This conflict, he believed, could only be ended by the introduction of responsible government. However, Durham wanted to be sure that responsible government did not result in Canadien control over the political life of Lower Canada. He believed that union of the colonies would prevent this.

Fearing a loss of their privileges, the Tory-dominated Family Compact of Upper Canada opposed the report's recommendations. Canadien political leaders in Lower Canada attacked Durham's argument that they should be assimilated. However, some Canadien leaders like Etienne Parent and L.H. LaFontaine were favorable to the idea of responsible government, as were Reformers like Robert Baldwin, in Upper Canada, and Joseph Howe, in Nova Scotia.

Under the governorship of Baron Sydenham, a union of the two Canadas was proclaimed in 1841. But the British government was as yet unprepared to grant responsible government to the newly-united colony. Reformers in Nova Scotia won an 1847 election making that colony the first to get responsible government.

In the Canadas, a succession of three colonial governors, Sydenham, Bagot and Metcalfe, fought against the Reformers' campaign for responsible government. Finally, the Reform alliance led by Baldwin in Canada West and LaFontaine in Canada East won a decisive election victory in 1848. In the next year, the issue of the Rebellion Losses Bill showed that responsible government had come to the Canadas.

REVIEW

Checking Back

1. Write one or two sentences to describe the significance of each of the following.

   Lord Durham   Louis-Hippolyte
   Lord Elgin   LaFontaine
   Robert Baldwin   Sir Charles Bagot
   Joseph Howe   Sir John Harvey
   Lord Russell

2. What was the "Canadian problem" and how did Britain hope to solve it?

3. Choose three important events that stand as milestones to the achievement of responsible government in the Canadas and explain why each was important.

4. What did Lord Durham cite as the real reasons for the rebellions of 1837-1838?

5. (a) One of Durham's suggested reforms was the union of Upper and Lower Canada. Read the reactions of Etienne Parent (page 60) and R.B. Sullivan (page 61) to the proposed union. Write a brief summary of each man's point of view.
   (b) If you had to decide whether to vote for or against union, after reading both arguments, which side would you support? Give reasons for your answer.

6. The Canadiens opposed the Act of Union, yet there was no rebellion following its passage. Suggest reasons for this.

Using Your Knowledge

7. Draw two cartoons: one showing the reaction of the Family Compact to the Durham Report and the other showing the reaction of the Canadiens.

8. One reason for the reforms presented in the Durham report was to prevent annexation of Canada by the United States. Record two pieces of evidence to support Durham's fears that some of the settlers were in favor of annexation. Which of Durham's suggestions do you think would stop the annexation movement? Explain.

9. Imagine that you had been a follower of William Lyon Mackenzie in the Rebellions of 1837-1838. Write a diary entry that reveals how you feel about life in the Canadas in 1849.

10. The year is 1849. The Rebellion Losses Bill has just been passed by the Legislature of the Canadas. Write a letter to Lord Elgin to persuade him to sign the Bill, despite his own feelings that the Bill is unfair.

11. Suggest one or two reasons to explain why responsible government was achieved in the Maritimes, without armed rebellion.

Chapter 4

British North America at Mid-Century

By the middle of the nineteenth century, British North America was experiencing rapid social, technological and economic change. It was a period marked by large-scale immigration and population growth, particularly in the Canadas. It was also an era of railway construction, which resulted in a dramatic increase in the speed of transportation and communication. As well, this period was marked by major changes in relations between the colonies and their two major trading partners, Britain and the United States. Following the end of mercantilism and the colonies' protected trading relationship with Britain, the colonies faced a serious economic depression. However, as you will learn, with the negotiation of a reciprocal trade treaty with the United States in the 1850s, British North America experienced new found prosperity.

At the same time as these changes were taking place, the Canadas were facing a severe political crisis. Achievement of responsible government had not ended the political problems in the Canadas. The constitutional arrangement provided by the Act of Union had brought the process of government in the colony to a standstill. Party politics and regional differences made it almost impossible for any one group to hold a majority of seats in the Assembly and to form a government. As you will see, a bold act of compromise and conciliation would be needed to break the deadlock.

As you read this chapter, the following key questions should be kept in mind:

- What social and economic forces were changing North America in the middle of the nineteenth century?
- What effect did the end of mercantilism have on the economies of the British North American colonies? How did the signing of a reciprocal trade agreement with the United States help bring prosperity to the colonies?
- Why was there a "deadlock" in the government of the Canadas during the 1850s and early 1860s? How was this deadlock broken?

North America at Mid-Century

The Industrial Revolution had taken firm root in mid-nineteenth century North America, drawing on the continent's vast resources. Centres such as New York, Montreal, Philadelphia and Toronto were rapidly growing, modern industrial cities. Railroads and telegraph lines linked these centres to rural towns and villages which had been isolated pioneer settlements only a few decades earlier. Along these transportation and communications lines flowed goods, ideas and people. **Entrepreneurs** and industrialists made great fortunes building railroads, shipyards and factories to meet the demands of a fast-growing economy.

Yet in the midst of this great wealth and strength, there was poverty and conflict. In the American South, black slaves were still being used to plant and tend crops on great plantations. Throughout North America, the westward movement of the railway and the immigrants it carried was changing the lives of Native peoples. Immigrant groups from Europe brought with them centuries-old political, national and religious rivalries.

Three key social and economic factors stood out dramatically in the two decades leading up to Confederation: immigration and population growth, changing patterns of trade, and changing methods of transportation. Each would play a major part in shaping the new Canadian nation.

THE END OF MERCANTILISM

Under mercantilism (see page 23), the British North American colonists had to buy most of their imported goods from Britain. In return, they had favored access to British markets for their grain, lumber and other products. As late as 1843, the British Conservative government had approved the Canada Corn [wheat] Act, which set the duty on wheat imported into Britain from Canada at only one-half that charged on wheat imported from the United States, France and other suppliers. This made Canadian wheat cheaper for British merchants to buy, while ensuring a good market for the colonial farmers and traders.

Three years later, the British government repealed the Corn Act. Canadian wheat merchants no longer enjoyed privileged access to British markets. The British government wanted to import grain at the lowest price, regardless of its origins, to feed Britain's rapidly growing population.

The end of mercantilism hit farmers and the business community in British North America with a sharp and sudden impact. By 1849, Canadian wheat farmers were getting half the profit they had received in 1843. Lord Elgin estimated that half the trading companies in Montreal, at this time the economic centre of the colonies, were forced into bankruptcy between 1846 and 1848. The end of mercantilism caused a depression in the economy of British North America.

A Movement for Annexation

Unhappy with the economic problems facing the colonies after the end of mercantilism, some Montreal merchants saw only one solution: join the United States. Some of these merchants had been among the mob that had attacked Elgin and burned the Parliament buildings (see pages 68-69). Now, they were ready to break with Britain completely. During the summer of 1849, the movement to seek **annexation** to the United States grew in strength and numbers.

The following document was published in the Montreal *Gazette* of October 11, 1849. Signed by 325 leading merchants of Montreal, among them, John and William Molson, founders of the famous brewing company, and J.J.C. Abbott, who would later become prime minister of Canada. The manifesto gave the annexationists' views on the situation faced by Canada at that time and their reasons for seeking union with the United States.

To the People of Canada

The reversal of the ancient policy of Great Britain whereby she withdrew from the colonies...protection in her markets, has produced the most disastrous effects upon Canada. In surveying the actual condition of the country what but ruin or rapid decay meets the eye!...our country stands before the world in humiliating contrast with its immediate neighbours, exhibiting every symptom of a nation fast sinking to decay.

With super abundant water power and cheap labour, especially in Lower Canada, we have yet no domestic manufactures;...Our institutions, unhappily, have not that impress of permanence which alone can impart security and inspire confidence, and the Canadian market is too limited to inspire the foreign capitalist. While the adjoining States are covered with a network of thriving railways, Canada possesses but three lines, which, together, scarcely exceed 50 miles [80 kilometres] in length...a fatal symptom of the torpor overspreading the land....

...Of all the remedies that have been suggested for the acknowledged and insufferable ills with which our country is afflicted, there remains but one to be considered...THIS REMEDY CONSISTS IN THE FRIENDLY AND PEACEFUL SEPARATION FROM BRITISH CONNECTION AND A UNION UPON EQUITABLE TERMS WITH THE GREAT NORTH AMERICAN CONFEDERACY OF SOVEREIGN STATES.

Within a week of the appearance of this manifesto, the Annexationist movement had more than 1000 prominent supporters in Lower Canada. Among them were several members of the Parliament of the Canadas. The group decided to press for union with the United States through the elected Assembly. The Annexationists were, for the most part, English-speaking members of the merchant classes. They soon found they had little support for their scheme outside of their own group. Most Canadiens were strongly opposed to annexation. They feared that there would be no protection for their way of life in any union with the Americans. The Loyalist population of Upper Canada, with its sentimental ties to Britain, likewise opposed the movement. Although some reformers favored annexation to the American republic, most, including Robert Baldwin, spoke out strongly against it. With so little popular support, the movement was soon abandoned.

1. In your own words, describe the economic problems of the Canadas as seen by the Montreal merchants in the Annexationist Manifesto of 1849.
2. Explain why Canadiens were not in favor of annexation to the United States.
3. The manifesto signed by the leading merchants of Montreal refers to "...cheap labour, especially in Lower Canada...." What does this statement indicate about the businesspeople's attitudes towards the Canadiens?

ANNEXATION COMES IN BY THE RAIL, WHILE LIBERTY FLIES OFF IN THE SMOKE.

What did the cartoonist see as the end result of annexation to the United States?

The Prosperous Years

Economic conditions in British North America began to change for the better in the 1850s. Because Britain was now buying far less timber from the colonies, colonial entrepreneurs had to begin finding new uses for it. In New Brunswick, Nova Scotia and Quebec, shipbuilders started using the timber to build schooners and other trading ships. These sailing vessels soon gained a worldwide reputation for their speed and grace. By the early 1860s, Canadian shipyards were producing as many as 700 wooden-hulled vessels each year.

Unfortunately, the success of this industry was short-lived. Shipbuilders in the United States and Europe were already turning to iron and steam, a change ignored in their prosperity by the shipyards of Nova Scotia and New Brunswick. By the 1880s, the wooden ship industry of those colonies was on its last legs, with no other major industry to take its place.

The Bluenose *was an outstanding example of the shipbuilding industry in the Maritime Provinces. By the end of the nineteenth century, steel ships had replaced wooden sailing vessels, destroying the livelihood of many people employed in the industry.*

Events in Europe and the United States at mid-century created an increased demand for many exports from the colonies. Britain's growing cities needed lumber to build homes and factories and grain to feed their populations. The immigrant-swollen population and strong industrial economy of the United States created a similar demand for Canadian exports.

War in both Europe and the United States played an important part in this economic boom. Manufacturing industries and trade were disrupted by war. Workers left their factories, farms, forest and mines to become soldiers. These soldiers had to be well-fed and supplied to fight effectively. The Crimean War of 1854-1856 between Russia and a British-French alliance, increased demand for the wheat, fish and timber of British North America. In the United States, the Civil War of 1861-1865 greatly expanded the market for British North American products in that country also.

1. What conditions in Europe and the United States created markets there for goods from British North America?

Reciprocity

Trade between British North America and the United States greatly increased as the result of a **reciprocity** agreement negotiated in the mid-1850s. Reciprocity is a fancy word for "you scratch my back and I'll scratch yours." It is a deal that provides some benefit for both parties. A reciprocal free trade treaty is a document signed by two nations that permits goods to pass freely across their borders without any barriers in the form of quotas, tariffs or duties.

During the late 1840s, Canadian merchants had been pressuring their political leaders to negotiate a trading agreement with the United States. The merchants needed access to the United States' market in order to make up for the losses they had suffered because of Britain's new free trade policy. But the American government was not in favor of such an agreement. It had listened to the concerns of manufacturers in Vermont, Massachusetts and other northeastern states. These manufacturers feared that free trade would lead to British manufactured goods being brought into the United States through Canada. Because manufacturing costs were lower in Britain than in the United States, British goods could be sold at a lower cost than similar American-made products.

Failure to reach a free trade agreement with the United States led to a meeting of delegates from the British North American colonies at Halifax in the fall of 1849. This meeting was the first-ever joint conference of Britain's colonies in North America. The colonial leaders knew that the Americans had long been seeking rights to the rich inshore fisheries of the Maritimes. Here was an opportunity to offer these rights in exchange for free access to the United States market.

In 1854, Lord Elgin, acting on behalf of the colonies, successfully negotiated a trade agreement with the United States. The treaty gave Newfoundland fish, Nova Scotia coal, New Brunswick timber and Canadian flour free entry to the United States. In return, the Americans were now able to fish freely in the waters of New Brunswick, Nova Scotia and Prince Edward Island. This agreement with the Americans gave the colonies an increased level of prosperity. As well, the Halifax Conference had established a basis for communication among the colonies on matters of mutual concern. It would be an important step towards Confederation.

Despite this new arrangement, the Atlantic colonies remained politically and economically isolated from the Canadas. Their only link with the rest of British North America was the St. Lawrence River, which was blocked by ice throughout the winter. Most of their trade and cultural contacts were with Britain, the area of the United States from Boston north, or the West Indies. Tense encounters between British ships and American gunboats during the American Civil War showed that these ties could be disrupted by foreign conflicts. These problems would have to be overcome before closer relations between the Canadas and the Atlantic colonies could be established.

1. What is reciprocity? Why did the British North American colonists want a reciprocal trade agreement with the United States in the 1850s?
2. What did the British colonies have to give up to get access to the American market?

Changes in Transportation: The Age of the Railways

One possible solution to the problem of transportation between the Atlantic colonies and the Canadas was building a railway. In 1850, British North America's only railway outside of the coal mines of Nova Scotia was the St. Lawrence and Lake Champlain Railroad. It stretched twenty-six kilometres south from Montreal, carrying passengers on day trip excursions. A decade later, there were

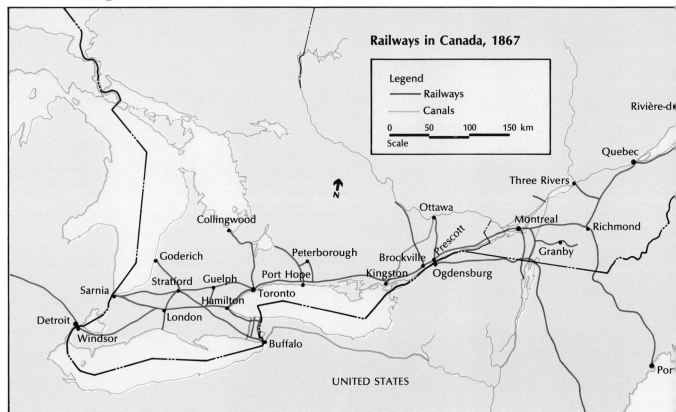

This map shows the extent of railway development in Canada up to 1867. Notice the strong ties to the United States using both rail and canal links.

3200 km of railway lines in British North America. Steam locomotives, products of the Industrial Revolution, had greatly revolutionized travel. They could pull heavy trains of goods or passengers at steady speeds no team of horses could match, regardless of the weather. The main railway was the Grand Trunk Western, completed in 1856, which joined Montreal and Toronto. It was later extended to Detroit in the west and Rivière du Loup in the east. On this line, a wood-burning locomotive could reach the then-breakneck speed of fifty kilometres per hour. The journey from Montreal to Toronto, one that had taken early explorers and pioneer settlers weeks of hard travel, could now be taken in less than a day. Admittedly, the trip took a little longer in winter. Passengers would often have to get out to help the train crew shovel heavy snow off the line, but that was part of the fun of getting there.

The Grand Trunk Western, welcomed by industry and commerce, was an expensive and ambitious project. Its owners repeatedly faced bankruptcy, only to be bailed out by loans from the

nouski

government of the Canadas, which added to the colony's debt. This pattern would be repeated throughout the history of railway building in Canada. Railway building required large areas of land and great amounts of money. Governments became involved in it almost from the start, giving land grants, providing surveys and, most importantly, assisting with the funding of these expensive projects.

Railways profoundly changed North American society. With the new age of high speed travel, cities began to take on a new importance. Small rural communities began to decline as manufacturing plants located in the cities began to supply farmers with tools once made by local blacksmiths. Mills closed down as logs and grain could be shipped by rail to the cities for processing. At the same time, the railways opened up new areas of the country to farming and other activities. New communities were created along the expanding networks.

Beginning in the 1850s, the railways, and the telegraph lines that ran alongside them, greatly increased the speed at which ideas could be communicated. City newspapers could now be purchased in frontier settlements within a day of their publication. The vast expanses of land to the west and north of the Canadas were no longer so daunting. Business leaders and politicians began to envision a future in which a web of rail lines would spread across the continent in all directions. This desire for a transcontinental rail system would play an important role in discussions leading up to the entry of Nova Scotia and New Brunswick and, later, British Columbia, into Confederation.

1. Why did the government get involved in railway building in the 1850s? In your opinion could railways have been built without government help? Explain your answer.
2. How did the growth of the railways affect rural and small-town industry?

Government in the Canadas: Conflict and Compromise

Although the colonial economic picture was bright in the mid-1850s, the political scene was less so. The process of government in the Canadas was deadlocked. It would remain so until, in 1864, a compromise solution was found. Below, you will first see how this political deadlock came about, then how it was broken.

The Deadlock Formed: Chaos in the Party System

Two major factors lay behind the problems of finding a stable government in the Canadas. The first was the equal distribution of seats in the elected Assembly between the two Canadas. No government could survive unless it had the support of elements in both the Canadas. The second was the large number of political parties and independent members holding seats in the Assembly. The Act of Union had created a political problem for the Canadas that appeared to have no solution. The division of power between Canada East and Canada West was so evenly balanced that no party could stay in power very long.

Durham had proposed the union of the Canadas to force the Canadiens to become part of an English cultural, political and social system. However, as Sullivan (see page 61) had predicted, the Canadiens were able to control the political life of Canada East. In doing so, they made their region the dominant force in the Assembly. Representation in the Assembly was equally divided between the two Canadas. With the representatives from Canada West split into Conservatives and Reformers, the Canadiens were easily able to control the Assembly. For example, a bill was passed in 1851 to extend support to Roman Catholic schools in largely Protestant Canada West.

This division gave rise to what became known as the problem of the **double majority.** Under responsible government, the party with a majority in the Assembly formed the government. The leader of the party forming the government became the prime minister. However, in the Canadas each government had to have both an English and a French leader and support from both regions in order to have a majority in the Assembly. This was the double majority. Although the Act of Union had created a single Legislative Assembly, no government could survive unless it had the support of elements in both the Canadas.

Meanwhile, old political alliances and parties in the Canadas were changing. The Conservative Party in Canada West, led by Alan McNab and John A. Macdonald, had become much more moderate. No longer just the party of the old land-owning elite, it was now committed to expansion of industry and commerce. In Canada East, the Bleus were a party of similar interests. Under the leadership of George-Étienne Cartier, this party had allied itself with the Conservatives of Canada West by the mid-1850s.

Reformers in Canada West were now divided into two main groups. On the one hand, there was the moderate Liberal Party, led by Francis Hincks, Baldwin's chief advisor. On the other hand, there were the more radical Clear Grits, led by George Brown, publisher of the Toronto *Globe*. Under Brown's leadership the Clear Grits gradually transformed themselves from a small, powerless group into a significant political force in Canada West. The Clear Grits were the party of the frontier farmers, opposed to big business, the Roman Catholic Church and the French language.

In particular, Brown was an outspoken advocate of **representation by population** in the Canadas. The equal division of seats in the Assembly made in 1840 had been designed to reduce the influence of the larger population of Canada East. However, the census of 1851 showed that Canada West now had 952 000 people, compared with 890 000 in Canada East. If, for example, there was to be one elected legislator for every 10 000 inhabitants, Canada West would have ninety-five seats in the Assembly compared to only eighty-nine for Canada East. Representation by population would now give Canada West a majority of the seats in the elected House of Assembly. Brown thus saw representation by population as a means to reduce the Canadien influence in the Assembly.

This anti-French aspect of the Clear Grit platform split them apart from their counterparts in Canada East, the Parti Rouge. Led by Antoine-Aimé Dorion, the Parti Rouge was opposed to big business in the form of the British merchants, bankers and railway builders. However, the Parti Rouge was a strong defender of the traditions of French-Canada. When the Clear Grits and the Parti Rouge attempted to work together in 1858, the result was the shortest-lived government in Canadian history, one that lasted less than a day.

To further complicate things, there was also a significant number of independents, tied to no party, sitting in the Assembly. Known as the **loose fish,** these independents often held the balance of power in the Assembly. They would cast their votes with whichever party or group of parties they could strike a deal.

The result was political chaos. Since no one party had enough seats to form a majority, two or more parties would have to agree to work together to form a coalition government. Such a government is faced with the difficult task of making decisions which all its parties support. As you learned in the previous chapter, under responsible government the executive branch (cabinet) must have the support of the elected Assembly. The tradition of responsible

CHOOSING A NEW CAPITAL

After the burning of the Parliament buildings in 1849, Montreal had ceased to be the capital of the united Canadas. Instead, the site of the capital alternated between Toronto and Quebec City. After several years of wrangling, the issue was submitted to Queen Victoria for royal arbitration, and in 1857 the Queen chose Ottawa as the site.

There was a rumor, widely circulated in the Canadas, that the queen had chosen the new capital by sticking a pin in a map while blindfolded. To many politicians and civil servants, this was the only possible explanation for the selection of the small lumber community of Bytown, renamed Ottawa in 1855. However, political and military reasons appear to have dictated this choice. The political consideration was the city's location on the Ottawa River, the dividing line between Canada East and Canada West. The military consideration was its location; several days difficult march away from the United States border.

government requires that a party or coalition enjoy the "confidence" or support of a majority of the elected members in order to govern. If a coalition government loses the support of one party, it may be defeated on a vote of **non-confidence.**

In 1854, the Liberals and the Conservatives formed a coalition, the Liberal-Conservative Party. This coalition was able to enlist the support of the Bleus in Canada East. Led by John A. Macdonald of the Conservatives and George-Étienne Cartier of the Bleus, the coalition formed a government following the 1857 election. However, the issue of finding a capital for the united Canadas led to their defeat.

Queen Victoria's choice of Ottawa as capital was put to the Assembly during the summer of 1858 for approval. The Rouges moved a motion calling for a rejection of the royal choice; the Bleus broke with the coalition to support the Rouge motion and the coalition government was defeated. The governor general invited George Brown, leader of the Canada West Clear Grits, and A.A. Dorion, the leader of the Canada East Rouges, to form a government. Despite bitter hatred for each other, the two leaders agreed. Less than twenty-four hours later, their government had fallen, defeated on a vote of non-confidence. Brown called for a new election to be held. Instead, the governor general called again on Macdonald and Cartier to form a new government.

Things became steadily worse. Between 1862 and 1864, for example, five successive coalitions attempted to govern the Canadas. None lasted more than a matter of months. The governmental process in the Canadas had come to a complete standstill.

1. Members of the Family Compact had opposed the Act of Union because they feared that the emergence of political parties would divide the people of Canada West. Were they right? What impact did political parties have on the process of government in the united Canadas?

2. In a chart form, summarize the information about each of the five major political parties in the Canadas during the 1850s. Use these headings: party, leader, power base, main concerns.

3. In your own words, explain the problem of the "double majority." How does it reflect the problems caused by the Act of Union?

4. Who were the "loose fish"? What role did they play in the Assembly of the Canadas?

This painting shows the Parliament buildings in 1866. Note the lock in the foreground.

The Deadlock Broken: the Great Coalition

George Brown, leader of the Clear Grits, was known as a hot-tempered giant of a Scotsman. His violent outbursts against Canadiens, Catholics and Conservatives had deeply divided colonial politics during the 1850s and early 1860s. He seemed an unlikely leader to offer a solution to the political deadlock in Canada. Yet that is exactly what George Brown did.

Brown's leadership in the search for a solution began with his role as chairman of an all-party committee formed to study the deadlock problem. This committee presented its report to the Assembly in June 1864. The report stated firmly that the deadlock could only be broken by a federal union, or confederation, of the British North American colonies. In the proposed federal union, power would be shared by the provinces and a central government. Each level of government would have its own elected Legislative Assembly. At the federal level, the legislature would have responsibility for those things that affected everybody within the union, such as currency, customs and excise taxes, the post office, criminal laws, and inter-provincial trade and transportation. The provincial assemblies would make laws dealing with local matters.

The day George Brown made his report to the Assembly, another government fell on a vote of non-confidence, the fourth in two

Born in Scotland and brought to Canada as a young boy, John A. Macdonald trained to be a lawyer. In 1856 he wrote to an English friend in Montreal: "The truth is that you British Lower Canadians never can forget that you were once supreme. . . . You can't and won't admit the principle that the majority must govern."

years. Brown stood up in the Assembly to announce that, to form a government, he was prepared to join with the Conservatives, the party he had been bitterly opposing for several years.

This bold move almost immediately broke the deadlock. Brown announced his willingness to put aside past conflicts, and to join with the Conservatives for the greater good of both colonies. The Assembly burst into wild applause. One of Brown's opponents from Canada East rushed across the floor of the Assembly to fling his arms happily around the feisty leader. Brown's action had required considerable compromise on his part. He had to side with a party that supported the bankers and industrialists, and, he had to join in an alliance with considerable support in French Canada.

Brown shared the leadership of this government with Macdonald, Cartier and Galt. The leaders of the Grits, Conservatives, and Bleus, had joined forces with Galt, a leading independent, to break the deadlock. Their government, known as the **Great Coalition,** committed itself to seeking a federal union of the Canadas and the Maritime colonies. If that effort should fail, the members of the coalition agreed that they would then form at least a federal union of the two Canadas.

The Great Coalition was led by a group of men rich in leadership and holding strong visions of what Canada might be in the future. Cartier, leader of the Bleus, had worked hard to ensure that the Canadien people were part of the mainstream of Canada's political life while preserving their culture and traditions. Galt, a successful financier, was an Independent-Conservative. He had first proposed a federal union in 1849 as an alternative to the annexationists' move to join the United States. A member of the English minority in Canada East, Galt was very mindful of the Canadiens' concern that their traditions be protected in any union of the British North American colonies.

One man, John A. Macdonald, emerged from the Great Coalition as a leader among leaders. Brown's bold action had created the coalition that had broken the deadlock but Macdonald's great political skills kept it working effectively. Macdonald is in many ways a strange figure in Canada's history. His life was marked by tragedy, scandal, corruption and controversy, yet this tall, friendly, ambling Conservative from Kingston in Canada West became a powerful and well-loved prime minister.

To a large extent, the quest for Confederation shaped the image people had of Macdonald. He would become known as the "Father of Confederation," yet, ironically, Macdonald was cool to the idea of Confederation almost to the time it was achieved. He had long fought to make the existing union of the Canadas work. In the end, the idea of a larger union put forward by Galt and Brown caught Macdonald's imagination. Once committed to the idea, his good-natured sense of humor and great skill as a tactful negotiator helped steer the tricky course of compromise that negotiations with the other colonies required.

1. Define "compromise." Suggest what could happen in a society or government if people are unable to achieve compromises.
2. What was the Great Coalition? What roles did George Brown play in its creation?
3. What is a coalition government? What problems might such a government face? Why would the leadership skills possessed by John A. Macdonald be so important in such a government?

Summary

In this chapter, you have learned that the mid-nineteenth century was a period of rapid social, economic and political change in British North America. In part, these changes were the result of forces at work in the Canadas and the Maritime provinces. To a very large extent, they were the result of events outside the colonies as well.

During the mid-1800s, large numbers of immigrants came to Canada from Great Britain. Many stayed in the Canadas; perhaps an equally large number went on to the United States. Immigration greatly increased the population of British North America, from 2 million people in 1840 to 4 million in 1867.

Events in Britain, as you have seen in this chapter, greatly affected the economic life of the colonies. The British government was now committed to free trade. Repeal of the "Corn Laws" saw the colonies' favored trading relationship with Britain come to an end, bringing hardship to many farmers and merchants.

Reactions to this changed trading relationship varied. On the one hand were the many merchants who saw their only hope for prosperity coming from annexation of the colonies to the United States. On the other hand were politicians and business leaders who felt that free trade with the U.S. would provide the colonies with the markets they needed. The process of negotiating a reciprocal trade agreement with the Americans saw the beginnings of co-operation among the British North American colonies.

The economic problems facing British North America were compounded in the Canadas by a continuing political deadlock. As you have seen, the Act of Union did not solve the problem of the division of power between the English- and French-speaking Canadians. Now, the problem was compounded by the large number of political parties represented in the House of Assembly. No party could form a majority without leaders from both the Canadas, and no party could form a government without the support of another party. Every government in the 1850s and 1860s was a coalition government, lasting only as long as the coalition held together.

George Brown broke this deadlock by the creation of the Great Coalition. He managed to unite the various major political parties into a government devoted to one end–Confederation of the British North American colonies.

REVIEW

Checking Back

1. Write one or two sentences summarizing the significance of each of the following in the economy of British North America.

   mercantilism   reciprocity

2. In one or two sentences, summarize the impact of the following on the social life of British North America.

   Industrial   railways
   Revolution

3. Who were the supporters of the annexation movement? Explain why they received little support in the Canadas.

4. In the late 1840s, why did Canadian entrepreneurs want to see a reciprocal trade agreement with the United States? Why were the Americans not interested in such an agreement?

5. Discuss how events in Europe and the United States affected economic growth in British North America.

Using Your Knowledge

6. The geography of Canada made it easier for the Maritimes to trade with Britain and the United States, than with the Canadas. Why?

7. Record at least one piece of evidence that supports the claim that one purpose of the Act of Union was the assimilation of the Canadiens.

8. In your own words, explain what is meant by political deadlock. Why was there a deadlock in the Canadas in the 1860s?

9. Why was George Brown's leadership important in solving the problem of political deadlock?

Chapter 5

Towards Confederation, 1865-1867

In this chapter you will examine events that led up to Confederation in 1867. The focus is largely on political events in the British North American colonies, but you will also learn how external pressures from Britain, the United States, and a group of Irish nationalists called Fenians, contributed to the union of Britain's North American colonies.

During the mid-1860s, the internal problems of the colonies were made worse by growing fears of invasion or annexation from the United States. It was also a time when Britain was changing its relationship with its colonies and worrying about the costs of maintaining and defending them. You will see how these internal and external forces led the leaders of the colonies to seek ways in which the colonies could be strengthened politically and economically.

To make the colonies stronger, the idea of uniting all of British North America, proposed by Durham in 1839, was once again raised. Yet, before such a confederation, or union, could be established, many questions had to be answered: Could regional differences among the colonies, particularly the distinctive culture of Canada East, be accommodated in the proposed union? What form of government would the proposed union have? Would the union of British North America prevent its invasion or annexation by the United States?

During the period 1860-1867 political leaders in the Canadas, New Brunswick, Nova Scotia, Prince Edward Island and Newfoundland weighed the costs and benefits of the proposed union. Opinion in the Atlantic colonies and Canada East was sharply divided over the proposal. These differences led to vigorous debate over what form the union should take, and whether it should take place at all.

You will learn that the process of shaping Confederation was marked by compromise, as the people who shaped Canada's Constitution worked out a solution to the issues raised in these debates. The result was the system of government that exists in Canada today, a federal union, with powers assigned to both the central government and the provinces.

As you read through this chapter, keep the following key questions in mind:

- What external forces helped shape Confederation?
- How did the British North America Act assign political power to Canada and the provinces following Confederation?

The Search for Support for Confederation

The leaders of the Great Coalition did not envision a fully independent Canada. Instead, they foresaw an **auxiliary kingdom,** one still closely tied to Britain. In the military defence of the united colonies and in their relations with foreign powers, Britain would still play the major role. The Great Coalition did not work out all of the details of the proposed federal union. Indeed, there were significant differences of opinion among its members over these details.

As well, one major obstacle still had to be overcome. The proposal had considerable support in the Canadas, but it did not have the support of the Atlantic colonists. During the years of 1864-1867, leaders of the British North American colonies met on three occasions to discuss some sort of union: in Charlottetown (September 1864), in Quebec City (October 1864) and in London (the winter of 1866-1867). Let us take a look at each of these three conferences.

The Charlottetown Conference

The leaders of the Atlantic colonies were concerned about their weak and isolated position in North America. The American Civil War had given rise to demands for a railway linking Halifax to Quebec City. Such a rail link would allow the quick movement of troops between the two cities if it became necessary to defend the colonies from American invasion. As well, merchants in Nova Scotia and New Brunswick were eager for the access to the Canadian markets that the railway would bring. Economic depression had hit the Atlantic colonies in the 1860s as demand for wooden ships declined. Civil war and the end of slavery in the United States had also caused reduced exports of salt cod, a major source of food for slaves on southern plantations.

For a while in 1861-1862, the three governments of the Canadas, New Brunswick and Nova Scotia seemed ready to have the intercolonial railway built. Then, in 1863, the government of the Canadas backed out of the scheme. It had already had to spend its scarce tax dollars to prop up the faltering Grand Trunk Western Railway. The Canadas would commit themselves to sharing the costs of surveying the proposed Halifax to Quebec City rail route, but nothing more.

Angered by the action of the Canadians, the colonies of New Brunswick, Nova Scotia and Prince Edward Island, the three Maritime colonies, decided to consider some form of union among themselves. They had already been united and divided in several combinations since 1713. Maritime union was still at the discussion stage when events in the Canadas during 1864 brought a new twist to the proposal.

The first event was renewed interest in the intercolonial railway in the Canadas. The Canadian government now approved a bill that called for a survey of the rail line, with the government of the Canadas paying the entire costs. The second event was the formation of the Great Coalition. The leaders of the coalition asked that

Delegates from New Brunswick, Nova Scotia, Prince Edward Island and the Canadas attended the Charlottetown Conference.

they be allowed to present their proposal for Confederation at the forthcoming Maritime Union Conference.

Encouraged by the renewed Canadian interest in the intercolonial railway, the Maritime colonists agreed to invite the Canadians to come and present their scheme. The date of the Conference was set for September 1, 1864; the place, Charlottetown, capital of Prince Edward Island.

It was a warm and pleasant September morning as fifteen men in black coats and top hats took their places at the great mahogany table in the Council Chamber of the Legislative building in Charlottetown. The fifteen were delegates from the three Maritime colonies: Newfoundland had chosen not to attend. As they took their seats, the Canadian party, among them Macdonald, Cartier, Galt and Brown, waited aboard the *Queen Victoria*, anchored in Charlottetown Harbour. With them on board their ship were several hundred bottles of champagne, brought along to help convince the Maritime colonists to join the proposed Confederation.

Inside the Council Chamber, the idea of a Maritime union was quickly rejected. The economies of the colonies were too similar, and their populations too small, for a Maritime union to bring many benefits. The discussion turned to the proposal for a larger union of the colonies brought by the Canadians. The plan was greeted by the Maritime leaders with cautious approval. They agreed that confederation of the British colonies in North America might be desirable, providing that suitable terms could be agreed upon. A second meeting was set for later that year, in Quebec City.

With the Charlottetown Conference over, the Canadians threw a gala ball for their hosts before leaving on a tour of the Maritime colonies. It was a triumphant occasion as the delegates danced, toasted each other with champagne and made speeches until three o'clock in the morning. The next day, the *Queen Victoria* left Charlottetown, carrying the Canadians to Nova Scotia. Everywhere they went, Macdonald and his companions gave speeches, claiming that confederation of the colonies would mark the beginning of a strong and prosperous nation. They received a mixed reception from the Maritime colonists, with Joseph Howe leading opposition to union with the Canadas.

1. What conditions within British North America encouraged the Maritime colonies to consider a union with the Canadas?

2. Why did the Maritime delegates to the Charlottetown Conference reject the idea of a Maritime union?

The Quebec Conference

One month after the Charlottetown Conference, the *Queen Victoria* made a second voyage to the Maritimes. This time, it returned with delegates from all four of the Atlantic colonies. Newfoundland, though still very wary of the Confederation proposal, had agreed to send observers to Quebec City.

The Quebec Conference began on October 10, 1864. The colonies brought different demands to the bargaining table. Nova Scotia and New Brunswick wanted assurances that the intercolonial railway would be built. Prince Edward Island wanted money to buy back the lands held by absentee landowners. The Newfoundlanders, unsure that they would receive any benefits from Confederation, were there mostly because of pressure from the British government. The delegates to the Quebec Conference vigorously debated the form of the proposed union. Some were committed to a federal union, while others favored a legislative union with a strong central government. Still others were not sure they wanted any form of union at all.

A legislative union would see one central government having all of the powers to make laws for all parts of the country. Each of the individual colonies would have to give up its own elected assemblies. Instead, elected representatives from local areas would be sent to sit in a central Parliament. This was the approach used then, and still used, in Great Britain. In such a union, people have only to deal with one level of government, one system of taxation and one set of laws.

The chief drawback to a legislative union is the fact that not everybody wants to be treated alike. In Britain, minority groups such as the Scots and Irish had seen their traditional customs and languages weakened under the legislative union. The Canadiens, remembering Durham's motives for the Act of Union, feared the same thing might happen to their language and religion. The Maritime colonies, with their small populations, feared their voices would not be heard strongly enough in a legislative union.

Gradually each of the issues was worked out. The unified colonies committed themselves to the construction of the Halifax-Quebec Railway and to the purchase from the absentee landlords of unoccupied lands in Prince Edward Island. The consensus among the delegates was that a federal union would be the most effective form of government.

Much of the discussion at the Quebec Conference focussed on how powers should be assigned to the federal and provincial levels

BROWN, CARTIER, GALT AND MACDONALD

GEORGE BROWN (1818-1880): Born in Scotland, Brown emigrated to North America at the age of twenty, moving to Toronto after five years in New York. In Toronto, he founded a newspaper, the *Globe*, which he used to publicize his political views. Elected to the Assembly in 1851, he remained politically active until 1867. In the elections of the autumn of that year, the first of the newly-formed Confederation, he failed to win a seat. He continued to work as editor of the *Globe* and to tend his cattle farm near Brantford, Ontario. An angry ex-employee of his newspaper shot Brown in the leg in 1880, and Brown died as a result of infection caused by the wound.

GEORGE-ÉTIENNE CARTIER (1814-1873): Born in St. Antoine, Lower Canada, Cartier was educated in Montreal, where he opened a law practice in 1837. He took part in the Papineau uprising of 1837, fighting with the rebels at St. Denis (see page 43). After a temporary exile in the United States, he returned to Montreal. There, he became Lafontaine's right-hand man. Cartier was first elected to the Assembly of the united Canadas in 1848. In the 1850s, he became involved with the Grand Trunk Railway, acting as legal advisor for its construction. In the early years after Confederation, he served as Minister of Militia and Defence. His unfortunate involvement in the "Pacific Scandal" of 1873 (see pages 194-195) spelled the end of his political career. He died that same year in London, where he had gone to seek treatment for a disease.

ALEXANDER GALT (1817-1893): Born in London, England, Galt emigrated to Canada in 1835 to work for the British American Land Company. He served as a land-agent in the eastern townships of Lower Canada, becoming president of the St. Lawrence and Atlantic Railroad in 1849. He was one of the men who signed the Annexationist Manifesto. In 1858, he became Finance Minister in the Macdonald-Cartier government. In the negotiations leading to Confederation, he worked out the plan to have the federal government assume the debts of the colonies. Unable to support either major political party, Galt retired from politics in 1872. In 1880, he began a three-year appointment as Canadian High Commissioner to London.

JOHN A. MACDONALD (1815-1891): Born in Glasgow, Scotland, Macdonald's family moved to Kingston when he was five years of age. He was raised and educated there, becoming a lawyer and getting involved in city politics. In 1844, he was elected member of the Assembly of the united Canadas for Kingston. He spent ten years with the opposition Conservatives, until in 1854 a Conservative-Liberal alliance won the election in the Canadas. He succeeded Sir Alan McNab as Conservative leader in 1856, and became premier of the united Canadas in the following year. During the next decade, he gradually came to believe that a larger federal union of the colonies was the best solution for the problems of colonial government. With the Confederation of 1867, he became Canada's first prime minister. Except for the years 1874-1878, he remained prime minister until his death.

of government within a federal union. All of the delegates were aware of the problems in the Constitution of the United States. It provided for a federal system with a weak central government and strong state governments. This system had contributed to the conflict over slavery that had led to the American Civil War. The delegates to the Quebec Conference wanted to avoid a similar situation in Canada. Their solution was to suggest a strong central government, with the individual provinces having limited, clearly defined powers under the constitution of the union. Any **residual powers,** not specifically assigned to the provinces would rest with the federal government.

The powers of each of the levels of government, and other details of the proposed Confederation, were outlined in a series of seventy-two resolutions passed by the delegates to the Quebec Conference. The central government would have powers to raise money through taxes and duties on imported goods. It would control interprovincial communication and transportation, operate the post office, issue currency and provide for military defence. All criminal law would be the responsibility of the federal government. The individual provinces, on the other hand, would be given powers over schools, roads and bridges, local trade and commerce, property and business contracts. The provincial governments would administer the local courts, both criminal and civil, having responsibility for building the courts, keeping records, providing juries, and so on. (A general court of appeal, now the Supreme Court of Canada, and any specialized federal courts that the central government might create, were excluded from provincial administration.) Judges for the higher provincial courts dealing with both criminal and civil matters would be appointed and paid by the federal government.

At the Quebec Conference, the Canadiens demanded and received assurances that their distinctive culture would be protected under the constitution of the new union. Public education, one of the main vehicles through which culture is preserved and transmitted, would be a provincial matter. So would civil law, allowing the Canadiens to maintain their land-ownership traditions and other customary ways of doing business.

The seventy-two resolutions approved by the delegates contained the basic framework of a constitution for the proposed union. Later, these resolutions would form the basis for the British North America Act. However, the proposed union still had to be approved by the government of each colony and to be endorsed by the British government.

As the colonists were to discover, it was not that difficult to get British support for the idea of a union. British views of empire were changing in the 1860s. Some British political figures were urging that the colonies be allowed to become independent states if they so desired. The colonies were costing Britain a great deal of money. Any crisis that might require Britain to send troops to defend its colonies, as in 1812, would be very expensive. When Cartier, Brown, Galt and Macdonald went to Britain in May of 1865 to test the British reaction to Confederation, they were so warmly received that they became suspicious. It seemed to them that the British could not wait to give the colonists their complete independence, something much more than the colonists wanted at that time.

Galt wrote a letter from Britain outlining his feelings about British reactions to the Confederation proposal:

> I am more than ever disappointed at the tone of feeling here as to the Colonies. I cannot shut my eyes to the fact that they want to get rid of us. They have a servile fear of the United States, and would rather give us up than defend us, or incur the risk of war with that country. Day by day I am more oppressed with the sense of responsibility of maintaining a connection undesired here, and which exposes us to such peril at home. . . .I much doubt whether Confederation will save us from Annexation. Even Macdonald is rapidly feeling as I do. . .

1. In your own words, state how a legislative union is organized. What are its advantages and disadvantages?
2. In your own words, explain the sharing of power in a federal union.
3. What reasons did the British have for giving the North American colonies their independence?

External Pressures on the Colonies

During the years 1865-1866, while the merits of Confederation were being debated in the provinces, all of British North America was confronted by several outside forces or pressures. These external pressures included changing trade patterns, raids by Irish rebels and the threat of invasion from the United States. They would bring the colonies in British North America closer together, helping to pave the way for Confederation.

American Threats

Deep divisions within the United States, the issue of slavery being the main one, resulted in a long and bloody civil war that began in 1861. The southern states, where slavery was legal, attempted to break away from the United States to form their own separate country, the Confederate States of America. After four years of war, the wealthier and more industrialized northern states finally defeated the Confederacy.

British support for the losing Confederate side gave rise to fears that Canada might be invaded in retaliation. Following the victory of the northern forces, a small but vocal group of Americans called for an invasion of Canada by the United States. Many Americans felt that it was their nation's manifest destiny, or God-given right, to rule all of North America. For them, it was merely a matter of time before the remaining British colonies in North America followed the original thirteen states into the Union.

Many Irish Catholics who immigrated to the United States during the first half of the nineteenth century remained committed to freeing their homeland from British rule. In 1857, they formed a

Flying their banners of Kelly green with gold harps, the Fenians met an army of volunteers near the Niagara frontier. The Fenians were pushed back to the Niagara River where they surrendered.

secret organization, known as the Fenians, to fight for Irish independence. After the Civil War, the Fenians had a membership of more than 10 000 veterans, organized into military clubs. They began to make plans to invade Canada because it was the closest place where they could attack the British. The Fenians were confident they would receive help for their invasion from the Americans. They also felt that Irish Catholics in Canada, and perhaps the Canadiens, would also support the Fenian cause.

The first Fenian raid on British North America came in April 1866. A small party of Fenian raiders attacked New Brunswick from Maine. The raid quickly collapsed in the face of local resistance. Its only real impact was to increase support for Confederation in the province of New Brunswick.

Less than two months later, the Fenians invaded British North America again. Shortly after midnight on June 1, 1866, more than 1000 Fenian raiders slipped across the Niagara River into Canada. They were armed with weapons left over from the just-ended American Civil War. Many had fought on the Union side during that war. Now, however, the enemy was the British, not the Confederacy. News of the invasion was quickly telegraphed to Toronto. Within forty-eight hours, 20 000 men from Canada West had answered the call for volunteers and were rushed to Niagara by train and steamboat. The Fenians were driven back to the banks of the Niagara River, where they surrendered.

A week later, another group of Fenian raiders invaded Canada East, just north of Lake Champlain. This incursion lasted less than forty-eight hours. The Fenians had found no support from the Americans or from the Irish Catholics and Canadiens for their attacks on British North America. However, the attacks forced many of the colonists to recognize just how difficult it would be to defend themselves against a major attack. The Fenian raids strengthened the arguments in favor of Confederation.

1. What was "manifest destiny" as perceived by Americans? How did it affect their attitudes towards British North America?

2. Who were the Fenians? Why did they wish to attack British North America?

3. Which groups in British North America would be most likely to sympathize with the Fenians? Why?

Reciprocity Ended

The Reciprocity Treaty between the United States and the British colonies expired in 1865, although it could have been renewed. At first, the treaty had been popular in both the United States and the colonies. However, support for the treaty dropped sharply during the Civil War. Some American business leaders and politicians wanted to end the Reciprocity Treaty in retaliation for British support for the Southern side in the conflict. Others wanted the treaty scrapped because they felt that the colonists had benefited most from the accord. There was some truth to this, as British North America owed its new found prosperity to the reciprocity agreements.

In March 1865, the United States government gave Britain the required one year's notice, stating that the Reciprocity Treaty would end in 1866. Many residents of the northern United States believed that an end to reciprocity would force the collapse of the colonies' economies. These Americans believed that, in the chaos that would ensue, the people of British North America would welcome annexation by the United States.

To counter the end of reciprocity, colonial leaders intensified their efforts to promote interprovincial trade within British North America. They also emphasized the role that the proposed federal union could play in increasing trade among the provinces. Macdonald and the other members of the Great Coalition, especially Galt, used trade concerns after the end of reciprocity to promote union during the Confederation debates.

1. In your opinion, what connection might there have been between "manifest destiny" and the cancellation of the Reciprocity Treaty by the government of the United States?

Confederation Achieved

The planned union had to be approved by the provinces before Confederation could take place. Over the two years following the Charlottetown and Quebec conferences, people throughout the colonies debated the idea of Confederation. These debates were often heated, even violent. In some colonies, elections were held on the issue of Confederation. Newfoundland's voters went to the polls in 1865, soundly defeating the pro-Confederation forces. In

THE VISION OF A GREAT NATION FROM SEA TO SEA

Many traditional histories of Canada focus on the internal political problems and external pressures that led up to Confederation. But some influential leaders had a more positive vision that helped guide them along the road to Confederation. During the late 1850s and early 1860s, in the minds of political leaders like George Brown and Thomas Darcy McGee, a vision was forming of a great nation from sea to sea, uniting all of the peoples of British North America.

Many things contributed to the shaping of this vision of a great nation, not the least of which was the fact that the United States had been steadily expanding westward for several decades. California became a state in 1850 and by 1862, despite the American Civil War, construction was underway on a great transcontinental railway that would link the eastern United States with the Pacific coast. The discovery of gold in British Columbia in 1856 was another factor contributing to the desire for westward expansion of Canada.

Thomas Darcy McGee, a poet and politician of Irish origin who would be killed by an assassin's bullet, had a more poetic vision of a nation from sea to sea. This was how he expressed his vision of a greater union:

I call it a Northern Nation–for such it must become, if all of us do our duty. I see in the future one great nationality, bound by the blue rim of the Ocean. I see communities, each disposing of its internal affairs, but all bound together by free institutions. I see the peaks of the Western Mountains and I see the crests of the Eastern Waves, the winding Assiniboine, the five-fold lakes. . . . I see a generation of industrious, contented, moral men, free in name and in fact.

McGee's vision of a larger, stronger Canada was not just poetic. He was very aware that American western expansion would spill over into the North West if the British colonies did not establish their control over the region. McGee was opposed to American-style democracy. He feared the absorption of the colonies by the Americans unless the British constitutional monarchy were strengthened on the North American continent.

1. The quotation from McGee is a brief but effective description of Confederation. What words does he use to describe how he foresaw a federal union of British North America?

New Brunswick, the anti-Confederation party won one election, only to be defeated by pro-Confederationists led by Sir Leonard Tilley a short time later. In Nova Scotia, Joseph Howe led a strong opposition to Confederation. In Prince Edward Island, the Assembly decided against both Confederation and Maritime union.

In the end, the legislative assemblies of three colonies, Nova Scotia, New Brunswick and the united Canadas, voted to support Confederation. The next step was out of their hands. The British government had to approve the plan. The three colonies appointed a delegation to take the seventy-two resolutions approved in Quebec to London.

The London Conference

In London, the delegates worked with British government officials throughout the winter of 1866-1867, drafting a bill to be put before the British Parliament as a treaty between two governments. As a treaty, the bill had to be approved or rejected by the British Parliament without any changes. Given the mood of the British government, rejection was unthinkable. Even so, one member of Parliament received a petition from Nova Scotia bearing the signatures of 30 000 persons opposed to Confederation. On behalf of those Nova Scotians, he argued unsuccessfully for defeat of the bill. Passage of the bill, titled the British North America Act, was swift. It received Royal assent on March 29, 1867. "One Dominion under the name of Canada" had been created by an act of the British Parliament.

The new Dominion had four provinces: Nova Scotia, New Brunswick, Quebec and Ontario. It had self-government in all domestic matters. But the new Constitution, the British North America Act, remained an act of the British Parliament. Canadians could not modify or revise it until 1949, when they obtained some limited power to amend the Act. It was not until 1982, under the government of Pierre Elliott Trudeau, that Canadians finally got a Constitution that could be changed in Canada. Even then, the British North America Act (renamed in 1982 the Constitution Act, 1867) remained the basic document of Canada's Constitution.

The Structure of Government under the BNA Act

The British North America Act established Canada as a **constitutional monarchy**. It assigned law-making powers to the Crown and to a Parliament comprising the House of Commons and the Senate. The lower chamber, the House of Commons, would be made up of elected members of Parliament. Representation, to the greatest extent possible, would be based on population. Each member of Parliament would represent a **riding** or **constituency** of approximately the same number of people. The number of seats in the Commons would not be fixed under the terms of the Constitution, but would be able to increase as the new Dominion's population grew.

Consistent with British Parliamentary tradition, the founders of Confederation saw the House of Commons as the place where most laws affecting the Dominion would be proposed, debated and voted on. All laws related to government spending and taxation would have their origins in the House of Commons. As well, the prime minister and most of the cabinet would be drawn from the elected members of the House of Commons.

The Senate was intended to be a parallel to the British House of Lords. In the words of one of the Fathers of Confederation, it was designed as "a power of resistance to oppose the democratic element." The Senate was also intended to represent the interests of Canada's regions. Fearful that Canada West, with its rapidly growing population, would control the House of Commons, delegates to the Quebec Conference from Canada East and the Maritimes insisted that each of the three regions have equal representation (twenty-four Senators each) in the Senate. (Today there are twenty-four Senators from each of Quebec, Ontario, the Maritimes and Western Canada; six from Newfoundland and two from northern Canada.)

Appointments to the Senate are made by the governing party in the House of Commons. Initially, Senators were appointed for life; now they must retire at age seventy-five. Senators are supposed to take "a serious and sober second look" at legislation passed by the elected representatives of the people. Yet the Senate, like the Legislative Councils before it, often served as a place where the party faithful could be rewarded or where those who could not be elected could be brought into government. The structure of Canada's government, as set out under the BNA Act, is shown in the diagram on page 102.

The roles of the government and opposition were not defined under the BNA Act, nor were the positions of the prime minister and cabinet ministers. In fact they were not even mentioned in the Act. This aspect of Canada's Constitution is unwritten, arising from British Parliamentary tradition.

The main purpose of the BNA Act was, and still is, to define the distribution of powers between the federal and provincial levels of government. Section 91 of the Act outlines powers of the federal government; Section 92 lists powers of the provincial governments.

1. In a chart, compare the House of Commons and the Senate using these headings:
   • selection of members
   • purpose
   • powers.

**The Structure of Government
as set up by the BNA Act**

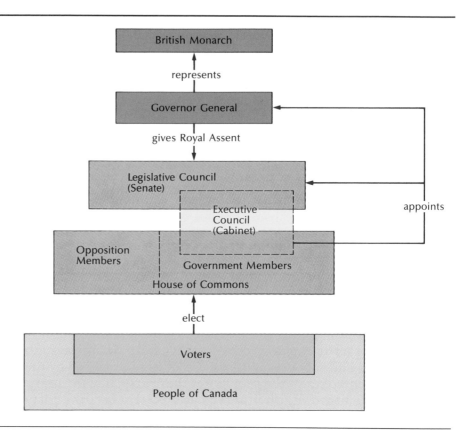

July 1, 1867

The new Dominion of Canada officially came into being on Monday, July 1, 1867. That morning, George Brown wrote the following editorial in his newspaper, the Toronto *Globe*:

> With the first dawn of this gladsome mid-summer morn, we hail the birthday of a new nationality. A united British America, with its four millions of people, takes its place this day among the nations of the world. The DOMINION OF CANADA, on this first day of July, in the year of grace, eighteen hundred and sixty seven, enters on a new career of national existence.

Not everyone in the new nation shared Brown's pleasure. As Brown was writing these glowing words, Joseph Howe, editor of the Halifax *Morning Chronicle*, was setting the type for his editorial. It would be a bitter attack on those he felt had sold-out Nova Scotia to Confederation. Outside the offices of the *Morning Chronicle*, black crepe, the symbol of mourning, hung listlessly in the muggy night air. Howe would campaign actively for the next two years seeking to have the BNA Act repealed. However, following his election to the House of Commons in 1869, Howe spent his final years as a strong supporter of what he once called the "Botheration Scheme."

In most cities and towns, joyful celebrations welcomed the birth of the new nation. Church bells were rung; cannons were fired in twenty-one gun salutes. People gathered in public places to hear the Queen's proclamation read. That night, there were lavish balls and great displays of fireworks.

Against the backdrop of the new Houses of Parliament, the governor general, Lord Monck, read the Royal Proclamation. Queen Victoria sent a message to the people of the new Dominion of Canada via the recently completed transatlantic telegraph cable. Included in her message was a knighthood for one of the leading architects of Confederation: Canada's first prime minister was now Sir John A. Macdonald. From platforms decorated with red, white and blue bunting, political leaders from all parties honored Macdonald and the new nation he and so many others had struggled to create.

Summary

Under the leadership of John A. Macdonald, along with Brown, Galt and Cartier, Confederation was achieved in 1867. Born out of internal political deadlock, and spurred on by external pressures, it was a significant act of skilful political compromise. Canada's political leaders had put aside their personal and political differences in an attempt to create a solution that would serve the greater good of all the colonists.

Conferences held at Charlottetown and Quebec City saw the framework for a federal union of the colonies worked out. But, the Confederation proposal still had to be endorsed by the governments of the individual colonies, then passed into law by the British government. The voters of Newfoundland and Prince Edward Island rejected the union, leaving Ontario, Quebec, Nova Scotia and New Brunswick to become the first four provinces of the new Dominion of Canada. The powers of these provinces and the federal government were defined in the British North America Act, passed by the British Parliament in March 1867. The result was the new

Dominion of Canada, extending from the western shore of Lake Superior to the Atlantic Ocean. But the Fathers of Confederation had no intentions of stopping with Canada as it had been shaped on July 1, 1867; they now turned their attention westward.

REVIEW

Checking Back

1. Write one or two sentences summarizing the significance of each of the following conferences in bringing about Confederation.
   Charlottetown   Quebec City
   London

2. Discuss the role the American Civil War played in the call for Confederation.

3. Who were the Fenians? Discuss the role they played in the call for Confederation.

4. In your own words, summarize how the seventy-two resolutions of the Quebec Conference proposed the power to make laws be divided between the federal and provincial governments.

Using Your Knowledge

5. At various times before Confederation, union of the Atlantic colonies was considered. Suggest advantages and disadvantages of a union.

6. Imagine you are one of the Canadien delegates at Quebec City. Write a letter to a delegate from New Brunswick explaining why you feel public education must be a provincial power.

7. Suggest one or two reasons for the unease felt by the Quebec delegates to the London Conference when they discovered how willing Britain was to grant independence.

8. Explain why the British government, in the 1860s, was eager to see a union of the North American colonies.

9. Examine the people profiled on pages 92-93. What characteristics did these people have in common?

10. Read Thomas Darcy McGee's vision of Canada's future (page 99). Did his predictions come true?

11. List the reasons for the creation of the Senate.

12. The colonies of British North America were legally joined together as of July 1, 1867. Since that time, do you think the regions of Canada have successfully formed one nation?

13. Design a poster that illustrates how either a pro- or anti-Confederationist might have felt on July 1, 1867.

UNIT 2

DEVELOPMENT OF THE WEST

Chapter 6

Western Canada: The Geographic Setting

The lure of the western frontier has played a major part in nation-building in North America. In the three chapters following this one, you will learn in detail about the development of the frontier in the lands that are now western Canada. This chapter will provide an overview of the geographic setting in which that development took place. You will first have a look at the early exploration and mapping of the West, then at the three major regions that make up the physical geography of western Canada.

As you read this chapter, keep in mind these key questions:

- What attracted Europeans, Americans and Canadians to the western half of North America?
- Who explored this area? What geographic features did they find when they came to the West?
- What are the three main regions of western Canada as defined in terms of physical geography? What are the major features of each one? What were the main resources used by the Native peoples of each area?

Exploring and Mapping the West

During the sixteenth, seventeenth and eighteenth centuries, the Pacific coast from Mexico to Alaska was explored, surveyed and mapped by Spanish, English, American and Russian seafarers. Details of the Arctic coastline were added to early maps as explorers searched for a Northwest Passage from Europe to China. Two things motivated these early explorers. One was the quest for a direct route from Europe to the riches of the Orient. The other, once the extent of the Americas was known, was the search for gold, silver, furs and other wealth in the New World itself.

EXPLORATION OF NORTH AMERICA

The explorations of the British Columbia coast begun by the Spanish were completed by the British. James Cook sailed into Nootka Sound in 1776. Ownership of the area was soon being contested by Britain and Spain, each attracted by the valuable fur trade that was being established along the British Columbia coast. The explorations of George Vancouver, who arrived in 1792, helped strengthen British claims to the region. He was to spend the next three years sailing and mapping the west coast from modern-day Oregon to Alaska.

Alaska had been discovered earlier by Vitus Jonassen Bering, who sighted the Alaskan coast in 1741. The voyage had been ordered by Peter the Great and led to Russia's only possession in North America–the present American state of Alaska.

The Hudson's Bay Company was also exploring and mapping the West in the search for furs. Men like Radisson and Groseilliers, Henry Kelsey and Anthony Henday travelled from Hudson Bay, following the many rivers and lakes of the western Canadian Shield. As they travelled, they kept notes and made maps.

During the late eighteenth and early nineteenth centuries, fierce competition between the Hudson's Bay Company and the North West Company saw a great expansion of the fur trade in the West. David Thompson, Alexander Mackenzie and Simon Fraser, employees of the North West Company, all explored and mapped various areas of the West from Oregon to the North West Territories. Mackenzie was the first non-Native to travel across North America on foot, reaching first the mouth of the Mackenzie River in 1789 and later the Pacific Coast in 1793.

French fur traders set out south and west from the St. Lawrence in the mid-seventeenth century. They explored and mapped much of the Great Lakes and the Mississippi River system as they searched for new sources of furs and for routes along which to carry their rich cargoes to the sea. Some, like Pierre de la Vérendrye, pushed westward, establishing fur trading posts as they went. La Vérendrye's sons travelled even further to the west, reaching the foothills of the Rockies in 1743. They were the first non-Natives to observe and record this imposing feature of the western Canadian landscape.

The exploration and mapping of the West was begun by the Spanish. During the early 1640s, Hernando de Soto crossed the Mississippi, reaching the edge of the Great Plains. At the same time, his countryman Francisco Vasquez de Coronado was exploring the plains and mountains of what is today the American Southwest. Other Spaniards explored and settled parts of modern California, Arizona, New Mexico and Texas during the late sixteenth and early seventeenth centuries. In 1774, seaborne Spanish explorers reached Vancouver Island.

The portions of the continent first explored and mapped in detail were the lands along the great waterways of North America: the Atlantic and Pacific oceans, the St. Lawrence River-Great Lakes system, and the Mississippi River. The areas between the Rocky Mountains in the west and the Great Lakes and Mississippi River in the east were explored only later. The mapping of the interior has continued into our own times. Two factors were most important in this process. One was the search for natural resources, among them gold and furs. The other was the need for transportation routes along which both resources and people could travel to and from the West.

The Physical Geography of the West

Three major landform regions, each running north-south, dominate the physical geography of western North America. These regions are the **Canadian Shield,** the **Great Plains** (or Western Interior Lowlands) and the Western Mountains (or Western Cordillera). Each has its own kind of climate, vegetation and animal life.

The Canadian Shield

The Canadian Shield is made up of ancient weathered rock formations surrounding Hudson Bay. These rock formations are among the oldest and hardest in the world. They are all that is left of a mountain range created several hundred million years ago. Over countless centuries, glaciers and rivers gradually eroded the mountains, leaving a generally flat and rocky landscape. The rivers and lakes that mark this landscape create a vast network of water transportation routes. The Native peoples and early explorers of Canada's West used these routes extensively.

The cool and rocky landscape of the Canadian Shield, with its many wet areas, has very little fertile soil. Much of the area is still covered by forests of coniferous trees, just as it was several centuries ago. Smaller trees, shrubs, and other hardy forms of vegetation create a sparse cover on the forest floor amid the fairly widely spaced trees. Wild rice, rushes and other plants grow alongside the lakes and marshes of the region.

When Europeans first visited the region, the forests and waters were home to a wide variety of birds and animals. Among them were many valuable species of fur-bearing mammals: beaver, musk-

Bare, exposed rock and many lakes and swamps tell of the force that gave this land its appearance–glaciation.

rat, otter, mink and fox. Most of the Native people of the region were hunters and trappers. They lived in small, nomadic bands, following the seasonal migrations of the animals.

Beneath the Canadian Shield lie many rich deposits of minerals such as nickel, iron, copper and uranium. These resources have only become known and used since the late nineteenth century, as the Native peoples of this region had no metal-working technologies.

The Great Plains

The Great Plains are usually called "the Prairies" by Canadians. This vast expanse of low, flat or rolling land extends from the sub-Arctic in the north to the coast of the Gulf of Mexico in the south. Millions of years ago it was covered by an ocean lying between the Western Mountains and the Canadian Shield and the Appalachian Mountains to the east. Erosional deposits from these three mountain systems gradually covered the floor of this ancient sea. Geological forces slowly produced a gradual rising of the entire region. The region rose most sharply in the West as the Rocky Mountains were formed. The Great Plains slope gently eastward toward Hudson Bay, the Great Lakes and the Mississippi River.

The Great Plains also fall away to the north and south from the centre of the continent. Two great river systems, the Mackenzie in the north and the Mississippi in the south, drain the region. These

The Great Plains are formed from flat-lying layers of sedimentary material deposited into a sea which once covered the area.

slow-moving rivers follow wide, meandering watercourses through the soft, sedimentary deposits of the plains on their way to the sea. Beneath the surface of the Great Plains lie vast reserves of coal, oil and natural gas. At the surface, the sedimentary deposits easily form rich, fertile soils.

When the first Europeans reached the Great Plains, the region was covered by prairie grasslands. Stands of deciduous trees such as aspens were also present along the rivers and lakes of the southern plains. Coniferous forests were found in the northern part of the region.

Some scientists believe that these forests were the true natural vegetation of this region. They think that the great grasslands seen by early European visitors were the result of human activity in the region. Native hunters, they suggest, may have used fire to drive deer, bison and other game from the forests and into pounds where they could be easily killed. This method of hunting may have cleared the forests and left vast expanses of fast-growing tough prairie grass in their place.

When the first non-Native explorers reached the Great Plains, the grasslands were home to many species of animals. Among them, the most important by far was the bison. Three centuries ago, the nearly 2 million km^2 of rolling hills and grasslands that make up the Great Plains were home to millions of these large, brown shaggy beasts.

The Native peoples built "buffalo pounds" to trap the bison that roamed the Great Plains. How were the pounds used?

The bison was a very valuable resource to the Native peoples of the Great Plains. Hunting on foot and using stone-age technology, the Native peoples could kill only small numbers of bison. To feed themselves, they also hunted other animals, among them elk, deer, antelope and rabbits, and gathered berries, roots and wild rice.

Some of the early Native groups of the Great Plains grew crops of corn, sunflowers, squash and beans in the rich prairie soils. Ironically, the introduction of horses and guns to the region through contacts with Europeans led many Native peoples to abandon farming to hunt bison for food. These innovations, combined with farm settlement after the coming of the railway, would quickly lead to the near extinction of the bison.

Today, the great expanses of prairie grass that once covered the Great Plains are almost completely gone. Human activity is again the cause. In order to farm the region it had to be stripped of its natural vegetation so the soil beneath could be ploughed and planted with crops such as wheat.

The Western Mountains

The Western Mountains are made up of a number of mountain chains running north-south from Alaska to the Isthmus of Panama. Among them are the Rocky Mountains, the Coastal Mountains, the

Mountains and valleys are the dominant features of the Western Mountain region. Less rugged plateaus fill in areas between mountain chains.

Cascade Mountains and the Sierra Nevada and Sierra Madre ranges. The mountains of the Western Cordillera are relatively young, in terms of geological time, having been pushed up between 60 million and 30 million years ago. Many of the western mountain ranges are made up of high, rugged peaks which have not yet been reduced and rounded by erosion.

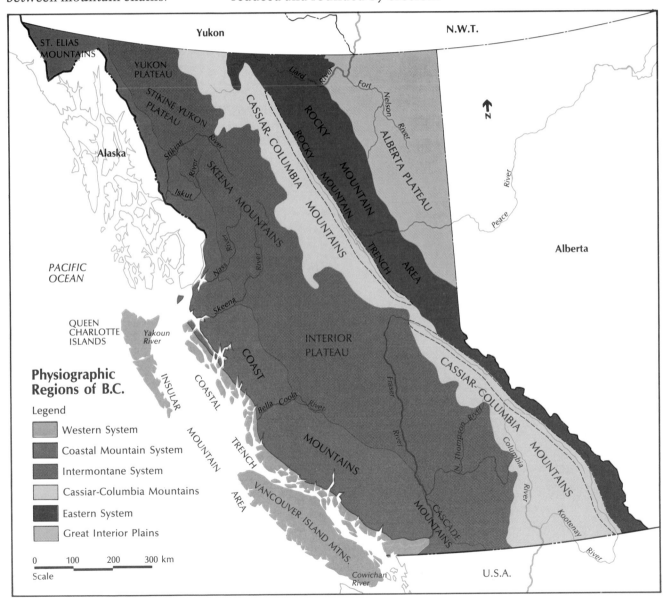

Physiographic Regions of B.C.

Legend

- Western System
- Coastal Mountain System
- Intermontane System
- Cassiar-Columbia Mountains
- Eastern System
- Great Interior Plains

Scale: 0 100 200 300 km

Mountains are not the only prominent landforms of this region. Lying between the mountain chains are a series of plateaus and valleys. Plateaus are upland areas of relatively flat land, while valleys are troughs cut by rivers or glaciers. Valleys formed by rivers flowing out to the sea between mountain chains may be accompanied by broad and fertile floodplains. Rivers flowing through sedimentary rock may carve deep and sharply defined canyons. The Fraser River Canyon, in the southern part of British Columbia's interior plateau, is an example of this geological process.

Rivers are an important feature of this region. The heavy moisture that falls as snow or rain on the western slopes of the Coastal Mountains feeds many fast-flowing streams and rivers. Among the great rivers that flow from the Western Mountains to the Pacific Ocean are the Yukon, the Stikine, the Skeena, the Fraser, the Columbia and the Sacramento.

The Fraser River, shown here near Lillooet, B.C., has eroded a steep-sided valley in the sedimentary rock of the area.

Not all of the rivers of the Western Mountains flow into the Pacific. Some, such as the Peace and the Parsnip, flow north and east to join the Mackenzie on its way to the Arctic Ocean. Others flow eastward from the Rocky Mountains, some to join the rivers of the Great Plains that form the great Mississippi River system, emptying into the Gulf of Mexico. Other eastward-flowing rivers, such as the North and South Saskatchewan, eventually drain into Hudson Bay. Still other rivers, such as the Colorado, follow routes along the

intermontane plateaus, carrying meltwaters from the mountains south through desert landscapes to the Gulf of California.

These rivers and their valleys were important transportation routes for the Native peoples of this region. Later, fur traders and explorers would use them. As non-Native settlement of the West progressed, rail lines and highways would follow the river routes through the mountains.

The rain-fed rivers that flow from the Western Mountains to the Pacific Ocean are home to several species of salmon and sea-run trout. Once present in uncountable millions, these fish were the major source of food for a large Native population when this region was first visited by European explorers.

The rain falling along the coast also nourishes the great forests of coniferous trees. Towering Douglas firs, red cedars, spruce and hemlock once crowded the mountain slopes in vast forest stands running right to the ocean's edge. Early European visitors were awed by the sight of these great trees rising 100 m or more above the forest floor. Red cedar was especially important to the Native peoples along the Pacific. They used its wood to build great longhouses and large ocean-going dugout canoes.

The forests and coastal margins were home to a wide variety of land and sea animals, including many species of waterfowl and shellfish. Native peoples obtained food from both the sea and the forests. They hunted deer, elk and mountain goat for food and skins. They also hunted and trapped the fur-bearing animals in this region, including beaver, marten, sea otters and seals.

The intermontane plateaus differ greatly from the surrounding mountains. Generally much drier than the mountains, the plateaus tend to support different species of plants and animals. East of the coastal mountains, the interior plateau of the southern third of the

A cross-section of the Western Cordillera.

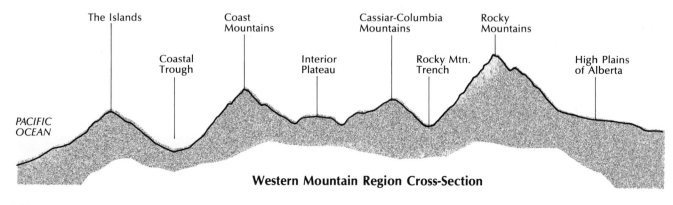

Western Mountain Region Cross-Section

province of British Columbia is largely covered by grassland and thin forests of small coniferous trees. Near water sources, larger trees and thicker plant cover are found. Willows, rushes, edible roots and berries found near these water bodies were important resources to Native peoples of the plateau lands. They used these foods to supplement the meat they obtained by hunting: deer, elk, mountain goats, rabbits, gophers, and fowl.

When European explorers first reached the Western Mountain region, they found large numbers of Native peoples, most of whom made their home along the Pacific coast, in the river valleys or on the intermontane plateaus. Within this region, several distinctive Native cultures evolved. To a large extent, this diversity reflected the ways each group had adapted to or made use of the differing environments of the region.

1. For each of the three physical regions of the West, list the following key information: geological beginning, present-day landscape, vegetation.
2. In each of the three regions, what resources of the local environment were used by the Native peoples?

Summary

Spaniards were the first people to map and explore western North America, followed by French fur traders as well as by representatives of the Hudson's Bay Company and North West Company. The chief motive of all these explorers was to search for natural resources and transportation routes.

In terms of physical geography, the three main regions of the West are the Canadian Shield, the Great Plains and the Western Mountains.

A mountainous region millions of years ago, the Shield is today a rocky area with little fertile soil. Its main attraction, both to Native peoples and to Europeans, was fur-bearing animals.

The Great Plains, formed from the bed of an ancient ocean, are rich in natural fuels and fertile soil. Grasslands covered the region when the first Europeans arrived. Yet some historians feel that the coniferous trees of the northern Prairies were once the natural vegetation of this entire region. Of all the animals of the region, the bison was the most important to its Native peoples.

Geologically speaking, the Western Mountains of the Cordillera are quite young. Valleys and plateaus are also prominent features of this region. Most, but not all, of the great river systems of the region drain into the Pacific. These river systems were important transportation routes both to Native peoples and to European explorers. While the coastal areas are heavily forested, the intermontane plateaus are often thinly forested or covered by grassland.

REVIEW

Checking Back

1. Write one or two sentences to summarize the significance of each of the following in the mapping of Canada's West.

   Hernando de Soto   Pierre de la
   Henry Kelsey   Vérendrye
   James Cook   David Thompson
   George Vancouver   Alexander
   Vitus Jonassen Bering   Mackenzie

2. Define and explain these terms which are found in this chapter: exploration, landforms, glaciation, sedimentary deposits, plateaus.

3. List two factors that encouraged exploration and two that discouraged exploration of the West.

Using Your Knowledge

4. Sketch a series of pictures to show the major characteristics of each of the western regions: the Canadian Shield, the Great Plains and the Western Mountains.

5. In a few sentences identify the problems people would face in settling on the Canadian Shield, the Great Plains and the Western Mountains.

6. On an outline map of North America, trace and label the following river systems.

   Mackenzie River   Colorado River
   Saskatchewan River   Mississippi River

7. Why were waterways important to the exploration of the West?

8. Write a letter to a real or imaginary friend in another country describing one of the three western landform regions. Include a sketch in your letter.

Chapter 7

The Opening of the West

European exploration of Canada's West began in the late 1600s. Over the next century and a half, fur traders, geographers, missionaries and scientific explorers would travel across the Prairies, through the Rocky Mountains, and along the Pacific coast, identifying resources, recording their impressions of the land and its people, and making maps.

The earliest Europeans to visit western Canada came in search of new sources of furs. The West had been home to Native peoples for thousands of years. There, they had developed ways of life closely tied to the West's varied environments. Yet the fur traders brought with them traditions, ideas and technology very different from those of the Native people. Many Native bands became dependent on the fur trade, abandoning traditional Native values and economic activities in the process.

The first fur traders to explore the region were French, soon followed by English traders from the Hudson's Bay Company. In the late eighteenth century, a fierce rivalry developed between the Hudson's Bay Company and the newly formed North West Company. This rivalry drove the fur traders to explore more and more of the West in search of furs. As well, it greatly changed the West, as both the environment and Native peoples were affected by the rapidly expanding fur trade. Ultimately, this rivalry would result in a merger of the two companies.

In this chapter, you will first examine in depth how the continental fur trade led to the exploration of the West. In doing so, you will study the roles of the Hudson's Bay Company and the North West Company, and the living conditions of fur traders and Native peoples. As well, you will also briefly study the short-lived Pacific coast fur trade.

- What role did the fur trade play in the exploration and settlement of western Canada?

- What were the working and living conditions of the people who worked in the fur trade?
- What impact did exploration and settlement have on the Native peoples of the West?
- How was the Pacific coast fur trade different from the continental fur trade?
- What was the impact on the West of the competition between the Hudson's Bay Company and the North West Company?

The Fur Trade and Western Exploration

The fur trade brought the first European explorers and settlers to western Canada. The fur-bearing animals of its forests, inland waterways and extensive coastlines were the first of its many natural resources to attract the attention of the European newcomers. Not long after the founding of New France, French fur traders began moving westward from the St. Lawrence. By the mid-1600s, the French were exploring and trading in the region around the Great Lakes. In 1670, with the establishment of the Hudson's Bay Company, English traders also became involved in the search for new sources of furs in western Canada. Out of this competition between the French traders and the Hudson's Bay Company would come the first European exploration of western Canada.

The Hudson's Bay Company charter had given it the exclusive right to trade in a vast region known as Rupert's Land, an area from which all rivers drain into Hudson Bay. Despite this monopoly, the French fur traders were the first to move into the West. They travelled by canoe and on foot into the area west of the Great Lakes. In western Ontario and southern Manitoba they found that the many lakes and rivers of the Canadian Shield made excellent routes along which to ship furs. These French traders established a network of fur trading forts. Each year, parties of traders from Montreal would travel west by canoe, stopping at the forts to get supplies. There they would also meet with Native people from nearby villages and camps who brought furs to trade.

But it was a Hudson's Bay Company man, Henry Kelsey, who in 1690 became the first European to visit the Canadian plains. He brought back glowing reports of the rich supplies of furs to be found there. He also brought back the first recorded description of the bison by a European. Kelsey's description of these great beasts must have been dramatic. Convinced that he had made up his account, the Hudson's Bay Company decided not to push farther inland. Instead, the Company decided to stay in its secure forts on the shores of Hudson Bay and to have the Indians bring furs to the posts there. The Hudson's Bay Company followed this policy for fifty years after Kelsey's trip to the West.

The success of the French fur traders who were trading in the West revealed the weakness of the Company's policy. The Indians of western Canada traded with the French who came to them rather than make the long journey to Hudson Bay. The Hudson's Bay Company saw its share of the fur trade drop sharply. The Company changed its policy in the 1750s and began sending fur traders like Anthony Henday into western Canada. Moving south and west from Hudson Bay, the English fur traders now established their own canoe routes and chains of trading forts in the West.

The fur trade had not penetrated far into the West by the middle of the eighteenth century. Most of the fur forts and much of the trading activity continued to be limited to the lake and forest lands of the Canadian Shield west of Lake Superior. Following the conquest of New France in 1756, however, exploration began to expand rapidly, spurred on by a new rivalry in the fur trade.

1. On what basis did the Hudson's Bay Company claim most of western Canada? Why would it be difficult to enforce this claim?
2. How were French fur traders able to capture a large share of the fur trade activity in the West?

The Great Rivalry

The Hudson's Bay Company was the largest fur trading organization in Canada in the late 1700s, but it soon had a powerful rival, the North West Company. Formed in 1784, the North West Company was a partnership of independent fur traders based in Montreal. These partners were mostly English, United Empire Loyalists, and Highland Scots who had moved to Montreal after the conquest of New France. These merchants had quickly gained control over the Montreal fur trade, hiring Canadiens for their skill and knowledge of the fur trade.

There were two types of partners in this new company. One group, based in Montreal, sold the furs and provided supplies and goods to be traded for furs. The others, known as *hivernants* or wintering partners, stayed in the West. There, they lived in the fur forts and travelled the waterways of the West, trading with the Native peoples for furs. Among them were men such as Simon Fraser, David Thompson and Alexander Mackenzie.

David Thompson had begun as a Hudson's Bay Company employee. However, frustrated at its failure to support his ambition to do further exploration and surveying in the West, he switched to the North West Company in 1797.

During the North West Company's short existence, its traders travelled and explored vast areas of the West. They followed the rivers and lakes of the Prairies and the Arctic, first to the Arctic Ocean, then to the Pacific. The "Nor'Westers" as the Company's men were called, became the first Europeans to enter Canada's Rocky Mountains. Assisted by Native guides, they travelled through broad river valleys and along dangerous, narrow, cliffside trails worn by years of use by Native peoples. From there they followed the westward flowing, snow-fed rivers to the Pacific. Everywhere they travelled, the Nor'Westers established new trading posts.

The North West Company was very successful. Because they were partners, the traders had a strong incentive to seek new and better supplies of furs. Each partner received a share of the profits at the end of the trading season. The Hudson's Bay Company, by contrast, was owned and run by businessmen in London, England. Most had never been to Canada to take part in the fur trade. Hudson's Bay Company fur traders were employees, paid an annual salary for their work.

As well, the Nor'Westers had the advantage of knowing the lands and the Native peoples of western Canada. At first, most Nor'Westers were Canadiens. These men lived much of their lives among Native peoples, trading for furs and learning the skills needed to survive in the wilderness. They were expert woodsmen and canoeists. They were soon joined by other adventurers, many of them Scots, hardy men eager for adventure, who quickly learned how to live and travel in the wilds of the West.

The men, known as *voyageurs*, who paddled the trading canoes were usually Canadiens or Natives. Many of the traders and *voyageurs* took Native wives. Their children were the first Métis. Able to speak English, French and Native languages, these Métis members of the North West Company played a very important part in the fur trade.

In contrast, the Hudson's Bay Company policy of having Native fur traders come to it on the shore of Hudson Bay discouraged

Both the Hudson's Bay Company and the Nor'Westers depended on river transportation to get furs from the West to the ships that would carry them to Europe. At first, both companies used canoes, usually paddled by Native crews. In 1749, the Hudson's Bay Company introduced York boats to the fur trade. Twice the size of the voyageurs' canoes, the York boats gave the Hudson's Bay Company a great advantage in getting furs from the West to the ships anchored in Hudson Bay.

exploration. For many years, its traders were caught in what one writer called "the sleep by the frozen sea." However, concern over falling profits resulting from the success of the French fur traders' aggressive expansion into the West forced the Hudson's Bay Company to change. The Hudson's Bay Company's new strategy was to set up trading posts upstream from the North West Company posts so that Native peoples bringing their furs by canoe to trade would reach the Bay men first. The Hudson's Bay Company also had a geographic advantage over the North West Company. The route from the Saskatchewan River to Hudson Bay was shorter and easier to travel than the one the Nor'Westers had to use to get furs to Montreal. Sailing ships operated by the Hudson's Bay Company brought trade goods to the posts. On their return trips, they would carry furs directly from Fort Churchill to Europe. The North West

Company furs still had a long canoe trip through the Great Lakes and St. Lawrence River before being loaded onto ships bound for Europe.

1. Which company began the expansion of the fur trade into the West? When did this expansion take place?
2. How did the trading practices of the Hudson's Bay Company and the North West Company differ? Which company was forced to change its trading practices? Why?

FUR TRADING RIVALS

1. How many Hudson's Bay Company forts are shown on the map? How many North West Company forts?

2. Which company had forts located furthest to the west? to the north? Suggest why they were so located.

3. On what geographic features were the great majority of fur trading posts located? Suggest some reasons why the posts would be so located.

4. Using an atlas, determine the distance from the North West Company posts on Great Slave Lake to Montreal, using the most direct water routes. Then, determine the distance from the Hudson's Bay Company post on the same lake to Fort Churchill on Hudson Bay. If an average fur trading canoe could travel eighty kilometres in a day, how long would it take to travel from Great Slave Lake to Fort William? to Fort Churchill?

5. Using your atlas and the map, identify each of the modern communities that are today located on the sites of former fur trading posts. Which communities still have the same names they had as trading posts?

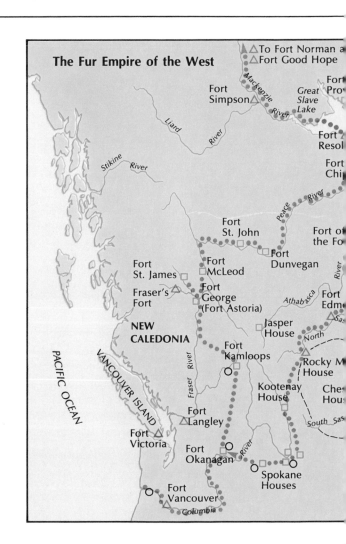

The Fur Empire of the West

3. What advantages did the North West Company have in its competition with the Hudson's Bay Company? What advangages did the Hudson's Bay Company enjoy?
4. In what ways were the fur traders dependent on the Native peoples?
5. Which company's traders were the first to cross the Rocky Mountains?

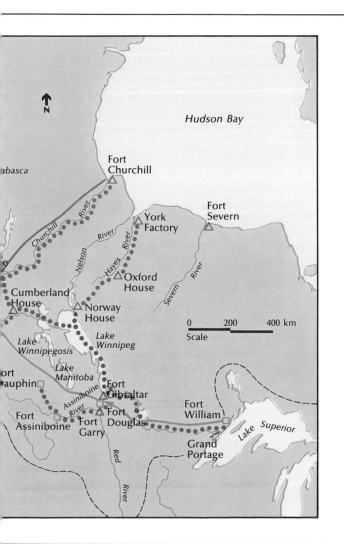

Legend

△	Hudson's Bay Company posts
□	North West Company posts
○	American Fur Trade posts
●●●● ▶	Major fur trade routes
◀——	North West Company from Montreal
◀——	Hudson's Bay Company from England
– – – –	Boundary of Rupert's Land

Fort William, a Fur Trading Centre

The centre of the North West Company's trading network was Fort William at the western end of Lake Superior. The area is today part of the city of Thunder Bay. The largest of the fur forts, Fort William was strategically located between the lakes and rivers of the Canadian Shield and the open waters of the Great Lakes.

Each spring, *hivernants* from the West would bring their furs to Fort William. There they would meet the large *canots de maître* which carried trade goods and supplies from Montreal. The *canots de maître* would then be loaded with furs to be shipped via the Great Lakes and St. Lawrence River to Montreal, and then to buyers in Europe. Later, small sailing ships were used to carry these cargoes to and from Fort William.

The North West Company's great "wilderness depot," completed in 1807, took nearly eight years to build. Its sturdy log walls, five metres high, enclosed an area 130 m by 160 m, room for two professional football fields. Its main gate faced the waters of Lake Superior. At the water's edge were wharves and ramps where canoes and cargo ships could be loaded and unloaded. Within the walls were more than twenty buildings. In them, furs were counted and pressed into bales, trade goods and supplies stored and the fur traders fed and housed.

Ross Cox, an Irish fur trader, wrote the following description of Fort William several years after its completion:

> The buildings at Fort William...consist of a large house in which the dining hall is situated, and in which the gentleman in charge resides; the council house; a range of snug buildings for the accommodation of the people from the interior [*hivernants*]; a large counting house; the doctor's residence (occupied by the first doctor west of the Great Lakes); extensive stores for the merchandise [trade goods] and furs; a forge; various workshops, with apartments for the mechanics [skilled craftsmen] a number of whom are always stationed there. There is also a prison....The whole is surrounded by wooden fortifications, flanked by bastions, and is sufficiently strong to withstand any attack from the natives. Outside the fort is a shipyard, in which the company's vessels on the lake are built and repaired. The kitchen garden is well stocked, and there are extensive fields of Indian corn and potatoes. There are also several head of cattle, with sheep, hogs, poultry etc., and a few horses for domestic use.

The country about the fort is low, with a rich, moist soil. The air is damp, owing to frequent rains...

At the peak of the fur trading era, as many as 3000 people would gather at Fort William each spring. The fort took on a lively, festive air as the *hivernants* arrived with furs from the winter's trading.

The dining room in the great hall, measuring ten metres by twenty metres, could hold 200 guests. With the partners gathered at the fort, a colorful and diverse group gathered there each night to dine. Wilderness-toughened traders from the West sat with the elegantly dressed Montreal partners. Old friendships were renewed, stories told and toasts drunk to the memory of traders and *voyageurs* who had not returned.

Fort William was more than just a meeting place. It was the nerve centre for all of the North West Company's activities in the West. Here, the partners would meet in the council house to plan the Company's activities for the coming year. Here, too, the supplies for a year's trading activities were gathered and organized. Trading goods, equipment and food supplies were set aside for each of the Company's western outposts and arranged by canoe loads. Early in the fall, men from each of the posts would come to Fort William, load their canoes and return for another winter of trading.

A fur trader's life meant long hours filled with backbreaking work, especially for the *voyageurs* who paddled the canoes. Ironically, paddling was not the hardest part of the job. The worst aspect of the journey was the portages, when the crew would have to carry the canoe and its heavy cargo overland to avoid rapids or waterfalls.

The men of the fur trade could carry few personal belongings with them in the canoes. Space was valuable and used to store trade goods and supplies. With little time to hunt or fish, the *voyageurs'* diet was mainly dried peas, beans, biscuits and salt pork during the journey to Fort William. Once they reached the fort, they depended on pemmican. At night, the fur traders slept under their overturned canoes drawn up on the bank of a river or lake. Their sleep was usually brief, as they had a long distance to cover each day. Many mornings they would rise at one or two o'clock to begin a day's journey that would not end until sunset.

1. Why was Fort William chosen as the major North West Company trading post?
2. Make a list of some of the activities that were carried on at Fort William.

This painting is titled "Dickering with the Factor" and it illustrates the relationship between the Native peoples and the fur traders. Which group benefited the most from trading?

The Fur Trade and the Native Peoples

By the early 1800s, both companies had a network of fur trading forts throughout the West. Their fierce competition led to trading practices which had harmful consequences for the Native peoples who provided the furs.

The Hudson's Bay Company required its employees to always give a standard amount of goods, such as blankets or tools, in exchange for furs of a given type or quality. The Company forbade the trading of alcohol to the Native peoples for furs. The Nor'Westers did not have a standard of trade, nor were they forbidden to trade brandy or rum for furs.

The Hudson's Bay Company found itself having to match the Nor'Westers' trading practices in order to compete effectively. The end of the Hudson's Bay Company trade standard forced the Native peoples to compete aggressively to supply furs when prices were high. They would abandon traditional hunting practices and spend all their time getting furs to trade. In doing so, some Native bands became dependent on the fur trade for survival. When changes in fashion and occasional economic recessions in Europe caused fur prices in Canada to drop, they suffered greatly. Native hunters and trappers would receive smaller amounts of food, ammunition and trade goods for the furs they brought to trade. With less food and ammunition, these Natives, who had largely abandoned their traditional hunting and food-storing practices, faced severe hunger and hardship.

The competition between the two companies also put great pressure on the resource base of the fur trade. In some areas, the animal populations on which the fur trade depended were virtually wiped out.

The use of alcohol as a trade good seriously disrupted Native life and further increased their dependence on the traders. Unfamiliar with alcohol, many Natives became dependent on the brandy or rum forced upon them by the traders. Soon, permanent Native villages were common around the trading posts. There, weakened by alcohol and increasingly dependent on trade goods, the Native bands often fell victim to European diseases such as smallpox. The

TRADE ITEMS

David Thompson recorded the following description of trade with the Native peoples while he was working for the Hudson's Bay Company in the late 1780s:

...everything is carried on by barter profitable to both parties but more so to the Indians than to us. We took from them furrs [sic] of no use to them, and which had to pass through an immense distance of freight and risks before they could be sold in the market of London. See the wife of an Indian sewing their leather clothing with a pointed, brittle bone, or a sharp thorn, and the time and trouble it takes. Show them an awl or a strong needle, and they will gladly give the finest Beaver or Wolf skin they have to purchase it. When the tents remove, a steady, careful old man or two of them are entrusted with the fire, which is carried in a rough wooden bowl with earth in it...to the place of the [next] camp...a flint and steel saves all this anxiety and trouble...tobacco was the great luxury and, like money, commanded all things. Iron heads for their arrows are in great request, but above all guns and ammunition.

Native peoples lacked immunity to these newly introduced illnesses and would often die from them even though the sickness was not fatal to Europeans.

1. Suggest some reasons why the introduction of alcohol, which was unknown to the Natives before the Europeans came, had a destructive effect on Natives. Why might some fur traders try to make the Native people dependent on alcohol?
2. What other factors contributed to the deterioration of the Native way of life around the trading posts?

Exploring the Pacific Coast: The Maritime Fur Trade

Two separate fur trades developed in the West during the eighteenth and nineteenth century. The first to develop was the one you have just studied. In effect, it covered practically all of the West from the Great Lakes to the Rocky Mountains. The second fur trade, however, was confined to the Pacific coast of North America. It involved the obtaining of sea otter pelts for sale in China. This fur trade also involved competition, in this case a struggle for control over the resource-rich Pacific coast.

Few, if any, non-Natives had visited the north Pacific coast of North America before the late 1700s. Native peoples of the region told stories of large sailing ships from across the sea. Chinese or Japanese vessels may have reached the Pacific North West as early as 1500 years ago, according to some historians. Archaeological discoveries including centuries-old iron tools in ancient Native villages suggest that this may indeed have happened. However, other than the account of Hwai Shan, who may have made a trading voyage from China to British Columbia in A.D. 458, there are no logbooks, maps or written accounts to confirm that such contacts occurred.

It is known for certain, however, that Russia and Spain began to explore this coast by sea during the mid-eighteenth century. By this time, Spain had a great empire in the Americas, which covered much of South and Central America, extending as far north as California. The Russian empire had expanded eastward far beyond the Ural Mountains to extend to the Pacific shores of Siberia.

Near the Arctic Circle, Alaska and Siberia are only a few kilometres apart. In 1728, the Russians sent an expedition led by Vitus

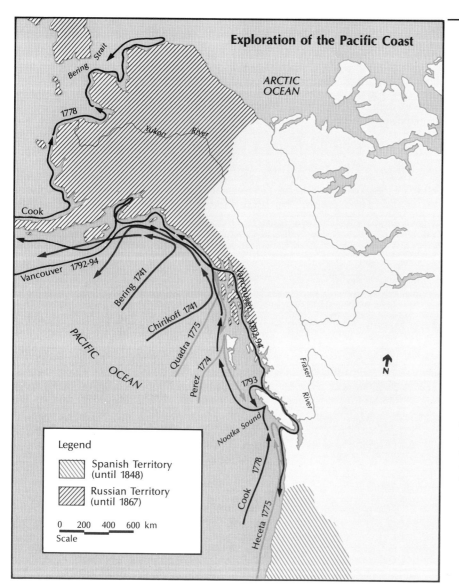

Exploration of the Pacific Coast

ARCTIC OCEAN

Bering Strait

1778

Yukon River

Cook

Vancouver 1792-94

PACIFIC OCEAN

Bering 1741

Chirikoff 1741

Quadra 1775

Perez 1774

Vancouver 1792-94

1793

Fraser River

Nootka Sound

Cook 1778

Heceta 1775

Legend

Spanish Territory (until 1848)

Russian Territory (until 1867)

0 200 400 600 km
Scale

Spanish and Russian sailors had explored portions of the west coast before the British arrived on the scene. Who first explored the coast of present-day British Columbia?

Bering, a Danish sea captain, to travel from Siberia to explore the coast of North America. On this voyage, Bering discovered the Strait that is named after him, proving that Asia and North America were not linked. His second expedition, in 1741, encountered severe difficulties, including the shipwreck of one of its vessels and scurvy aboard the other. Yet the expedition managed to explore the coast of present-day Alaska as far south as Mt. St. Elias, claiming this land for the Russian Empire. The survivors of the expedition also returned to Siberia with a heavy load of pelts from the sea otter, a marine mammal which lived in great numbers on the islands off the coast of Alaska. Its thick and lustrous coat was highly prized in Russia and China. Soon, many Russian trading vessels were coming to this area to obtain sea otter pelts.

News of Russian exploration and trading activities along the coast of Alaska upset the Spanish, who believed that they had a rightful claim to all of the Pacific coast of the Americas. In 1774, Juan Josef Perez Hernandez sailed north from Mexico to establish Spain's claim to all of the Pacific coast of North America. He came in sight of the Queen Charlotte Islands before being driven back by a fierce storm. On his return voyage, he found a safe harbor at a place he named San Lorenzo, near Nootka Sound on Vancouver

COOK AT NOOTKA SOUND

Captain James Cook was the first European to record a description of the coastal landscape of British Columbia's Vancouver Island.

The country had a very different appearance to what we had seen before. It was full of high mountains whose summits were covered with snow; but the valleys between them, and the land on the coast, high as well as low, were clothed with forest.

This was the scene that Cook recorded in his diary as his vessels entered Nootka Sound:

March 29th: We no sooner drew near the inlet, than we found the coast to be inhabited; and at the place where we were first becalmed, three canoes came off to the ship...Having come pretty near to us, a person in one of the two last stood up...inviting us to land.

March 30th: A great many canoes, filled with natives, were about the ship all day; and a trade commenced betwixt us and them, which was carried out with the strictest honesty on both sides. The articles which they offered for sale were the skins of...bears, foxes, wolves, wildcats, deer, martens, ermine, squirrels and of seals and sea-beaver [the sea otter]...

The most important of these was the sea otter, which commanded the highest prices in Europe. The Nootka were shrewd traders; glass beads and trinkets would not do in trade for the valuable furs. Cook wrote in his journal:

Our articles of traffic (trade) consisted for the most part of mere trifles....Beads and such other toys...were in little estimation. Nothing would go down with our visitors but metal....Before we left the place, hardly a bit of it was left in the ship, except what belonged to our necessary instruments. Whole suits of clothing were stripped of every button; bureaus of their furniture and copper kettles, tin canisters, candlesticks and the like all went...

Cook also noted that the Natives of Nootka Sound had already acquired European trade goods, most likely from the Spaniards or from Canadien fur traders who had come into contact with Natives on the mainland who, in turn, traded with the people of Vancouver Island.

Island. There, he obtained sea otter pelts from local Natives who came out to his ship in their canoes. The following year, another Spaniard, Juan Francisco de la Bodega y Quadra, sailed north as far as Alaska.

Thirty years later, Britain joined the maritime fur trade. In 1778, the great British sea captain and explorer, James Cook, was sent to explore the northwest coast of North America. His task: to determine once and for all whether a northern passage linking the Atlantic and Pacific oceans existed. Sailing northeast from the Sandwich Islands, Cook made his first North American landfall on the coast of northern California or southern Oregon. Heading northward, Cook's ships, *Resolution* and *Discovery*, were forced away from the coast by fog and storms. When they finally came in sight of land again, Cook thought they were still on the mainland coast. Instead, the *Resolution* and *Discovery* had blundered into an inlet on the west coast of Vancouver Island.

Cook's crew repaired their ships and set out again on the search for the northern passage. He carefully explored and mapped the coast as far north as 60° north latitude, a point which Bering had reached heading southward. Cook also explored the coastline of Alaska and the Aleutian Islands, then sailed into Bering Strait. Here, a solid wall of ice four metres high blocked his progress and he was forced to turn back, having reached just north of the Arctic Circle. The great explorer headed back to the Sandwich Islands where he was killed. Sea otter pelts taken to China by his crew, however, attracted much attention and commanded high prices. Cook's journals, published in 1784, also excited a great deal of interest, particularly his accounts of the sea otters to be found on Vancouver Island. Several British trading companies were formed to take part in the maritime fur trade.

Soon, many British trading vessels were coming to this coast to gather sea otter skins for sale in China. American traders from ports as far away as Boston joined them, and a fierce competition for control over the sea otter fur trade began. The Spaniards played only a small part in the sea otter trade but they moved swiftly to protect their claim to the area. They built a fort at Friendly Cove, on Nootka Sound, where much of the sea otter trade was centred. Since there was no agreement as to who had possession of the North Pacific coast, the Americans, Russians, Spanish and British argued continually over who had the right to control trading in the area. Spanish ships sometimes attacked British trading vessels, seizing their cargoes. The British continued to explore and map the area they claimed as theirs, sending explorers such as Captain George Vancouver to survey the coast.

In 1795, Britain and Spain signed the Treaty of Nootka Sound, giving the British control over the area south of Alaska. Twenty years later, the British and Russians also signed a treaty limiting Russian fur trading activities to the area north of 54° 40′ north latitude.

By the time these treaties were signed, competition between the Russians, British and Americans for their valuable furs had left the sea otters virtually extinct. Once found in the millions from California to Alaska, the sea otter population was reduced to a few thousand animals by the end of the nineteenth century. Ironically, so many sea otter pelts had been shipped to China that the market had become glutted. The price of sea otter pelts dropped sharply, and the Pacific maritime fur trade came to an end.

JOHN MEARES

The sea otter trade came close to causing a war between Britain and Spain. John Meares, a former British navy officer who ran a trading business out of Calcutta, India, arrived at Nootka Sound in 1786 to trade for sea otter pelts. An ambitious person, he devised a plan to gain control over the sea otter trade. He returned to Nootka Sound in 1789 with fifty Chinese and Portuguese laborers, who built a fortified trading post on land bought from the Natives. These workers also constructed a 40-tonne vessel, *The Northwest America*, to be used to carry furs along the coast.

At first, the Russian, Spanish and American traders took little notice of Meares' trading post. Then, in 1790, while Meares was on his way to China with a load of furs, the Spanish Viceroy in Mexico decided that Meares' trading post was a threat to Spain's long-standing claim to all of the Pacific coast of North America. A Spanish warship was sent to Nootka Sound. Meares' fort and several ships anchored nearby were destroyed and their contents seized. The Spanish built a fort where Meares' trading post had stood, its cannon pointing at the anchorage.

Meares went to London to protest the Spanish action to the British monarch, and to demand compensation. The British government agreed to support Meares, recognizing an opportunity to claim the region for the empire. Two million pounds and fourteen ships were committed to avenge the Spanish insult to Meares at Nootka Sound.

The war that might have taken place over Nootka Sound never happened. In Europe, Spain was involved in the French Revolution and did not wish to stand alone against the might of the British Royal Navy. In October 1790, Spain agreed to give up its exclusive claim to the Pacific region and to pay compensation to Meares. The following year, Britain sent Captain George Vancouver to claim and survey the north west coast.

MAQUINNA: NATIVE MIDDLEMAN

The Native leader who greeted Cook's ships at Friendly Cove in 1778 was Maquinna, one of the leading chiefs of the Nootka. Maquinna was a key figure in the maritime fur trade. He acted as a "middleman" between the traders and the Native peoples, keeping both sides honest. For this role, he took a portion of the proceeds for himself. Maquinna was also involved in negotiations with both Spanish and British delegations who visited Nootka Sound asserting claims to the region.

Maquinna emerged as *the* dominant chief of the Nootka during the fur trade. While he had reached his position as one of the leading chiefs through traditional means, his power and prestige were greatly enhanced by the wealth he acquired through the fur trade.

Maquinna faced the difficult task of leading his people through a period of rapid and dramatic change resulting from European contact. In doing so, he showed great skill and wisdom. Maquinna's reputation was so great that his name became a title of rank adopted by all subsequent Nootka chiefs.

The maritime fur trade brought not only European traders to the Pacific North West, but also claims of ownership by their governments. Russia secured a foothold in Alaska, while further south, the British had taken control of Vancouver Island and laid claim to the coast of British Columbia. The British now blocked the northward expansion of the Spanish empire in Mexico and California. As well, the maritime fur trade had resulted in a strong American presence on the Pacific coast of what are today Oregon and northern California. The stage was now set for later struggles over the settlement and control of this area during the nineteenth century.

1. Name the four countries which became involved in the struggle for control over the maritime trade along the Pacific coast during the period 1741 to 1815.
2. Why did the maritime fur trade last only a short time?
3. In your own words summarize the role played by each of the following in the maritime fur trade: James Cook, Maquinna, John Meares.

From Exploration to Settlement: The Red River Colony

Until the early nineteenth century, European activity in the West was confined to trading and exploration. With the establishment at Red River of the first European settlement on the Prairies, however, the pattern of western development would begin to change. In this section, you will first look at the founding of the Red River colony.

You will then look at how the establishment of this colony led to conflicts involving both fur trading companies as well as Métis, Native peoples and the settlers themselves. Finally, you will see how this conflict helped bring about a merger of the two companies, from which the Hudson's Bay Company emerged more powerful than ever.

The Founding of the Colony

At the start of the nineteenth century the economy of western Canada was based on hunting, trapping and fishing. The numerous Native groups from the Pacific coast to the Canadian Shield depended almost entirely on hunting or fishing for the food they ate. Many of the things they used in their daily lives, including their shelter, clothing and tools came from the animals they hunted or trapped. Any goods of European origin that they used, such as iron tools, cooking pots or rifles, were obtained through the fur trade.

The Métis, like the Native peoples of the Prairies, depended on the great buffalo herds for their food. They traded surplus buffalo meat to the fur traders. For their part, the fur traders, the only Europeans in the region, depended entirely on the Native and Métis hunters and trappers of the West for their livelihood.

There was almost no agriculture in the Canadian West at this time although some of the Native peoples of the region had been farmers centuries before. After the introduction of the horse, brought to the New World by the Spanish, most Native peoples of the Plains obtained their food through hunting bison. Some of the Hudson's Bay Company trading posts had small garden plots and kept some livestock, but there was nothing that could really be called a farm west of Upper Canada. Then, in 1812, events began to take place which would change the economic life of western Canada forever.

In August of that year, a small group of Scottish settlers reached what is today southern Manitoba and began clearing land along the Red River for farms. They arrived too late to plant a crop that first year. Poorly provisioned and ill-equipped to face the harshness of the climate, these settlers barely survived their first winter.

A wealthy young Scottish nobleman, Thomas Douglas, the fifth Earl of Selkirk, was the driving force behind this establishment of a colony at Red River. Selkirk, who owned a controlling interest in the Hudson's Bay Company, persuaded the Company in 1811 to give him a grant of nearly 300 000 km² in what is now Manitoba, Minnesota and North Dakota.

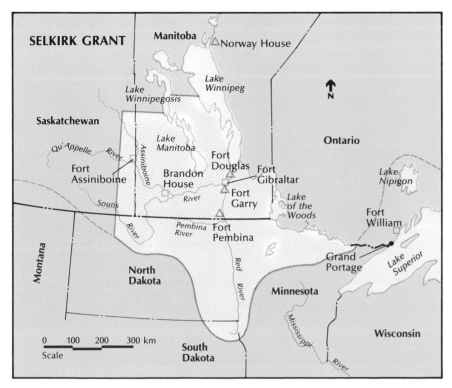

The Selkirk Grant. Selkirk was strongly anti-American and he saw the relocation of peasants from Scotland to the West as a way of ensuring a British influence in the area.

Selkirk's motives for establishing the colony were rooted in the problems of the poor rural peasant crofters and farmers of his native Scotland. Evicted from their small farm holdings by landlords who wanted to create large sheep farms, the displaced peasants drifted into Britain's industrial cities, or left the British Isles. Those who emigrated often chose the United States, rather than the British North American colonies. At his own expense, Selkirk assisted many Scots to emigrate and settle in Prince Edward Island and in Upper Canada. Now, in the Red River country, he was prepared to undertake an even bigger settlement program for his countrymen.

The Hudson's Bay Company directors had mixed feelings about Selkirk's plans. To ensure the supply of furs, they preferred to disturb the Native way of life as little as possible. On the other hand, they also recognized that a permanent colony, sponsored by the Hudson's Bay Company, would help to reinforce its claim to the territory covered by the grant of 1670. They also saw that the settlement could become a source of food and men for the Hudson's Bay Company, and a place where employees of the Bay could retire and settle with their families.

The Earl of Selkirk

The Hudson's Bay Company also saw that farming in the Red River area would disrupt the bison-hunting economy of the Métis, most of whom lived in the Red River and Assiniboine River valleys. All the major fur trading canoe routes passed through this region. The Métis living there provided the North West Company with pemmican, the basic food of the fur trade. A mixture of dried bison meat, fat and berries, pemmican was a high-energy food that kept for a long time.

Selkirk's proposed Red River colony would occupy the same lands as did the bison on which the Métis depended for the production of pemmican. If its supply of pemmican was cut off or reduced, the North West Company would be less able to compete in the fur trade. The Hudson's Bay Company men hoped that the ploughs of the new settlers would break up the prairie grasslands on which the bison grazed. They also saw a chance for the Company to use the produce from the Red River farms to supply its own fur traders.

1. Why was pemmican so important to the fur trade? What did the Hudson's Bay Company hope to achieve by disrupting the Métis bison-hunting grounds?

2. Who was Lord Selkirk? Why did he wish to start an agricultural colony at Red River?

3. Why did the Hudson's Bay Company originally not wish to see settlement in the West? What benefits did they see in Selkirk's Red River colony proposal?

Conflict at Red River

The Red River colony's population increased with the arrival of another seventy men, women and children from Scotland in 1813. However, the colonists' wooden ploughs were unable to break much of the tough prairie grass that covered the fertile soil beneath. Few crops were planted, and the colonists faced another winter of near-starvation.

Miles Macdonell, governor of the Red River colony, had been both a soldier and a farmer in Upper Canada, but his experience failed him in the Red River settlement. Macdonell thought his authority extended to all residents of the Red River area. When he learned in 1814 that more colonists would be arriving from Scotland, he issued an order prohibiting the export of pemmican from the Red River colony. Macdonell wanted the pemmican kept in the colony so the settlers would have an assured supply of food for the winter. Macdonell's proclamation outraged the North West Company. Without access to the region's pemmican supplies the Nor'Westers faced a hard winter in the Western interior. The Métis, ignoring Macdonell's orders, went on driving the bison herds, killing the animals and making pemmican to sell to the North West Company. Angered by the Métis' refusal to obey his orders, Macdonell seized pemmican supplies that had been stored by the North West Company, along with two cargo canoes. The result was the "pemmican war."

Outraged at the seizure of its pemmican, the North West Company sought revenge. Its agents encouraged the Métis to harass the colonists and drive them out of the Red River area. The Métis did not require much encouragement for they considered themselves to be the rightful owners of the lands around the Red River. They attacked the settlers' farms and homes, breaking down fences and burning crops and buildings. Macdonell was arrested and taken as a prisoner to Fort William.

With the colony in the hands of the Métis and the North West Company, some of the colonists decided to resettle in Upper Canada. The rest journeyed to Norway House, a Hudson's Bay depot at the head of Lake Winnipeg. After wintering at Norway House, the settlers returned to the Red River colony under the leadership of Colin Robertson. They were soon joined by a fresh group of immigrants and a new governor.

The Hudson's Bay Company sent the new governor, Robert Semple, to the Red River colony in the spring of 1815. Semple chose to put up a show of strength against the Métis. In March of 1816, he had an empty North West Company trading post, Fort Gibralter, burned as a warning to the Métis. On June 19, 1816, Semple's bravado resulted in tragedy. A party of Métis was spotted passing close to the Red River colony. Semple gathered a group of twenty-one armed colonists to face the Métis, thinking that a show of courage would repel an attack.

A second group of Métis on horseback rode out to meet the colonists, cutting Semple and the others off from the safety of their houses. For some reason, Semple reached out to grab the bridle of a Métis' horse. A shot was fired, followed by a volley of gunfire. Within minutes, Semple and the other men lay dead or dying on the ground. The settlers were evacuated and the colony burned. This incident is known as the Battle of Seven Oaks.

An artist's interpretation of the Battle of Seven Oaks.

Following this clash, the struggle for control of the Red River Valley widened. Hudson's Bay Company men clashed directly with the Nor'Westers. Each company attacked and burned posts belonging to the other.

Meanwhile, in 1815 Lord Selkirk had received news of the earlier events at Red River. In the spring of 1816, he organized a private army of one hundred soldiers in Upper Canada. On the way to Red River, news of the Battle of Seven Oaks reached Selkirk. He decided to divide his forces. Some were sent directly to the Red River colony, while Selkirk led a party of his mercenaries in a successful attack on

Fort William. There, he took several members of the North West Company prisoner and seized the entire contents of the Company's richest storehouse. Selkirk and the Hudson's Bay Company now took legal action against the North West Company for its harassment of the Red River colony. Despite a long and costly court battle lasting from 1817-1819, neither side won. The costs were so great that Selkirk lost both his personal fortune and his health in the process. He lived long enough, however, to recruit another party of colonists for Red River before his death from tuberculosis in 1820.

This time, settlers from Switzerland as well as Scotland were sent to the fertile valleys of the Red and Assiniboine rivers. Selkirk realized that the colony needed large numbers of settlers to be successful. He made grants of land available to the soldiers who had come west with him, to retired Hudson's Bay Company men and to the Métis.

Pioneer settlers from both Upper and Lower Canada joined the Red River colonists. These settlers were better prepared and equipped for the tasks of clearing land and farming on the Canadian frontier. Soon, the fertile Red River soil was producing crops of hay, wheat, barley and potatoes, with the Hudson's Bay Company purchasing any surplus food produced in the colony.

The agricultural settlement at Red River had shown that farming could succeed on Canada's fertile western plains. A new economic activity, potentially more valuable than the fur trade, had been established. However, the distance from major markets and the lack of land transportation would slow agricultural settlement in the Canadian West. As you will see in Chapter 8, the full benefits of the fertile Prairies would only be realized with the building of a railroad linking the West to eastern Canada. The fertile lands around Winnipeg would then truly become the crossroads of the continent.

1. Why did the Métis and the North West Company oppose the Red River settlement? What was the outcome of their opposition?

2. What problems did the Red River colonists face getting to this region? What routes could they take? from Europe? from the Canadas?

3. On what basis could the Hudson's Bay Company justify creating the Red River colony on lands occupied by the Métis and used by the Nor'Westers? In your opinion, were they justified in doing so? Why?

The Triumph of the Hudson's Bay Company

The conflict between the Hudson's Bay and North West companies over the Red River greatly disrupted the fur trade. The cost of the court battle added to the companies' financial problems and neither company showed a profit for several years. By 1821, the struggle had proved too costly for the North West Company to continue the competition. In the end, the conflict was resolved by a decision to merge the two great rivals into a single company.

The Nor'Westers negotiated an agreement which appeared to give them control over the combined fur trading operation. The Hudson's Bay Company received forty-five shares [45 percent of the ownership] in the new company. The North West Company received the remainder of the 100 shares in the company. Thirty went to the Montreal partners and the *hivernants* received twenty-five shares. The new company would continue to be known as the Hudson's Bay Company, because the royal charter granting exclusive trading rights in Rupert's Land was in that name. In 1821, the British Parliament passed a bill confirming that the newly merged company would continue to have a monopoly over trade in Rupert's Land and extending that control to include the North West Territory as well.

At first it appeared the old Nor'Westers had gained control over the new Hudson's Bay Company. However, the route to Europe via Hudson Bay still proved faster and cheaper than the canoe route to Montreal, and Fort William's importance as a fur trading post lessened. The Montreal partners found themselves forced to close their doors as they no longer had furs to sell. The western fur trade remained firmly in the hands of the old Hudson's Bay Company men, but now they found themselves working side by side with old rivals.

The Hudson's Bay Company emerged from the merger of 1821 much stronger than before. It controlled, under the royal charter of 1670, all the territory drained by rivers flowing into Hudson Bay. The merger gave them an exclusive license to trade in the lands opened by the North West Company, all the unsettled lands west of the Great Lakes and north of the 49th parallel. As well, it had a complete monopoly over the fur trade in all unsettled lands north of the St. Lawrence River and the Great Lakes. The Hudson's Bay

The insignia of the Hudson's Bay Company. What symbols can you identify?

THE LITTLE EMPEROR

From 1821 to 1860, the directors of the Hudson's Bay Company entrusted complete control over its fur trading empire in North America to one man, George Simpson. During his nearly forty years as governor of the Hudson's Bay Company, Simpson showed that the directors' faith in him was well-founded. During the years that this tough, intelligent Scot was governor, the Hudson's Bay Company never failed to show a profit.

Rather than sitting behind a desk in London or York Factory, Simpson constantly travelled throughout the Company's vast territory. He crossed and recrossed the continent many times, ensuring that trading posts were being run in an efficient and economical fashion. He also took great care to ensure good relations between the traders and the Métis and Native peoples on whom they depended. The governor often acted as judge when he found that a crime had been committed or a contract broken within the Company's territories. He tried to ensure that all persons, whether British, Canadien, Métis or Native, received fair treatment. Recognizing the destructive impact liquor had on the Native peoples, Simpson actively sought to prevent its use in the fur trade. He also insisted that the Company's standards of fairness in trade be maintained at all times.

Governor Simpson's single-handed rule earned him both respect and fear. He became known as the "Little Emperor" within the Company for the way he carried out his role as "Overseas Governor of the Honourable Company." Dressed in a high beaver hat and frock

coat, Simpson would arrive at a remote trading post by canoe with a kilted bagpiper standing at the bow to pipe him ashore.

Simpson's rule not only made the Company's fur trading operation highly profitable, it also brought stability to Canada's western frontier. Simpson managed to avoid the kinds of conflict and "wild West" lawlessness that marked much of the American frontier during this period.

Company now controlled nearly one-third of the North American continent. It was the supreme authority, governing and controlling all aspects of trade on a resource-rich frontier covering nearly six million square kilometres.

1. When and how was the conflict between the North West Company and the Hudson's Bay Company finally resolved?
2. What did the Hudson's Bay Company gain from the merger of the two firms? What did the North West Company gain?

Summary

During the late 1700s and early 1800s, European traders pushed further and further west along the rivers and lakes of the Canadian Shield and the Prairies. Rivalry between the Hudson's Bay Company and the North West Company spurred this process of exploration and trade. The North West Company, with its major centre at Fort William, followed the practice of the earlier French fur traders, travelling by canoe deep into the West in search of furs. At first, the Hudson's Bay Company was content to have Native peoples bring furs to its post on the shores of Hudson's Bay. However, the success of the Nor'Westers forced the Bay men to change their policy. By the early 1800s, the two companies were locked in a fierce and often bitter rivalry for control of the fur trade.

This rivalry also led to dubious trading practices such as the selling of alcohol, unknown before the Europeans came, to the Native peoples who provided the furs. The fur traders depended on the Native peoples to supply them with furs, guide their canoes and carry their loads. In turn, however, the fur trade left the Native peoples increasingly dependent on the traders for their survival. Many did not survive: weakened by alcohol abuse and malnutrition, they fell victim to European diseases such as smallpox, to which they had little or no natural resistance.

On the Pacific coast, the fur trade, based on sea otter pelts, gave rise to rivalry not between companies, but nations. Traders from Spain, Britain, Russia and the United States came to the Pacific Northwest. Each of these nations claimed the area. The rivalry saw Spain give up its claims to Vancouver Island to the British, while Alaska remained part of the Russian empire. As well, American interest in the West Coast was strengthened.

The first farmers in the West were brought by Lord Selkirk to the Red River area of what is now Manitoba. The Hudson's Company hoped that farming would destroy the buffalo grazing lands on which the Nor'Westers depended for their supplies of pemmican. The establishment of an agricultural colony at Red River resulted in armed clashes between the colonists and Bay men on one side and the Nor'Westers and their Métis allies on the other.

These clashes were costly to both companies. Yet by 1821, the two rivals had merged to create a new company, which kept the name of the Hudson's Bay Company. Following the merger, the Hudson's Bay Company held a monopoly on all trading activity in the West. It was also the sole source of law and government for this vast and sparsely populated area.

REVIEW

Checking Back

1. Write one or two sentences summarizing the significance of each of the following in the western fur trade.

   Hudson's Bay Company's   pemmican
       charter   sea otters
   Fort William   beavers

2. Members of the North West Company received a share of the profits, rather than set wages. Imagine you are on the board of directors for the North West Company. How would you divide the year's profits from the fur trade among the Montreal merchants, *hivernants*, Nor'Westers and the *voyageurs*?

3. The early fur trade was successful because of the skill and knowledge of the Native people. Do you agree or disagree with this statement? Record at least two facts that support your point of view.

4. Create a chart to compare the west coast and western interior fur trades. Some headings you might use are: Types of furs, Rivalries, Markets, Role of Native people.

Using Your Knowledge

5. Use the written description of Fort William found on page 124 to help you draw a sketch map of the fort. Remember to label all important buildings.

6. Imagine you are a *voyageur* working for the North West Company. Write a diary entry describing a typical day during the trading season.

7. David Thompson made this statement about the trade between the Hudson's Bay Company and the Native people: "... everything is carried on by barter profitable to both parties but more so to the Indians than to us." Do the facts given in this chapter support Thompson's views?

8. Imagine you are a judge deciding whether Britain, America, Russia or Spain will gain control of the west coast fur trade. What evidence will you use to help you decide the issue? Based on that evidence, to which nation would you award the trading rights?

9. Write a newspaper article summarizing the events of the "pemmican wars." Write a headline to accompany your article.

Chapter 8

Manitoba: Canada's Fifth Province

European exploration and settlement of western Canada began with the fur trade. Of the West's many valuable resources, furs were the first to be exported. Up to the early 1800s, the fur trade had brought only a small number of non-Native people to western Canada. Yet, it had already significantly changed the environment and the Native people who lived there.

At the time of Confederation, western Canada was still under the complete control of the Hudson's Bay Company. In order to preserve the fur trade, the Company's policies had limited the number of non-Native settlers in the region. However, the discovery of highly fertile prairie soils had attracted European farmers to what is now Manitoba as early as 1812. There, they found themselves in conflict with the fur traders, the Native people and the Métis over control and ownership of the western lands.

These fertile lands in the West also attracted the attention of both political leaders and farmers in Canada, particularly Ontario. At the same time, westward expansion of the United States added to Canadian interest in this region: the British government began to fear possible conflict with the Americans over control of the West.

In this chapter, you will learn how Canada's fifth province, Manitoba, was created against the backdrop of these changes and conflicts. As you do so, consider the following key questions:

- How did the purchase of Rupert's Land by Canada contribute to the creation of the province of Manitoba?
- How did the conflicts between the Métis and the Red River settlers lead to provincial status for Manitoba?
- What impact did annexation of Rupert's Land by Canada, and the creation of Manitoba, have on the Métis and Native people of the West?

The New Dominion Expands

Confederation took place at the time when the United States was expanding westward and, it was hoped by many, northward. During the period 1864-1890, nine new states were established in the northwestern quarter of the United States. Four of these states lay along a broad stretch of the Canada-United States border. Of concern to the Canadians was the fact that the day after Queen Victoria signed the British North America Act, the United States purchased Alaska from the Russians.

During the late 1860s, a number of factors fuelled the expansionist mood in the United States. One was an economic boom that followed the end of the Civil War. Entrepreneurs were once again able to invest money in land, build railways and develop the resources of the American West. Many of these entrepreneurs were eager to see the United States frontier pushed north of the 49th parallel believing that it was their nation's "manifest destiny" to rule all of North America. Another factor was the lingering resentment toward Britain, which had supported the defeated Confederacy during the Civil War (see pages 96-97).

In the late 1860s, American traders and settlers began eagerly eyeing the vast and thinly populated Canadian Prairies. These lands were still largely home only to Native and Métis fur traders and hunters. American politicians and newspaper writers of this period spoke increasingly of a time when the British North American provinces and territories would become part of the United States of America.

Faced with these expansionist threats, the new Canadian government entered into negotiations with the Hudson's Bay Company to buy the lands to the north and west of Canada. These negotiations were begun even before Confederation, and provision was made in the British North America Act, Section 146, for the eventual inclusion of Rupert's Land as part of the new Dominion. Both the British and Canadian governments believed that the Americans were less likely to annex these lands if they belonged to Canada than if they remained in the hands of the Hudson's Bay Company.

For its part, the fur trading company was finding it difficult to maintain its control over the region. American traders were making inroads into the Prairies and the western mountains, and settlers were moving into the region drawn by the gold rushes and fertile lands. Also, by this time the western fur trade was declining in importance. The Company was now turning its attention to the profits to be made from providing supplies to miners, settlers and the crews of trading ships. Opening up the West to Canadian settlers would benefit this aspect of the Company's operations.

The Canadian government and the Company reached an agreement on November 19, 1869. It was George-Étienne Cartier (see page 92) who did most of the negotiation for the government of Canada. In exchange for Rupert's Land, the Hudson's Bay Company received £300 000 and 2.8 million hectares of Prairie farmland from the Canadian government. As well, it was able to continue its fur trading activities. Rupert's Land was officially transferred to Canada on June 23, 1870. With the addition of this land, renamed the North West Territories, Canada more than doubled in size.

The purchase of Rupert's Land brought the promise of a larger, stronger Canada. The North West Territories were rich in resources, but the acquisition of these lands also brought problems for the new nation to deal with.

What present-day provinces and territories lie within the area transferred to Canada in 1870?

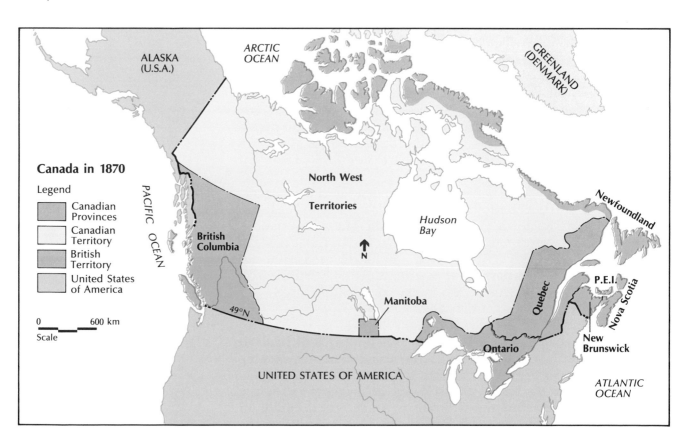

146

THE AMERICAN POINT OF VIEW

The following statements made in the United States in the 1860s show the strength of expansionist sentiment in that country.

The first statement is from a report made to the United States Senate on the need to build a transcontinental railway.

The opening by us first of a North Pacific Railroad seals the destiny of the British possessions west of the 91st meridian. They will become so strongly Americanized in interests and feelings that...annexation will be but a question of time.

The second is a statement made by William Seward, the American Secretary of State who negotiated the purchase of Alaska in 1867. Seward's statement not only sums up the "manifest destiny" view, but also clearly states the expansionist position with regard to Canada.

I look upon Canada and see how a clever people are occupied with bridging rivers and making railroads and telegraphs. I say, "It is very well: you are building excellent states to be hereafter admitted to the American Union."

I know that Nature designs that this whole continent, not merely these thirty-six states, shall be, sooner or later, within the magic circle of the United States.

1. Use your atlas to find the 91st meridian [91° West Longitude]. Which British territories does the Senate report see falling into the hands of the United States? Which present-day provinces and territories of Canada lie within those territories?
2. In the view of the authors of the Senate report, how would completion of an American railway to the Pacific affect Britain's territories in the West?

1. Suggest reasons why Americans would consider expanding north of the 49th parallel into Canadian lands.
2. Why did the Hudson's Bay Company want to sell Rupert's Land? Why did the Canadian government want to buy the land?
3. Suppose you had been in charge of the Hudson's Bay Company during this time period. Would you have sold the land? Explain your answer.

Manitoba: Creation of a New Province

The non-Native population of the North West Territories in 1870 was only 12 000 people, most living along the Red River. Of these, 10 000 were Métis. Most were French-speaking and Roman Catholic, although some were of Scottish or English background as well.

Even before negotiations with the Hudson's Bay Company were completed, the government of Canada sent surveyors to the Red

Educated in Montreal, Riel was a serious, thoughtful person, dedicated to helping his people. While he opposed the actions of the Canadian government, he strongly resisted the idea that the Red River area should become part of the United States.

River Valley. From the surveyors, the Métis learned of the Canadian government's planned purchase of the area. This news shocked and outraged the Métis who had never been consulted by either the Hudson's Bay Company or the Canadian government during the period of negotiations. Some of the surveyors treated the Métis quite badly, responding to their protests with verbal and physical abuse and ignoring their claims to ownership of land. The surveyors' presence led the Métis to fear the Canadian government was going to take away their lands. The Métis remembered the earlier efforts of the Hudson's Bay Company and the Red River colonists to destroy their buffalo hunting lands and they had seen the slow but steady growth of pioneer agricultural settlements along the Red River.

The Métis reacted quickly to the threat posed by the Canadians. Gathering for the annual fall buffalo hunt in October 1869, they selected as their spokesman Louis Riel, a well-educated young man fluent in both French and English. Riel formed an organization called the *Comité National des Métis* to defend the rights of his people.

Many of the recent non-Métis settlers in the Red River area were from Ontario and wished to see the area added to that province. Known as the "Canadian Party," this group was led by men who were anti-French and anti-Catholic. Their leader was Dr. John Christian Schultz, a newspaper publisher. In his newspaper, Schultz called for massive immigration of English-speaking, Protestant Ontarians to the western territories. Schultz began organizing armed resistance to the Métis.

Back in Ottawa, the government at first showed little concern for the problems of the Métis. However, as reports of Métis opposition slowly made their way eastward, the leaders of the new Dominion became increasingly alarmed. They decided to delay the formal takeover of the Hudson's Bay Company lands until the issues were resolved.

William McDougall, the newly appointed lieutenant-governor for the North West Territory, was already on his way to Red River when the government in Ottawa took this decision. Therefore, he was unaware that his authority in the North West did not yet have legal status. He travelled by the only easily accessible route to Fort Garry, the route through the United States west to St. Paul, and then north. (See page 146.) McDougall attempted to enter the Red River area from the United States, expecting to declare the North West officially part of Canada on December 1, 1869. However, the Métis met McDougall at the border on October 31 and blocked his entry into the area.

Three days later, Riel and his comrades seized the Hudson's Bay post at Fort Garry. With its strong stone walls and supply of weapons, Fort Garry gave the Métis a secure military base. By their seizure of the fort, Riel and his committee hoped to gain a better bargaining position with the Canadian government.

Riel then organized a **provisional government** to look after the region's affairs until a suitable arrangement could be made with Ottawa. A provisional government has no formal, constitutional basis. It exists for a short period of time until a properly constituted government can be established. Riel's provisional government was intended to ensure law and order in the area until an elected Assembly, comprised of local residents and recognized by the government of Canada, was created. The Métis were not opposed to becoming part of Canada. However, they were upset that the Canadian government had not bothered to discuss its plans for the area with the Métis or even to inform them of its intentions.

During their negotiations with the Canadian government, the Métis sought to ensure that the rights of all people in the Red River area should be protected, whether they were French- or English-speaking, Protestant or Catholic, Native or newcomer. Above all, the Métis wanted to be sure that their lands and traditional way of life would be preserved when they became Canadians. This would soon become a key issue, as the Métis did not issue titles or deeds to the lands their people occupied.

During the first week of December 1869, Riel and his committee held meetings in Fort Garry and at Winnipeg to discuss the terms under which the region should become part of Canada. At these meetings, they drew up a Métis "List of Rights," specifying their demands.

This List of Rights was not a declaration of independence by the Métis. In creating their provisional government, the Métis leaders had sworn allegiance to the Queen. They emphasized that their only wish was to see their rights as British subjects protected. They wanted similar protections to those given the Canadiens under the terms of the Quebec Act and other constitutional documents.

Response to the Métis provisional government came swiftly from Quebec, Ontario and the United States. The people of Quebec felt strong sympathy for the Métis struggle to preserve their rights and traditions. In Ontario, the powerful Orange Order agitated against the rights the Métis wanted protected. The Order strongly opposed

THE MÉTIS LIST OF RIGHTS

The following are some of the items on the "List of Rights" drawn up by the Métis and carried to Ottawa by their negotiating committee:

1. That the people have the right to elect their own Legislature.
2. That the Legislature have the power to pass all laws local to the Territory...
4. That all Sheriffs, Magistrates, Constables, School Commissioners, etc., be elected by the people...
6. That a portion of the public lands be appropriated to the benefit of Schools, the buildings of Bridges, Roads and Public Buildings.
7. That it be guaranteed to connect Winnipeg by Rail with the nearest line of Railroad, within a term of five years...
10. That the English and French languages be common in the Legislature and Courts, and that all Public Documents and Acts of Legislature be published in both languages.
11. That the Judge of the Supreme Court speak the French and English languages.
12. That Treaties be concluded and ratified between the Dominion Government and the several tribes of Indians in the Territory to ensure peace on the frontier.
13. That we have a fair and full representation in the Canadian Parliament.
14. That all privileges, customs and usages existing at the time of transfer be respected.

any constitutional move that would entrench the rights of Catholics, especially Catholic schools. In the United States, the Annexationists hoped that the Métis would turn to them for help in their conflict with the Canadians.

The federal government sent negotiators to the Red River in January 1870. After a series of public meetings, agreement was reached: the Red River area would become a self-governing province, separate from the rest of the North West Territory. A group of Métis leaders was chosen to go to Ottawa to negotiate the terms and conditions for joining Confederation. They carried with them the Métis List of Rights when they left for Ottawa in April 1870.

The Canadian Parliament passed the Manitoba Act on May 12, 1870, creating Canada's fifth province. The name had been chosen by the provisional Métis government for the new province. "Manitoba" was an Assiniboine word meaning "water of the prairie." It was an apt description of the region, with its vast network of lakes and rivers.

The provisions of the Act included most of the major clauses of the Métis List of Rights. All lands held by the Métis and other settlers in the area would be protected, but the rest of the territory would be the property of the Dominion of Canada. Both French and English would be the official languages of Manitoba. There would be two publicly supported school systems, one Roman Catholic, the other Protestant. However, no provision was made for French language education in the Manitoba Act. This would later create great conflicts in Manitoba, as the Métis had assumed that Roman Catholic education would take place in French. However, under the terms of the British North America Act, the province's legislators would have to determine the language of instruction in the schools.

The Manitoba Act of 1870 now became Manitoba's provincial constitution and joined the British North America Act in forming Canada's constitution. The new province of Manitoba was to officially come into existence on July 15, 1870. At this time, the population of Manitoba was fewer than 12 000 people. According to a census conducted in 1870, there were 558 Natives, 5757 French-speaking Métis, 4083 English-speaking Métis and 1585 whites.

1. Describe the reaction of the Métis people to the purchase of Rupert's Land by the Canadian government.
2. In your own words, explain the role of each of these figures in the events leading up to the seizure of Fort Garry by the Métis: John Schultz, William McDougall, Louis Riel.
3. Did the actions of the Métis constitute a rebellion? Explain your answer.
4. What agreement did the Métis reach with the government of Canada in 1870?

The Death of Thomas Scott

While the Métis negotiation with the government of Canada was underway in the spring of 1870, an event occurred that was to affect French-English relations in Canada for a long time.

When the Métis provisional government took over, it arrested the leader of the Canadian Party, John Schultz, and some of his followers. Riel feared that the Canadian Party might invite McDougall, the appointed governor, into the region to govern it according to the wishes of the Canadian Party. However, Schultz and some of his followers escaped and began organizing an armed attack on Fort Garry. Before the attacking forces were ready, a skirmish took place between the raiders and the Métis. One man was killed on each side; however, the combatants withdrew before a full-scale battle could develop.

The Métis leaders decided that the Canadian Party agitators had to be detained in order to demonstrate the provisional government's authority. One of those arrested was Thomas Scott, an Orangeman from nearby Kildonan, one of the most anti-Métis members of the Canadian Party. Many of the Métis believed Scott was responsible for the drowning death of a young Métis boy after the skirmish.

While in jail in Fort Garry, Thomas Scott constantly abused his Métis guards and threatened the life of Louis Riel. Scott's abusiveness and attempts to incite the other prisoners to violence angered the Métis. He was tried, found guilty of making threats against Riel's life, abusing his guards and encouraging hostility toward the Métis. On March 4, 1870, Scott was executed by a Métis firing squad.

News of the execution of Scott reached eastern Canada after the completion of negotiations, causing a storm of angry protest. The Orange Order increased its pressure on the federal government to put down the "rebellion" in the western territory. In many Ontario towns, angry public meetings were held to protest the death of Scott. They demanded that Prime Minister Sir John A. Macdonald send troops to the Red River. In Quebec, the response was one of sympathy for the problems faced by the Métis. There, the death of Scott was seen as a sad but necesary part of the Métis' struggle to protect their rights.

Macdonald bowed to anti-French and anti-Catholic sentiment in Ontario. He ordered 1200 soldiers sent west under the command of

This political cartoon illustrates John A. Macdonald's situation. He is seen as stuck between two horses going in opposite directions. Riel is the "monkey on his back," an image used to refer to annoying problems that cannot be shaken off easily.

SOMETHING'S GOT TO GO SOON!

Colonel Garnet Wolseley. Macdonald's government argued that the military expedition was not intended to punish the Métis, but only to assert a strong Canadian presence in the North West, to prevent the Americans from taking advantage of events there.

In the summer of 1870, the troops set out on an arduous ninety-six day trek across the rugged landscape of the Canadian Shield, reaching Red River on August 23. Most of the soldiers were volunteers, eager to avenge Scott's death. They were disappointed when they met no resistance from the Métis on their arrival at Fort Garry. The gates of the great stone fort were open, and the place deserted. Riel had fled to the United States, and the other Métis had returned to their homes. The troops stayed on in Manitoba to ensure the orderly transfer of power to the new provincial government.

1. What reasons did Louis Riel and the Métis give to explain the execution of Thomas Scott? What reasons do you think John Schultz would have claimed for the execution of Scott?
2. In several sentences, describe how each of these groups felt about Scott's execution: the Métis, French-speaking Canadians, Ontario Orangemen.

Land and Life in the West

Manitoba's entry into Confederation differed from that of the other four provinces in one key respect. Under the Manitoba Act, Ottawa held all of the powers it was given through the British North America Act plus one extra power, control over public lands. This power, which extended to all of the North West Territory as well, was intended to ensure the orderly settlement of the West. It would prove to be a source of conflict between Westerners and the federal government for more than one hundred years.

The first to feel the impact of this provision were the Métis of Manitoba. They were unable to get legal possession of their traditional lands in the area until these lands had been surveyed by the federal government and titles issued. The survey was not completed until 1873; two years later many Métis families were issued with **scrip** (paper, resembling a bank note) entitling them to 160 acres (64 ha) of land. Coming from a society with no written laws, land deeds or money, and unfamiliar with the Canadian legal system, many of the Métis did not recognize the real worth of the scrip.

CHANGING VIEWS OF HISTORY

Canadian history books written in the late nineteenth century and the early part of the twentieth century usually portrayed the Métis, and their leader Louis Riel, as villains in the events that led to the creation of Manitoba as a province. These histories were usually written by English-speaking Protestants. In recent years, however, Canadian historians have stressed the importance of seeing the events at Red River from both the point of view of the Métis and that of the Canadians.

The Métis saw the Canadians as intruders into an area that had been their home for nearly a century. They remembered the attempt to destroy their way of life that had been made when the Red River colony had been established a half-century earlier. The English-speaking Ontarians who moved west to settle in the area saw the Métis as primitive people who stood in the way of progress. They believed that agricultural settlement was superior to a hunting way of life. They also brought with them anti-Catholic biases and they remembered the French Canadians who had rebelled against British rule in 1837.

Given this combination of values and experiences, conflict between the two groups was almost inevitable. Problems of communication, and the failure of the Canadian government to discuss its plans for the region with the Métis, combined with these ingredients to result in the "rebellion."

Unscrupulous speculators acquired much of the Métis land, giving them whisky or a few dollars for their scrip.

Disillusioned, many of the Métis left Manitoba for the lands along the Saskatchewan River to the west of the new province. There, as you will learn in Chapter 10, the conflicts at Red River would be repeated a decade later.

1. How did the terms of Manitoba's entry into Confederation differ from those of the eastern provinces?
2. How did these terms affect the Métis?

Declining Native Population in the West

Native populations in the West declined sharply during the period 1780-1870. When the first Europeans reached the Prairies, as many as 100 000 Native peoples may have lived there. By 1880, out of a total population of 120 000, there were only about 30 000 Native people.

The major cause of this decline in population was disease, particularly smallpox. Weakened by alcohol and malnutrition, as fur trading replaced hunting, the Native peoples had low resistance to diseases brought by Europeans. Epidemics of European-introduced diseases struck the people in 1781, 1819, 1837, 1845, 1864 and 1869.

The smallpox epidemic of 1781, for example, is estimated to have reduced the population of the Blackfoot from 10 000 to 7000 in just a few months. By 1900, the number of Blackfoot was just over 4000.

Problems of disease were compounded by the destruction of the buffalo herds, the major food source for the Métis and Native peoples. Starvation and malnutrition further reduced the Indian population of this region. Attempts to make farmers of Native people placed on reserves, usually located on the poorest soils, were largely unsuccessful. With the introduction of improved medical care in the 1930s, Native populations in western Canada began to increase again.

This photograph illustrates the mingling of cultures that had unhappy consequences for the Native peoples. The Red River cart was a new technology introduced by European traders and settlers. Why would the Native people have started to use it?

Summary

Manitoba was the fifth province to join Confederation. The path the people of the Red River colony took on their way to becoming citizens of Canada was very different from that taken by the colonists living in the first four provinces. This difference reflects the distinctive ways in which the lands around the Red River were settled and developed. Originally part of the Hudson's Bay Company's western operations, the Red River colony was the first part of the Prairies to experience agricultural settlement. In 1869, recognizing the region's rich potential for agriculture, and fearing American expansion into the area, Canada purchased Rupert's Land from the Hudson's Bay Company. Surveyors were sent west to prepare for the orderly settlement of the North West Territory, the new name given to the area.

This move, taken by the Canadians without the knowledge or consent of the Métis, sparked the Red River Rebellion. Led by Louis Riel, the Métis kept the governor from entering the area and set up a provisional government themselves. The Métis demands that their traditional rights be preserved led to the creation of Manitoba as Canada's fifth province in 1870. The execution of Thomas Scott during the rebellion added to conflicts between French- and English-speaking Canadians in Ontario and Quebec. A military expedition was sent to put an end to the uprising, but no battles were fought as the Métis had returned to their lands after the new province had been created.

While the Métis appeared to get all they wanted, their traditional way of life was soon disrupted. Confederation brought new settlers to the Red River, new land laws and a new way of life very different from that of the Métis. Many Métis left the Red River for lands further west in the hope of preserving their distinctive way of life. However, as you will learn in Chapter 9, the westward expansion of settlement would again bring the Métis into conflict with the government of Canada.

REVIEW

Checking Back

1. Write one or two sentences summarizing the significance of each of the following in the Riel Rebellion (1870).

   Purchase of Rupert's Land

   Louis Riel

   Thomas Scott

   John A. Macdonald

   Dr. John Christian Schultz

   Manitoba Act

2. List all the groups that sought control over Rupert's Land. In your own words, summarize how each group saw the future of the West.

3. What benefits did the Hudson's Bay Company gain from the sale of Rupert's Land?

4. The Canadian Party opposed Riel's actions in setting up a provisional government. Who were members of the Canadian Party? How did they propose to settle the West?

Using Your Knowledge

5. Rank in order the causes of the Riel Rebellion, from the least important to the most important.

6. Imagine you have the ability to travel through time. What actions would you take to prevent the Riel Rebellion?

7. Compare the demands made by the Métis in 1870 with those of the Patriotes in 1837. Suggest one or two reasons for any similarities you find.

8. Did the Riel Rebellion achieve its goals? Record at least two pieces of evidence to support your answer.

9. What rights were guaranteed to the Métis in the Manitoba Act of 1870? How does the Manitoba Act relate to the British North America Act?

Chapter 9

British Columbia: From Colonies to Confederation

The province of British Columbia, like Manitoba, was created out of former Hudson's Bay Company territories. Here, too, resources other than furs attracted settlers to the area. As well, fears of annexation of this region to the United States played a role in British Columbia's entry into Confederation. However, unlike Manitoba, British Columbia was for several decades a British colony before becoming a province of Canada.

In this chapter you will learn how natural resources, including coal, gold and timber, began to attract attention to Vancouver Island and the mainland of British Columbia during the period 1830-1860. Concerns about possible American expansion into this area led to the creation of the Vancouver Island colony in 1849 and of a second colony on the mainland in 1858. Ten years later, the two were united into a single colony, British Columbia.

As in the Canadas and the Maritimes, the two Pacific colonies experienced the struggle to achieve responsible government. The colonies faced the problems of economic booms and depressions, with the colonial governments having to borrow money to provide services such as roads and land surveys. Just as in the East, you will learn that these problems led first to a proposal for union of the colonies, and then to their entry into Confederation in 1871.

As you read through this chapter, consider the following key questions:

• What events led to the formation of the crown colony of Vancouver Island?

- What role did the gold rush play in the creation of the British Columbia colony?

- Why did British Columbia agree to enter Confederation? What events led to this agreement? Under what conditions did British Columbia agree to become part of Canada?

The Pacific Coast in the Early 1800s

The central Pacific coast of North America was disputed territory at the beginning of the nineteenth century. A boundary treaty, signed by Britain and the United States following the War of 1812, had established the 49th parallel of latitude as the border between Canada and the United States. But the treaty only covered territories extending as far west as the Rocky Mountains. Beyond the Rockies, both Britain and the United States claimed the coastal area lying north of California. This disputed area was known as the Oregon Territory. In the absence of an agreement between the two rivals, the territory was left open to settlement. Most of the settlers came from the United States.

Fur trading companies from the United States established posts along the Columbia River as early as 1808, but by 1821 the Hudson's Bay Company had taken control of the area. However, American fur traders and land developers continued to encourage settlers from the United States to come to the fertile lands of the Columbia River Valley. Most of this settlement took place around Fort Astoria, operated by the American Fur Company at the mouth of the Columbia. Soon, these American settlers in the Oregon Territory began to pressure political leaders in the United States to annex the Pacific Northwest.

The Americans had effectively established a claim to the area through settlement. John McLaughlin, the man in charge of the Hudson's Bay Company's Columbia Department, was ordered to build a new fort to counter the American presence. The new trading centre was to be located at the junction of the Willamette River and the Columbia, 150 km upstream from Fort Astoria.

Fort Vancouver, the name given to this new post, was to be the main shipment point for the Company's fur trade in the area drained by the Columbia. It was also to be the centre of the British fight against American expansion in the West.

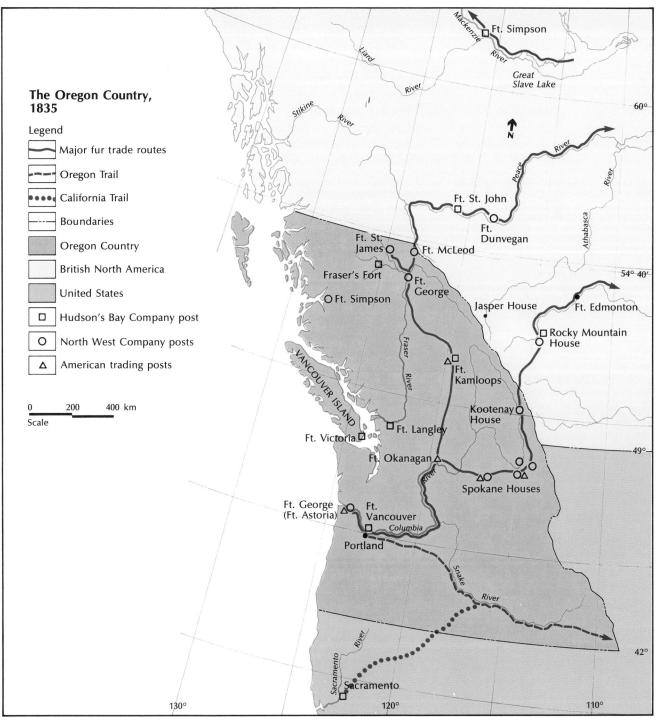

The Oregon Country, 1835

Legend

Major fur trade routes	
Oregon Trail	
California Trail	
Boundaries	
Oregon Country	
British North America	
United States	
□ Hudson's Bay Company post	
○ North West Company posts	
△ American trading posts	

0   200   400 km

Scale

Ft. Simpson

Mackenzie River

Liard River

Great Slave Lake

Stikine River

60°

Peace River

N

Athabasca River

Ft. St. John

Ft. Dunvegan

54° 40'

Ft. St. James

Ft. McLeod

Fraser's Fort

Ft. George

Ft. Simpson

Jasper House

Ft. Edmonton

Rocky Mountain House

Fraser River

Ft. Kamloops

VANCOUVER ISLAND

Kootenay House

Ft. Langley

49°

Ft. Victoria

Ft. Okanagan

Spokane Houses

River

Ft. George (Ft. Astoria)

Ft. Vancouver

Columbia

Portland

Snake River

42°

Sacramento River

Sacramento

130°   120°   110°

The Company encouraged British settlement and the establishment of farms in the Columbia Valley. These settlements would not only provide supplies for the fur traders, they would offset American colonization in the region. Hudson's Bay Company traders worked aggressively to dominate the fur trade in the area.

The Hudson's Bay Company governor, George Simpson, took other actions on the west coast to counter American expansion. In 1827, he had McLaughlin send men north to build Fort Langley on the Fraser River. As well, Simpson ordered the establishment of trading posts along the Pacific coast just south of Alaska to compete with American fur trading ships operating in the area. Despite these moves, Simpson still feared that further waves of American settlers might sweep into the area. His fears were well-grounded.

A treaty negotiated by the Russians and the Americans in 1824 had divided the coast into a series of trading areas. The southern limit of Russian fur trading in North America was set at 54° 40′ north latitude, (just north of present-day Prince Rupert). South of this latitude, trading was to be jointly controlled by Britain and the United States. However, the British government, which had not taken part in the negotiations, did not recognize the Russian-American fur trade treaty.

In 1844, James Polk campaigned for election as president on a promise to gain for the United States all of the area under joint British and American control. He threatened to go to war if necessary to obtain this territory. Polk's campaign slogan was "54-40 or fight." Polk won the election, but chose not to fight. Some historians have suggested that Polk did not really want to obtain control over the entire Pacific Northwest. His slogan, they believe, was just a campaign ploy.

In the negotiations that followed Polk's election, the British hoped to see the boundary set at the Columbia River. But, as a result of Polk's threat, the Americans were able in 1846 to have the boundary between British and American territories in the Northwest set at the 49th parallel, 500 km north of the Columbia. However, all of Vancouver Island would remain British. This agreement became known as the Oregon Boundary Treaty.

1. What actions did the Hudson's Bay Company take to ensure British control over portions of the Pacific Northwest?

2. In your own words, explain the meaning of "54-40 or fight."

Fort Victoria

George Simpson had suspected that the lands along the Columbia would become part of the United States, and that the Company would lose both the Oregon fur trade and also its main access route, the Columbia River. Fort Langley, on the Fraser River, was the first site chosen for the Company's new headquarters, to replace Fort Vancouver. However, the route through the Fraser Canyon proved too difficult and dangerous for use by the fur traders. As a consequence, Simpson turned his attention to Vancouver Island as a possible site for the new trading post.

The man sent out by Simpson to select this site was James Douglas. As you will see, Douglas would come to play a key role in the region's history over the next two decades. Some historians have called him "the father of British Columbia." The child of a West Indian mother and a Scottish merchant father, Douglas was described by his contemporaries as a mulatto, the Caribbean equivalent of Métis. At age sixteen, he came to Canada to work as a clerk-apprentice for the North West Company. He stayed on to work for the Hudson's Bay Company after the two companies merged in 1821. Simpson described Douglas as "a stout, powerful, active man of good conduct and respectable abilities." At Fort Vancouver, Douglas became the chief Hudson's Bay Company trader in 1835 and **chief factor** in 1839. Three years later, he travelled north to Vancouver Island to select the site for the new fort.

Sir James Douglas

The site of the new headquarters would have to have the following qualities: a well-protected harbor, fertile soil and abundant stands of timber. Douglas recommended one such location based on a report made by Captain W.H. McNeill, skipper of the Hudson's Bay Company steamboat *Beaver.* In 1837, McNeill had explored the southern end of the island and reported that he had "found an excellent harbour, of easy access with good anchorage, surrounded by a plain of several miles in extent, of an excellent soil."

In the spring of 1843, the Company's managers approved a resolution calling for construction of a post, to be called Fort Victoria, at the site chosen by Douglas.

Under Douglas' direction, a crew of Hudson's Bay Company men and Native workers set about building Fort Victoria. When they were finished in 1844, Fort Victoria looked much like any other fur trading post. The fort was surrounded by a rectangular stockade one hundred metres by ninety metres, with an octagonal bastion or tower at one corner. Inside, there were eight buildings, including

THE SITE FOR THE NEW FORT

James Douglas submitted the following report to Governor George Simpson on July 12, 1842:

...At Camosack [the name of an Indian village, now known as Camosun] there is a pleasant and convenient Site for the Establishment [fort] within Fifty Yards [forty-six metres] of the Anchorage, on the Border of a large tract of clear Land, which extends Eastward to Point Gonzalo at the South-east extremity of the Island and about Six Miles [ten kilometres] interiorly being the most picturesque and decidedly the most valuable Part of the Island that we had the good Fortune to discover...

Being pretty well assured of the Capabilities of the Soil as respects the Purposes of Agriculture, the Climate also being mild and pleasant, we ought to be able to grow every Kind of Grain raised in England...We are certain that Potatoes thrive and grow to a large Size, as the Indians have many small fields in cultivation, which appear to reward the Labour bestowed upon them, and I hope that the other Crops will do as well...

As a harbour it is equally safe and accessible. An abundance of timber grows on it for home consumption and exportation....

1. Summarize the reasons why Douglas thought that Camosack would make a good site for the new fort.
2. List the resources found at the site whose commercial potential Douglas identified in his report and letter.

Fort Victoria

Fort Victoria was built with an eighteen foot (5.5 m) stockade and an octagonal bastion in the southwest corner for defence. Galleries, platforms for soldiers to stand on to see over the stockade, were built in other corners.

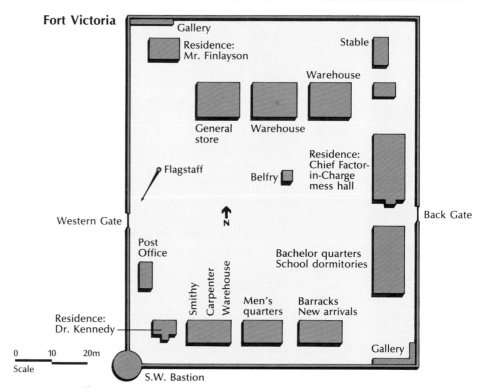

warehouses for furs and other goods, a trading store, accommodations for the traders and quarters for the officers of the Company stationed there. Later, a house for the chief factor would be built inside the fort as well.

Slow but steady expansion of the fur trade on Vancouver Island marked the first five years of Fort Victoria's existence. The Hudson's Bay Company traders soon learned that the area's richest resources were not furs, but forests and fisheries. As well, they discovered deposits of coal on the Island. Several decades would pass, however, before these resources would draw significant numbers of settlers to Vancouver Island.

The farming community around Fort Victoria grew slowly, despite the rich soils. Grants of land were given to retired Hudson's Bay Company employees who wished to start farming. They soon were able to earn a good living supplying the fort and the steadily increasing number of British naval ships that were coming to explore the area.

1. What events led to the founding of Fort Victoria? Who chose the site?
2. What characteristics were necessary for the site of a major trading post and fort?

Creation of the Vancouver Island Colony

Two events in the late 1840s served to focus British attention on Vancouver Island. The first was the signing of the Treaty of Washington in 1846, commonly known as the Oregon Boundary Treaty. This treaty defined the 49th parallel of latitude as the boundary between the United States and the British territories west of the Rockies. The second was the annexation of California to the United States in 1848. The British government feared that its resource-rich territories along the Pacific might be the next to fall to the Americans and their "manifest destiny."

George Simpson's fears of American expansion had not been reduced by the Oregon Boundary Agreement of 1846. If anything, they had become stronger. He believed that American settlers from the Columbia River and Puget Sound regions would move north into the thinly populated and poorly defended British territories on the Pacific coast. The British government shared Simpson's belief that more effective occupation of Vancouver Island was needed to defend its claim to the region. In January 1849, Vancouver Island was proclaimed to be a crown colony, with Fort Victoria its capital. The British government issued a special royal charter to the Hudson's Bay Company, giving it a monopoly on trade and commerce on the Island. This charter was similar to the one given the Company in 1670, but it had one important difference. The Company was to actively encourage settlement, something it had once opposed in Rupert's Land. Now, however, the Company had a strong motive for encouraging settlement. Its charter stated that if no colony had been successfully established within five years, control over Vancouver Island would revert to the British government. Under the terms of the charter the Company was instructed to sell land on the Island to British settlers. It would be allowed to keep 10 percent of money earned from such sales. The rest was to be used for public works such as roads, bridges, and wharves.

In 1849, Fort Victoria became the centre of the Hudson's Bay Company's west coast operations. In that year, James Douglas was transferred from Fort Vancouver, now in the United States, to Fort Victoria. He arrived before the newly appointed governor of the Vancouver Island colony, Richard Blanshard. Blanshard arrived to find that he had no salary, no officers and, above all, no power. He quickly learned that the only authority in the Vancouver Island colony was the Hudson's Bay Company. The real power was in the hands of the chief factor–James Douglas. After less than two years of bitter struggles with Douglas over control of the new colony, Blanshard resigned and returned to Britain. He was replaced by James Douglas.

Settlement of the colony began in earnest after Douglas became governor. Douglas wanted to encourage settlers who would be willing to work hard. He suggested that grants of 80-120 ha (200-300 acres) should be given free of charge to families wishing to settle on Vancouver Island. But the British government had a different view of settlement. Once again, the old memory of the humiliating loss of the American colonies surfaced. The British decided that to prevent a similar situation on Vancouver Island, the best system of settlement for the new colony would be one that recreated the class structure of England. Settlers were required to purchase a minimum of twenty acres (eight hectares) at one pound per acre. Any settler buying one hundred acres (forty hectares) or more was required to bring five workers or three married couples with him to the colony. In this way, the colony was meant to be peopled by "the better class" of Englishmen, those who could bring servants with them to work the land.

When Douglas arrived in 1849, the colony had only fifteen settlers. The largest and longest established farms belonged to the Hudson's Bay Company and its employees. But the colony was quickly changing its fur-trading origins. Town plans were being laid out for Victoria and for a naval base at nearby Esquimalt. Fine homes were built for the colony's "leading citizens." In them, the manners of British country society were maintained, replacing the rougher social graces of the fur fort.

RESIDENCE-OF-HON-JNO-ROBSON-   RESIDENCE-OF-JES-HUNTER

By the early 1850s, there were schools and churches in the colony, formal dances and polite social evenings. At the same time that these elements of British society were being introduced to the colony, many prominent British Columbia families were being founded as young English gentlemen married the daughters of the fur traders and their Métis or Indian wives.

The growth of the colony was spurred by the discovery of new resources in the form of lumber and coal. Equally important was the sudden appearance of a rich market for the colony's products close at hand. Gold was discovered in California in 1849. News of the gold rush reached Victoria in the form of a shipload of miners who

This engraving of homes in Victoria was made in the 1880s, but gives a view of what the leading citizens were striving for as they constructed the community. Why were bricks and stone not common as building materials for homes?

had come to the colony seeking provisions and supplies. Their arrival marked the beginning of a period of economic boom for the colony as regular steamship service between California and Vancouver Island was established. The Hudson's Bay Company now added to its profits by selling supplies to the prospectors who often paid for their purchases with gold nuggets.

The colonists also found a ready market for lumber in the fast-growing mining communities of California. Commercial lumbering operations began at Sooke in 1850. One enterprising settler, Captain Cooper, brought with him a small iron schooner in pieces. When the *Alice* was reassembled, Cooper began a highly successful business shipping sawn timber to San Francisco. So completely export-oriented were the Island's timber merchants that local residents had trouble getting building supplies.

Despite this boom the colony grew slowly. By 1852, there were fewer than 450 non-Native settlers on Vancouver Island. In that year, the Hudson's Bay Company established several large coal mines in the area around Nanaimo, north of Fort Victoria on the east coast of Vancouver Island. Coal was a major natural resource in the mid-nineteenth century. Steam was replacing sail as the source of power for the world's shipping fleets, creating a great demand for coal. Miners were brought out from Britain to work the mines, bringing the non-Native population of Vancouver Island up to more than 1000 by the mid-1850s. Soon settlements were springing up around the mines at Cumberland, Wellington and other places near Nanaimo.

In 1858, however, the discovery of gold on the mainland briefly but dramatically overshadowed the coal mining industry on Vancouver Island. The gold rush was about to bring a sudden influx of settlers to the region and would cause the Hudson's Bay Company to lose control over the colony.

1. How did the annexation of California by the United States increase fears of American expansion into British controlled territory?

2. According to the Royal Charter of 1849, what obligations did the Hudson's Bay Company have on Vancouver Island?

3. Furs were the natural resource that led to the establishment of Fort Victoria. What other natural resources contributed to its growth?

The Fraser River Gold Rush

One evening in 1857, during dinner in the mess hall at Fort Victoria, James Douglas casually showed his fellow diners a few grains of gold dust which had been found along the North Thompson River by a fur trader. Among the people in the mess hall, Douglas alone seemed to attach any importance to the find. By the end of the year, employees at the Hudson's Bay Company posts on the mainland were being warned that they should prepare for the gold rush Douglas felt was soon to come.

And come it did. During the fall of 1857, hundreds of miners from Washington and Oregon began prospecting along the Thompson River. From there, they moved on to the Fraser. Both north and south of its junction with the Thompson, they found gold along its banks. News of these finds spread quickly to California when a Hudson's Bay Company shipment of gold arrived in San Francisco just as the California gold rush was tapering off. Miners flocked to the San Francisco waterfront to find passage north to the gold fields of the Fraser.

The first shipload of miners arrived in Victoria aboard the wooden side-wheeler *Commodore* on April 25, 1858. Residents of Victoria, returning from morning church services, watched the scene in the harbor with fascination as 450 men, most wearing red flannel shirts and carrying packs filled with prospecting gear, left the ship at Victoria.

Some watched the disembarkation with anxiety. Governor Douglas feared that the gold rush would mean that a large "anti-British element" would come to the colony. He was concerned that the gold rush might result in annexation of the mainland by the United States.

Some fifty of the new arrivals decided to stay in Victoria. Among them were thirty-five blacks fleeing from persecution in California. They were to become valued members of Victoria's community as prosperous merchants, firemen and members of the militia. While they faced some discrimination from the British population of Victoria, these black settlers did not experience the persecution that their race suffered in the United States. Eighteen of their number would be the first naturalized British subjects in the colony.

The rest of the ship's passengers headed off for the gold fields. At the time of their arrival, there was no large vessel in Victoria to carry them to the mainland. The miners set off in any boat they could find. They used small sailboats, canoes, rowboats and even

Compare this miner's rude cabin to the fine homes of Victoria.

rafts to cross the Strait of Georgia and head up the Fraser. Some were lost in the crossing, others drowned in the eddies and currents of the river, but nothing could deter the men who pushed into the area in search of gold. Every sand bar along the Fraser was tried. By the start of summer, 1858, 10 000 men were on the river. Their numbers would swell to 25 000 before the year was over.

For their part, the merchants of Victoria welcomed the newcomers who brought a great increase in business to the young town. The Island's farmers prospered from the miners' demands for food provisions for the gold fields. The hotels of Victoria, few in number, quickly filled. Settlements of tents and shanties grew up around the fort. Soon there were more American than British residents in Victoria. The appearance of the town began to change rapidly. Within a period of six weeks in the spring of 1858, 223 buildings, nearly all of them stores, were put up. Land values rose quickly.

The gold rush brought an end to the Hudson's Bay Company monopoly on economic activities in the colony. Both the new merchants and the Island's settlers were competing with the Company, which was powerless to stop the growth of these businesses. Then, news arrived from Britain that, on May 30, 1859, the Hudson's Bay Company's special position as proprietor of Vancouver Island would end. The Liberal government in Britain was strongly committed to free trade and competition. The monopoly enjoyed by the

Hudson's Bay Company was, in their view, a long out-dated carry-over from mercantilism.

1. Using your atlas, find Victoria, the Strait of Georgia and the Fraser River. How long a trip is it from Victoria Harbour to the mouth of the Fraser? to the junction of the Thompson and Fraser rivers where gold was first discovered?
2. What problems did the prospectors face in getting to the gold fields from Victoria?
3. Suggest the impact that the arrival of 25 000 miners in one year would have on the environment of an area that was largely wilderness. What impact would there be on the Native people of the area whose way of life was based on fishing in the river for salmon? on the economy of the region?
4. Why was Governor Douglas concerned about the arrival of the gold miners?

The Founding of the Mainland Colony

The Fraser River gold rush did more than just spur the growth of the Vancouver Island colony. It led to the creation in 1858 of a second crown colony, this one on the mainland. The new colony was created to ensure the maintenance of law and order in the gold fields. It was also to reduce the growing fears of American annexation of the mainland.

A song, popular in Oregon at the time, announced the Annexationists' sentiments:

Soon our banner will be streaming,
Soon the eagle will be screaming,
And the lion–see, it cowers,
Hurrah boys, the river's ours.

At this time, there were more American than British residents in Victoria and on the mainland as well.

Britain's new colonial secretary, Sir Edward Bulwer Lytton, wanted to provide the new colony with sound leadership while reducing the influence of the Hudson's Bay Company. He offered James Douglas the governorship of both Vancouver Island and the new British Columbia colony. There was one condition attached to the offer. Douglas would have to resign from the Hudson's Bay Company. He did so, to serve the Crown with the same determination and loyalty that had marked his thirty years of service to the Hudson's Bay Company.

Ceremonies marking the official establishment of British Columbia were held at Fort Langley, the colony's first capital, on November 19, 1858. The colony's only judge, Matthew Begbie, was sworn in by Douglas. Begbie, in turn, read Her Majesty's commission naming James Douglas as governor of British Columbia. Ironically, Douglas' first official duty that day was to read a proclamation revoking the Hudson's Bay Company's exclusive right to trade on the mainland. Governor Douglas and Judge Begbie, along with Colonel Richard Moody, Commissioner of Lands and Works, would be the three most important figures in the public life of the young colony. They faced the very large task of bringing good government, law and order and public works to the 25 000 settlers and miners in the remote and rugged colony.

The early character of British Columbia was shaped largely by two forces. On one hand were the miners, on the other Douglas, Begbie and Moody. The miners were a mixed lot, in Begbie's words: "Englishmen (staunch royalists), Americans (Republicans), Frenchmen very numerous, Germans in abundance, Italians, several Hungarians, Poles, Danes, Swedes, Spaniards, Mexicans and Chinese." There were also Native miners, and even Hawaiians too. British Columbia's multicultural character was established right from the earliest days of the colony.

In their ethnic diversity, the miners were joined by two common bonds: their rugged individualism and their burning desire to get rich through their efforts in the gold fields. Douglas and his public servants, for their part, sought to establish an orderly and well-governed society along British lines.

Matthew Begbie played a key role in the attempt to bring law and order to the rough-and-tumble communities of the gold seekers. He travelled many thousands of kilometres on horseback, making his lonely circuits through the frontier colony, holding court in tents, bunkhouses and even saloons. Begbie soon earned the respect of the miners and settlers. His approach to the administration of justice earned him a reputation for being fair but often unorthodox. The British government, in particular, was concerned about the speed of Begbie's trials. Some American settlers were upset by Begbie's insistence that the full protection of British law be extended to Native peoples, Chinese and other non-white ethnic groups. He learned three Native dialects, and held trials in the Native languages. He also organized Native courts, in which tribal chiefs would judge cases in which only Natives were involved.

Begbie's blunt comments to defendants and the juries who tried

Sir Matthew Baillie Begbie

them were frequently quoted in the colony's newspapers. In 1865, the *Cariboo Sentinel* reported how Begbie handled juries which returned verdicts he did not like. According to the newspaper, Begbie threatened to "lock the jury up until they had come to a conclusion which he might conceive to be correct."

Colonel Moody and his Company of Royal Engineers had the task of creating roads and other public works to serve the colony. They were also given the responsibility for building a capital city and a seaport for British Columbia.

The Royal Engineers' greatest accomplishment was the construction of the Cariboo wagon road through the rugged Fraser Canyon. In 1860, more gold was discovered in the Cariboo region, north of the Fraser gold fields. These new fields, especially the ones discovered at Williams Creek in 1861, proved to be far richer than those along the Fraser. At Barkerville, the mining town that grew up along Williams Creek, a single panful of gravel could produce as much as $1000 worth of gold. By comparison, most workers in Victoria at this time earned two to three dollars a day.

These rich gold deposits were located in isolated areas beyond the coastal mountains. A road was needed because of the high costs of supplying the mining communities by horseback along narrow mountain trails. In 1862, therefore, Douglas ordered the construction of a wagon road up the Fraser Canyon and into the Cariboo. While civilian contractors built most of the road, the Royal Engineers constructed the most difficult parts. From Yale to Boston Bar, the road had to be blasted out of solid rock walls. Hanging down the cliffs on ropes, workers drilled holes in the rock and set the dynamite charges. To Douglas' delight, the Cariboo Wagon Road, 600 km long and 6 m wide, was completed in less than four years.

1. What two purposes was the mainland colony to serve when it was created in 1858?

2. Explain what role each of these people played in the new mainland colony: James Douglas, Matthew Begbie, and Richard Moody.

3. The song verse on page 169 refers to an eagle and a lion. What do these symbols mean?

4. Explain why the Cariboo Wagon Road was vital to the economic health of the new colony.

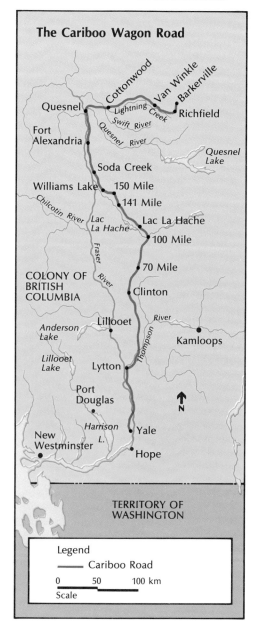

The Cariboo Road from Yale to Barkerville was built between 1862 and 1865. Why did the government undertake such an expensive project?

Choosing a Capital for British Columbia

The decision about where to locate a capital and a seaport for the new colony brought Douglas and Moody into conflict. Along with most of the residents of British Columbia, Douglas assumed that the capital would remain on the south side of the Fraser at Fort Langley, known this time as Derby. He had selected a site for the seaport on the north bank of the Fraser across from Annacis Island, some 30 km from the Fraser's mouth. For his part, Moody had decided even before leaving England, that the capital should be located on the north side of the Fraser River. Such a location, argued Moody, would better protect the new capital if it were attacked by the Americans. Following an inspection tour of the river, Moody recommended that the site chosen by Douglas for a seaport be used for the new capital as well.

Moody's reasoning was militarily sound but politically unpopular. Many Victoria investors had bought land around Fort Langley in anticipation of the capital's construction there. They expected that land values would rise significantly when the capital was built. Now, those lands would be worth less than the **speculators** had paid for them.

Douglas eventually accepted Moody's recommendations, announcing in July 1859, that the colony's capital and seaport would be on the north side of the Fraser. The city to be built there would be named New Westminster after Westminster, the site of the British Houses of Parliament in London.

Moody further upset Douglas with his plans for the new capital. His sketches showed fine squares and plazas, broad avenues and magnificent buildings. Douglas rebuked Moody, saying: "I would suggest to you that the colony itself must first become great and flourishing before we can undertake works on a scale of magnificance." By the end of 1859, after Moody had already spent £15 000 on surveys, not a single street had been laid out.

The following year, however, construction of the capital city was well underway. Homes, churches, offices and commercial buildings were being constructed. They were practical frontier buildings, not the elegant European-style structures that Moody hoped to see built in New Westminster. The city was incorporated in 1860 and responsibility for local improvements passed out of Moody's hands to the new town council. When Moody left the colony in 1863 to return to Britain, his plans for a magnificent capital city existed only on paper.

Colonel Richard Clement Moody

The Cariboo gold rush brought prosperity to New Westminster. It was easier and less costly to supply the gold fields from the new capital than from Victoria. New Westminster quickly found itself in a strong and sometimes bitter rivalry with Victoria. In particular, the mainlanders resented the fact that Douglas and most of his senior officials lived on the Island. They were further upset when Douglas declared Victoria a **free port**, so that importers bringing foreign cargoes into Victoria no longer had to pay customs duties. This gave Victoria merchants a great advantage in competition for the gold rush trade.

The commercial rivalry between Victoria and New Westminster would continue for more than half a century. It ended only when Vancouver established itself as the leading commercial centre of the province at the beginning of the twentieth century.

1. What was Moody's reason for wanting a capital located on the north side of the Fraser River?

The Struggle for Responsible Government

The two colonies on the Pacific coast differed in their forms of government. In 1856, after protests from the colonists and pressure from the British Colonial Office, Douglas had reluctantly created an elected Assembly for the Vancouver Island colony. But without responsible government, the Vancouver Island Assembly had little power. The right to vote was limited to property-holders. As a result, fewer than forty of the 450 residents of the colony were entitled to vote or run for the Assembly. Most of the power rested in the hands of Douglas and his appointed Legislative Council.

The British Columbia Act of 1858 made no provision for an elected Assembly on the mainland. There, all power rested with Douglas and his appointed Legislative Council, most of whom were Hudson's Bay Company officers. A small reform group began almost immediately to demand changes in the way the mainland colony was governed. The reformers were led by John Robson, publisher of the newspaper *The British Columbian*. Robson's supporters were mainly New Westminster merchants who had come from the Canadas and the Maritimes. They wanted British Columbia to have an elected Assembly with responsible government, as recently achieved by the other British colonies in the East.

**Organization of Government
1858–1863**

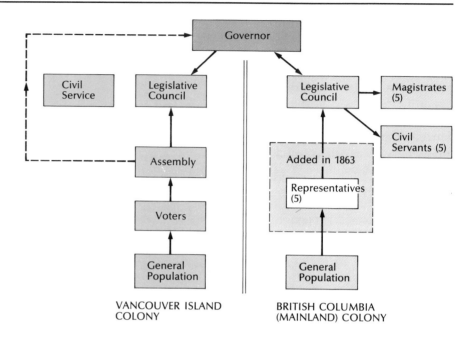

VANCOUVER ISLAND
COLONY

BRITISH COLUMBIA
(MAINLAND) COLONY

Amor de Cosmos (William Alexander Smith)

The reformers believed they had a legitimate complaint. The British Columbia Act of 1858 gave Governor Douglas the authority to make any laws he wanted. In three years he raised taxes three times. In spite of Robson's vigorous campaign through his newspaper, the reformers found little support among the miners who liked and trusted Douglas. The taxes he raised helped to build better roads and other services needed by the miners.

A reform movement emerged on Vancouver Island as well. As was so often the case in Canadian history, it also was led by a newspaperman. He was William Smith, publisher of a Victoria paper, *The British Colonist.* Smith had changed his name to Amor de Cosmos, which he mistakenly believed to be Latin for "lover of the universe."

Amor de Cosmos was harshly critical of the government. Douglas took little heed of the elected Assembly's decisions and referred to it for none of his. Virtually every piece of important legislation during the period 1856-1863, was made by the governor and his Legislative Council. De Cosmos protested strongly against Douglas and what he called the "family compact" of senior Hudson's Bay Company men who ruled the colony. He demanded the establishment of responsible government along the lines of that achieved by Joseph Howe, for whom de Cosmos had worked, in Nova Scotia.

Douglas ignored the reformers: he had little time for politicians or reformers demanding change. Douglas disliked politics. He was a man of action who wanted to see his colonies grow and prosper, secure within the British Empire. He saw himself as the father of British Columbia, and made plans for its economic growth and territorial expansion. Unfortunately, his public works projects cost more money than the colony was raising through taxes. To meet these costs, the colony's government had to borrow money. The mounting debts led the British to doubt his ability as governor.

In 1863 the British Columbia Act was due for a five-year review. Up to this time, the Colonial Office had ignored the reformers, who had sent four petitions to London complaining about Douglas' high-handed rule. But now it began to pressure Douglas to hear the reformers out. Accordingly, Douglas created a partially elected Legislative Council for British Columbia. But this was not responsible government: two-thirds of the Council would still be appointed by the governor.

In 1863, the Colonial Office decided that it was time for Douglas to retire. It did so by announcing that, beginning the following year, each colony would have its own governor. Reluctantly, Douglas resigned. His last official act as governor was to attend the inaugural meeting of the partially elected Legislative Council on January 21, 1864.

On the eve of his retirement, Douglas was knighted by Queen Victoria. Sir James Douglas, as he was now called, and his wife were treated to rounds of banquets and speeches of praise as they waited for the new governors to arrive. Douglas returned to private life in Victoria, proud of his accomplishments in building roads and bringing law and order to the gold rush frontier.

1. The Vancouver Island colony had an elected Assembly, but did not have responsible government. Explain how this was possible.

2. Under the terms of the British Columbia Act of 1858, how was the mainland colony to be governed? How did this differ from the system of government on Vancouver Island?

3. What reforms were Amor de Cosmos and John Robson seeking for the colonies? Why?

4. What event in 1863 changed the way the two colonies were governed? Did it satisfy the reformers' demands for responsible government?

Union of the Two Colonies

As governor of both the Vancouver Island and British Columbia colonies, Douglas had ruled the two as if they were one, despite their different populations and economies. Now, the two governors who followed him, Arthur Edward Kennedy on Vancouver Island and Frederick Seymour in British Columbia, arrived to find their colonies facing great economic difficulties.

The British Columbia colony had borrowed money to build the roads into the gold fields. To repay these loans, it badly needed to raise money through taxation, but the miners were doing everything they could to avoid paying taxes. Despite the fact that gold production was increasing, the colony's revenues were decreasing.

On Vancouver Island, Governor Kennedy faced not only economic but also political problems. He found himself in conflict with elected members of the Assembly, including Amor de Cosmos. The members fought against some of his proposals, such as taxes on income and real estate, measures which would have cost them personally. Kennedy did gain some popular support in areas of the Island other than Victoria, where residents in the past had felt neglected. He managed to have the Royal Navy establish its major Pacific base at Esquimalt, assuring the coal mines at Nanaimo of a major market.

Less than a year after his arrival, Kennedy appealed to the Colonial Office in London for assistance in dealing with the colony's problems. His requests were ignored. The colonial secretary had begun to consider forcing Vancouver Island to join the mainland in a united colony. Running one colony rather than two would be much less expensive for the British government because only one set of government officials and offices would be required. Some of the Vancouver Island legislators recognized these economic advantages, but they wanted to be able to preserve their colony's own identity in a **federal union**. They wanted Vancouver Island to be a separate province, with its own elected Assembly, within the united colony. In the midst of a worsening economic depression on the Island, the idea of a federal union was dropped. Such a move would be too costly given that the tax revenues of both colonies were dropping as the gold rush came to an end.

In January 1865, Amor de Cosmos rose in the House of Assembly and called for the immediate and complete union of the two colonies. To test public support for the proposal, he and another legisla-

A view of Esquimalt Harbor taken around 1867.

tor then resigned their seats, forcing by-elections to be held. They ran their by-election campaigns solely on the issue of the proposed union, winning easily at the polls. A year later, the British Parliament approved a bill uniting the two colonies. On November 19, 1866, the union was officially proclaimed. As one newspaper editorial described it, British Columbia had "married its debt of $1 002 983 to that of Vancouver Island, a mere child of $293 698." The united colonies were given the name British Columbia.

The most vigorously debated question in the newly united colony was where should the capital be located, Victoria or New Westminster? Seymour, who had been made governor of British Columbia, put the question to the House of Assembly. Assembly members in Victoria, such as John Helmcken, argued that the Island city should be the capital. Even though a majority of the Assembly's members were from the mainland, the Islanders, led by Helmcken, won the debate. In 1868, Victoria was proclaimed the capital.

1. What was the British government's reason for promoting union of the two colonies?

British Columbia and Confederation

July 1, 1867, passed by largely without notice in Victoria and New Westminster. In Victoria, disheartened businessmen were more interested in the possibility of a union of British Columbia with the United States. In September 1866, they had issued a public statement calling for the union of British Columbia with the United States. Such a move, they believed, would bring them access to growing markets along the west coast of the United States.

Amor de Cosmos sought to head off the annexationists. He introduced a motion in the House of Assembly aimed at joining British Columbia to the rest of British North America. His motion called on the British government to ensure that the British North America Act, then being debated in the British Parliament, would allow for the eventual inclusion of British Columbia in Confederation.

Governor Seymour had already sent a similar request to the Colonial Office. He received a reply telling him that consideration of British Columbia's entry into Confederation would have to wait. Rupert's Land, still held by the Hudson's Bay Company, would have to be incorporated into the new Dominion before British Columbia, otherwise, British Columbia would be geographically isolated from the other Canadian provinces .

British Concerns about the Pacific Colony

It is doubtful whether British Columbia would have joined Confederation on its own initiative. The divisions in the colony were too deep to allow compromise or agreement among the various factions. But, by the late 1860s, a number of external forces were pushing British Columbia toward Confederation. In the end, it was the wishes of the British government, rather than the colonists themselves, that brought about British Columbia's entry into Confederation. In the words of a Colonial Office document, the British government now believed the "political and economic interest" of both Britain and British Columbia "would be best advanced through union" with Canada.

British Columbia's location on the Pacific was important to Britain, which had considerable economic and military interests in both the Orient and the islands of the Pacific. Britain was facing strong competition from Russia, the United States and France. The Pacific region was a long way from Britain for purposes of either defence or communication. It was in Britain's interest to have a strong naval outpost on the Pacific, such as the base at Esquimalt. However, the British government was concerned about the costs of maintaining and defending the far-distant British Columbia colony. It did not want to pay for the administrative costs or the increasing debt of the colony. Union with Canada would offer an easy, safe and cheap way to solve the colony's problem.

During the period 1867-1870, the pro- and anti-Confederation forces in British Columbia vigorously debated the idea of union with Canada. While this was going on the economic problems of the colony continued. Fires wiped out Barkerville and the business district of Victoria. The gold rush was over, and the production of the gold fields was dwindling. The non-Native population of the mainland had dropped to about 11 000, about a third of what it had been at the peak of the gold rush. There was little agreement as to the solution of these problems, as factions organized behind three separate options: to stay a British colony, to join Confederation, or to seek annexation to the United States.

The chief spokesman of the anti-Confederation forces in British Columbia was J.S. Helmcken. He did not want to see the traditional ties between the colony and Britain broken. As a prominent member of the House of Assembly, Helmcken argued forcefully against union with Canada. Loyalty to Britain aside, Helmcken had four objections to Confederation. He felt that the distances involved were too great to make Confederation work, given the transportation and communication systems of the time. He feared that British Columbia would have little political influence in the proposed union, and therefore it would be forced to follow policies set in eastern Canada. Third, he was very concerned that British Columbia's fledgling industries could not compete with established firms in the East. Helmcken further argued that Britain's withdrawal from the colony would leave British Columbia isolated and defenceless on the Pacific coast.

Helmcken's strongest support came from the residents of Vancouver Island, including most of the senior government officials in Victoria, among them the governor, Frederick Seymour. The anti-Confederationists lost a key supporter when Seymour died in 1869.

The strongest voice heard in support of British Columbia's entry into Confederation was that of Amor de Cosmos. The feisty and eccentric newspaperman was the leader of the opposition party in the House of Assembly. There, he was as passionate an advocate of Confederation as of responsible government. In fact, the two causes were linked in his mind. Amor de Cosmos saw Confederation as the means of achieving a fully elected and responsible government for British Columbia. His strongest support came from the mainland area of the colony, despite the fact that de Cosmos himself lived in Victoria.

The new governor of British Columbia, appointed after Seymour's death, was Anthony Musgrave, a strong advocate of Confederation and a former governor of Newfoundland. A friend of Sir John A. Macdonald, he shared Macdonald's enthusiastic vision of a great Dominion that would extend from sea to sea. Musgrave arrived in the colony ready to bring about its entry into Confederation. But he would have to use a great deal of diplomatic skill to get all sides to agree to British Columbia joining Canada.

Confederation was the key issue in the British Columbia election of November 1868, which resulted in a further deepening of the division in the colony. The anti-Confederation forces swept every seat on Vancouver Island. Even Amor de Cosmos was defeated. On the mainland, the pro-Confederation forces were triumphant.

The division in the House of Assembly was further complicated by the colony's system of government. The British Columbia colony still did not have a government that was truly representative. The colonial officials, who were also part of the government, were all British. The pro-Confederation forces saw them as the major obstacle to union with Canada.

Sir Anthony Musgrave

A vote on a resolution calling for entry into Canada was taken at a meeting of the colony's Legislative Council in December 1868. The motion was defeated by senior colonial officials, who held appointed positions on the Council. These officials feared that Confederation might bring financial hardship on them through loss of their lucrative positions. As employees of the British government, they had no assurances that the Dominion or the new province would employ them.

CONFEDERATION, FOR AND AGAINST

The following excerpts summarize the views of the various factions in British Columbia in the late 1860s.

Anti-Confederation

We are a Colony of England; and I don't know that many people object to being a Colony of England; but I can say that very many would object to being a Colony of Canada...

No union between this colony and Canada can permanently exist, unless it be to the material and pecuniary [financial] advantage of this colony...Therefore, no union on account of love need be looked for. The only bond of union outside of force–and force the Dominion has not–will be the material advantage of the country and the pecuniary benefit of the inhabitants....

Confederation so far as it has at present gone, is only an experiment. It is absurd to ally ourselves with a people two thousand miles [3200 km] away, without any settlements in between, with no communication except through the United States.

[Excerpts from speeches made by J.S. Helmcken 1868-1870.]

Pro-Confederation

Shall we hestitate to accept our destiny? Canada wants us, and she is willing to pay our debt, spend a million making our end of the railroad, give us full powers of self-government, and send us population. The cry of the government at Ottawa is "From the Atlantic to the Pacific." Shall we be content to be as we are, struggling under crushing debt...or shall we join the Confederation and be free, prosperous, wealthy?

[A speech to the electors of the District of Yale by F.J. Barnard, April 9, 1868.]

Annexationist

We view with great alarm the intention of Her Majesty's government to Confederate this colony with the Dominion of Canada. Such a move can only deepen our economic depression for the following reasons:

• It cannot open to us a market for the products of our mines, forests or waters.
• It cannot bring us population (our greatest need). The Dominion itself suffers from a lack of people.
• In view of these facts, we request that you try to get Her Majesty to consent to the transfer of this colony to the United States.

[Adapted from a petition to the President of the United States, signed by 104 Victoria merchants, November 1869.]

1. List some problems that the British Columbia colony was facing at the time its entry into Confederation was being debated.

2. Summarize the positions of each of the following groups regarding British Columbia's entry into Confederation:
   (a) Anti-Confederationists
   (b) Pro-Confederationists
   (c) Annexationists.
3. Why did senior civil servants in the British Columbia colony oppose Confederation? What might Governor Musgrave have done to overcome their opposition?

Confederation Achieved

It was Governor Musgrave who engineered a solution to the divisions in the colony over Confederation. In fact, when the Colonial Office had appointed Musgrave governor of the colony, it had instructed him to do everything possible to get the colony to agree to Confederation. Musgrave knew that he had to overcome the opposition of both the government officials and the Vancouver Island faction led by Helmcken.

To win over this first group, Musgrave worked out a system of pensions that would allow any colonial officials not hired by the Dominion to retire in comfort. The governor's action enraged many of the government officials, who now felt betrayed and abandoned by the mother country. Many applied for transfers to other colonies. Others, like Judge Matthew Begbie, decided to stay and support Confederation.

The Annexationists in Victoria unintentionally helped Musgrave's cause. The petitions and letters from the Victoria merchants asking for union with the United States angered several colonial officials, among them Attorney General Henry Crease and Commissioner of Lands and Works Joseph Trutch. Both men had opposed Confederation. The Annexationist petition led them to change their position. If it was a choice between union with Canada and union with the United States, they much preferred the first choice. On March 9, 1870, these two men introduced a motion in the Executive Council calling for union with Canada.

Musgrave still had to win over the Vancouver Island faction led by Helmcken. To do so, he chose Helmcken and two of his allies to form a delegation that would go to Ottawa. This delegation would call for the federal government in Ottawa to assume the colony's massive debt and to undertake construction of a transcontinental railway. Both of these moves had been unanimously approved in the

Legislative Council of the British Columbia colony. Therefore, while in Ottawa, Helmcken and the B.C. delegates would be able to claim that they were speaking for the entire colony, not just for one faction.

The warm and favorable reception given the British Columbia delegates in Ottawa surprised them. The Canadians were prepared to accept all of their terms, including a guarantee to start construction of a transcontinental railway within two years. Macdonald's cabinet promised the British Columbians that the railway would be completed within a decade.

Amazed by their success, the delegates returned home. They appeared to have gained more than they had asked for. In the election of November 1870, supporters of Confederation were elected in every riding. The following January, the negotiated terms of union were approved unanimously by the Legislative Council. The agreement between Victoria and Ottawa was sent to London for approval by the British government in April of 1871. The British quickly approved the union. July 20, 1871, was set as the date for British Columbia's entry into Confederation.

Crowds gathered in the streets of Victoria and New Westminster on the night of July 19, 1871. Fireworks lit up the night while bands played and politicians cleared their voices in preparation for their speeches. At the stroke of midnight, a roar went up from the crowd, cannons were fired and a new era began in the history of British Columbia.

In the midst of all the excitement, few people seemed to realize that politicians are often better at making promises than at keeping them. As you will see in the next chapter, the building of a railroad across the continent was one such promise easier made than kept.

1. Name the two key terms of the union with Canada negotiated by the British Columbians. Why were these terms important to them?

Summary

British Columbia was the sixth province to join Confederation. Originally part of the Hudson's Bay Company's western operations, this region, unlike Manitoba, experienced colonial status within the British Empire before joining Canada.

The westward expansion of the United States forced the Hudson's

Bay Company to shift its centre of operations on the Pacific coast northward to Fort Victoria on Vancouver Island. In 1849, continued fears of American expansion along the Pacific saw the British create the Vancouver Island colony under the leadership of Governor James Douglas. The Hudson's Bay Company was given monopoly over trade on Vancouver Island. In return, the Company was required to bring settlers to the colony. While it had been founded on the fur trade, the Vancouver Island colony developed on the basis of its coal and timber resources, its farmlands and its location as a commercial centre.

In 1858, the discovery of gold along the Fraser River brought hundreds of would-be miners to the mainland and prosperity to Victoria's merchants. Most of the miners were Americans, adding to British fears of American expansion. Again, the British responded by making the area a colony. Colonial status ensured that law and order were effectively maintained when a second gold rush took place in 1860.

Under the strong leadership of Governor James Douglas, both colonies enjoyed political stability and economic prosperity during the gold rush period. However, the lack of responsible government resulted in opposition by people such as John Robson in British Columbia and Amor de Cosmos on Vancouver Island. Responsible government was not achieved until British Columbia entered Confederation in 1871.

Political and economic problems arose as the British Columbia gold fields were exhausted. Douglas' ambitious public works projects had left the British Columbia colony deeply in debt at a time when the colonies were experiencing an economic depression. Merchants in both Victoria and New Westminster faced sharply reduced markets for their products after the miners left. In 1864, two years after Douglas' retirement as governor, the two colonies were united. This union, however, failed to bring an end to economic problems facing the colony.

At the same time, Britain was growing increasingly concerned about the cost of keeping its isolated colony on the Pacific coast. Following Confederation in 1867, several attempts were made by the British government to get British Columbia to unite with Canada. However, opposition among the residents of Vancouver Island, and the fact that Rupert's Land was still owned by the Hudson's Bay Company, delayed this union until 1871. The terms of union negotiated by the British Columbians included a promise that a transcontinental railway would be built within ten years.

REVIEW

Checking Back

1. Write one or two sentences summarizing the significance of each of the following in the history of British Columbia.

   "manifest destiny"   Amor de Cosmos
   George Simpson   J.S. Helmcken
   California gold rush   Sir Anthony
   James Douglas   Musgrave
   John Robson

2. Find in this chapter and list in your notebook details which show the role played by Native people in the early history of British Columbia.

3. List all the contributions made by James Douglas to British Columbia. Based on your list, would you agree that Douglas was the Father of British Columbia?

4. Read the excerpts from Douglas' report to Governor George Simpson (page 162). In your own words, state five facts that suggest Douglas' conclusion that Victoria was the ideal site for a new fort.

5. Record two pieces of evidence that show Judge Begbie respected the traditions of the Native people.

6. In one or two paragraphs, explain the importance of the gold rush in the creation of the British Columbia colony.

7. What tasks did Colonel Moody and his Company of Royal Engineers have to complete to build the Cariboo Road?

Using Your Knowledge

8. Write a series of advertisements for a Victoria newspaper in the days of the California gold rush.

9. The year is 1858 and you are a merchant in Victoria. Write a letter to your family describing the changes brought by the Fraser River gold rush.

10. List the internal and external forces that led British Columbia into Confederation.

11. In your own words, summarize the position of the Annexation, pro-Confederation and the anti-Confederation movements. Which movement would you have supported in 1867? Explain your choice.

12. List the advantages and disadvantages of Confederation from the point of view of both British Columbia and Canada.

Chapter 10

The Western Frontier, 1871-1905

Between 1871 and 1905, change came rapidly to the West. At the beginning of this time period, the government of Canada established the North West Mounted Police as an agency to maintain law and order throughout the region. This force played a major role when Native and Métis people, responding to conflicts with white settlers and the government, rebelled against the government of Canada. Important to the success of the NWMP in putting down the North West Rebellion was the Canadian Pacific Railway. It allowed police and militia reinforcements to be brought in quickly from eastern Canada. The completed railway had other influences as well, and led to a greatly increased population in the West.

The trains carried large numbers of immigrants, attracted to the West by grants of free land. At the end of the century, the railway would also carry large numbers of fortune seekers west, bound for the Klondike Gold Rush. This rapid settlement of the Prairies led to the creation in 1905 of two new provinces, Alberta and Saskatchewan.

In this chapter, you will first see how the life of the Native peoples in the West changed during the 1870s. Next, you will look at the construction of the CPR, then at the North West Rebellion of 1885. Finally, you will examine some major events in the Canadian West in the two decades following 1885. As you read the chapter, keep in mind these key questions:

- How did the arrival of the North West Mounted Police and, later, the CPR, affect the Native peoples of the West?
- What problems had to be overcome in building the Canadian Pacific Railway?
- What were the causes and results of the North West Rebellion of 1885? What role did Louis Riel play in the rebellion?
- What role did the Canadian government and the CPR play in the settlement of the West? Why did it take on this role?
- When and how were the Yukon Territory and the provinces of Alberta and Saskatchewan established?

Problems on the Prairies

Life changed greatly for the Native peoples of the Prairies during the 1870s. Some of these changes involved the whisky trade and the establishment of the North West Mounted Police. Other changes resulted from the treaties by which the Native peoples gave up much of their lands.

The Whisky Trade

In the early 1870s, Prime Minister Macdonald received several reports about problems on the Prairies. Missionaries such as Father Lacombe and railway surveyors such as Sir Sanford Fleming wrote to him that whisky traders, nearly all of them from the United States, were selling their product to the Native peoples of the West. For bottles of cheap "rotgut" whisky, Native peoples were trading valuable buffalo robes, furs, horses, food, and some even their wives and daughters. Many deaths and murders had followed drinking sessions in the Native camps. Disease and malnutrition were rampant as alcoholism interfered with traditional Native hunting and food-gathering activities.

The centre of the whisky trade was Fort Whoop-Up, in what is now southern Alberta. It was an impressive fortified trading post, with log walls more than four metres high. Two bastions with rifle slits and brass cannon guarded the fort from attack by rival whisky traders or Native people.

A bleak and isolated place, Fort Whoop-Up was a world of outlaws, men hardened to loneliness and violence. Most of these men had come from Fort Benton, 100 km to the south in Montana. Many were rough veterans of the American Civil War, finding new adventure in buffalo hunting. These frontiersmen were now bringing their lawlessness to Canada's North West Territories.

Few Canadians had travelled to the West in the early 1870s. The canoe routes of the fur traders were still the main link between the Prairies and eastern Canada. Most visitors to the Prairies had to go through the United States, then travel north by horse to Canada. As a result, the whisky trade around the isolated and distant fort went largely unnoticed in the rest of Canada. Macdonald and other political leaders knew about the situation, yet there was little public pressure on them to do anything about it.

Public attitudes changed significantly when an event that became known as the Cypress Hills Massacre brought the whisky trade to the attention of eastern Canadians. The Cypress Hills straddle the Alberta-Saskatchewan boundary, close to the border with the United States. In early May of 1874, a party of whisky traders attacked a band of Assiniboine whom they believed to have stolen some of their horses. The traders, thoroughly drunk themselves, rained shot after shot from rapid fire rifles into the Assiniboine camp. When the firing was over, thirty of the Assiniboine were dead. In their vain attempt to defend themselves with their ancient muzzle-loading rifles, the Assiniboine had managed to kill only one of their attackers.

News of the Cypress Hills Massacre eventually spread across North America. Newspapers in the United States wrote about brave American frontiersmen facing hostile savages. Canadian newspapers described the event as an attack by American ruffians on the innocent Assiniboine. The Canadian public called for an end to the lawlessness on the Prairies.

Warned of the whisky trade problems, the federal government had already passed a bill to establish a police force in the West to be known as North West Mounted Police. However, nothing had been done to recruit members for this force. News of the massacre and the public reaction to it forced the government to begin this recruitment hastily.

The newly formed police force was trained in the Winnipeg area during late 1873 and early 1874. In July 1874, they began their patrol of the Prairies. During the march west to Fort Whoop-Up and to other centres like Fort Edmonton, the 300 new NWMP recruits travelled 2000 km across the Prairies in the summer heat. They reached Fort Whoop-Up only to find that the whisky traders had fled. The hot and gruelling march took a great toll on both men and horses as they trekked from Fort Garry to the foothills of the Rocky Mountains. It was far tougher than any of the Mounties had imagined. But it was just a brief taste of what would lie ahead for them as they patrolled the vast North West Territories over the next thirty years.

"No person shall be appointed to the Police Force unless he be of sound constitution, active and able-bodied, able to ride, of good character, able to read and write either the English or French language, and between the ages of eighteen and forty."
[excerpt from the Act of Parliament establishing the NWMP, 1873]

1. How did the whisky trade affect the Native peoples of the Prairies? Suggest some reasons why the traders might want to sell alcohol to the Native peoples.
2. When and why did the government of Canada create the North West Mounted Police?
3. What differences in attitude are revealed in the American and Canadian newspaper accounts of the Cypress Hills massacre?

4. In the United States, settlement of the West took place before effective government and police services were introduced. The result was the legendary "Wild West" portrayed in western movies. In Canada, the police came to the West before the settlers. Can you suggest how the presence of the police might have affected the settlers? the Native population of the area?

The Aboriginal Treaties

Nomadic Native bands had occupied the vast Prairie grasslands for centuries, moving seasonally with the migrating bison herds. When the Dominion of Canada bought the region from the Hudson's Bay Company, the government decided that it had to end any claims Native peoples might have to these lands before the West was settled. Through a series of treaties, the Natives gave away their claim to ownership of vast areas of western Canada. In return, they received a small portion of their lands as reservations, some money and a promise from Ottawa that they would be looked after by the Canadian government. Many people argue that this promise has never been kept.

Seven treaties were signed by the government of Canada and the Native peoples during the period 1871-1877. The first treaty, signed at Fort Garry in 1871, saw bands of Cree and Ojibwa give up vast areas of Manitoba. In return, they received reserves amounting to sixty-five hectares for each family of five, a small yearly payment and some food.

Another treaty gave the Cree heartland, more than 350 000 km² along the North and South Saskatchewan rivers, to the Canadian government. The Cree chiefs were given military uniforms (to be replaced every three years) and silver medals. They were also given horses, wagons and agricultural tools. The Canadian government hoped that the Cree chiefs would encourage their people to give up their nomadic hunting way of life to become farmers. Each member of the tribe was given reserve land, a yearly payment of twelve dollars and a promise by the government to provide aid and rations if the Indians faced hard times.

The last treaty to be negotiated resulted in the Blackfoot Confederacy surrendering 150 000 km² of very fertile land in what is now southern Alberta. Let us look in more detail at the ceremonies that led to the signing of the treaty.

ABORIGINAL RIGHTS

The seven treaties negotiated by the Dominion of Canada with the various Native groups in the North West gave the government title to lands once occupied by wandering bands of Native hunters. It is doubtful that the Native people fully understood the importance or impact of these treaty negotiations. They were seminomadic hunters, who moved with the seasons and with the animals they hunted. They had no concept of individual land ownership or even fixed boundaries to their hunting territories. The people were one with the land; it gave them food and shelter and they respected it as a sacred spirit-filled place. The idea of buying and selling land was totally foreign to these Native hunters. The land was theirs–but they did not own it.

However, the Native peoples of the North West were well aware of the fate of their brothers in the American West. There, the settlers and the United States army were engaged in constant warfare with the Native peoples. It was a one-sided war that saw heavy losses on the Native side and left bitter divisions between the newcomers and Natives for decades afterwards. The Natives of the Canadian West feared the same would happen north of the forty-ninth parallel. The promise of the Canadian government to help and protect them held great appeal. It is likely that it was the promise of protection, not an understanding of the implications of giving up their lands, that led to Native leaders signing the treaties.

Today, in many parts of Canada, Native peoples are concerned about the loss of their "aboriginal" rights as non-Native settlers have occupied the land. In most of Quebec, British Columbia, the Yukon and Northwest Territories, no treaties were negotiated with the Native peoples. In these areas of Canada, Native peoples are using the courts and other political and legal channels to press for restoration of their lands or compensation for the loss of lands traditionally occupied by their people.

Negotiations with the Blackfoot began in the spring of 1877, with the signing ceremony taking place in September of that year. The signing had to wait for fall because the Blackfoot were busy hunting bison during the summer. On September 17, the lieutenant-governor of the North West Territories, David Laird, arrived at Blackfoot Crossing, the site of the signing. He was accompanied by the NWMP Commissioner, Colonel James Macleod, and an escort of 108 Mounted Policemen. Here is how one of the NWMP men who accompanied Laird described the scene at Blackfoot Crossing that day:

There must have been a thousand lodges. They were plentifully supplied with meat, having only just left a large buffalo herd downstream to the east. Their horses covered uplands to the north and south of the camp in thousands. It was a stirring and picturesque scene: great bands of grazing horses, the mounted warriors threading their way among them and as far as the eye could reach the white Indian lodges glimmering among the trees

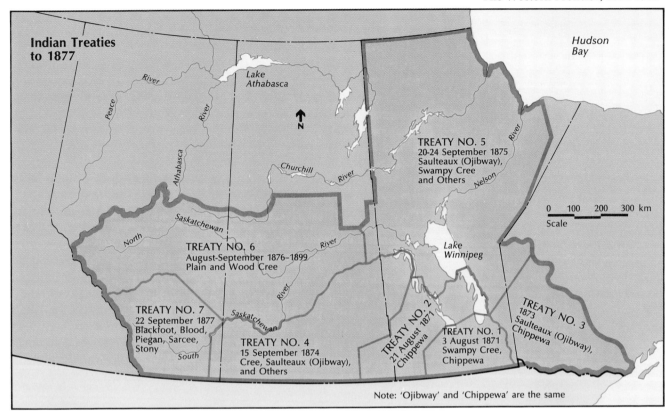

Indian Treaties to 1877

TREATY NO. 5
20-24 September 1875
Saulteaux (Ojibway),
Swampy Cree
and Others

TREATY NO. 6
August-September 1876–1899
Plain and Wood Cree

TREATY NO. 7
22 September 1877
Blackfoot, Blood,
Piegan, Sarcee,
Stony

TREATY NO. 4
15 September 1874
Cree, Saulteaux (Ojibway),
and Others

TREATY NO. 2
21 August 1871
Chippewa

TREATY NO. 1
3 August 1871
Swampy Cree,
Chippewa

TREATY NO. 3
1873
Saulteaux (Ojibway),
Chippewa

Hudson
Bay

Lake
Athabasca

Peace *River*

Athabasca

North *Saskatchewan*

Saskatchewan River

Churchill *River*

Nelson *River*

Lake
Winnipeg

Saskatchewan

South

N

0 100 200 300 km
Scale

Note: 'Ojibway' and 'Chippewa' are the same

along the river bottom. By night the valley echoed to the dismal howling of the camp's curs [dogs] and from sun to sun drums boomed from the tents. Never before had such a concourse of Indians assembled on Canada's western plains.

Two days later, some 4000 men, women and children gathered on the grass to watch the signing of the treaty. The chiefs of the Blackfoot, Blood, Peigan, Stoney and Sarcee seated themselves in front of the Council tent to hear Lieutenant-Governor Laird address the Blackfoot Confederacy. NWMP Sergeant-Major Sam Steele, another officer who was present at the signing, wrote down Laird's words as he spoke to the Indians:

...the Queen has sent Colonel Macleod and myself to ask you to make a treaty....in a few years the buffalo will be destroyed, and for this reason the Queen wishes to help you to live in the future in some other way. She wishes you to allow her white children to come and live on your land, and raise cattle and grain, and thus

This map shows the extent of the territory acquired through treaties with the Native peoples between 1871 and 1877.

give you the means of living when the buffalo are no more. She will also give you and your children money every year, which you can spend as you please....Cattle will be given to you and potatoes, the same as are grown at Fort Macleod.

The commissioners strongly urge you to take cattle, as you understand cattle better than you will farming, for some time at least, and as long as you continue to move about in lodges....as soon as you settle, teachers will be sent to you to instruct your children to read books like this [Laird held up a Bible] which is impossible so long as you continue to move from place to place. I have now spoken....Go, therefore, to your councils, and I hope you may be able to give me your answer tomorrow.

The next day, Steele listened and took notes as Crowfoot, speaking through an interpreter, replied to Laird:

The plains are large and wide; we are the children of the plains; it has been our home and the buffalo have been our food always. I hope you look upon the Blackfeet, Bloods, Peigans and Sarcees as your children now, and that you will be indulgent and charitable to them.

The advice given to me and my people has proved to be very good. If the police had not come to this country, where should we

The signing of the treaty between the Blackfoot and the government of Canada involved much ceremony. The NWMP played a central role by representing the authority of the government.

all be now? Bad men and whiskey were indeed killing us so fast that very few of us indeed would have been left today. The Mounted Police have protected us as the feathers of the bird protect it from the frosts of winter....I am satisfied. I will sign the treaty.

The other chiefs followed Crowfoot, each speaking in favor of the treaty. It was signed on September 21, 1877. The first to make his mark on the document was Crowfoot. With the treaty signed, a thirteen gun salute was fired, and the police band played "God Save the Queen." The tribes had given up their land and, with it, their independence. Soon the buffalo, too, would be gone, marking the end of the plains peoples' traditional way of life. Out of these changes would come a bitter conflict. The harmony and trust that had marked the signing of the treaty would be shattered.

1. Why did the Canadian government want to sign treaties with the Native peoples on the Prairies? Why were the Native peoples prepared to sign these treaties?
2. What did the Native peoples give up under the terms of the treaties? What did they receive?
3. What was the role of the NWMP in the negotiations with the Native peoples? Why were they so important to the negotiations and to the creation of a climate of harmony and trust?
4. What problems would seminomadic hunters face in suddenly becoming ranchers or farmers?
5. In your opinion, were the treaties between the Native peoples and the government of Canada fair deals? Give your reasons.
6. Suggest what might have happened in the Canadian West if no treaties had been signed with the Native peoples prior to large-scale non-Native settlement.

Building the Railway

By 1875, Canada was a vast nation stretching from sea to sea. There were now seven provinces. (Prince Edward Island had joined Confederation in 1873.) These provinces and the North West Territories had a combined area of nearly 10 million square kilometres, but they were thinly populated and joined in a political union that had few economic, communication or transportation links, particularly in the West. It would take a cross-country railway, as promised to British Columbia in 1871, to provide these links.

Starting the Railroad

Construction of a 5000 km long rail line from the Pacific to central Canada involved many tasks. An appropriate route through the Canadian Shield and across the Rocky Mountains had to be selected and surveyed. Sufficient financial backing had to be found. Also needed were engineers and laborers to plan, build and operate the railway. As well, government support would be necessary, particularly assistance to secure financing for the rail line and to acquire land for the line's right of way.

The terms of union that had brought British Columbia into Confederation in 1871 called for construction of the railway to begin within two years. Macdonald's Conservative government realized that they would have to increase taxes to build the railway, an action unpopular with voters in the East. Instead, they looked for private investors to take on this great project.

In the United States, the men who had just constructed the Northern Pacific Railroad were eager to get the contract for the Canadian rail line. Their motives went beyond the profits they hoped to make. They hoped to see the trans-Canada rail line linked with the American route south of the Great Lakes. This link would reduce construction costs and, if sections of the line ran through the United States, the rail line would effectively be placed under American control.

The American railroad builders saw this control as an important step toward annexation of western Canada to the United States. But the government of Prime Minister Macdonald, suspicious of the Americans' intentions, insisted that there be Canadian participation in the financing of the railway. This would ensure at least partial Canadian control. In 1872, Sir Hugh Allan, a Montreal businessman, agreed to act as head of the company that would build the railway.

In exchange for the railway contract, Allan secretly paid thousands of dollars to prominent members of the government, including George-Étienne Cartier, Hector Langevin, and Macdonald himself. Much of this money came from Allan's American colleagues.

When Macdonald urged Allan to break off his connections with his American partners, the businessmen were outraged. They sold to Liberal members of Parliament a number of letters and telegrams showing that bribes had been paid. Aided by numerous newspapers, the Liberals made these documents public.

The resulting public outcry over these bribes was enormous. The affair became known as the "Pacific Scandal," and it led to the resignation of Macdonald's government in November of 1873. The Liberals, led by Alexander Mackenzie, were called upon to form the government. In the election of 1874, Mackenzie won an overwhelming majority. The new Liberal government inherited the pledge to begin construction of the railway to British Columbia.

However, Mackenzie decided that the federal government could not afford the cost of building the complete transcontinental railway. Instead, he focussed on smaller railway building projects. West of the Great Lakes, only two short sections of rail line were laid down in the first two years of Mackenzie's government. Construction of the first section, running seventy-five kilometres west from Fort William, was begun on June 1, 1875, and marked the actual start of the long-awaited rail route to the Pacific. The second section was in Manitoba, linking Selkirk to Emerson, and joining the railroad running north from St. Paul, Minnesota.

1. In your own words, explain the "Pacific Scandal." How did it affect the government of Sir John A. Macdonald?
2. Using your atlas, locate where the first two western sections of the transcontinental railway were built.
3. Suggest some reasons why the first two western sections were built so far apart. What is the physical geography of the region between the two sections?

Railway Building in Western Canada

The first steam locomotive in western Canada, the *Countess of Dufferin*, arrived in the fall of 1877 at St. Boniface, on a Red River barge. The rail link with Ontario to the East had not yet been completed but construction of the rail line across the Prairies had begun. The first spike of the St. Boniface branch of the transcontinental railway was driven on September 29, 1877, ten days before the arrival of the *Countess of Dufferin*. People were already beginning to call the new railway the Canadian Pacific. Soon, the *Countess of Dufferin* proudly sported the words "CPR No. 1" painted in white against the gleaming black paint of its cab. There was a sense of excitement in the towns and villages of the West, now that the long-awaited railway was finally under construction.

The western settlers' excitement was not generally shared by the politicians and businessmen of eastern Canada. Mackenzie saw

MACDONALD'S NATIONAL POLICY

Canada in the mid-1870s was suffering from an economic depression. Despite large-scale importation of manufactured goods from the United States and Britain, Mackenzie's Liberals refused to increase tariffs to protect Canadian industries. They failed in 1874-1875 to negotiate a **reciprocity** agreement with the United States. Macdonald and the Conservative Party campaigned in 1878 on the promise of a "National Policy" with increased tariffs to protect Canadian manufacturers. The Conservatives won the election on their protectionist platform. In the budget of 1879, Macdonald set out a nationalist program that would strengthen Canada's economy and restore Canadian confidence in the development of the country. Duties were increased on imported manufactured goods, but decreased on imported raw materials used by Canadian manufacturers.

Over the next fifty years, Macdonald's National Policy became the central theme of the Conservative Party in Canada. This policy was expanded to include construction of the CPR, settlement of the West, harbor developments and support for fast steamship service to Europe and Asia.

construction of the railway as costly and unnecessary. He publicly stated that "all the power of man and all the money of Europe" would not be enough to build a transcontinental railway in Canada in the ten year period promised by Macdonald. Others, like Sir Richard Cartwright, a prominent Liberal politician, claimed the venture would bankrupt the country. Cartwright claimed that building the railway "would place upon every man's farm a mortgage so heavy that it would take two or three generations to clear it off."

Vast in area and thinly populated, western Canada appeared to have little value in the eyes of critics of the transcontinental railway. With few farms or other economic activities, the West was unattractive to most Canadian and British investors. Their fears were reinforced by articles in British magazines, such as one in *Truth*, which stated that "the Canadian Pacific Railway, if it is ever finished, will run through a country as forbidding as any on earth." Manitoba was described in the article as a place where "men and cattle are frozen to death in numbers that would rather startle the intending settler if he knew." British Columbia was dismissed as "a barren, cold mountain country that should never have been inhabited."

Sir John A. Macdonald did not share the gloomy view of the West as presented by *Truth*. He saw the railway as a means of bringing prosperity, security and settlers to western Canada. Macdonald fought the 1878 election on a promise to restore the country to economic health: his "National Policy" emphasized the importance of the railway and western settlement. The voters of Canada returned the Conservatives to power.

Macdonald quickly set about getting the railway construction project back on track. In 1879 Macdonald and two of his cabinet ministers, Leonard Tilley and Charles Tupper, the former premiers of New Brunswick and Nova Scotia, went to London, England, to seek funding and British government support for the railway. They failed completely in their efforts to obtain British backing for the project.

Macdonald's failure to obtain support for the transcontinental railway could not have come at a worse time. The people and government of British Columbia were outraged that the railway had not been built. Canada had not lived up to the terms of union, negotiated when the province agreed to join Confederation. By 1880, George Walkem, the premier of British Columbia, was threatening to have the province secede from Canada.

Macdonald now realized that the government of Canada itself,

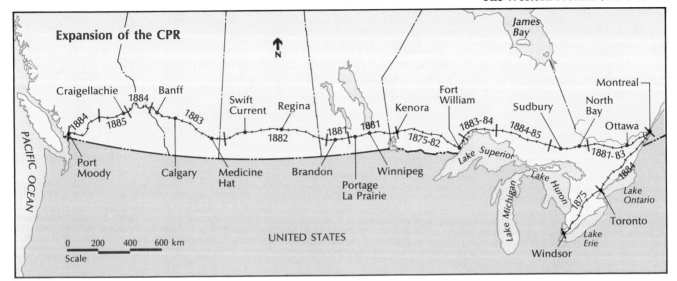

Expansion of the CPR

By 1880, nine years after British Columbia joined Confederation, little of a transcontinental railway was built. Still to be crossed were the Prairies and the formidable mountains.

without help from Britain, would have to finance construction of the railway. To honor the commitment to British Columbia, Macdonald committed his government to the building of a rail line west of Lake Superior, linking Port Arthur to Winnipeg. Contracts were quickly signed for construction of the railway through the Fraser and Thompson river valleys of British Columbia. The contracts were awarded to Andrew Onderdonk, a young American railway builder.

Onderdonk started work on the Fraser River section of the line in the fall of 1880. Work on the rugged mountain section was hard and dangerous; hundreds of the railway builders were killed by falling rock and other hazards. Construction of the railway progressed slowly. By 1881, just over 400 km of track had been laid down. The federal government already had spent millions of dollars on the project, with very little to show for the money. With few remaining government funds available, Macdonald and his fellow Conservative politicians realized that private money had to be raised to build the railway.

In the fall of 1880, a group of Canadian, American, British and French investors came together to finance the building of the railway. Led by the former president of the Bank of Montreal, George Stephen, this group had the money and the skill needed to build the railway. Stephen and his cousin Donald Smith, head of the Hudson's Bay Company, had earlier purchased a bankrupt railroad in Minnesota. They had not only turned the railroad into a profitable operation, they had become multimillionaires in the process.

Stephen drove a hard bargain during negotiations with Macdonald's government. His demands were enormous: 10 million hectares in land grants and $25 million (more than $650 million in 1986 dollars) in subsidies for construction of the rail line. Macdonald's government was staggered by these demands. In the end, however, the Conservatives agreed to the terms set by Stephen. They had no choice. No other investors were willing to take on the enormous challenge.

1. What factors caused Mackenzie and other government and business leaders of Canada to be pessimistic about finishing the transcontinental railway within a few years? In the end, did it take "all the power of man and all the money of Europe" as Mackenzie had predicted?
2. How might newspaper accounts, such as the one quoted from *Truth* on page 196, have affected the British government's decision in 1879 regarding financial support for the railway?
3. Potential builders of the railway demanded huge sums of money from the government and enormous areas of land in western Canada. Did the government of Canada get a fair deal? Give reasons for your answer.

The CPR Incorporated

The act incorporating the Canadian Pacific Railway Company was approved by Parliament on February 15, 1881. In addition to the 10 million hectares and the $25 million agreed to by the government, the legislation included other terms favorable to the syndicate formed by Stephen. The lines being built in Manitoba and British Columbia were to be turned over to the CPR on completion. No charters were to be granted to any competing company seeking to build a railway within twenty-five kilometres of the Canada-U.S. border for a period of twenty years. During those twenty years, the CPR would not have to pay any taxes on the vast amounts of land it had been given. In return, Stephen and his partners were committed to building the transcontinental rail line by the end of 1890.

Meeting that commitment would require more than just money and land. It would take tens of thousands of workers, and the rail, wooden ties, dynamite and tools needed to run a ribbon of steel from the Pacific Ocean to the St. Lawrence River. The workers needed to be fed and housed during this enormous task. They needed someone who could inspire them to the almost superhuman effort the work would require. Stephen found this leadership in the person of William Cornelius Van Horne, an experienced railwayman who had been superintendent of the Chicago, Milwaukee and St. Paul Railroad.

Van Horne arrived in Winnipeg to take up his new duties as general manager of the CPR on January 1, 1882. He was a huge, burly man, hard as a **navvy's** hammer, and filled with boundless energy. When he gave orders, he made sure that they were carried out. He provided the organization and equipment needed to ensure that the rail line could be built efficiently. Five thousand men and 1700 teams of horses were brought to the Prairies to build that portion of the CPR. Construction camps were set up, tonnes of food were made available and the best cooks hired to keep the men happy and well-fed. Trains reached the railhead at regular intervals, each carrying the rails, ties and hardware needed to build 1.6 km of track. Van Horne would show up at the construction site at any time of day or night, standing on a flat car or wagon to urge the workers to go faster. Under his direction, the railway advanced steadily westward from Winnipeg at a rate of six kilometres a day.

Sir William C. Van Horne

Van Horne had pledged to lay 800 km of track across the Prairies before freeze-up. By October 1882, trains were running between Winnipeg and Regina, then known as "Pile o' Bones." By the time snow and cold stopped work that fall, the railhead had reached Medicine Hat, Alberta.

Steel rails and sunbleached bones were symbols of the changes in Canada's West. The great herds of buffalo that once roamed the Prairies were all but gone and the Native people who had followed them were on reserves. Now, the trains brought settlers who took advantage of the free or low-cost land being offered by both the CPR and the government.

The Indians and Métis watched as the grasslands were turned into farms and the buffalo killed off by white hunters. In Alberta, the rail line was being laid on lands set aside as part of the Blackfoot reservation under Treaty 7. The Blackfeet were angered and prepared to attack and drive off the railway builders. Only the quick-witted intervention of Father Lacombe prevented bloodshed. He promised the Indians that he would make sure that the railway gave them land to make up for where tracks had been laid. When the CPR reached Calgary in August of 1883, both Chief Crowfoot and Father Lacombe were Van Horne's guests for dinner in his private car. Each was given a lifetime pass on the CPR; Crowfoot wore his proudly from his neck until his death.

Building the railway across the Prairies was relatively easy. The section north of Lake Superior was another matter entirely. This route had been chosen to ensure an all-Canadian route. As a result, the tracks had to run through the bare rocks, **muskeg** and waterways of the Canadian Shield. Van Horne himself called the route north of the lake "200 miles [320 km] of engineering impossibilities." But he liked nothing better than to make the impossible possible.

Van Horne hired 12 000 laborers, offering them "two dollars a day and upwards" to attract them to this rugged land. Five thousand horses and a newly-invented track-laying machine were brought in. Three dynamite factories were built to provide explosives needed to blast the rail line through the solid rock of the Shield. In other places, workers watched in frustration as newly-laid track vanished into the swamps. One section of track near Rat Portage (now Kenora) was swallowed by the muskeg seven times before a stable route was found. Some sections of track cost as much as $250 000 per kilometre to lay.

Still more challenging problems lay ahead as the rails neared the

In many places in the Canadian Shield and the Western Cordillera, huge volumes of rock had to be cut away to prepare the track bed. Trains cannot manage steep inclines so cutting and filling is necessary to smooth out the features of the natural landscape.

Rocky Mountains. Survey crews and engineers had been working in the Rockies since the summer of 1883. The railhead reached Lake Louise, on the British Columbia-Alberta border, by the end of that year. From this point west, the steep slopes and solid mountain rock would make construction of the rail line north of Lake Superior seem simple by comparison. In the Rockies, construction costs often exceeded $300 000 ($6 million in 1986 dollars) per kilometre.

CHINESE WORKERS ON THE CPR

More than 15 000 Chinese workers were brought to Canada during the period 1881-1885 to help build the CPR. Labor shortages in western Canada forced Onderdonk to import workers to build the railway. He also had an economic motive–Chinese laborers were paid seventy-five cents to a dollar a day, 50 percent less than other workers doing the same work. These wages, however, were much greater than they could earn in China or the colony of Hong Kong at this time.

Chinese agents were hired by the railway builders to recruit work gangs in China. The Chinese workers were carried to British Columbia in cargo ships, as many as 1000 to a ship. Crowded beneath the hatches of the cargo holds, hundreds died on route to Canada. Once in Canada, the workers were divided into gangs of thirty laborers, a cook and a "bookman," or overseer, who spoke both Chinese and English.

Many Chinese railway workers were killed in dynamite explosions, rockfalls, and other accidents. Their deaths were not counted in official CPR records of workers who died on the job. They also died of scurvy and other illnesses largely because their diet consisted mainly of rice and stale ground salmon. Ill-fed and ill-dressed, the Chinese workers suffered greatly during the harsh winters in the western mountains, yet their labor contributed enormously to the completion of the British Columbia section of the railway.

Faced with such tremendous costs, Stephen's syndicate ran out of money in 1883. A loan of $20 million had to be obtained from the Canadian government. To secure the loan, Van Horne offered to complete the railway in five, not ten years.

In the spring of 1885, the syndicate had again run out of money. The $20 million had not been nearly enough to cover the enormous costs of building the final section of the CPR through the Rocky Mountains and to complete the section through the Canadian Shield north of Lake Superior. Although most of the line had been completed, the most difficult and costly sections in the mountains remained unfinished. The CPR was on the verge of bankruptcy. The government turned down a request for an additional $5 million. In July, however, it changed its mind and passed a bill to authorize the loan. Earlier that year, during the North West Rebellion, examined in the next section of this chapter, the government had realized the railway's importance as it had been able to send troops quickly to the West to suppress the rebellion.

1. What aspects of Van Horne's character made him an effective person to take charge of building the railroad?
2. In what ways did the coming of the railway change the way of life on the Prairies?
3. How did the geography of British Columbia and of the Canadian Shield affect the construction of the CPR? Why was construction of the railway cheaper and faster on the Prairies?
4. In the spring of 1885, the government turned down a request for a loan of $5 million to finish the railway through the mountains. What would have been the likely outcome of this action had they not reconsidered several months later?

THE FIRST TRAIN TO THE COAST

Sam Steele, who was present for so many important events during the early history of western Canada, was among those who stood and watched the driving of the last spike. He rode the first train as it travelled through the mountains to Port Moody. Here is how he described that trip in his journal:

...the train rushed along at the rate of 57 miles per hour [90 km/h], roaring in and out of the numerous tunnels, our short car whirling around the sharp curves like the tail of a kite, the sensation being such that when dinner was served Dickey [the Dominion Engineer], the manager [Onderdonk] and I were the only ones not suffering from train sickness. I think this was one of the wildest rides by rail that any of us had ever taken, and was, to say the least of it, dangerous, for had the train left the rails it would have plunged down a precipice a couple of hundred feet [65 metres] into the wild waters of the Fraser...

The Last Spike

With the additional loan of $5 million, in the summer of 1885, work resumed on the railway. By the end of September, Onderdonk's crews had completed the western section through the mountains. In October, the eastern and western sections were joined at Craigellachie, near Salmon Arm, B.C. All that remained to be completed was a short section in the Rockies, a task that took less than a month. The last spike was driven on November 7, 1885.

The ceremony marking the completion of the CPR was a simple one. Contrary to popular belief, there was no gold spike to mark the event. The CPR could hardly have afforded such an extravagance. Called upon to make a speech, Van Horne simply said, "All I can say is the work has been done well in every way." A few minutes later, a train whistle blew. The conductor called out, "All aboard for the Pacific."

In 1887, the western terminus of the CPR was moved twenty kilometres westward from Port Moody to where the city of Vancouver now stands. There deeper water permitted large ocean-going vessels to dock. The CPR now owned and operated 8000 km of railway lines. Of these, nearly 5000 km were mainline tracks stretching from Montreal to the Pacific. The CPR had a monopoly of transportation through western Canada and owned vast areas of fertile land, just waiting to be settled.

Riel and Rebellion

The North West Rebellion of 1885 was a relatively brief episode in the history of western Canada. It lasted fewer than four months, but it would have lasting effects, both in western and in eastern Canada.

Background to Rebellion

Following the events of 1870 (see pages 147-153), many Métis moved west from Manitoba as settlers crowded into the new province. Seeing their traditional way of life threatened, the Métis sought lands where they could continue to hunt buffalo and create their own farms. Many of them settled along the Saskatchewan River, where, as they had traditionally done, they established long, narrow farms running down to the river banks.

Métis, Native peoples and the few white settlers in the area lived peacefully together for nearly fifteen years. Gradually the three groups became unhappy with the government in Ottawa.

Settlers in the area were faced with high costs and weak markets for their farm products. They wanted economic assistance from Ottawa and a stronger voice in the political affairs of the region. There was no elected Assembly for the North West Territories: power lay in the hands of a lieutenant-governor appointed by Ottawa. Unlike the provinces, the North West Territories did not have responsible government, and they had no elected members of Parliament in Ottawa to speak on their behalf.

The Métis resented the way land was being divided as the federal government readied the Prairies for the settlers expected to come with the railway. Government surveyors divided the landscape into townships in a square, grid pattern similar to that used in Ontario. The long thin Métis farms, similar to those of Quebec, did not fit into this gridwork system. Without proper surveys, the farmers could not receive title to their lands.

The Native peoples faced far more severe problems during the early 1880s. Over the short time the West had been open to settlement, they had suffered many hardships. They had been exposed to smallpox, sold rotgut whisky and seen the loss of their lands. The destruction of the great buffalo herds left many Native bands facing starvation.

In an attempt to save money, Macdonald's government had slashed the funds given to the Indian Department in both 1883 and

1884. The rations and supplies promised the Natives by treaty were now cut back and the number of Indian Agents appointed to carry out the terms of the treaties was reduced sharply. The hungry Natives were becoming more and more angry over the government's failure to live up to the terms of the treaties:

Early in 1884, a group of starving Salteaux attacked a government food storehouse on their reserve. They took a white employee hostage and carried off sacks of flour and bacon. A NWMP detachment was sent to arrest the Salteaux, who had barricaded themselves in a building on the reserve. While the incident ended without bloodshed, the Native people no longer saw the NWMP as their protectors.

Métis and Indian frustrations reached the boiling point late in 1884. Repeated petitions to Ottawa had brought only vague replies and no results. The Métis sent for Louis Riel who was living in Montana at the time. They still remembered his leadership during the events of 1870 that had resulted in Manitoba becoming a province of Canada. After the Rebellion of 1870, Riel had been declared an outlaw—$5000 was offered for his arrest and conviction. Nevertheless, the people of Red River elected him to the Canadian Parliament, but he had not been able to take his seat in the Commons. In 1874, Riel was granted an amnesty by the Liberal government of Alexander Mackenzie on the condition he remain in exile for another five years. Rejected by Protestant Ontarians because of the death of Scott and shunned by many francophone Catholics for his religious views, the now bitter and frustrated Riel suffered a breakdown and began a period of emotional despair. In 1876, friends smuggled him back into Quebec where he spent two years in mental hospitals. By 1881 he was back in the American West, in Montana, where he taught school.

The delegation that visited Riel in Montana convinced him to come back and to help his people. He arrived in the summer of 1884, welcomed eagerly by both the Métis and white communities. Riel felt that the same strategies that he had used in the Red River settlement fourteen years earlier would work effectively in the new territory.

Riel undertook a speaking tour of the region, seeking to unite Natives, Métis and white settlers in a common effort to get a better deal from the federal government. After four months of efforts, a Petition of Rights was sent to Ottawa in December 1884, outlining the demands of the Métis and the settlers. Foremost among the demands was the Métis concern over land titles.

Macdonald and his government ignored the demands sent by Riel, whom they considered to be a dangerous agitator; so did the government administrators sent to the North West. Only a few NWMP officers tried to call attention to the increasing resentment in the area. They could not understand why the government was unwilling to respond to what they saw as the not unreasonable demands of the Métis. Catholic Church leaders, fearful that their authority was being undermined by Riel's presence, also sent a warning to Ottawa. They urged that Riel be bribed to return to Montana. Macdonald rejected the suggestion:

We have no money to give to Riel and would be obliged to ask for a Parliamentary vote. How would it look to confess we could not govern the country and were obliged to bribe a man to go away? This would never do. He has a right to remain in Canada, and if he conspires we must punish him, that's all.

Talk of the proposed bribe, combined with the government's refusal to address the Métis' concerns, fuelled Riel's anger. In early 1885, his speeches became more powerfully emotional, ringing with calls to take up arms. Repeatedly, phrases like "striking a blow against Ottawa" and "ruling this country or perishing in the attempt" were heard spoken by Riel over the next few months as he drummed up support. Alarmed at these meetings, the local NWMP officers sought and received additional Mounted Policemen for the area. The force grew from eighty to 200 Mounties, and new police posts were established and fortified. Riel's speeches also alarmed the white settlers, who abandoned their support for him. Many of them armed themselves to defend their homesteads against possible attack. The settlers were aware of Native uprisings in the 1870s against settlers who had occupied their lands in the western United States. Now, they feared similar uprisings might occur on the Canadian Prairies.

In March 1885, Riel gained support for his planned rebellion from starving Cree bands led by Big Bear and Poundmaker. Riel promised them that the Mounted Police would be "wiped out of existence" in less than a week.

1. Summarize the discontent the Indians, Métis and settlers felt towards the government in Ottawa in the early 1880s.

2. Why did the Métis and Indians turn to Riel for leadership in 1884? What did they hope to gain?

3. Some recent historians have suggested that the reports of Riel's mental breakdown and emotional despair were either created or exaggerated by people in eastern Canada. Why would eastern Canadians believe that Riel was unbalanced? Would all people in eastern Canada share that view? Explain.

Rebellion Breaks Out

On March 13, 1885, Superintendent Lief Crozier of the NWMP sent a telegram from Battleford to Ottawa saying "Half-breed [Métis] rebellion liable to break out at any moment. If half-breeds rise Indians will join them." Five days later, after hearing a rumor that 500 NWMP were on their way to arrest the Métis leader, some of Riel's Métis followers cut the telegraph line at Batoche. They seized the government buildings there, raided the stores and took the employees hostage. At Batoche, Riel declared a provisional government with himself as leader. Riel then sent a message to Superintendent Crozier demanding the surrender of the police post at Fort Carlton. The Métis leader vowed that, should Crozier not surrender, full-scale war would follow. Crozier did not surrender his post: the rebellion had begun.

The first battle between the Métis and Indians and the government forces was at Duck Lake. Sites of other battles are shown on the map.

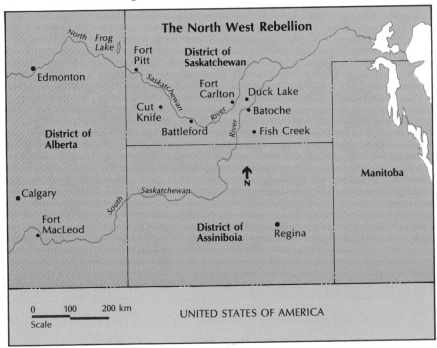

206

Blood was first shed on March 26, 1885, when Crozier led a force of ninety-eight men to attack the Métis rebels near Duck Lake. Crozier's party of Mounted Policemen and volunteers from Prince Albert was eager, but ill-equipped and poorly trained. What the excited attackers thought would be a picnic turned into a nightmare.

Travelling in sleighs and dragging a seven-pounder artillery piece, Crozier's fifty-five NWMP men and forty-three Prince Albert volunteers were forced to follow a narrow trail through the sticky, deep, wet snow. About three kilometres from Duck Lake, Crozier's party halted in what one policeman called "a wretched position, in an exposed hollow, surrounded on three sides by scrubby bush." Concealed in the trees on the hillsides were several hundred Métis, led by Gabriel Dumont, Riel's deputy and military commander.

Two Natives approached Crozier and his Métis intepreter, Joe McKay. After a brief discussion, Crozier realized that his force was in a vulnerable position and turned to withdraw. As he did so, one of the Native men tried to seize Crozier's pistol. As the two struggled, McKay shot the man. McKay's shot was answered by deadly fire from the Métis positions less than 150 m away. The Battle of Duck Lake lasted less than thirty minutes. When the firing ceased, twelve of Crozier's men lay dead or dying. A similar number, including Crozier himself, were wounded.

Four Métis and one Indian were killed at Duck Lake; three were wounded, including Gabriel Dumont whose scalp was grazed by a bullet. Without their commander, the Métis forces were reluctant to pursue the retreating NWMP force. Louis Riel, who had watched the battle from a hillside armed only with a crucifix, refused to order the Métis to press their advantage. Had he done so, Crozier's ill-advised raid might have been a greater failure than it was.

The events of Duck Lake forced Louis Riel to change his strategy. Riel had hoped that the threat of force, combined with negotiations, would yield the results the Métis were seeking. This strategy had worked well for the Métis at Red River in 1869-1870, but fifteen years later it was doomed to failure. The telegraph and railway allowed the Canadian government to respond quickly to the threats and they were not willing to negotiate. A force of 260 militiamen was dispatched from Winnipeg on March 27, 1885. Using the newly-constructed CPR line, they reached the Duke Lake area the following day.

The Métis victory over Crozier's forces strengthened their cause. It also brought the active support of Natives led by the Cree leaders

Big Bear

Big Bear and Poundmaker, who had earlier been reluctant to join the rebellion. On March 29, Poundmaker marched on the small community of Battleford seeking food. The 600 residents of the town took refuge in the police fort. From there, they watched as the Cree leaders spoke with the Hudson's Bay trader, William McKay. The Cree promised to leave if they were given food, clothing and ammunition, but McKay was unable to obtain government approval to meet their demands. Frustrated, the Cree looted the town, out of range of the NWMP rifles. Nearby farms and homesteads were attacked and burned, and two settlers were killed. The rebels occupied Battleford for almost a month before abandoning it to an advancing party of Canadian militia led by Colonel William Otter.

Even less fortunate was the small settlement of Frog Lake. There, on April 2, 1885, a party of Cree led by Big Bear's war chief, Wandering Spirit, attacked during a mass at the Frog Lake mission. They seized food and attempted to lead the settlers off as hostages. The local Indian Agent, Thomas Quinn, resisted and was shot dead. Two Catholic priests and nine settlers also were killed. The rest of the settlers were taken prisoner.

The Cree then besieged Fort Pitt, a small NWMP post on the banks of the Saskatchewan River. Two weeks after the Frog Lake killings, Fort Pitt was abandoned to the Cree. It would be the last major victory for the Indian and Métis rebels, as news of the rebellion had reached Ottawa swiftly along the recently strung telegraph lines. A large militia force of 5000 men was being assembled in Ontario and Quebec. Van Horne approached the government, offering to move these men and their equipment to the West.

Four sections of the railway north of Lake Superior, totalling 140 km, were unfinished. Men had to march and equipment be moved by horsedrawn sled over these sections. Nevertheless, Van Horne was able to move the troops from Ottawa to the Prairies in less than five days. By mid-April, all of the troops had reached their jumping off points at Qu'Appelle, Swift Current and Calgary.

The value of the newly arrived troops was immediately known. The Métis came close to winning the Battle of Fish Creek on April 24, when Gabriel Dumont and 150 of his men surprised Major General Frederick Middleton's column of Canadian Militia. The Métis held the upper hand killing ten militiamen and wounding forty-three others, but withdrew when reinforcements arrived to relieve Middleton's troops.

On May 2, Poundmaker and his Cree warriors scored one final victory against the militia at Cut Knife Hill, just west of Battleford.

Anxious to end the conflict with the Canadian government, how-ever, Poundmaker restrained his warriors and kept them from wiping out the retreating troops.

On May 12, 1885, following a four-day assault on their headquar-ters at Batoche, the Métis rebels were convincingly defeated. Before Batoche fell, both Riel and Gabriel Dumont escaped. Dumont fled to exile in the United States. There, he built for himself a career as one of the attractions of Buffalo Bill Cody's Wild West Show. Riel surrendered to two NWMP scouts two days after the fall of Batoche. He was taken to Regina to await trial on charges of leading an armed rebellion against the government of Canada. On hearing of the defeat of the Métis at Batoche and the capture of Riel, Poundmaker surrendered to the soldiers on May 24, 1885.

Following an intense but inconclusive battle at Frenchman's Butte (with a militia force led by Sam Steele), Big Bear withdrew from the rebellion when he heard of Poundmaker's surrender. His Cree warriors, led by Wandering Spirit, continued to hold their hostages for another month as they moved north across the Prairies and into the woodlands, trying to avoid the soldiers searching for them. Big Bear and his people finally surrendered to the NWMP on July 2, 1885, at Fort Carlton. The North West Rebellion was over.

The railway had played a major part in the defeat of the rebels. Had troops from eastern Canada not reached the Prairies swiftly, the rebels might well have won. The North West Rebellion had proved to Ottawa the importance of the rail link to western Canada. In return, the government agreed to provide the financing needed to complete the railway to the Pacific.

Poundmaker

1. In your opinion, who started the Rebellion of 1885? Give rea-sons for your opinion.
2. What role did the railway play in the Rebellion of 1885?
3. Suppose the Métis and Indian forces had been able to push back the NWMP and the militia. What do you think the gov-ernment would have done then? What would the rebels have done?

The Trial of Louis Riel

While the shooting had stopped, the aftermath of rebellion had yet to be played out. Dozens of Cree and Métis were tried for crimes related to the rebellion. Eleven Cree were sentenced to death; eight, including Wandering Spirit, were sent to the gallows in the NWMP

THE JURY JUDGES RIEL

After the trial and execution of Louis Riel, members of the jury that had convicted him made these comments:

We, on the jury, recommended mercy. The prisoner was guilty and we could not excuse his acts. But, at the same time, we felt that the government had not done its duty. It did nothing about the grievances of the Métis. If it had, there would never have been a second Riel Rebellion. We strongly condemned the dawdling of Macdonald and his government. If they had been on trial as accessories, the jury would have shown them little mercy. We tried Louis Riel for treason, but he was executed for the murder of Thomas Scott.

Riel at his trial in 1885.

barracks yard at Battleford, and three had their sentences commuted to prison terms. Five other Cree were jailed for treason, among them Poundmaker and Big Bear, who each spent two years of their three-year sentences in the Stoney Mountain Penitentiary. Within six months of leaving jail both would die, old and broken men. Eighteen Métis were convicted of treason and given sentences of one to seven years.

One trial, that of Louis Riel, caught the attention of the nation. Although Riel was charged with treason resulting from the Rebellion of 1885, many Canadians felt he was really on trial for the 1870 rebellion in which Thomas Scott had died. English-speaking Protestants demanded that Riel be convicted and executed. Many Quebeckers saw Riel as a hero, who had simply been fighting to defend the rights of French-speaking Catholics. A Riel Defence Committee was set up in Quebec. Money raised by the committee was used to hire three Quebec lawyers to defend the Métis leader.

Riel's trial took place in a small, rented building in Regina. The makeshift courtroom was crowded on the afternoon of July 20, 1885, as it began. Newspaper reporters from all over Canada had gathered to observe the trial. Their stories, sent by telegraph, would appear in newspapers of eastern Canada the next day. It was a trial that fascinated the public, not only because of the crimes of which Riel was accused, but also because of the complex nature of his personality.

Riel's lawyers hoped to win an acquittal using a defence based on the Métis leader's apparent madness. They urged Riel to plead not guilty by reason of insanity. But Riel undermined this defence by making an impassioned speech insisting that he was sane. The Métis leader did not wish to see his mission and his struggle dismissed as the actions of a madman. Riel told the judge and jury that he had led his people into rebellion only because the Canadian government had done nothing to help the Métis. He cried out to the crowded courtroom that he would rather die than see his actions dismissed as those of an insane man.

Louis Riel, a bilingual, Catholic Métis was tried before a judge and jury who were all white, English-speaking Protestants. The jury took only one hour and twenty minutes to find Riel guilty of treason. The jurors added a recommendation for mercy to their verdict. This recommendation was ignored by Judge Hugh Richardson who sentenced Riel to be hanged on September 18, 1885. The execution was twice delayed while the sentence was appealed. Many Canadians, both French- and English-speaking, appealed to

Prime Minister Sir John A. Macdonald to intervene. Macdonald replied that he found the sentence "satisfactory," saying "He shall hang though every dog in Quebec bark in his favour." Finally, on November 16, 1885, Louis Riel went calmly to his death on the gallows in the Regina police barracks.

News of Riel's execution quickly reached Montreal. The night of his death, 400 students marched through the streets of the city. They carried red, white and blue flags draped in black. As they marched, they sang *La Marseillaise*, the anthem of the French Revolution. The protest marchers stopped only once, to burn a straw dummy dressed as Sir John A. Macdonald.

Quebec's French language newspapers all carried angry editorials denouncing Riel's execution. They accused the Conservatives of betraying the rights of all French-speaking Canadians. Many Montrealers agreed with these sentiments. The following Sunday, 40 000 Montrealers gathered in the Champs de Mars at a mass meeting to protest Riel's death. There, they heard thirty prominent speakers defend Riel and the cause he had died for. Wilfrid Laurier, the future prime minister, told the crowd "If I had been on the banks of the Saskatchewan, I would have shouldered my musket too." Honoré Mercier, another speaker, drew wild cheers as he opened

THE LEGACY OF RIEL

The North West Rebellion of 1885, combined with the execution of Thomas Scott during the earlier Red River Rebellion of 1869-1870, would leave many bad feelings, specifically toward the Métis and more generally toward Catholics and the French language. In 1890, the government of Manitoba created an English-only school system, without making any provision for separate schools. The move, which had the support of Ontario Conservatives, badly split the federal government of the day. Prime Minister Macdonald recognized that the Manitoba government's action was in violation of the terms of the Manitoba Act, but he felt powerless to stop it.

Following only five years after the execution of Riel, the Manitoba schools question added to deepening divisions between French- and English-speaking Canadians, leaving wounds that have endured to the present. Macdonald and his Conservative Party were seen to be the supporters of English-speaking Protestants in Canada. The Manitoba schools question saw the people of Quebec swing their support strongly to the Liberals led by Wilfrid Laurier. The Conservatives were defeated in the 1896 federal election. In 1979, and again in 1985, the Supreme Court of Canada ruled that any Manitoba laws that did not conform to the terms and conditions of the Manitoba Act of 1870 were unconstitutional.

with the words "Riel, our brother, is dead, victim of his devotion to the cause of the Métis of whom he was leader, victim of fanaticism and treason." Jeers and shouts of anger filled the air as speaker after speaker attacked Sir John A. Macdonald and his government. The hanging of Riel produced conflicts and tensions that would trouble Canadian unity for many years to come.

1. Why was Louis Riel hanged after the Rebellion of 1885? How was the hanging viewed in Quebec? in Ontario?
2. Do you believe that Riel's execution was just? Give reasons to support your position.

Towards the Twentieth Century

The two decades from 1885 to 1905 saw still more changes in western Canada. Three developments dominated those years: the settlement of the West, the Klondike Gold Rush, and the creation of two new provinces, Alberta and Saskatchewan.

Settlement of the West

The completion of the Canadian Pacific Railway made large-scale settlement of the West possible. The potential for wheat farming on the fertile Prairie lands had been recognized for some time. However, the lack of an effective means of shipping the grain to markets had kept agricultural settlement to a minimum in the years before the railway.

The CPR owned vast areas of the Prairies. It started immediately to sell many of these lands, making them available to settlers at a cost of $6.25 per hectare. Half the purchase price was to be refunded for every hectare cleared and ploughed. It was in the company's interest to see these lands become working farms. With its twenty year monopoly, the CPR stood to profit from the shipment of grain eastward from the farms and from the transportation of supplies and people westward to the farming communities.

The CPR advertised Prairie farmland heavily in both eastern Canada and Europe. Special steamship and rail fares were introduced to lure settlers to Canada's West. In 1891, a bumper wheat crop ripening on the Prairies created a huge demand for farm workers. Thousands of young men and women took advantage of the railway's offer of a special fifteen dollar one-way fare from any place in Ontario. The "Harvest Specials" ran each fall from 1891 until the early 1920s. Many of those who rode on the wooden seats of the Harvest Specials' coaches stayed in the West. Others returned to tell their friends and neighbors of the opportunities the West presented.

The population of western Canada grew steadily after the CPR was completed. In 1881, there were 118 706 people living in the North West and the two western provinces, British Columbia and Manitoba. A decade later, the population had more than doubled to exceed 250 000.

In 1896, the Liberal Party, led by Sir Wilfrid Laurier, came to power. Laurier had campaigned on a platform that emphasized increased immigration and expanded settlement of the West. Laurier named Clifford Sifton, a Manitoban, to be Canada's Minister of Immigration. Sifton was committed to building a strong and independent Canadian economy within North America. He believed that Canada needed a larger population to develop industries and find markets for its products. Immigration was a key part of Sifton's development policy for Canada.

In his mind, bringing settlers to the West was linked to a national transportation policy, greater use of Canada's rich natural resources and development of manufacturing industries. Sifton stated his views in a speech made in 1896: "The place to which our merchants and manufacturers of eastern Canada must look for enlarged markets is Manitoba and the North West Territories. There will be no markets until we have the population." He set out boldly to bring that population to western Canada.

Sifton believed that the best possible immigrants for western Canada were hardy peasant farmers. These men and women were more likely to be able to endure the harsh conditions and humble circumstances of pioneer life. Sifton offered the following description of the ideal immigrant: "I think a stalwart peasant in a sheepskin coat, born on the soil, whose forefathers have been farmers for generations, with a stout wife and a half-dozen children, is good quality." Many of these settlers came from dryland regions of central and eastern Europe, where conditions are similar to those of the Canadian Prairies.

Such people, Sifton argued, would bring Canada the best possible return on its investment, year after year. He began a major advertising campaign in Europe, Britain and the United States. The Canadian government offered 160 acres [65 ha] of free land on the Prairies to would-be immigrants, and promised to pay their passage to Canada.

Advertisements such as this were used throughout Europe to attract settlers to western Canada. Do you think the image of western Canada shown by the poster was realistic? Explain your answer.

Sifton's views angered many English Canadians. They regarded his "peasants in sheepskin coats" with suspicion at best, more often with undisguised hostility. They regarded the ideal immigrant as being of "the right class of British immigrant from the Old Land." A prominent Conservative politician rebuked Sifton saying: "The quality of population counts much more than the quantity. Five thousand first-class immigrants are much better than 50 000 of a class that it would take a generation or two to bring up to the right standard." Fortunately for Canada, Sifton's views prevailed.

Clifford Sifton was Minister of Immigration from 1896 to 1905. In those years, the population of western Canada grew from 300 000 people to more than one million. Soon there were thousands of family grain farms in Manitoba and the North West Territories. By 1905, western Canadian farmers were producing more than 2 million tonnes of wheat each year. Sifton could say proudly "the world's bread basket is western Canada."

Sifton's immigration policies added a new dimension to the population of Canada. Drawn by the promise of free land and increased opportunities, hundreds of thousands of European immigrants– Germans, Poles, Ukrainians and Scandinavians–came to Canada. A Winnipeg clergyman and political leader, J.S. Woodsworth, recognized both the promise and the problems of such immigration. In "Strangers at our Gate," an anti-immigration pamphlet written in 1909, he noted:

Within the past decade, a nation has been born. English and Russians, French and Germans, Austrians and Italians, Japanese and Hindus–a mixed multitude, they are being dumped into Canada by a kind of endless chain. They sort themselves out after a fashion, and each seeks to find a corner somewhere. But how shall we weld this heterogeneous mass into one people? This is our problem.

1. What development made large-scale settlement of the West possible? How did this settlement change the Prairie landscape?
2. (a) Why did Clifford Sifton advocate large-scale immigration and settlement of the West? Do you think his position was a wise one? Why?
   (b) What would Canada be like today if a more restricted immigration policy had been followed? Would this be a good or bad thing? Why?

3. Who did Sifton feel would make the best settlers for western Canada? Why did he feel this way? Why did some people disagree with him?
4. What did the federal government do to attract settlers to the West during the 1890s? What did the CPR do? Why?

The Klondike Gold Rush

Mineral exploration was being carried out all over Canada in the late 1890s. Gold, silver and metals for industrial use were being mined in British Columbia and on the Canadian Shield. Other prospectors were pushing northward into the areas along the Klondike and Yukon rivers. One day, in 1896, a prospector named Robert Henderson told his friends: "Go to Bonanza Creek, boys. You're sure to find gold there."

George Washington Carmack and two Native companions, Tagish Charlie and Skookum Jim, took Henderson's advice and began panning for gold in the creek. On August 17, 1896, they struck paydirt: a single shovelful of gravel yielded ten dollars worth of gold. Henderson had been right. There was gold along the Klondike.

News of the Bonanza Creek discovery soon spread, carried by newspapers in New York, Toronto, London and San Francisco. Thousands of men and women read the stories of the riches to be found in the Yukon. They travelled by train or ship to Vancouver, Victoria, Seattle or Edmonton, jumping off points for the Klondike Gold Rush. In these cities, the would-be prospectors loaded up with supplies, then began the long journey north. A few travelled overland from Edmonton, but most sailed to Alaska. Life aboard ship was rough and dangerous. Many of the gold seekers were seasick. Some gambled away all of their money and supplies during the voyage. Others never reached the north at all; their ships were lost on the stormy seas of the North Pacific.

Those Klondike-bound prospectors who survived the voyage came ashore at Skagway, Alaska, a lawless, violent frontier town. From there, the gold seekers set out on foot over the steep Chilkoot Pass into Canada. They stopped on the shores of Lake Bennett to build boats, which they used to travel north along the lake. Then they followed the Yukon River north of Dawson where the richest gold fields had been discovered.

Tens of thousands of miners made the difficult trip north to Dawson. By 1900, the gold rush had made Dawson the largest town

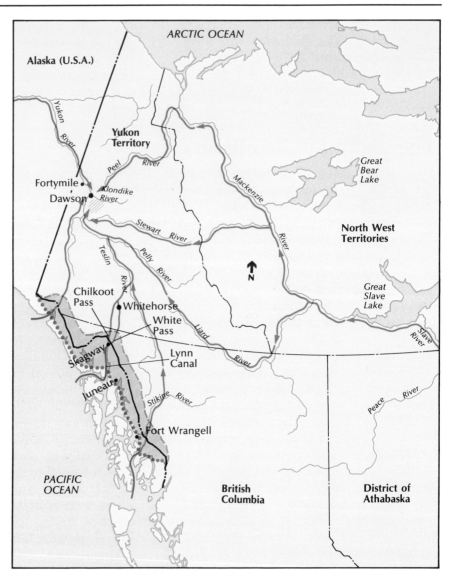

The shortest routes to the gold fields involved crossing the Alaska Panhandle, an area whose boundaries were in dispute. Alternate routes involved long, hard journeys up wild northern rivers.

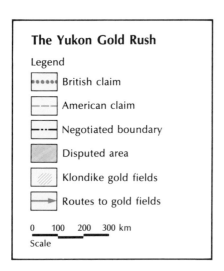

The Yukon Gold Rush

Legend

•••••• British claim

— · — American claim

— ·· — Negotiated boundary

Disputed area

Klondike gold fields

→ Routes to gold fields

0   100   200   300 km

Scale

in Canada west of Winnipeg. The town's population grew as a steady stream of people arrived by sternwheelers travelling along the Yukon River. They brought not only miners but gamblers, tourists, thieves, journalists, dance-hall girls and merchants. All of them were seeking to profit from the gold rush.

The sudden arrival of thousands of people in the region caused concern in Ottawa. The Canadian government had received reports of the lawless conditions in Skagway, and officials were also con-

While miners worked getting gold from the streams and rock, others worked getting gold from the miners' pockets. This is a street in Dawson at the height of the gold rush.

cerned about the large number of American miners pouring into the Klondike. A detachment of Mounted Police officers, among them Sam Steele, was sent there to maintain law and order. In 1898, the western section of the North West Territories was officially incorporated as the Yukon Territory, with its capital at Dawson. From this location, the Mounted Police could patrol the area more effectively.

ALASKA BOUNDARY DISPUTE

When the United States bought Alaska from Russia in 1867, it acquired a "panhandle" of territory extending as far south as 54°40' (see the map on page 216). A long-standing dispute between Canada and the U.S. over this region came to a head during the Klondike Gold Rush. The U.S. claimed the entire coastline of the panhandle, which is deeply cut by long fiords. Canada demanded control over the heads of certain fiords, especially the Lynn Canal, which gave access to the Yukon. Negotiations through the Joint High Commission of 1898-1899 failed to resolve the dispute.

The matter was then referred to an international tribunal composed of three American judges, two Canadian judges, and Lord Alverstone, Lord Chief Justice of Britain. Alverstone sided with the Americans, supporting their claim to a boundary line lying behind the heads of the fiords. The result was a wave of angry anti-British and anti-American sentiments in Canada. Prime Minister Sir Wilfrid Laurier asserted that Canada's lack of treaty-making power, as the Dominion was still technically a British colony in international matters, made it difficult for the country to assert itself in international disputes.

The boom of the gold rush ended a few years later. Some of the miners had made great fortunes along the Klondike. One young man made $40 000 during one winter's digging, 10 percent of which was collected by the NWMP for payments of royalties to the federal government. Many others left the Yukon with just what they had when they arrived. Dawson became little more than a ghost town, but the Klondike Gold Rush had left its mark on the history of Canada.

Alberta and Saskatchewan Become Provinces

Population growth and plentiful harvest brought prosperity to Canada's West during the opening years of the twentieth century. Where great herds of buffalo had roamed thirty years earlier, there was now a checkerboard pattern of grain farms. Small towns and villages marked by tall grain elevators could be seen at regular intervals along the railway lines. A network of roads and rail lines linked these small farming communities to fast growing cities such as Calgary, Edmonton and Regina.

In the large cities and small towns of the North West Territories, citizens were beginning to seek a greater say in how they were governed. Responsible government had been granted to the North West Territories in 1891, but the Territories' budget was still controlled by Ottawa until 1897. In 1905, the federal government decided that the people living between Manitoba and British Columbia were ready for their own provincial governments. The acts that created these new governments were set by the federal government without any negotiation with the people of the region.

On September 1, 1905, two new provinces were added to Confederation. The North West Territories south of the sixtieth parallel was divided into two sections. The western province was named Alberta, after Queen Victoria's husband Prince Albert. The eastern part of the territory became the province of Saskatchewan a name taken from the Cree word for "swift-flowing." The sparsely settled area north of the sixtieth parallel remained known as the Northwest Territories. It was governed directly from Ottawa until the establishment of a territorial capital at Yellowknife in 1967.

There had been little opposition to the two Prairie provinces' entry into Confederation. The West was booming. Its farms were prosperous and more settlers were arriving each day. The railway

Western Boundaries, 1905

By 1905, the boundaries of the three western provinces were established. The boundaries of Manitoba were extended in 1881 and 1884 and finally set along their present lines in 1912.

had been built, and mail service and telegraph lines linked the Prairies to all parts of Canada. The people of Alberta and Saskatchewan were proud of their new provincial status.

Three controversial issues, however, marked the entry of the two new provinces into Confederation.

One issue involved the location of the boundaries and capital cities which had been decided by the government in Ottawa. Albertans wanted their eastern boundary at 110° west latitude, but had to accept 107°. Within Alberta, rivalry developed between Calgary and Edmonton over which was to be the capital city. The dispute was settled in favor of Edmonton. Regina, previously capital of the North West Territories, became Saskatchewan's capital.

The second issue was the question of separate schools for Catholics. The Conservatives had greatly angered many English- and French-speaking Catholics over their handling of the Manitoba schools question a few years earlier. Now, the Liberals, led by Sir Wilfrid Laurier, would take steps to ensure that a separate Catholic school system would exist in each of the new provinces. This action upset some of Laurier's Protestant cabinet ministers, among them Clifford Sifton. When Sir Wilfrid Laurier took part in the ceremonies in Edmonton on September 1, 1905, marking that province's birth, Sifton was not there. The man who had played such a big part in bringing settlers to the West had resigned as minister of immigration over the separate schools issue.

The third and most enduring controversy arose from the federal government's retention of control over crown lands and mineral resources. Twenty-five years would pass before these responsibilities were transferred to Alberta and Saskatchewan. In the 1970s and early 1980s, federal-provincial conflicts over control of energy resources brought back bitter memories of this controversy.

1. Describe the political process used by the federal government in the creation of the provinces of Alberta and Saskatchewan.

Summary

The Prairie region of Canada changed dramatically between 1871 and 1905. The Canadian government created the North West Mounted Police in 1873 because of fears that American westward expansion might spill over into the Prairies. One of the NWMP's first duties was to keep out American whisky traders. The force also helped to negotiate treaties with the Native peoples of the Prairies during the 1870s. These treaties were intended to prevent the bloody conflicts between Native peoples and settlers that were taking place in the United States. The treaties resulted in the creation of reserves for Native peoples, ending their nomadic, hunting way of life forever and making them dependent on the government for support.

Construction of a transcontinental railway was one of the conditions on which British Columbia entered Confederation in 1871. The railway was to be completed in ten years. However, because of political and financial problems, the last spike of the Canadian Pacific Railway was not driven until 1885. The construction of the Canadian Shield and Western Cordillera portions of the railway proved to be enormously difficult and expensive.

The coming of the railway greatly altered the West. Faced with the loss of their traditional ways of life, the Native peoples and Métis rebelled against the Canadian intruders in 1885. Both the NWMP and the CPR played important roles in the suppression of the North West Rebellion, led by Louis Riel. Riel's arrest and subsequent execution deepened the divisions between English- and French-speaking Canadians.

Completion of the railway greatly changed both the landscape and the population of the West. The trains carried large numbers of immigrants, mostly from northern and eastern Europe, attracted to the West by grants of free land. Two new provinces, Alberta and Saskatchewan, were created as a result of the rapid settlement of the Prairies. Further north, the Klondike Gold Rush led to the creation of the Yukon Territory.

REVIEW

Checking Back

1. Write one or two sentences to summarize the role each of the following played in the history of the West.

   North West Mounted Police
   aboriginal rights
   "Pacific Scandal"
   Bonanza Creek

   Battle of Duck Lake
   Manitoba schools question
   "Harvest Specials"
   Alaska boundary dispute

2. How did the arrival of the North West Mounted Police and, later, the CPR, affect the Native peoples of the West?

3. Record two pieces of evidence that suggest the government of Canada did not understand the Native people's attitudes towards the Prairies.

4. What problems did Macdonald have to overcome in order to fulfil his promise to British Columbia of a transcontinental railway?

5. Why did the strategies that brought success to Riel in 1870 fail in the Rebellion of 1885?

Using Your Knowledge

6. Imagine that you are watching a debate between Louis Riel and Sir John A. Macdonald. Write a dialogue for the debate.

7. Wilfrid Laurier said "If I had been on the banks of the Saskatchewan, I would have shouldered my musket too." Do you agree or disagree with Laurier? Support your point of view with facts.

8. Explain how the Manitoba schools question described in the close-up on page 211 is linked to issues which have not been resolved since the time of Riel.

9. Design an advertisement to encourage immigration to Canada's West in the year 1890. Now create an advertisement for modern-day immigrants.

10. How did Clifford Sifton change the West?

11. Suppose you are a Prairie farmer in the year 1896. Will you leave your farm to pan for gold in the Klondike? Give the reasons for your decision.

12. In your own words, summarize the three controversies that developed over the creation of the provinces of Alberta and Saskatchewan. Explain how each controversy was settled.

UNIT 3

CANADA'S ECONOMIC ACTIVITIES

Chapter 11

Canada's Changing Economy

The story of Canada's economy is a fascinating one. From the early days of fishing and furs to the computerized offices of the present, it has been the interaction of people and resources that has created our economy.

The Canadian economy was originally based on the extraction of **natural resources,** first by Native peoples and later by Europeans. As you saw in earlier chapters, the various Native peoples of western Canada had a traditional economy based on hunting, food-gathering and trading between tribes. Following Native routes, and often led by Native guides, the first European fur traders used the network of lakes and rivers stretching throughout the country to get the natural resources they wanted. The early nineteenth century timber trade of the Maritimes and the St. Lawrence Valley was an early use of the forest resource in Canada. Farming often followed the cutting of the forest. Other examples of the extraction of natural resources include the Fraser and Cariboo "gold rushes" of the 1850s, described in Chapters 9 and 10.

This early period of the Canadian economy was followed by a stage in which resources were not merely extracted, but also **processed.** Wood from the forests was turned into ships' timber and railway ties; iron ore was smelted and refined into farm implements and other tools; wheat was ground into flour. This second stage began around the middle of the nineteenth century in eastern Canada, but not until the late nineteenth century in western Canada.

Since roughly the middle of the twentieth century, our economy has entered a third stage. Most working Canadians now earn their living in **service industries,** rather than in activities which directly involve the extraction and processing of resources.

The first section of this chapter will provide definitions of some key economic concepts. An understanding of these concepts will help you to better appreciate the development of the Canadian economy. The chapter's next section will look at this development in each of the five major regions of Canada. The final section will provide you with an overview of how changes in the structure of our economy have led to changes in the lives of working Canadians. As you read the chapter, consider these key questions:

- What is an "economy"? an "economic region"?
- What are the five major economic regions of Canada?
- What resources were important in the early development of each of the regions?
- What have been the major resource-processing industries in each of the regions?
- How is the growth of service industries changing the Canadian economy?
- How do changes in Canadian society and changes in the Canadian economy affect each other?

Key Economic Concepts: Some Definitions

The concept "economy" often suggests a picture of rich bankers in pinstripe suits, with charts of complicated figures in front of them. Yet the economy is far wider than this picture. The economy is just as much something that happens at home as it is something to do with banks. In fact, the word "economy" comes from Greek and Latin words meaning "management of the household." No less than the bankers, you and your family are participants in the economy of Canada. In its most common understanding, an economy might be defined as a process of buying and selling goods and services.

Let us take a common household item–the television set–and look at how it represents the three basic kinds of economic activities. These are **production, exchange** and **consumption**. Each of these three can be broken down into further kinds of activities.

In the economic sense of the term, production means the action by which goods and services are created or brought about. Production usually begins when **raw materials** are harvested from nature. A raw material is anything that people use to make something else: most of the components of the television set originated as minerals.

Because the harvesting of raw materials must occur at the beginning, activities of this nature are called **primary activities**.

Some aspects of production are **secondary activities**, those in which the value of resources is increased by changing their form. The metals used for the television set had to be transformed or manufactured into parts, which were then assembled. "Manufacturing" means the processing of raw material into another form.

Economists distinguish between two basic kinds of exchange: of location and of ownership. When your television set was shipped from the factory where it was manufactured, an exchange of location took place. The manufacturer who sold the television set to the store was involved in an exchange of ownership, just as was the store which in turn sold the set to your family.

Consumption means the use of an object or service by people to satisfy their needs or desires. If you buy and use toothpaste advertised on television, you are "consuming" the toothpaste.

The toothpaste and the television set are both examples of a **finished product**. Most items which consumers buy and use are finished products. **Semifinished products** are items which are exchanged but are not ready to be consumed. For example, the casing for the television set may have been manufactured by one company which in turn sold it to a second company. In the assembly of the television set, the second company will use the casing, or "semifinished product," to make the television set, or "finished product."

Some types of activities do not fit neatly into any of our production, exchange or consumption categories. For example, into which category do insurance companies, teachers, or social workers fit? These service functions are grouped together as **tertiary activities**: they include jobs that do not fit into primary (getting the raw materials) or secondary (making the products) activities.

Another key concept in understanding an economy is **capital**; we usually think of capital as money. More specifically, capital can be defined as the amount of money or property used to carry on economic activity. Businesses use capital to buy machinery or equipment needed for their activity, and to buy the raw materials they require to make their products.

On a personal or family level, capital has two basic uses. The first is to obtain necessities: food, clothing and shelter; all those things which we must have just in order to stay alive. The second use of capital is to obtain luxuries: a new television set, or a trip during summer vacation; all those things which may make us happier, but

Describe the pattern of growth shown by the statistics in the table. What factors might have accounted for the decrease in number of workers between 1951 and 1961?

which we do not need in order to stay alive. Because most households have a limited supply of capital, families must make decisions about how to spend their money. Some families have to use all their capital just for necessities. More fortunate families have enough left over for luxuries. Most families must manage their capital, often by setting up a budget. Your money (capital) is important in Canada's economic system. Your capital is the means by which you can purchase, and then consume, goods and services.

Growth in Manufacturing in Canada—1921-1981

	1921	1931	1941	1951	1961	1971	1981
Number of Establishments	20 836	23 049	26 241	37 021	33 357	31 908	35 395
Number of Workers	371 253	437 041	801 931	1 010 588	939 413	1 167 810	1 884 400
Salaries and Wages (000s$)	370 934	415 197	977 906	2 459 566	5 701 651	12 129 897	37 415 600

Source: Statistics Canada

Growth of Selected Canadian Manufacturing Industries—1921-1981

	1921	1931	1941	1951	1961	1971	1981
Number of Textile Manufacturing Plants	343	378	509	892	884	915	952
Number of Rubber & Plastic Manufacturing Plants	44	48	56	67	93	664	1030
Number of Wood Industry Manufacturing Plants	4716	5193	6905	11 976	5243	3164	3394

Source: Statistics Canada

Which of the three industry groups in the table showed the largest increase in number of plants since 1961? Suggest some reasons for this growth.

1. In your own words, explain what is meant by these terms.
   economy   semifinished product   consumer
   raw material   capital

2. Give two examples of each of the three major types of economic activity: primary, secondary, and tertiary.

HOW GOVERNMENTS "BUDGET": LOOKING AT YOUR SCHOOL SYSTEM

The various levels of government in Canada also have to manage their capital. They must do so in order to provide the goods and services that the Canadian people need and want. To help you understand how governments have to "manage their capital," consider the operation of schools. Some of the school board's money comes in the form of local property taxes; other money comes in the form of grants from the provincial government. Therefore, both your local and provincial governments are involved in the production of educational services. To provide these services, schools must be built and maintained, teachers' and caretakers' salaries paid, and textbooks purchased. Both your provincial government and your local school board have to "budget" their available capital in order to decide how to divide the money among these items.

Since the school system is only one responsibility of your local and provincial governments, education is often affected by the expenses involved in other government responsibilities. For example, if more money is spent to provide services such as highways and hospitals, less money may remain for education.

Canada's Economic Regions

Your community is made up of different individual households: some big, some small; some rich, some poor; some with many skills, some with few. Likewise, Canada itself is made up of different groups of communities. When the communities within an area share common economic activities, economists say that this area is an **economic region**. Since the economic activities of one area are often very different from those of another, the idea of economic regions helps us to understand the differences.

Depending on the criteria used, the mapping of Canada's economic regions can be very broad and general, or very narrow and specific. A "broad" mapping would show a small number of large regions, such as the Atlantic Provinces or the North. A "narrow" mapping would show a large number of small regions: the Lower Mainland or the Central Business District of a community. This chapter will use a broad definition of economic region. The five regions you will study are shown on the map on page 228. In many ways, as you may notice, some of these regions correspond to regions based on physical geography.

Each of these economic regions could be further subdivided. Some of the subregions would be centred on sizable urban centres, others would have very little population within them; some would be based on one kind of resource or industry; other subregions would have a variety of activities. This chapter will make some

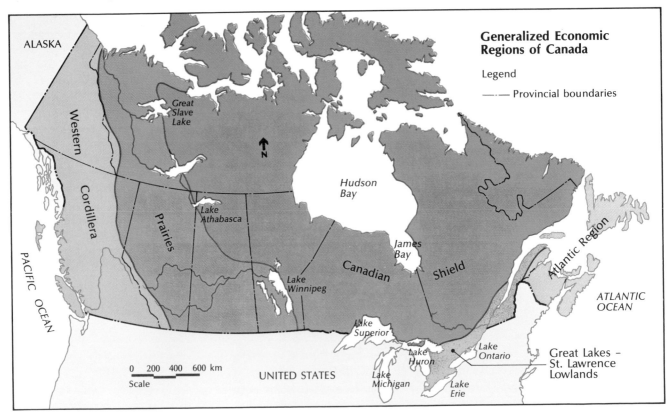

Generalized Economic Regions of Canada

Legend

—·— Provincial boundaries

Places which share economic features can be grouped together to form an economic region. Can you suggest one or two industries found in each of the economic regions shown?

references to such subregions, but the emphasis will be upon five broad regions: the Atlantic, the Great Lakes-St. Lawrence Lowlands, the Canadian Shield, the Prairies, and the Western Cordillera.

The Atlantic Region

In 1497, John Cabot and a crew of eighteen men sailed from England for the shores of North America. This voyage marks the beginning of the non-Native portion of Canadian economic history. Cabot took back news of seas teeming with fish, which prompted further English voyages to the New World. Yearly fishing expeditions to the coastal areas of what are today Newfoundland and Nova Scotia began almost immediately. French as well as Portuguese ships also began to search for fish in the rich coastal waters over the Grand Banks and other shallow water "bank" areas.

With their plentiful supplies of salt, the French and Portuguese fishermen used this method to preserve the fish. The fishermen caught the fish and then stored them in barrels of heavily salted water, or "brine." This method, called the "green" or "wet" fishery, meant that ships did not have to land. Therefore, no French settlements occurred along the coasts at this time.

The British, with poor supplies of salt, had a different method for fish preservation. The fish were caught, brought ashore, cut open and allowed to dry on drying racks or "flakes." The warm summer sun and winds soon dried the fish so that they could be shipped long distances, even to tropical areas, without spoiling. This "dry" method required the fishermen to land and establish some sort of permanent base on the coast. In 1610, the English began a winter settlement on the shores of Conception Bay in Newfoundland, close to the fishing grounds.

Codfish provided the staple diet for the British navy and for all ships' crews sailing to hot climates. Several towns in England depended on profits from the fisheries. While much of the fish caught by British fishermen was used to feed the population of Britain, other markets were developed as well. Some of these markets were in the colonies which Britain had established in the West Indies. Cheap food in the form of dried fish was exported to these colonies to feed the slaves who produced tobacco, fruit and sugar for Britain. The sale of fish to Spain provided gold and silver for Britain.

As demand for North Atlantic cod grew, more and more ships sailed to Newfoundland to catch fish for sale in Spanish and other markets. These ships sailed to the New World without a cargo. It was not long before the ship owners were looking for settlers they could carry to the new lands. Even so, estimates put the population of Newfoundland at fewer than 2000 by 1650.

In other parts of the Atlantic region, the climate and physical conditions were less harsh than in Newfoundland. Here, the population grew a little more rapidly. Land was more easily farmed, even if forests had to be cleared to make farmland. The felled trees, viewed as a nuisance by the struggling farmers, were usually burned. The earliest Maritime farmers were the Acadians who grew peas and wheat in the fertile marshes around the Bay of Fundy. Three decades after the 1755 Expulsion of the Acadians by British Forces, the Maritimes saw the arrival of Loyalists. Many of the Loyalists took up farming, both around the Bay of Fundy and in inland areas.

In the early nineteenth century, the agricultural development of the Atlantic region was hampered by competition from the United

States. Nova Scotian farmers did raise livestock and dairy products because these products were costly to transport from the United States. They avoided growing wheat, as the Acadians had done, because it was now cheaper to get it from the United States. As well, a lack of population and good roads in the Atlantic region meant that transport and markets for farm products were limited. Investment money and business interests were focussed on overseas trade rather than on local agriculture. The farmers had little incentive to produce a surplus over and above their own requirements. In the 1830s, however, Prince Edward Island began to export some wheat to Britain. At about the same time, Prince Edward Island farmers began to harvest crops of potatoes.

The timber of the Atlantic region was eventually to become important as an export product. By the early 1800s, England's forests had become largely depleted. A French naval blockade of Britain during the French Revolutionary Wars cut the British off from their foreign sources of lumber in Scandinavia and Northern Europe. Thus, Britain had turned to the lumber from Canada's forests. In the hills of central New Brunswick and Nova Scotia, an economic region based on lumber began to take shape. At first, the pine forests of Nova Scotia provided the Halifax dockyard with masts to repair the naval ships of Britain damaged in conflicts or in storms. Soon, the dockyards in England relied on New Brunswick for pine masts.

By mid-century, the Port of Saint John had developed its own shipbuilding industry, and had become one of the largest building centres in the world. But the transition from wooden clipper ships to iron steamships by the 1890s, effectively ended the Maritime shipbuilding industry.

In later years, the forests of the Atlantic region were used for purposes other than shipbuilding. In central Newfoundland and New Brunswick, pulp and paper mills were built to produce newsprint for the large newspapers of British, American and Canadian cities. Their locations were based on the abundant forests and on hydro power sites that could be developed easily. The plants were located where rivers emptied into lakes, or into the Atlantic. Such locations allowed for cheap water transportation. The economic subregions based on pulp and paper exist today, little changed over the last fifty or sixty years. For example, the Abitibi-Price pulp mill in Grand Falls, Newfoundland, and the New Brunswick International Paper Company newsprint mill at Dalhousie, New Brunswick, are still vital to their respective communities.

Sawmills and fish processing plants are two activities that still flourish in the Atlantic region. Their locations are related to their source of the raw materials. The numbers and sizes of the processing plants have varied since the turn of the century. Many smaller sawmills have closed because of an inability to compete, a lack of demand for lumber or a lack of quality wood.

In the nineteenth century, some mining of coal began on Nova Scotia's Cape Breton Island to supply local steam engines. By the time of Confederation, Cape Breton coal miners were producing two-thirds of all coal mined in Canada. A small manufacturing subregion developed on Cape Breton Island around Sydney. It was based on the manufacture of iron and steel, using furnaces fuelled by coal. The major advantages for location here were the local supply of coal and cheap transport of iron ore across the 150 km stretch of the Cabot Strait from Newfoundland.

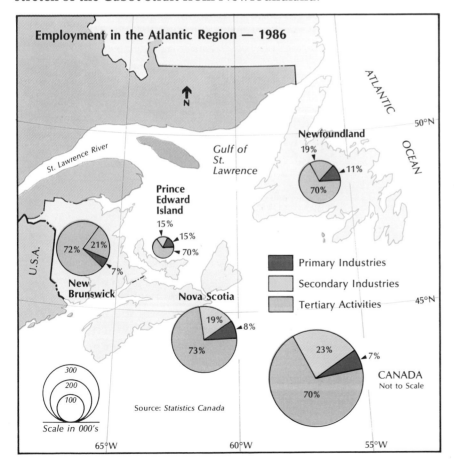

Employment in the Atlantic Region — 1986

How does employment in the Atlantic region compare to the Canadian average?

Unfortunately, the Atlantic region does not have a sufficiently large population to act as a market for goods produced by large manufacturers. In general, manufacturing in the region consists of simple processing. The region has only a few plants producing complex manufactured goods, notably the three Michelin tire plants in Nova Scotia. One food processing firm, McCain's of New Brunswick, does a worldwide business in frozen foods.

During the twentieth century, the size of the Atlantic region's economy has declined proportionate to the size of the national economy. In 1890, the three Maritime provinces accounted for 16 percent of the nation's total economic activity. This figure had shrunk to 3.5 percent by 1980. (If Newfoundland is included, the figure is 4.5 percent.) This loss in relative economic strength shows the poor performance of this region's economy. Other parts of the country have simply grown and developed at a faster rate. Differences in economic performance, **regional disparities** as economists call them, are found in other parts of Canada as well. But, in no other region have they persisted for as long as in Atlantic Canada.

1. Explain the difference between the wet and dry fisheries of the seventeenth century in the Atlantic region. How did each one affect patterns of settlement?
2. In your own words, summarize the development of each of these industries in the Atlantic region: (a) agriculture; (b) timber.

Great Lakes-St. Lawrence Lowlands

When Samuel de Champlain arrived at the site of present-day Quebec City in 1608, he met groups of Algonquian Natives, such as the Montagnais. These tribes, plus the Hurons of the Great Lakes area, soon proved useful to the French. They provided the furs–especially beaver–that brought high prices back in France, where beaver hats had become the fashion. Here was the beginning of a second economic region, one based on the fur trade. The French fur traders were able to procure large quantities of beaver pelts through their contact with the skilled Indian trappers and hunters. The French influence spread along the St. Lawrence and up the Ottawa and Saguenay rivers as the search for high quality furs expanded.

A trading system in the Great Lakes-St. Lawrence region, with its base in Quebec City, was firmly established by 1623. The Huron Indians, who were semi-agricultural, supplied northern tribes with food and European goods which they had received in exchange for furs traded to the French. This system was an obvious advantage to the French, as it cut their travel time and costs and therefore increased their profit in the markets of Europe.

In order to make the fur trade still more efficient, the French formed trading companies. These companies were more organized and productive than individuals or small groups trading on their own. The French government awarded control of the fur trade to these companies on the condition that they bring settlers from France. Generally, this settlement was not effectively carried out. Many of the men who came to New France were reluctant to work as farmers. They preferred to lead the life of *coureur-de-bois* ("runners of the woods"), travelling the forests and waterways in search of furs.

The few agricultural settlements that did get started were not very successful. When Champlain died in 1635, there were fewer than twenty-five actual settlers at Quebec; thirty years later, there were only 2500 settlers in all of New France. (This figure was less than 1 percent of the population of the British colonies to the south.) Those who were farming only produced goods for themselves, or for the few people in the settlements. By 1663, the economic situation of New France had become so difficult that the French government took direct control of the colony out of the hands of the companies. Over the next decade, increased immigration, directly sponsored by the government of France, enlarged the tiny population along the St. Lawrence to about 7000. Small farming settlements began to grow up along the banks of the river, yet furs remained the economic staple of the Great Lakes-St. Lawrence region in the era of New France. By the middle of the eighteenth century, fur trading still accounted for about 70 percent of New France's exports.

By the time of the British Conquest in 1759 (see page 3), New France had a population of about 60 000. British settlers began moving into the area, especially Loyalists fleeing the rebellion in the United States. While the French had burned the forests to clear the land, the British saw a commercial value in the forest. A shortage of English oak – an important timber in the construction of ships – caused the British to search for new supplies in their colonies. In the early years of the nineteenth century the British naval timber trade began to shift to Quebec, obtaining pine for masts and oak for the hulls and planking. The navy could obtain all the timber it needed from the St. Lawrence Lowlands, but the price was high due to high transportation costs. In order to assure Canadian companies of a reasonable profit from this industry, Britain placed high import taxes on timber coming in from Scandinavia and other countries. Thus, for the British, Canadian timber became cheaper than other sources, and the Canadian timber industry flourished.

It was not long until the Ottawa Valley had a booming lumber industry. Trees were cut, rafted down the river and shipped to England. The cutting of "square timber" for export to Britain tended to be wasteful. First of all, only the best trees were cut; then these trees had their four sides made flat by a broad axe, so the timber would pack tightly.

The centres of lumbering moved steadily inland. By 1820, rafts were coming down the St. Lawrence River from the eastern end of Lake Ontario. But, by 1840, lumber was arriving in Quebec from the Lake Huron area.

In the first decade of the twentieth century, lumber was the main Canadian export. The forests of the St. Lawrence Valley, the Ottawa Valley and the Great Lakes Lowlands were the main sources of the timber. Agriculture quickly followed lumbering, with the lands cleared of timber used for farming. Quebec agriculture shifted from wheat-growing, for which the local soils were not especially suitable, to dairying and stock-raising, meeting the needs of the growing

This painting shows the entrance to the Rideau Canal at Bytown in 1839. Notice the rafts of square timbers. This was the most efficient way of transporting the timber to the Port at Quebec City.

communities. In Ontario, different areas of the province developed their own specializations: orchard farming in the Niagara area, tobacco in the southwestern end of the province.

The mineral resources of the Great Lakes-St. Lawrence region were also developed to some extent during the eighteenth and early nineteenth centuries. Iron was first made in Canada by the Forges St. Maurice, near Trois Rivières, Quebec, in 1733. In 1822, the Marmora Ironworks, near Peterborough, Ontario, began operating. It was, at that time, one of the most technologically advanced ironworks in North America. In both places, the iron was processed from local sources of ore.

In western Ontario in the late 1850s, a Welshman named John Williams drilled wells that produced the first oil in North America; as well, Williams built a small refinery. Until the advent of the automobile in the early twentieth century, these small Ontario refineries converted the raw petroleum into buggy-wheel grease and kerosene lamp fuel for sale to the local market. The oil and gas fields in Ontario were too small to lead to large-scale developments, yet, these early refineries would provide a basis for later expansion of the industry.

The development of manufacturing in the Great Lakes-St. Lawrence Lowlands was greatly influenced by the region's geographical position. The late nineteenth century saw the concentration of manufacturing and capital in the northeastern part of the United States. It was inevitable that the Canadian businesses in the Great Lakes-St. Lawrence Lowlands, closest to this centre of American activity, should benefit from the new inventions, the easy movement of people and ideas, and the capital. The other regions of Canada were not able to take the same advantage of this growth because they were not as well endowed with population, rail and water connections linking the centres of population, available capital for investment, or sources of energy.

Manufacturing plants using raw materials from local primary industries produced iron and steel ingots, sawn lumber, pulp and paper, packaged fish, milled flour, beer and other alcoholic beverages. Hamilton, Ontario, became the early centre of heavy manufacturing because of its protected harbor and its location, roughly midway between iron ore from the Lake Superior region and coal from Pennsylvania.

As the United States developed into the world's foremost industrial and financial economy, American businesses began to influence the Canadian economy. Troubled by this outside presence, the

Workers in the bar mill at Stelco in Hamilton, Ontario, circa 1915. Note the absence of protective equipment.

Canadian government erected tariff barriers to protect young Canadian manufacturing industries against competition from products manufactured in the United States. To get around these tariffs, American companies established "branch-plant" operations in Canada to manufacture goods locally, using Canadian labor. The automobile, paper, chemicals and electrical products industries in Canada were (and are) almost all branch plants. These operations were set up mostly in southern Ontario and southern Quebec. Here there was hydro power, an efficient modern transportation system, and productive agriculture already in place. There were few barriers to the growth of these branch plants.

The extent of American involvement in the Canadian economy can be seen by examining the amount of foreign investment in Canada. The American portion of foreign investment in Canada grew from 14 percent in 1900 to over 80 percent in 1985. During the same period, Great Britain's investment dropped from 85 percent to less than 10 percent. The American influence in the Canadian economy will be examined in detail in Chapter 13.

1. What was the first dominant economic activity of the Great Lakes-St. Lawrence region? Which activity was next? What is the dominant activity today?
2. What advantages does the Great Lakes-St. Lawrence region have as a centre of manufacturing?

The Canadian Shield

As in the Great Lakes-St. Lawrence Lowlands, the fur trade was the Canadian Shield's first industry. Around 1700, as the fur bearing animal populations of the lowlands region became depleted, the fur trade began to move into the Shield. It continued over the next century until British-French and HBC-NWC rivalries pushed the centre of the fur trade further west.

With the decline of the Shield's fur trade in the early nineteenth century, timber became the region's predominant resource. However, unlike the Great Lakes-St. Lawrence Lowlands, where lands cleared of forest were eventually farmed, the cleared timberlands of the Shield did not prove suitable for agriculture. Consequently, the region remained dependent on foresty alone. By the 1840s, Britain began to lower its tariffs on the price of Scandinavian lumber. The square timber of the Shield that had been so much in demand could no longer compete in Britain. Exports of this product declined, along with the economic fortunes of the region, until new markets were found in the United States.

In the early twentieth century, mining became an important industry of the Shield, beginning in the Sudbury area. Mining then spread into northern and northwestern Ontario and east into northern Quebec. The mining companies set up plants to process the ore, further developing the economy of the area. The plants "concentrated" the metals and thus reduced shipping costs to smelters outside the region. Concentration is a process by which the waste rock of the ore is removed, leaving the valuable mineral in a more pure form. Hydro plants provided the mining companies with inexpensive energy supplies.

Private American capital was responsible for the development of iron ore mines in Quebec and Labrador, particularly during the two decades before and after World War II. The economic subregion that resulted, centred around Sept Îles and Labrador City, soon had railway links, hydro installations, concentrator mills, and ocean ports. This mining area, in a remote part of the Shield, fell on hard times in the 1980s.

As the railway was extended farther north and east during the early part of this century, the economic importance of the Shield expanded. Lumber and pulp and paper mills, utilizing the boreal forests of the region, developed near the southern edge of the Shield, close to water and hydro power. The plants are large and

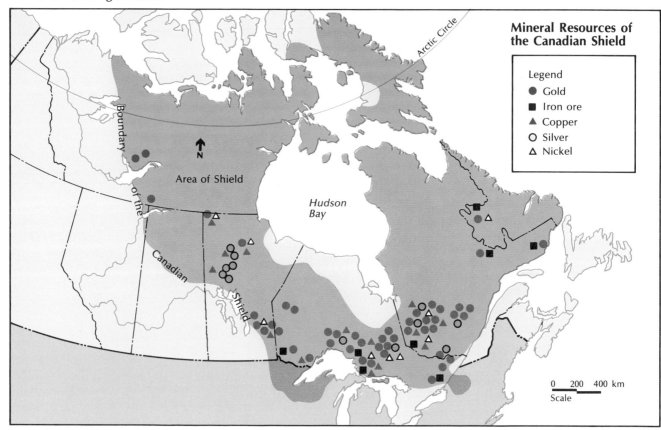

Mineral Resources of the Canadian Shield

Legend
● Gold
■ Iron ore
▲ Copper
○ Silver
△ Nickel

What problems are associated with mining in the Canadian Shield?

efficient; their market is the large newspapers of cities in the southern part of the country and in the United States.

Several new mills in the Shield, such as that at Amos in northwestern Quebec, have been built in the past two or three decades. Such mills have often been subsidized by the government, especially in Quebec. Government money helps these remote towns to build the necessary services like schools and hospitals.

The pattern of capital investment in the Canadian Shield since the 1950s shows a substantial increase in foreign, especially American, investment. These investments have brought with them an advanced technology which has strongly stimulated the economic growth of the Canadian Shield.

1. When and where did mining become important on the Canadian Shield?
2. Why would it be advantageous for mines to be located near railways and near sources of hydro power?

The Prairies

The activities of the Hudson's Bay Company were a major influence on the early economy of the Prairies, since many of the rivers flowing into Hudson Bay also flow through the Prairies. While the fur trade was the dominant activity, a small agricultural settlement (the Selkirk colony) was established in 1812 on the Red River, in what is now Manitoba.

Agriculture began to develop around the Red River settlement, but grain was not as yet a major money-making product because of transportation costs. It would take the coming of the railway (see Chapter 10) to create a strong agricultural economy on the Prairies, allowing products to reach the markets of eastern Canada and, from there, Europe. The focus of the railways on Winnipeg made that city a major growth area. Similarly, since the markets were located to the east, railheads (where a railway meets a water route) such as Port Arthur and Fort William (now merged as Thunder Bay) became important grainhandling ports. Here, the products were transshipped from railway to freight ships for movement down the Great Lakes.

Today, the Prairie region is by far the largest agricultural region in Canada, accounting for over 80 percent of the country's farmland and over 70 percent of the country's revenue from agricultural crops. Of these crops, cereal grains–wheat, barley, oats, rye and

Some grain elevators on the Prairies, such as this one at Biggar, have come to symbolize the important role of wheat in the Prairie and Canadian economies.

corn–are overwhelmingly dominant, with the Prairie region producing over 90 percent of the national total. While Saskatchewan leads in the production of wheat and rye, Alberta leads in barley and oats.

In 1914, what one writer called "the British Empire's...potentially richest petroleum asset" was discovered in southern Alberta. This discovery was made when oil was found seeping up through the ground at Turner Valley, south of Calgary. By June of 1929, there were 103 producing wells near Turner Valley, some as deep as 2000 m. After World War II, the search for oil and gas across Canada resulted in the discovery of the important Leduc field, just south of Edmonton. One after another, new oil districts were found. As a result, a dozen or so petroleum refining plants sprang up. The effects of the petroleum industry on the economy of Alberta, in particular, have been extremely important. With its heavy dependence on the oil and gas resource, the economy of the province has boomed and slumped according to changes in the world petroleum market.

As in the other economic regions of Canada, the Prairie region has manufacturing plants located in larger communities. However, in only a few instances do Prairie factories produce for international or world markets: distance from major centres of population has been a disadvantage for these manufacturers. One exception is the potash-mining district in Saskatchewan, where fertilizers are manufactured for distribution to Africa and South America. Since transportation costs for the raw potash would be high, refining goes on near the mine site. Another exception is the SED Systems Company of Saskatoon, a high-technology firm that manufactures fibre-optics products. In this case, low transportation costs, as compared to the value of the products, mean location is a relatively minor concern.

1. Where was western Canada's first agricultural settlement? When was it established?
2. Why have railways been so important for Prairie agriculture?
3. Suggest some reasons why manufacturing has not become a dominant form of economic activity on the Prairies.

The Western Cordillera

The early development of British Columbia has already been treated in earlier chapters of this book. Chapter 9 showed that, as with the Great Lakes-St. Lawrence Lowlands, the Canadian Shield and the

Prairies, the fur trade was the first important non-Native economic activity on the Pacific coast. Unlike in the other regions, however, sea otter pelts, rather than the furs of land mammals, were the most significant items of the Pacific fur trade.

Other chapters yet to come will deal with the early history of the various economic activities of the region. Chapter 16 will relate how development of the lumber industry in British Columbia began in the mid-nineteenth century on Vancouver Island, with construction of lumber mills along the coast following shortly thereafter. Chapter 18 will trace the early development of the fishing industry; in 1870, British Columbia's first fish cannery opened. The Fraser River Gold Rush of 1857 did much to open up the southern British Columbia interior.

Canada's Working People: A Brief History

Since the early days of fishing, furs, lumbering and farming, the lives of working Canadians have undergone two major sets of changes. The first such changes began in the mid-nineteenth century, as secondary industries gradually overtook primary industries as the dominant form of economic activity in Canada. The second set of changes began in the middle of our own century. Since then, tertiary or "service" industries have displaced secondary industries as the country's leading kind of economic activity. This section will look at how each of these two transformations has affected Canada's working people.

Canadian Workers and the Industrial Revolution

Until the mid-nineteenth century, most Canadians earned their living in one of two ways: either as hired workers or as independent operators. Hired workers usually did hard physical labor; for example, chopping trees for a lumbering operation, or handling a team of horses in the construction of a canal. Such work was often seasonal, lasting only a few months of the year. The workers tended to move a great deal to wherever unskilled jobs were available. Many hired workers never had anything like a permanent job. Independent producers included farmers and tradespeople such as shoemakers,

Work crews, some coming from as far away as Ontario, harvested the grain crops of the Prairies before machinery became capable of doing the job. These hired hands worked only a few weeks and then were unemployed once again.

blacksmiths, tailors and carpenters. For the most part, these people ran their own businesses, creating a product, then selling it.

The emergence of factories, starting around 1870, changed the lives of both hired workers and independent producers. By that time, textile plants, iron foundries and railway supply shops were springing up in eastern cities such as Hamilton, Toronto and Montreal. People whose families had been hired workers, farmers or tradespeople a generation earlier, now found themselves working in these factories. Conditions were crowded, dirty, harsh and dangerous. Children as young as ten years were sometimes employed as unskilled laborers. Wages were low, hours long, and injuries common.

As the number of factories grew, the independent tradespeople had a hard time competing. An independent shoemaker, for example, could not produce as much as a factory which used modern sewing machines to make footwear. The transition from independent tradespeople to factory manufacturing was, by 1920, almost complete. After that time, few Canadians (unless they were farmers) made a living as independent producers. Within a couple of generations, tens of thousands of skilled tradespeople had in effect been transformed into hired workers.

Fed up with dangerous and difficult working conditions, some hired workers began to look to unions for help in getting better conditions. Unions were not unknown before the onset of factories. In the 1830s and 1840s, for example, Irish immigrant laborers employed in canal-building along the Great Lakes-St. Lawrence system had formed labor organizations. These organizations sometimes demanded higher wages from the contractors, and sometimes the workers walked off the job when the demands were not met. But these early workers' organizations were small, locally based, loosely structured and short-lived. They had little resemblance to the large, powerful unions of our time.

Both governments and businesses were extremely hostile to early unions. Governments at all levels would outlaw unions and sometimes send in the police or militia to discipline striking workers. Businesses would not hesitate to hire "scabs" (replacement workers) if their regular employees went out on strike. Some employers demanded that their workers sign a pledge promising never to join a union. Refusal to sign meant being fired on the spot. Given these obstacles, unions experienced very slow and difficult growth during the nineteenth century.

By the 1890s, only about 20 000 Canadian workers belonged to unions, a figure representing less than 2 percent of the labor force of that time. Twenty years later, the figure was 8 percent. Most of these workers were skilled tradespeople, and many of their local unions were affiliates of a national union, the Trades and Labor Congress (TLC), which had been founded in 1883. Since their skills were in demand by employers, people with a trade could sometimes demand better wages and working conditions.

Unskilled workers were much slower to unionize. The threat of a strike was, in many cases, not much of a weapon for them. With the waves of immigration into the country in the late nineteenth and early twentieth century, there was a ready supply of unskilled labor. Unlike skilled workers who were often in short supply, unskilled workers could be easily replaced. When workers set up picket lines, the employers, backed up by police or militia, would force passage for "scabs." Violence could result. In 1909 and 1911, the coal miners of British Columbia were involved in labor strife of this sort.

THE TORONTO PRINTERS' STRIKE OF 1872

Perhaps the most famous strike of the early post-Confederation period was the Toronto Printers' Strike of 1872 in which George Brown (see page 92) played a role. As publisher of *The Globe*, Brown led a campaign of Toronto businessmen to hold down wages and keep up the hours of the typesetters and printers. The Typographical Union, representing the workers, rallied behind the "Nine-Hour Movement," an attempt to get the working day down from twelve to nine hours. Brown's response to the workers was representative of the views of business and political leaders of the time. "If this agitation for shorter hours continues," he wrote in *The Globe*, "let the employers shut their doors and starve the men into submission." A crowd of 10 000 marched in downtown Toronto in support of the workers when they went out on strike, but, after a walkout that lasted almost two months, the Typographical Union failed to get its demands met.

THE WINNIPEG GENERAL STRIKE

The most dramatic expression of labor strife in all of Canadian history is the Winnipeg General Strike of 1919. It was the highlight of a year that saw labor unrest all over Canada.

The First World War (1914-1918) was a period of full employment for Canadians. Tens of thousands of workers at home toiled in the munitions factories and garment shops to supply weapons and uniforms for Canadian soldiers in Europe. Yet the wages of most Canadian workers failed to keep up with the spiralling cost of living created by wartime conditions. The war years were marked by numerous strikes.

When the soldiers returned to Canada at the war's end, they found no jobs awaiting them. Many workers in the war-supply industries found themselves out of jobs as well. Some union leaders in Canada, as elsewhere, were openly talking radical politics in the wake of

Shortly after this picture was taken on June 21, 1919, armed mounted police charged the crowds and arrested the leaders.

Through this century, the relationship of Canadian and American unions has been a thorny issue. The TLC, representing mostly skilled workers, had strong ties with the United States. Some TLC affiliate groups, however, grew unhappy with their domination by American unions. In the late 1920s, they left the TLC and grouped together to form an all-Canadian organization. After many changes of name and structure, this group established itself as the Canadian Congress of Labour (CCL) in 1940. In 1956, the CCL and TLC united to form the Canadian Labour Congress (CLC). The affiliate local unions of the CLC today represent about 60 percent of unionized workers in Canada. However, only about a third of working Canadians today belong to unions. (In British Columbia, the most the 1917 Communist revolution in Russia. In western Canada, this radicalism was more marked than anywhere else in the country.

Winnipeg, with a population of 200 000, was western Canada's largest city in 1919. Throughout the spring of that year, the Winnipeg Trades and Labour Council, representing both skilled and unskilled workers of the city, had been trying to negotiate higher wages and reduced working hours. But the negotiations collapsed, and on May 15th the Council called a general strike. Within hours, almost 30 000 Winnipegers had walked off their jobs. Factories, stores and public transportation in the city promptly ground to a halt.

Leading the opposition to the strike was the Citizens' Committee of 1000, a group of Winnipeg's most influential bankers, manufacturers and politicians. The Winnipeg *Citizen*, a newspaper representing the committee's viewpoint, called the strike "a serious attempt to overturn British institutions in this country and to supplant them with the Russian Bolshevik system of Soviet rule." The Winnipeg city government, the government of Manitoba and the federal government all allied themselves with the committee in an attempt to break the strike. For the first few weeks of the strike the city remained paralysed and essentially peaceful, but tensions were growing. The eyes of the country focussed on Winnipeg.

Then the strike gradually weakened as several prominent strike leaders were arrested. Some groups of strikers, destitute after weeks with no income, drifted back to work. The streetcar workers were the first such major group to return to the job, in the strike's fifth week.

Yet some groups of workers held out. Among the most militant were the war veterans, who had no jobs to return to anyway. At a massive demonstration by the veterans on "Bloody Saturday," June 21, North West Mounted Police charged the angry crowd. Thirty demonstrators were injured, and federal troops moved in to occupy the city's streets. Four days later the Winnipeg General Strike was over.

A Royal Commission appointed to investigate the causes of the strike later concluded that there had been no real threat of "revolution," as political and business leaders had claimed. The strike's major cause, said the commission's report, was "the dissatisfied and unsettled conditions of labour at and long before the beginning of the strike...the high cost of living [and] inadequate wages."

heavily unionized province in Canada, the figure is close to one-half.)

In the past two decades or so, one big change in the character of Canadian unions has been the unionization of working women. By the mid-1980s, women represented 40 percent of the labor force in Canada and accounted for 30 percent of union memberships.

Another major change has been the steady unionization of civil servants (government employees). In the mid-1980s, 80 percent of civil servants in Canada were unionized. (By contrast, only 25 percent of Canadians in the private sector are unionized.) Three of the four largest unions in Canada are public service unions. These three are the Canadian Union of Public Employees (municipal civil servants), the National Union of Provincial Government Employees (provincial civil servants, except in Quebec and New Brunswick) and the Public Service Alliance of Canada (federal civil servants). All three organizations are part of the CLC.

1. Explain the difference between hired workers and independent producers.
2. Why were most early unions composed of skilled workers?
3. Why did unions grow so slowly in the period up until about 1920?
4. Suggest some reasons why most workers in the public sector are unionized, while most in the private sector are not.

Canadian Workers and the Growth of the Tertiary Sector

Consider the number of tertiary or service activities that you encounter in a typical school day. In the morning, your radio alarm wakes you with music from the radio station. You visit the bathroom to use running water and flush toilets which have been installed by plumbers. The milk, juice and cereal you have for breakfast come from a retail store. The bus that takes you to school, and the police officer who is at the corner, are part of the tertiary sector. At school, your teachers and other school employees, such as the secretaries, cafeteria staff or caretakers, are part of the service industry. As you relax in front of the television set in the evening, the programs you watch are the result of tertiary activity; they involve the work of technicians, actors, actresses, film crews, communications workers and advertisers.

In highly developed nations such as Canada, tertiary economic activities are very widespread. Although the different economic regions of Canada do not always have the same level of access to such services, almost all enjoy the services of retail stores, radio and TV stations, doctors, lawyers, teachers, police and fire protection. During the period 1930-1960 tertiary industries employed around 40 percent of the labor force, but during the 1960s this figure leapt to over 50 percent. In 1984, the figure was 74 percent. Service industries are the fastest growing segment of the Canadian economy. What accounts for this growth?

For one thing, the increase in tertiary employment is linked to the decrease in primary and secondary employment. Agriculture, for example, employed about 30 percent of Canadians at the end of

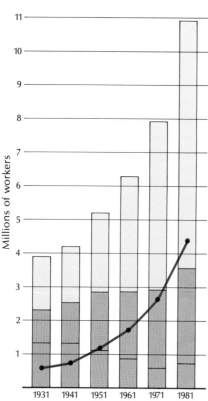

Distribution of Labor Force in Canada, 1931-1981

Legend

Tertiary Industry:
Transportation and communications, Trade, Finance and real estate, Service

Secondary Industry:
Manufacturing, Electricity, Construction

Primary Industry:
Agriculture, Forestry, Mining, Fishing and Trapping

●—● Females in labor force

Source: *Statistics Canada*

Which sector of the labor force has grown most rapidly for the time period shown?

World War II. The figure is now less than 5 percent. With the **mechanization** of farming, machines now do the work of many laborers. In the secondary sector, manufacturing and construction laborers made up over 30 percent of the work force at the end of World War II. They now comprise less than 20 percent. In these industries, new technologies have also meant that fewer workers are needed.

A second reason for the growth of the tertiary sector is the growth in the size of government in the past four decades (especially since the 1960s). In the late 1940s, government spending at all levels accounted for a yearly average of 23 percent of Canada's Gross Domestic Product. In the early 1980s, the figure was 44 percent. Much of the money spent by governments goes towards wages. Virtually all government employees are, of course, part of the tertiary sector.

The growth in employment in tertiary industries is also related to the dramatic increase in the number of women working outside the home. Until the early 1950s, women made up about 15 percent of the total labor force. Within three decades, this figure climbed to over 40 percent. Now, almost the same number of women as men work in the tertiary sector. In some occupations, such as teaching, health care and clerical work, there are more women than men. Women are making rapid progress in traditional male areas of employment: business, medicine, engineering, law enforcement and politics. However, women are still not adequately represented in many professions, including political office and executive-level business positions.

Another significant change in the work force has resulted from the increased use of computers. The automobile industry, a secondary activity, is installing computers at a fast pace. It is estimated that a computer-controlled robot on the assembly line can replace the equivalent of 2.5 workers per shift. Such automation has dealt a devastating blow to employment in manufacturing. However, as robot prices decline and industry turns increasingly to these "mechanical workers," a new work force will be needed to design, produce, control and service robots. But the unskilled assembly-line workers displaced by robots will have to look elsewhere for employment.

More than half of Canadian workers are now employed in offices. Many of these employees are facing changes in their work because of the increased use of computers. This automation may bring about a significant change in working hours. By the year 2000, the

Employed Labor Force by Category, 1984

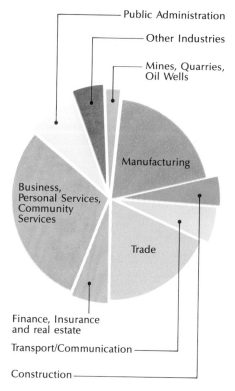

Source: *Statistics Canada*

Which categories would you expect to see grow most rapidly over the next decade?

247

work week as we know it may no longer exist, as the trend continues toward the widespread use of part-time employees, job-sharing techniques and "flextime." In job-sharing, two employees divide the work normally done by one. One employee may work mornings, while the other works afternoons. One employee may work for six months of the year, then do something else while the second employee does the job for the other six months. In flex-time arrangements, working hours are made more flexible. Employees may choose, for example, to work from 7 a.m. to 3 p.m. instead of the usual 9 to 5. These trends, some people argue, mean that Canadians will have more time available for leisure activities, perhaps as much as ninety hours per week by the twenty-first century.

The growth in service industries is particularly important for young people. Just consider where you or your friends find jobs after school or on weekends—working in a fast food outlet, clerking in a store, babysitting, washing cars. These are all part of the broad range of service jobs. Also consider where you and your parents spend a great deal of money: grocery stores, service stations, restaurants, movies, video stores, sporting clubs, or on things like insurance, dry cleaning, or plumbing. If you choose a career in computers, accounting, teaching, law enforcement or firefighting, you will still be part of the service sector. The future of workers in Canada, as elsewhere in the western world, is tightly linked to patterns of employment in the service sector.

1. What factors account for the increase in the size of the tertiary sector?

Summary

Economic activity is of three basic kinds: production, exchange and consumption. Production is of two kinds: primary, where natural resources are extracted, and secondary, where finished goods are produced. Secondary production is often called manufacturing. Tertiary activity involves the production of services, rather than of goods. In all forms of economic activity, money, or capital, is important.

Economic regions designate areas in which the various communities share similar economic activities. A broad definition of economic region could look at Canada in terms of five regions: the Atlantic, the Great Lakes-St. Lawrence Lowlands, the Canadian Shield, the Prairies, and the Western Cordillera.

Until the mid-nineteenth century, most working Canadians were either hired workers or independent producers. The growth of manufacturing from the mid-nineteenth century onward increased the numbers of hired workers, many of whom worked for low wages and under difficult conditions in the factories. Unions gradually emerged as a means for workers to improve their lot.

Three of the four largest unions in Canada are today public service unions. Public servants make up part of the tertiary sector, the sector in which most Canadians now work. Canada's labor force has undergone extensive changes with the increased use of computers, a change which has displaced many secondary-sector workers.

REVIEW

Checking Back

1. In one or two sentences, distinguish between finished and semifinished products. Give two examples of each produced in British Columbia.

2. Each of Canada's economic regions was influenced by many factors, with the most dominant largely shaping the economic situations we find today. Compare the four economic regions (Atlantic, Great Lakes-St. Lawrence Lowlands, Canadian Shield, Prairies) described in this chapter using a chart format, with these headings: Time of Earlier European Activities, Earliest Economic Activities, Major Influences, Significant Problems.

3. In a few sentences, distinguish between primary, secondary and tertiary activities. Describe the trends in employment that have taken place in these categories over the past few decades.

Using Your Knowledge

4. Use a series of small labelled sketches to show the sequence of steps from primitive forest to a thriving community.

5. What would be your reaction if the workers in a major industry in your area went on strike to get better working conditions? Write a "letter to the editor" of a fictitious local newspaper. The letter should be either in favor of the strike or against it. Give reasons to support your view.

6. Explain how the growth in the service sector has changed the Canadian economy. In your answer include information about the kinds of work done, the skills required by employers and opportunities for young people.

7. Explain the term "economic disparities." In which region of Canada do you predict the most improvement in the next twenty years?

Chapter 12

Canadians Trade to Live

As you learned in the previous chapter we all have a place in Canada's economy. In turn, Canada's economic system has a place in the world economy. Our businesses must buy and sell outside of Canada as well as inside it.

In this brief chapter, you will look at Canada's role in the international economy. First you will see what resources and goods Canada has traded with other nations and how this pattern of trade is changing. Then you will take a glance at who our major trading partners have been. Finally, a short "case study" will show you the role of a Japan-based international company in Canada's automotive industry.

While reading this chapter, think about these key questions:

• What kinds of goods has Canada traditionally imported? exported?
• How is this pattern of import and export changing?
• Which two countries have traditionally been Canada's trading partners?
• What role do foreign corporations play in Canada's international trade?

Canada as an Importing and Exporting Nation

As you have seen in Chapter 11, an "economy" is a process of buying and selling goods and services. To understand this process in its international context, you should know the meanings of some key terms. Among these terms are some you have already studied in the previous chapter: raw material, natural resource, finished product and semifinished product (see pages 224-226). Two other key terms are **import** and **export**. The items we sell to other countries are called exports; items we buy from them are imports. When Canadians sell lumber to Japan, we are exporting; when we bring in cassette recorders manufactured in Japan, we are importing.

A large portion of Canada's exports have traditionally been raw materials–coal (shown here being loaded at the Port of Vancouver), wheat, pulp, lumber, minerals, furs, and so on. In more recent years other sectors have developed as well, but a large proportion of exports still leave in unprocessed forms.

Canada is an importer and exporter of both raw materials and finished products. Traditionally, however, most of our exports have been raw materials and natural resources. Most of our imports have been finished products. In Chapters 13 and 14, you will look in detail at our trading relationship with the United States and with the countries of the Pacific region. As you do so, you will see how and why we have developed this pattern of import and export.

Despite our traditional reliance on resource-based industries, it is becoming much more difficult for Canada to achieve growth in these industries. In the past, our resource exports had steadily increased through greater extraction of raw materials from the land, employment of larger numbers of workers and investment of more money in plants and equipment. We now face stiff competition from developing countries with ample natural resources of their own and lower labor costs. For example, coal, copper and pulpwood from South American companies now compete for the same markets (mainly in the United States) as do Canadian products.

The Challenges and Problems of International Trade

Because they are so import- and export-oriented, Canada's industries are highly affected by changes in world economic patterns and trading relationships. Upward or downward moves in world prices of raw materials or energy resources can help or hurt Canadian producers and consumers. A series of global economic crises in the 1970s and 1980s made Canadians highly aware of the extent to which our economy is linked to that of other nations.

The first crisis came in 1973, with the collapse of an international agreement that had kept the value of foreign currencies pegged to the United States dollar. Since that time, **currency rates** may change at any time, making the international pricing of goods unpredictable. In recent years, the Canadian dollar has fallen sharply against the U.S. dollar, making Canadian exports more competitive in the world market. During the early 1980s, a British Columbia lumber executive noted that "each drop of one cent in the value of the Canadian dollar against the U.S. dollar means an extra million dollars in profits for our company." On the other hand, Canadians had to pay more for imported goods, especially those coming from the United States.

A second global crisis resulted from a rapid rise in world oil prices. A cartel (price-setting group) of major oil producing nations known as the Organization of Petroleum Exporting Countries (OPEC) raised their prices dramatically in 1973. This crisis was fuelled by fears and rumors of a world oil shortage. Rising oil prices drove up costs of producing both raw materials and finished products all over the world. As oil importing countries were forced to pay more for petroleum, they had less money with which to buy other foreign resources and goods. Because fewer foreign goods were purchased, the producers of these goods suffered. They often had to lay off workers, or even went bankrupt. Falling employment, incomes, and investment all served to reduce economic growth. World trade declined.

During the period of rising prices, Canada experienced a period of rapid oil exploration and development. At the same time, rising oil prices drove other prices up, fueling inflation. A decade later, sharply dropping world oil prices left Canada's oil companies and government oil policies in disarray. However, Canadian consumers benefited from dropping oil prices, both when they filled up at the pumps and in lower prices for many goods and services.

The world oil crisis, and the global economic slowdown that followed severely depressed prices for Canadian resources such as copper, nickel and iron ore. Technological change is another factor. Copper, one of B.C.'s major mineral exports, is being replaced in some electrical circuits by fibre optics. Aluminum and plastics are replacing steel in some products such as automobiles. Since iron ore is used in making steel, the market for Canada's iron ore has suffered. Nickel is an important alloy used to strengthen steel. So as the demand for steel decreases, the demand for nickel also drops. Iron mines have had to shut down, and many nickel mines have reduced production and laid off hundreds of workers. In the Schefferville region of Quebec, the Iron Ore Company of Canada closed its Knob Lake mine in 1982, laying off over 550 workers. The giant operations of the International Nickel Company (INCO) at Sudbury, Ontario, suffered a cycle of shut-downs and layoffs throughout the early 1980s. In the recession of 1982, Sudbury had the highest unemployment rate of any Canadian city, with almost one-quarter of its labor force unemployed.

Changing Patterns of Trade

Canada's resource exports continue, but are declining as a percentage of our total exports. For example, Canada's resource exports in 1964 were valued at approximately $7 billion, accounting for 84 percent of our export dollars. In 1984, our resource exports were $64 billion, but only 70 percent of our export dollars.

Canadian businesses and governments are aware that they have to meet the challenge of declining resource exports. They are attempting to do so by exporting more finished products such as cars, trucks and automotive parts. Since 1964, as a result of the **Auto Pact**, an automobile trade agreement between the Canadian and United States governments, vehicles and parts have increased from 2 percent of total exports, by value, to over 23 percent in the mid-1980s.

In addition, many Canadian firms are marketing the very latest modern technology. Some of them design and build portable electrical transformers that are shipped worldwide. Canadian built electric-powered trains for urban mass-transit are being marketed around the world. The use of the Canadian manufactured Canadarm in moving goods on space platforms or on space shuttle flights has put Canadian technology in the spotlight. Canadian telephone systems are being installed in Middle Eastern countries. Candu nuclear reactors have been or are being built in South America and India. Canadian-made computers have been adapted for use as cheque-sorting machines in New York banks. In the long run, competition from developing countries may be beneficial. Canadians are being forced to make creative use of new technology.

Composition of Canadian Exports

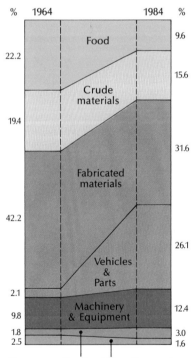

Source: *Statistics Canada*

Which export group had the greatest increase over the twenty-year period? Which export group had the greatest relative decline?

Imports and Exports by Major Groups, 1983-1985

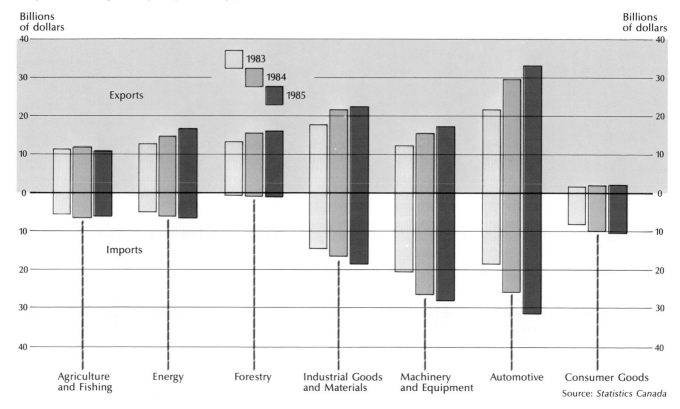

Billions of dollars

Exports

1983
1984
1985

Imports

Agriculture and Fishing | Energy | Forestry | Industrial Goods and Materials | Machinery and Equipment | Automotive | Consumer Goods

Source: *Statistics Canada*

1) How might Canada's trading partners have reacted to our balance of trade pattern during the decade 1975-1985? Why?

2) The period 1981-1983 was a time of worldwide economic recession. How did this recession affect Canada's imports and exports? Why?

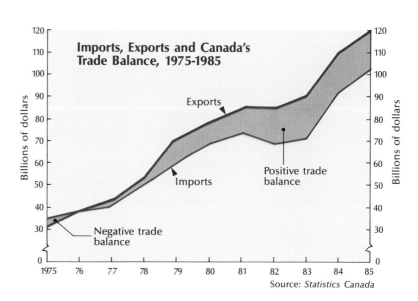

Imports, Exports and Canada's Trade Balance, 1975-1985

Billions of dollars

Exports

Imports

Positive trade balance

Negative trade balance

1975 76 77 78 79 80 81 82 83 84 85

Source: *Statistics Canada*

1. Look at the bar graph to answer these questions:
   (a) What was the main export commodity group, by value, in 1985?
   (b) Import commodity group?
2. Canadians are both importers and exporters of most commodity groups shown on this chart. Which group do we almost entirely export? import? Suggest why this is so.
3. The first three categories on this chart are resource commodities, the last four processed or manufactured goods. In which of the latter four categories is Canada a net importer? exporter?
4. Suggest some reasons why Canada is both a large-scale importer and exporter of automobile products.

Canada and Its Trading Partners

Just as the products involved in Canada's international trade have changed, so too have the trading partners.

The United Kingdom was Canada's main trading partner throughout the 1800s and took 60 percent of Canada's exports even into the early 1900s. During the 1920s, the United States began to become an ever-larger market for our exports. By the end of World War II, the United States had overtaken Britain as our major trading partner. Today, trade with the U.S. accounts for about 70 percent of Canada's imports and exports. In Chapter 13, you will have an in-depth look at Canada-United States trade. While the United States continues to be our most important trading partner by far, Canada began during the 1970s to develop wider trade with the countries of the Pacific region, a development you will learn about in Chapter 14. As our trade with the Pacific region has increased, our traditional economic ties with the North Atlantic European countries have weakened.

Illustrating the importance of these Pacific countries to Canada is the fact that Japan now ranks second to the United States as the leading trading partner (5 percent of exports and 6 percent of imports by value in 1985). From Japan and other East Asian nations, Canada buys electronic equipment, photographic equipment, textiles, clothing, footwear, automobiles and even wood products. In turn Canada sells them raw materials such as wood pulp, copper, rapeseed and coal.

1. Suggest three possible reasons why the United States replaced Britain as Canada's leading trading partner.
2. Canada's trade with the United States is ten times as great as with Japan. Suggest two reasons why Japan is not likely to replace the United States as our leading trading partner.

Trade and the Automobile Industry

Canada is both an importer and an exporter of automobiles. Most of the automobiles exported from Canada are shipped to the United States. An automobile trade agreement (known as the Auto Pact) between the United States and Canada permits cars made in this country to be sold in the United States duty-free. As a result, all of the major American car manufacturers–General Motors, Ford, Chrysler and American Motors–operate large-scale production and assembly plants in Ontario and Quebec. Cars and trucks produced in these plants and shipped to the United States are the largest single source of export revenue in Canada.

Canadians buy automobiles from many nations, but the United States and Japan are by far the two most important sources. In particular, Japanese car sales in Canada have risen dramatically over the last twenty years, chiefly at the expense of North American produced vehicles. In 1963, Canadians purchased only $300 000 worth of Japanese vehicles. Six years later, the value of Japanese cars and trucks sold in Canada had jumped to $71 million, and by 1985 Canadians were buying $800 million worth of Japanese vehicles each year.

Japan is today the world's leading producer of automobiles. The Japanese achieved this status in 1983, when they produced 11.1 million vehicles (28 percent of the world's total), compared to 9.2 million (23 percent) in the United States. In every year from 1980 to 1986, Japan's automobile manufacturers produced more than 10 million vehicles. These cars and trucks are built in some of the world's largest and most highly automated production plants, where robots are used extensively.

Japan is the world's leading exporter of automobiles. Because of its smaller population and densely populated cities, Japan is not as large a car market as is the United States. Much of Japan's automobile production is intended solely for export, a fact that worries automobile manufacturers in countries like Canada. Japanese manufacturers have been able to capture large portions of the automobile market in Canada and other industrialized nations because of a well-established reputation for producing high quality, fuel efficient vehicles at a reasonable price.

In Canada, rising demand for imported Japanese cars has led to reduced demand for domestic cars and trucks. As domestic sales dropped, plants in Canada and the United States were closed and many auto workers laid off. To compete more effectively with the Japanese, Canadian companies and auto workers' unions pressured the government to reduce imports of cars from Japan or to require the Japanese to use a number of Canadian-made parts in cars shipped to this country.

In the early 1980s, faced with pressure from Canadian automobile workers and car companies, the Japanese entered into a voluntary restraint agreement. The Japanese government, at the request of the Canadian government, restricted the number of cars leaving Japan for export to Canada. Each year the two countries established the number of cars that would be shipped. This action was different than a quota because the exporting nation voluntarily exercised restraint in one commodity in order to keep good relations with its trading partner. As of 1986, the Japanese had not exceeded their voluntary limit.

Government and automobile industry officials believe, however, that voluntary restraint agreements and quotas are only short term measures. They believe that greater Canadian participation with the Japanese auto industry is necessary to help Canada's economy grow, while allowing consumers greater access to popular Japanese models of cars and trucks. The giant Japanese car manufacturer,

Japanese automobiles have earned a reputation for durability and economy, giving them an expanding share of the North American automobile market. Who benefits from the importation of foreign vehicles?

257

Toyota, provides two examples of how this increased participation might work.

Toyota is the largest of Japan's eleven major auto firms, producing 30 percent of the cars and trucks manufactured in Japan in the mid-1980s. Only the two giant American-owned multinational car makers, General Motors and Ford, are larger than Toyota. While Toyota has made cars in Japan for many years, it only began to export them to Canada in the early 1960s. The first Toyotas imported to Canada were sturdy and reliable economy cars. Today, Canadians may choose from a wide range of economy, sports and luxury models. Toyota has captured 40 percent of the Canadian market for cars imported from Japan.

There has long been a Canadian component to Toyota and other Japanese cars. Canadian iron ore and coal are used to make the steel needed by Japan's auto industry. Copper, zinc and other metals from Canada are used to make wiring, mufflers and other components. Increasingly, Toyota and other car companies are using other raw materials in the cars they ship to this country.

A Toyota plant in Delta uses aluminum made in Canada, and much of the machinery used in the plant was manufactured in Canada. Other products made in Canada and used by Toyota include laminated glass, wiper blades, radial tires, batteries and headlights.

Toyota has set up the plant at Delta, B.C., to make aluminum wheels for its cars. Aluminum is an "indirect energy product," one of a number of commodities where Canada's abundant low-cost energy resources give us an advantage over the Japanese who must import all of their energy sources. Indirect energy products are petroleum-based or electronically produced products such as chemicals, plastics, aluminum, smelted metals and alloys. Cars and trucks of the 1980s have higher proportions of these products in engines, bodies and interiors. For example, in 1975 a typical car was 74 percent plain carbon steel and iron, whereas in 1985 this proportion was down to 53 percent. Much of this reduction was made possible by the use of aluminum and high-strength steel and plastic, up from 9 percent in 1975 to 30 percent in 1985. Canada is in a position to supply many of these lightweight indirect energy products to Japan.

The market for Toyota vehicles in Canada and the United States is so large that the giant automaker is constructing two assembly plants, one in Kentucky and the other, valued at $400 million, in Cambridge, Ontario. The U.S. plant will have the capacity to pro-

BRANCH PLANT OPERATIONS

Multinational corporations often set up new plants in other nations, such as the one built by Toyota at Cambridge, Ontario. These operations, known as branch plants, may be established for a variety of political and economic reasons. Toyota built the plant in Ontario, taking advantage of a number of government incentives, in order to get around the limits on its sales in Canada caused by the quota system. Other reasons for building branch plants may include assured sources of raw materials, energy, parts or low-cost labor.

Toyota branch plants benefit both the company and the people of Canada. The branch plant creates jobs and increases government revenues from taxation, while Toyota receives profits from the sale of cars made or assembled there. However, should sales in Canada drop sharply, most foreign owners tend to close branch plant operations first in order to protect jobs at home.

duce 200 000 cars per year; the one in Canada, 50 000 per year, by the end of the decade. These are to be metal stamping and assembly plants using parts manufactured in Japan. Eventually, Toyota may join the North American auto pact and use parts manufactured here rather than in Japan. This would allow Toyota to export cars made in Canada to the United States.

Toyota Canada Incorporated has invested heavily in Canada since 1964, with distribution plants and dealerships all across the country. The vehicles are shipped in specially designed car-carrying ocean freighters. They arrive on Canada's West Coast after a twelve-day voyage from Japan. There they are offloaded at the Fraser Wharves Port facility on the Fraser River in Richmond, British Columbia. They are then sent from the 10 000 vehicle storage facilities to other parts of Canada by rail and truck. There are additional storage facilities in Toronto, Montreal and Halifax for distribution to dealers. All told, Toyota directly employed over 3500 Canadians by 1986. This figure will rise by as many as 1000 more when the Cambridge assembly plant is fully operational. (The company also provides indirect employment to transportation workers and customs officers.) Indirect employment is created for thousands more workers by over 2000 Canadian companies which supply Toyota with everything from accessories and replacement parts to automotive fluids and advertising.

1. Make a chart to show the path of a Toyota car from its manufacture to its purchase by a Canadian consumer.
2. Why do Canadians import cars, such as Toyotas, from Japan?

3. Why do Japanese car manufacturers use raw materials and manufactured parts imported from Canada? What does this tell us about the interdependence of the two countries as trading partners?

4. Should there be quotas on imported cars? Explain your answers.

5. What concerns might each of the following groups have about a Japanese car company opening a branch plant in Canada?
   - North American automobile manufacturers
   - the managers/owners of the Japanese company
   - Canadian car workers
   - Canadian consumers

6. Suggest why Toyota located its branch plant in Ontario rather than British Columbia or Prince Edward Island.

Summary

Traditionally, most of Canada's exports have been natural resources, while most of its imports have been finished products. With the global economic slowdown that began in the 1970s, Canada has had a more difficult time selling its resources abroad. However, technological innovations have opened up new markets for Canadian exports in areas such as telecommunications.

Until the start of the twentieth century, Britain was Canada's chief trading partner, but by the end of World War II, the United States had overtaken it. While the U.S. is still by far our largest trading partner, Canada is now doing more and more business with the countries of the Asia Pacific region, particularly Japan. The case of the Toyota Motor Corporation illustrates the importance of a single Japanese automaker to Canadian-Japanese economic relations.

REVIEW

1. For each of the following statements, record three pieces of evidence from this chapter that support the conclusion given.
   (a) Canada's industries are highly affected by changes in world economic patterns and trading relationships.
   (b) Canadians are aware that they will have to meet the challenge of declining resource exports and so are attempting to export more finished products each year.
   (c) Branch plant operations in Canada benefit Canadians.

2. Check the current value of the American dollar relative to the Canadian dollar. How does this affect Canadians travelling to the United States?

Chapter 13

Canada and the United States

In the previous chapter, we saw that Canada is a nation whose economy is heavily dependent on trade with other countries. To a large extent, our trading relationships are based on sales of raw or semiprocessed natural resources to other nations, and on purchases of finished goods from them. This chapter will now focus on our economic ties with the United States of America, our most important trading partner.

The first section of this chapter gives a brief historical overview of the long and often rocky economic relationship between the two nations. The middle portion of the chapter explores that relationship as it is today, with the key feature being the debate over trade protection versus free trade. The final section of the chapter is a case study of this debate as it applies to the softwood lumber trade. This example illustrates the complexity of trading relationships between countries.

As you read this chapter consider these questions about our trading ties with the United States:

- What factors have encouraged a strong economic relationship between the two countries?
- How has each country benefited from trading ties?
- How might ties with the United States hurt our economy?

Looking Back: A Historical Overview

Today, the United States is Canada's most important trading partner. Our relationship with our neighbor has not always been this strong. At one time, British colonies in North America enjoyed special trading privileges with Britain; their goods could enter the mother country with little or no duty added. In 1845, however, Britain ended these special privileges and began a **free trade** policy: goods from all countries could enter Britain duty-free. Businesses in the colonies then lost their market advantage and suffered badly.

Realizing the limitations of their small home markets, businesses in British North America began looking elsewhere for sales. The American population to the south offered some opportunities. In 1854, the Reciprocity Treaty was signed; its terms allowed natural products like wheat and livestock to move across the border without duties being added. Colonial businesses flourished once again and the United States quickly became the most important trading partner. However, a series of disputes in the following decade, including American resentment over Canadian tariffs on some goods, led to the termination of the agreement by the Americans in 1866.

In the years following Confederation the Canadian government acted to protect domestic (of one's own country) businesses. In 1878, John A. Macdonald's National Policy established new tariffs on American manufactured goods, increasing the cost of these goods and making Canadian-made products relatively cheaper.

The National Policy had other goals besides the protection of businesses. Macdonald wanted to create strong economic ties between eastern and western Canada in order to hold the country together. New settlers in the West became the market for eastern manufactured goods. Safe behind the high tariff "fences," the businesses grew. The wheat produced in the West fed the cities of the East, and the surplus was exported to bring much needed foreign money into the new nation.

As the West became more established, farmers and businesspeople there sought freer trade with the United States. After all, the manufacturers of farm machinery in Chicago and the Midwest were as accessible to them as were the companies in Hamilton and Montreal. But the greater population of central Canada held the reins of power. Because of its reliance on manufacturing, this part of the country was reluctant to open the border between the two countries to tariff-free U.S. goods.

In 1891, Macdonald's Conservatives, still supporting their National Policy, narrowly missed being defeated by the Liberals who favored unrestricted trade. The election of 1896 saw the Liberals under Laurier take power although their stand on free trade was much softer than before. When they tried to institute free trade agreements with the United States in 1911, they were bitterly opposed by the Conservatives under Sir Robert Borden. The Conservatives won the election that year, 134 seats to eighty-seven for the Liberals.

The desperate economic conditions of the Great Depression of

Value of Foreign Trade, Selected Years, from 1886 (in millions of dollars)

Year	Imports from				Exports to		
	U.K.	U.S.	Total		U.K.	U.S.	Total
1886	39	43	96		37	34	85
1896	33	54	105		63	38	116
1906	69	169	284		127	84	247
1916	77	371	508		452	201	742
1921	214	856	1 240		313	542	1 189
1929	195	894	1 299		290	523	1 182
1931	110	394	628		172	257	605
1939	114	497	751		329	390	936
1946	138	1 387	1 842		596	905	2 299
1948	294	1 799	2 618		685	1 520	3 087
1950	401	2 090	3 125		471	2 050	3 143
1954	382	2 871	3 968		656	2 359	3 926
1956	481	4 041	5 566		817	2 866	4 839
1960	589	3 689	5 495		925	3 039	5 390
1961	620	3 870	5 718		923	3 217	5 903
1975	1222	23 616	34 691		1777	21 074	32 466
1977	1279	29 815	42 332		1929	30 404	43 684
1978	1609	35 436	50 102		1985	36 651	52 259
1979	1928	45 571	62 871		2589	43 519	64 317
1980	1974	48 473	69 128		3187	46 828	74 259
1981	2234	54 131	78 665		3321	53 667	80 895
1982	1904	47 866	67 856		2727	57 685	84 530
1983	1810	54 103	75 587		2509	66 333	90 964

Export Canada, the Marketing Directory for Canadian Trade. Surrey, B.C.: CanExpo Publishers, 1983; Statistics Canada *Statistical Review*. Monthly. Catalogue no. 11-003.

the 1930s encouraged both the United States and Canadian governments to continue to protect their businesses through tariff increases. During World War II, tariffs were relaxed to facilitate trade in war materials.

Following World War II, many countries moved to protect their war-torn industries. The high tariffs they imposed discouraged imports, giving their domestic industries a chance to become stabilized. Because of this use of tariffs, international trade relations became so tense that twenty-three countries, including Canada, decided to look for ways of improving them. The General Agree-

Prior to Confederation the British colonies relied on Britain for markets. Sales to the United States accounted for only a small part of exports. Since Confederation, the United States has become increasingly important, both for exports and as a source of imports.

ment on Tariffs and Trade (GATT), negotiated by these countries in 1947 came into effect at the beginning of 1948. This agreement is an example of **multilateral** (among many countries) negotiations.

The promise of broader international trade connections was one of the reasons for Canada's enthusiastic involvement in GATT. In spite of trade protections, this country had grown very dependent on trade with the United States. The manufacturing sector of Canada's economy, which had grown tremendously in the twentieth century, was heavily linked to American markets and suppliers. Canadians viewed this dependence with some concern. With both markets and sources of materials in the United States, that country had a powerful influence on our economy. Some people viewed this

GENERAL AGREEMENT ON TARIFFS AND TRADE

The General Agreement on Tariffs and Trade is a set of conditions under which trade takes place. By the mid 1980s, ninety countries had signed the GATT agreements, indicating they would abide by a code of conduct in trade matters. Members pledge:

• to reduce tariff barriers between member nations
• to ensure that trade policies are applied equally to all member nations
• to work towards the gradual elimination of trade restrictions.

The intent of these practices is to encourage freer trade between countries by removing barriers and discriminating policies.

Annually, the members of GATT meet to conduct business and plan for the future. One important feature of this organization is that it provides an ongoing forum for countries to discuss trade problems and attempt to deal with trade issues. More and more, concern about the economic stability of developing countries

has become a topic of discussion. From time to time, this agency sponsors talks aimed at negotiating further reductions in trade restrictions.

Although GATT has produced a general reduction in tariffs, it has not been effective in broadening Canada's foreign trade. With each new decade, the trade connections between Canada and the United States have increased rather than decreased. Analysts say this has occurred for three reasons. First, GATT only regulates goods: services, the largest sector in industrial economies are not covered under GATT policies. Second, agricultural products are ignored. Together, these conditions mean that a large part of Canada's economic activity, the production of agricultural products, and services such as telecommunications and international banking, are not regulated by GATT.

A third reason is also important. Protection measures other than tariffs are not included ("Buy Canadian" policies are an example). These three factors have meant that policies under the agreement have been largely ineffective. The result is that trade between Canada and other countries has not been stimulated enough to counterbalance a strong trade pull to the United States.

as "putting all our eggs in one basket." More trade with other countries was seen as a way to reduce the influence the American economy had over the Canadian economy.

In 1972, the Canadian government announced new actions to broaden trade: this program was known as the "Third Option." The government believed it had to choose one of three alternatives. The first option was to make no policy decisions and let nature take its course. The second was to move towards closer connections with the United States. The third option was to strengthen trade with other countries so that dependence on the United States was reduced. This last one was clearly designed to move Canada away from a **bilateral** (two country) trade orientation.

The government of Pierre Trudeau encouraged trade links with European and other countries around the world. It tried to reduce American ownership in Canadian industries by setting up policies that made it more difficult for foreigners to get control of businesses in Canada.

However, this determined attempt by the government to reduce American influence failed. The natural attraction of the two economies was too strong and Canadian-American trade continued to grow throughout the 1970s and 1980s.

THIRSTY OR HUNGRY?

This cartoon appeared in 1970 and shows a perception of Canada-U.S. relations on the use of natural resources. In one or two sentences, describe the cartoonist's message.

1. Describe how and why Canada's trading relationship with Britain changed between the early 1800s and the twentieth century.
2. How have concerns about national unity and independence influenced Canada's trade with the United States?

Canadian-American Trade Today

Some Canadians believe Canada should be less dependent on trade with the United States. Others believe that our economy would benefit from even closer ties with the United States. In this section, we will look at both sides of the argument. But first of all, let us take a look at the size and shape of this trade relationship.

The Mouse and the Elephant

Close ties to our huge neighbor to the south are a reality we cannot avoid. The question we should ask is not "Should we trade with the United States?" but rather "What should our trade relationship be?" Former Prime Minister Trudeau once compared the relationship of Canada to the United States with that of a mouse and an elephant living next door to each other. In such a relationship, it pays to consider your actions carefully.

The extent of the relationship between the Canadian economy and that of the United States is staggering. In 1984, we exported about $86 billion worth of goods and services to the United States. This figure represents 75.6 percent of our total exports, and 19 percent of their imports. Imports from the United States totalled over $66 billion, or 71.4 percent of all our imports. Canada accounted for 16 percent of their exports. These percentages have generally been growing.

Some products rely on the American market more than others. Live animals, such as pigs and beef cattle, are traded almost exclusively with the United States. This is largely because of the high transportation costs and the delicate handling required with livestock. Other goods, such as food, beverages and raw materials, are easier and cheaper to transport. Therefore, sales to and purchases from other countries are possible.

The differences between imports and exports cause some Canadians to be concerned about trade with the United States. They point out that many of our major exports are raw or semifinished natural

Canadian petroleum and natural gas are transported by pipelines to customers in the United States. What other unprocessed or semiprocessed natural resources are sold in large quantities to American businesses?

resources: coal, wheat, lumber, pulp and paper and electricity. Most of our imports are finished manufactured goods: computers, plastics, aircraft and automobile parts. These Canadians are upset that we send our natural resources south of the border to be made into finished goods which we then buy. If we manufactured those products ourselves, they argue, we could then export them, creating many more Canadian jobs at the same time.

As it is, American industries often buy the materials they need from Canadian suppliers. They do so because they cannot get these materials from domestic sources, or the price there is too high. Canadians buy manufactured goods from Americans because we have not developed our own industries, or because prices here are too high. This interchange creates strong economic ties between the two countries.

ECONOMIES OF SCALE

One reason why American industries can often sell goods at a lower price than Canadian businesses has to do with their larger population. Here is how a bigger market is an advantage.

Suppose Amcorp and Cancorp are two companies about to set up factories to produce a new high-strength, puncture-resistant widget. One firm will sell to the United States market and the other to the Canadian market. Both firms build factories and buy the specialized machines needed to produce the widgets. These capital costs are identical: $1 000 000 for each company.

The Amcorp president calculates that they can sell a total of 100 000 widgets in the United States. With a market population only one-tenth the size of the United States, the Cancorp president believes her firm can sell only 10 000 widgets. The costs of labor and raw materials are the same on both sides of the border: $100 per widget. The total production costs are found by multiplying the unit costs

times the total number of widgets made.

In order to calculate the total costs of producing widgets we need to add the capital costs (factory and machinery) to the production costs (labor and raw materials).

Amcorp

Capital Costs	$ 1 000 000
Production Costs ($100 × 100 000)	10 000 000
Total Costs	$11 000 000

$$\text{Cost per widget} = \frac{\$11\,000\,000}{100\,000} = \$110$$

Cancorp

Capital Costs	$ 1 000 000
Production Costs ($100 × 10 000)	1 000 000
Total Costs	$ 2 000 000

$$\text{Cost per widget} = \frac{\$2\,000\,000}{10\,000} = \$200$$

The larger market in the United States means the costs per unit are lower than in Canada. These savings in costs as a result of high rates of production are called **economies of scale.**

Let us now look in detail at the debate over what the trading relationship should be between Canada and the United States. First, we will consider the case for trade protection; second, the case against it; third, the case for free trade; fourth, the case against it.

Trade Protection: The Case For It

When economic growth is slow, people and governments instinctively want to protect what they have. It is reasoned that if foreign goods cannot enter the country, or at least must enter under a price handicap, then domestic businesses will have an advantage. Protection is really a policy to assure that domestic firms have a safe, secure market. Throughout history, most countries have used some form of trade protection.

PROTECTING THE AMERICAN SUGAR INDUSTRY

The United States sugar industry provides a good example of how domestic businesses are protected or defended by trade policies. In 1982, the price for sugar throughout the world was low. Sugar and sugar products produced in other countries could be sold in the United States for a lower price than American producers could charge. Their costs for growing and refining the sugar were too high to allow their price to be reduced any further. American sugar refiners could not compete against the lower priced imports without some protection.

In May of 1982, the United States government set up a series of **quotas** to control the amount of sugar entering the country. Once the amount of the quota was reached, imports of sugar were stopped. American producers were then in a position to supply their domestic market without competition from lower priced foreign sources. In June 1983, and again in November 1984, controls were expanded to include liquid sugar, sugar blends (sugar replacements made of a mixture of sugar and cornstarch) and food products with a high sugar content.

In spite of these controls, Canadian businesses were finding good United States markets for some products unaffected by quotas, such as cocoa, chocolate, candied nuts, pudding mixes, drink powders, and the like. In fact, exports to the United States in these products doubled from 1983 to 1984. A strong American economy and the relatively low value of the Canadian dollar made Canadian products attractive south of the border.

The growing share of the market taken by Canadian and other foreign producers led to even stronger demands for protection of the American sugar industry. As a result, in 1985, the United States placed a wide variety of food products containing sugar under quota. Since most processed foods contain at least some sugar or sugar product, this action was widely felt by Canadian industries. Without the American markets, Canadian food processors were forced to lay off an estimated 400 workers, and lost about $100 million in sales the first year alone.

Trade between Canada and the United States has normally been controlled by protection measures. Occasionally some products have been allowed to move across the border freely, but these have been special cases where specific agreements have been worked out. The automobile industry is one example discussed later in this chapter. Totally free trade between the two countries has never occurred.

There are two ways in which protection can be used to help domestic businesses. The first way is as a *defensive* measure; the other is as a *retaliatory* ("fighting back") measure.

Defensive measures are used in cases where foreign competitors are able to sell better or less expensive products in another country. Perhaps they can do it because their wage rates are lower, because they have better technology or more favorable economies of scale, or because they have a better source for raw materials. In any case, these outside producers are able to take the market away from local firms. Trade protections are meant to defend the home economy from the competition of outside forces.

Retaliatory measures are sometimes used to combat what is seen as unfair assistance to industries. Often governments help domestic businesses by giving them loans or grants or tax breaks, usually in exchange for the jobs these businesses create. Government help of this sort reduces the costs of manufacturing the goods and lets the businesses sell the goods for a lower price. It may also mean that the goods can be exported to another country and compete in that market. This competition hurts the businesses there. To compensate for the help given by the foreign government, protection measures may be taken. A case involving the pork industry shows how protection measures can be used as a weapon.

The use of tariffs as a trade protection measure is common. Tariffs have the effect of raising the price of goods or services which come from outside the country. For tariffs to be effective, the total cost of a foreign item to a consumer should be higher than the price of a similar item produced within the country. Tariffs eliminate the competitive advantage imported goods may have and give the domestic goods an edge in the marketplace.

Tariffs help maintain a strong, vital industry for many goods, but for some others, personal preference works even against higher prices. Even though wines imported from France, Italy, Germany and California carry higher prices, the Canadian wine industry still struggles to compete with them.

Other import-control methods, besides tariffs, are used as well.

THE PORK INDUSTRY: A CASE OF AMERICAN RETALIATION

Thirty percent of the pork produced in Canada is exported; 83 percent of exports go to consumers south of the border. In 1984, Canadian producers exported $542 million worth of pork to the United States–1.2 million live hogs and 145 000 t of dressed pork (prepared carcasses and packaged meat). Sales to the United States were expected to grow.

However, the United States Department of Commerce identified what they considered an unfair advantage for Canadian producers. In order to stabilize the industry, both federal and provincial governments had programs which guaranteed a minimum or base price to farmers. These programs, Americans argued, amounted to a form of **subsidy.** Canadian farmers could sell their pork for a low price knowing that the government would make up their losses. Here is how the programs worked.

Suppose farmers on both sides of the border need to get $120 per hog to break even; on the Canadian side, this price is guaranteed. A Canadian farmer could sell pork to the United States, getting only $110 per hog, knowing the extra $10 will be made up by government programs. American farmers, without such help, could not compete with the lower priced imported meat.

In order to protect the domestic industry, the United States Department of Commerce in 1985 imposed a tariff of 11.6¢/kg on all shipments of Canadian pork. The effect of this tariff was to make American meat more competitive with Canadian exports. Canadian producers could still try to sell in the United States, but now their market advantage was gone.

The American tariff affected prices in Canada. Because pork that was expected to be exported was not, a surplus was created. Pork prices fell about 10 percent. These lower prices created a good situation for consumers, but a real concern for pork producers. Even with a guaranteed base price, the loss of a competitive advantage in a large market meant producers' earnings were reduced because they could not sell as many hogs and would have to reduce their output.

This use of a tariff to counterbalance an unfair trading relationship is known as a **countervailing duty.**

Livestock raised in Canada often ends up as the main course on American tables. This photograph shows dressed carcasses being inspected in a Canadian meat-packing plant.

They are often referred to as **non-tariff barriers.** These methods also protect businesses, but in different ways.

For example, quotas control the amount of imports allowed into a country. Once a specified level is reached, imports are stopped for the remainder of the year. The example of the sugar industry (see page 268) shows how quotas work. Occasionally quotas are voluntary; that is, the exporting country agrees to limit the flow of goods into the importing country. In the mid 1980s, the Japanese government agreed to voluntary quotas on automobiles sold in Canada, and regulated the number of cars shipped to this country. In 1985, only 197 000 cars were imported from Japan. The automobile manufacturers did this because sales of Japanese autos in North America were threatening the domestic industry and prompting cries for higher tariffs on foreign cars. Most quotas, though, are set and controlled by the importing country.

A second non-tariff barrier to trade is the use of **content restrictions.** These controls force the purchaser to buy goods which are produced in the home country. In the United States, cities receiving government money for some projects must ensure that at least 51 percent of items purchased originate in that country. In order to qualify for available funds these cities must make sure the majority of their money is spent on American products; imports are at a disadvantage. Canadians also use similar techniques. The British Columbia Ministry of Education, like that of most provinces, gives first preference to textbooks written, published, and printed in Canada. Elementary and high school textbooks that originate outside the country are less likely to be purchased because of the preference given to Canadian materials.

The National Energy Program (NEP), introduced in July 1980, is a third example of non-tariff barriers to trade between Canada and the United States. In this case, government policies unfavorable to foreign businesses were used to limit trade. Here is how it worked. Throughout the 1970s, world oil prices went wild, rising from $3.00 a barrel at the beginning of the decade to over $30.00 a barrel at the end. The high energy costs and instability in prices made it difficult for businesses to produce and market their goods. The federal government believed that by controlling the rate of increase of Canadian domestic oil prices they would be protecting the Canadian economy against sharply rising world oil prices. Companies would be able to predict energy price increases and adjust their way of doing business. The government believed the whole country would benefit from the NEP.

Canadians are so used to seeing bilingual labels that we fail to realize syrup bottles in the United States are in English only. Explain why packaging requirements can be considered non-tariff barriers.

271

American businesspeople generally felt Prime Minister Trudeau's policies hindered Canada-U.S. relationships. The National Energy Program was developed during his term in office.

Americans objected to the NEP because it favored Canadian businesses. It did so by forcing foreign oil companies with operations in Canada to make maximum use of Canadian goods, services, and labor, regardless of cost. Also, certain grants and other benefits were made available to Canadian corporations but not to foreign-owned companies. In some cases, licences to extract oil were only given to companies with at least 50 percent Canadian ownership, or to foreign companies in partnership with Canadian firms. Clearly these policies hit hard at American companies, along with their suppliers.

The effects of the NEP reached further than just the oil industry. Energy costs in Canada were low in comparison with those of the United States and Canadian industries benefited. American businesses charged that low Canadian energy costs were in effect a subsidy from the government and that Canadian firms were competing unfairly.

American businesses and government tried to change the NEP using three different techniques. First, they applied pressure through international organizations such as the Organization for Economic Co-operation and Development (OECD). They argued that Canada was bound by existing trade agreements and that the NEP violated those agreements. Secondly, they used informal diplomatic channels between Ottawa and Washington. A series of speeches, letters and meetings between officials from both governments made the American views known. Thirdly, threats of retaliation were made. American officials pointed out that the United States could impose new tariffs or other protections to match the Canadian actions.

In the end the threats of retaliation did not lead to action. Throughout 1981 and 1982, the Canadian government relaxed some of the restrictions on foreign oil companies, making the NEP less of a problem for the United States. As well, falling world energy prices in the mid-1980s, made the program less important than it had been. In 1985, the Conservative government under Brian Mulroney dismantled the NEP. Nevertheless, the NEP was a thorny issue that clouded Canadian-American relations throughout the early part of the decade.

1. Write definitions for "tariff" and "quota." Explain how each of these works to protect domestic industries.
2. Give two examples of non-tariff barriers and explain how they discriminate against foreign businesses.

Trade Protection: The Case Against It

Trade protection can sometimes create problems for an economy. Let us look at three such problems.

The first one might be called "failure to adapt." When businesses are safe from outside competition, they sometimes lose their incentive to adapt to new conditions and they grow less and less able to compete. Some people have argued that the Canadian clothing and textiles industry falls into this category. Protected by quotas and tariffs, the industry has not had to deal fully with the competition from Third World countries. If the doors were opened wide to imports from these areas where wages and other costs are only a fraction of Canadian rates, the industry would likely not survive. Competition forces businesses to constantly improve: reducing costs, improving products, finding larger markets. In the business world, as in the natural world, failure to adapt to changing conditions usually leads to extinction.

Another problem is that trade protections have often led other countries to take countermeasures in order to protect their industries. As we have seen, tariffs were applied to Canadian pork to balance what Americans considered an unfair trade subsidy. In the case of the National Energy Program, countermeasures were seriously considered by the Americans in response to Canadian actions.

Foreign ownership is a third problem that is encouraged by trade protections. If firms cannot sell their goods in other countries, one option they have is to build factories in those countries. In this way, they are able to get around trade protections. Foreign ownership is considered a problem by some governments because profits leave the country, and because foreign-owned companies are not necessarily good corporate citizens. They may make decisions which benefit the company but seriously harm the country in which they are located.

Throughout our history, American corporations have established factories and offices in Canada. In fact, some critics of foreign ownership have argued we have only a "branch-plant economy." But there are Canadian companies opening branch plants south of the border. The Bombardier Company, a Canadian-owned business, has established a plant in Vermont to get around the "Buy American" requirements attached to government funding. They build subway cars for the American market, especially for New York City. To meet the regulations, Bombardier makes sure that at least 51 percent of

Many large companies in Canada have American parents.

the material in the cars originates in the United States. Other Canadian firms, particularly in the communications industry, have taken similar action.

1. List some ways in which trade protection helps typical Canadians. List some ways in which it might harm them.

2. Explain how import quotas affect businesses on both sides of the border.

3. Explain why each of the following could be considered non-tariff barriers to American trade:
   • metrication
   • bilingualism
   • Canadian content requirements.

4. Give some examples of domestic industries that could or should be protected by trade barriers. Explain how and why.

Free Trade: The Case For It

While it has never truly existed between Canada and the United States, free trade has often been suggested as a cure for economic woes. Completely free trade would mean that all goods and services could pass between the two countries with no tariffs or barriers imposed. Forest products from British Columbia would find open markets in California; cotton from the southern states would be worn across Canada; data bases would link businesses and institutions throughout the continent. In short, economic exchanges would take place as if political boundaries did not exist.

Access to larger markets for businesses in both countries would be the key advantage of free trade between Canada and the United States. Our southern neighbor is ten times larger than Canada; this figure means ten times more consumers. For ambitious Canadian firms, the potential for growth is enormous. But American businesses are also interested in larger markets. They see Canada as a country of over 25 000 000 customers, most of whom share the same language as themselves and have similar purchasing patterns. In addition, the Canadian government is stable and has generally been friendly towards them. Many Americans view the Canadian market as a natural extension of their own.

Benefits of Free Trade

The people who support free trade argue that open competition could make the Canadian economy stronger. With more foreign competition, firms will be forced to be very aggressive, or they will die. Businesses will have to become better at identifying opportunities and following them up, and more efficient at eliminating waste and unprofitable activities. Without the benefit of a secure domestic market, companies that are not aggressive and efficient will not be successful. Those that do not measure up will find themselves falling farther and farther back, until it is unprofitable to continue in business.

One way businesses could adjust would be **specialization.** In a report on the problems and opportunities of free trade between Canada and the United States, one economist says:

> With the elimination of trade barriers between the two countries, Canadian producers would rationalize–that is, they would specialize in a smaller range of goods, producing each good at higher volume and frequently at lower cost.
> [R.J. Wonnacott, *Canada/United States Free Trade: Problems and Opportunities*, March 1985.]

Rather than producing a variety of goods for the Canadian market, Canadian firms would produce a few goods for sale to a much larger market. Here is an example. Suppose that under trade protections, the Acme Canning Company produced three "lines" of products: a budget "no name" brand, a higher priced name brand, and an expensive diet product line. All lines do well and make a profit. But conditions change because of a free trade agreement. Now low priced canned food from the American West and South is crossing the border and underselling the Acme brands.

The Acme board of directors studies the situation. It makes a decision to drop the lower priced lines and to specialize in high profit diet products. The company has an established reputation for these products and knows it can take a good share of the American market. Because of the higher volume in this one profitable area, its net profit becomes even higher.

Specialization usually is more profitable because activities are focussed. Highly specialized machines and tools, while more expensive to buy, usually have lower production costs, particularly if they are producing high volumes. Workers can be trained to do very specific tasks, and so do them well. Rather than attempting to produce many goods, specialized firms produce those which they do best.

There are a number of different ways in which firms could change their operations. They might sell some of their equipment and ideas to other companies who are specializing in that product. They might modify their equipment so that it is more useful to them. Or, they might simply close down their operations. On the other hand, the new approach to business may mean that they need to build new facilities and to expand existing plants. Whatever the case, free trade would force companies to make adjustments.

Some economists argue that free trade will benefit consumers in Canada. Because businesses will have rationalized and become more profitable, they will eventually be able to increase wages paid to workers, or reduce their prices, or both. In fact, supporters of free trade suggest that Canada's economy would grow by 5 to 10 percent if barriers with the United States were removed. Canadian consumers would also benefit by the inflow of lower priced American products.

Canada and the United States have, in fact, been gradually moving towards freer trade. Eighty percent of Canadian exports to the United States enter that country duty free while 65 percent of their exports to Canada cross the border without duties.

1. In one or two sentences, explain how specialization could help a business become or continue to be competitive.
2. Suggest reasons why the Americans would consider free trade with Canada. What do they have to gain by such an agreement?

Free Trade: The Case Against It

What would be the effect on Canada of a free trade agreement with the United States? People opposed to completely open trade argue there are several crucial issues that need to be examined. Let us look at five of the issues.

The first issue is that some sections of the economy may need protection because they could not survive in open competition. Four sectors would be hit especially hard by free trade, largely because their labor costs make them uncompetitive with their American counterparts. People employed in these sectors–furniture, chemicals, food and beverages, plastics and rubber–are generally opposed to completely free trade. An official of a large Canadian brewery estimated in late 1985 that completely free trade would lead to the loss of almost two-thirds of the 19 000 jobs in the Canadian brewing industry.

Opponents to total free trade suggest that **sectoral free trade,** where specific sectors of the economy have free trade and others do not, is a more desirable option. Those industries that would likely benefit by free trade would be able to operate without barriers, while those which need protection would have a secure domestic market.

A second issue is the loss of jobs that would result when branch plants of American companies closed. As we have seen, one method of getting around tariff barriers is to establish a branch plant in another country. Many American companies have opened outlets in Canada. Under free trade, these companies could find it more efficient to close the smaller branch facilities and supply Canada from the home base in the United States. In 1985, Lynn Williams, the Canadian president of the powerful international union, the United Steelworkers of America, remarked: "There is a much larger market in the United States. Canada is the northern fringe of that market. What incentive will [American companies] have to provide manufacturing facilities in Canada?"

A third issue is that of job displacement. People who are in favor of free trade point out that people who lose their jobs in one sector of the economy will find work in another, more active sector, but those opposed to it wonder if people can change jobs that easily. Tool and die makers laid off from the appliance industry may find it difficult to get work in the electronics or telecommunications fields. They will likely have to take retraining courses, and begin their careers again, probably at a lower salary. As well, if they are unable to find suitable jobs in the area where they live, they may have to move to find new employment. In any case, laid-off workers will find their lives disrupted, their incomes reduced, and their futures uncertain.

The fourth issue is Canada's potential loss of political freedom or **autonomy** in international relations. Because of the unrestricted movement of goods that would come about with free trade, our business activities would be impossible to separate from those of the United States. Businesses in Canada would be dependent on suppliers in the U.S.A. for equipment and materials, and on American consumers for purchases. Any disruption in trade would mean hardships for the economy. Under these circumstances it would be difficult for the government of Canada to do anything that might

What does this cartoon seem to be saying about free trade with the United States?

SECTORAL FREE TRADE: THE AUTO PACT

In 1965, Canada and the United States signed the U.S.-Canada Automotive Agreement, or Auto Pact, making the two countries a single market for automobiles and parts. Until that time, high tariffs had effectively created two separate markets, even though the major manufacturing companies were the same on both sides of the border.

The Auto Pact came about as a result of both consumer and industry pressure. Because of defensive trade barriers, Canadians were paying at least one-third more than Americans for the same make of car. To meet Canadian demands and get around paying tariffs, manufacturers had separate plants in Canada producing small quantities of a wide variety of models. Economies of scale meant costs per unit were higher in Canada than south of the border. Still, these prices were lower than those on American-made products placed under tariffs. The industry wanted to eliminate tariffs in order to avoid this duplication and make manufacturing more efficient. Consumers wanted to pay lower prices for automobiles.

Under the Auto Pact, vehicles made in either country can be moved across the border without tariffs being paid. Manufacturers in Canada soon developed specialized plants; instead of making three or four models a year, these plants now turn out only one model. From these assembly plants, the vehicles are shipped throughout the continent.

During negotiation of the Auto Pact, Canadian auto workers expressed concern about their future under a sectoral free trade situation. They thought the auto companies might shift some manufacturing out of Canada and into the United States, leaving them without jobs. As a result of their concerns, the Auto Pact contains safeguards which protect the Canadian auto industry. The agreement ensures that the number of vehicles produced in Canada is roughly equal to the number purchased here each year. In this way, the Auto Pact is not really free trade, but managed trade.

The graphs show the importance of Canadian-American automobile trade. But the graphs point out a situation that has led to dissatisfaction with the Auto Pact. Canada has become an assembler of automobiles: large

jeopardize free trade. Suppose the United States government decided to take some action against another country, as they did when they put a trade embargo (an order forbidding trade) on Nicaragua in 1985. Could the Canadian government oppose such an action?

The fifth issue has to do with Canada's cultural sovereignty, our ability to remain culturally separate from Americans. The strong economic ties we have to the United States have encouraged close cultural linkages. We watch American television programs and films, read American magazines and books, and listen to American recording artists. Clothing fashions for Canadians are influenced by trends in New York and southern California. Ideas, too, about education, politics, the environment, are shaped by American per-

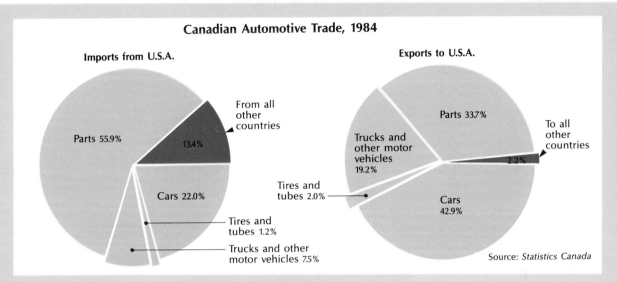

Canadian Automotive Trade, 1984

Imports from U.S.A.

Parts 55.9%
From all other countries 13.4%
Cars 22.0%
Tires and tubes 1.2%
Trucks and other motor vehicles 7.5%

Exports to U.S.A.

Parts 33.7%
Trucks and other motor vehicles 19.2%
To all other countries 2.2%
Tires and tubes 2.0%
Cars 42.9%

Source: *Statistics Canada*

volumes of parts are brought into the country and many completed vehicles leave. While this activity provides many jobs, they are generally the less-skilled, manual labor positions. The highly paid technical jobs, such as designing and testing and the manufacture of high-value parts, are centred in the United States. While the number of jobs in Canada is in proportion to the number of automobiles purchased, the dollars going into the Canadian economy as wages are less. Throughout a large part of the Auto Pact's history, Canada has had a trade deficit in automotive parts; more money leaves Canada than enters.

Recently, problems with the Auto Pact have been overshadowed by concerns about competition from offshore manufacturers. The North American industry has had to be very aggressive to hold its own against low-priced imports from Japan, Germany, Korea, and the Soviet Union.

spectives that have been transported across the border. Opponents of free trade argue that Canada's radio, television, magazine, film and publishing industries would be overwhelmed by American competition should the current protections be taken away by new trade agreements.

Since 1970, Canadian radio and television stations have had to meet minimum Canadian content regulations. For TV stations that are part of the Canadian Broadcasting Corporation (CBC) this means they must give at least 60 percent of their time to "Canadian" programs. To qualify, shows must have some Canadians in key positions, such as writers, producers, actors, composers, or directors. Private TV stations must have 50 percent Canadian content and radio stations are to meet a 30 percent requirement. The

The Conservative government under Prime Minister Mulroney encouraged freer trade with the Americans under President Reagan. What would the Americans gain from freer trade? What would Canadians gain?

magazine publishing industry is regulated in other ways that have similar goals. These content regulations have protected the broadcasting and publishing industries from American competition. A free trade agreement that required the removal of content regulations would put Canada's cultural industries in a very vulnerable position.

Issues such as these have hindered a free trade agreement between Canada and the United States. These issues involve problems for which there are no easy solutions.

1. Make a chart in your notebook showing the case for and against protected trade, and the case for and against free trade.
2. Summarize the advantages of specialization for a company.
3. If labor costs make a Canadian manufacturing company uncompetitive, what might the company do to overcome this problem?

Case Study: The Softwood Lumber Trade

The Canadians are playing with fire; you do have to defend yourself at some point.

With these words, Idaho Representative Larry Craig summed up his feelings about the growing volume of Canadian lumber imported into the United States. He had just finished introducing a bill in the United States Congress to limit sales of Canadian lumber in that country. In that year, 1985, a total of six bills aimed at protection of the American forest industry from Canadian imports made their way into Congress. Finally, in 1986, a bill imposing a tariff on Canadian softwood lumber products imported into the U.S. was signed by President Reagan.

Mr. Craig's words were representative of the feelings of protectionism that had sprung up in the lumber industry in the early and mid-1980s, but these feelings were relatively new. With the exception of a few brief years, there had been free trade in forest products between the two countries since the turn of the century. For all practical purposes, there was a single, continental forest economy.

Canadian softwood products were indeed enjoying strong sales south of the border. In 1978, they took 28 percent of the market; in 1984, 32 percent. (Supporters of protection measures claimed the

1984 figure was actually closer to 37 percent.) While this looks like a modest increase in percentage points, it represents millions of American dollars leaving the country. Remember, the demand for lumber is great; about 3000 to 4000 rail carloads of lumber *every day* in North America. Canadian lumber exports to the United States were worth over $3 billion in 1984. The American producers and workers were concerned about the erosion of their market.

The American industry based its claim for protection on the differences in **stumpage fees** between Canada and the United States. Stumpage fees are the costs producers must pay to harvest timber from publicly owned land. In Canada, these fees range between $15.00-$40.00 per million board feet (mbf) [1 mbf = 2360 m³], while in the United States they go as high as $100.00/mbf. The American producers claimed that the lower fees charged by the Canadian government amounted to a subsidy. Because of the subsidy, there was unfair competition. If the American producers could prove their case, they could get tariffs added to the price of Canadian imports.

In their defense, the Canadian forest companies argued that stumpage fees were not a fair way to compare the two industries.

Lumber destined for markets in the United States.

They point out that fees vary in different parts of the United States as well: $13.79/mbf in the American Rocky Mountains to $100.52/mbf in the Pacific Northwest. Stumpage fees reflect the conditions under which the timber can be harvested and marketed. Timber that grows fast and is easy to reach can be harvested at low costs, so stumpage fees can be high and the producer still makes a reasonable profit. Where timber is hard to get at, and grows slowly, stumpage fees must be lower or the timber companies will not make a profit. Differences in stumpage fees between the two countries only shows the differences under which the industries operate, and so is not a fair way to compare the two.

Continuing their defense, the Canadian companies pointed out that stumpage fees were not an issue in the boom times of the '60s and '70s. The Americans were not upset by differences in the fees then, and the method of setting the fees had not been changed. What had changed were the market conditions. Hard times in the early 1980s led the forest industry to become much more protective of its market. The Americans saw the differences in stumpage fees and blamed their loss of business on them. But that was not the real reason; the whole industry was just part of a huge economic system.

After the rough years of the early 1980s, the United States economy improved more quickly than that of most other countries. Its huge economy became more active, and so the strength of the U.S. dollar grew compared to other currencies. One U.S. dollar could buy more and more in other countries. In the mid-1970s, one U.S. dollar could buy a dollar's worth of goods in Canada; in 1985 it could buy goods worth about $1.38 in Canadian currency. In effect, Canadian lumber became cheaper than American lumber, so consumers bought the imported wood products. This lower price, the Canadian forest companies argued, was the real reason for their increasing share of the American market.

These arguments did not stop the American industry from pressing ahead with action to limit the Canadian influence. The United States companies were not even deterred by a 1983 decision of the United States Department of Commerce and the International Trade Commission that stumpage fees did *not* give Canadians an unfair advantage. After all, profits and jobs were at stake.

Officials in Canada were concerned about how American trade protections would affect relations between the two countries. Barriers in this industry would almost certainly bring cries for Canadian barriers to American products. Business people would not be prepared to let other countries put up protections without using

Canadian $ vs. U.S. $

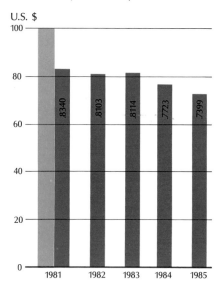

By 1985, a Canadian dollar could buy only about seventy-four cents' worth of American goods. This change in value meant the American dollar could buy more Canadian products.

some themselves. The situation could easily get out of hand and seriously affect trade patterns with the United States. With so much of Canada's employment dependent on sales across the border, the issue could not be taken lightly.

With the coming of the tariffs on shakes and shingles in 1986, the whole issue became even more thorny. Canadian officials did indeed respond by adding tariffs to a number of goods coming into the country. But, this action did little to quiet the voices of the American lumber interests. They pressed for even more tariffs while the Canadian industry argued for more open trade. A great deal of tension existed in the industry.

The problems of the North American softwood lumber industry illustrate the complex nature of international trade. This industry is part of a global economic system and responds to a multitude of forces and pressures. Friction between the two countries has occurred because of the changing value of Canadian and American currency on the world market. Industry officials cannot look for simple causes, such as blaming stumpage fees, nor look for simple "band-aid" remedies, like tariffs. Only by understanding the complexity of the problems will sophisticated solutions be found.

Despite the problems that do occur, millions of Canada-U.S. transactions occur smoothly every year. Remember, trade between the two countries totals over $150 billion a year: each country is the other's best customer.

1. Summarize the Americans' arguments for trade protections for their softwood lumber industry. Summarize the Canadian counterargument.
2. Why do simple solutions to international problems usually fail?

Summary

In the early history of Canada, the colonies were dependent on Britain for both markets for their raw materials and supplies of manufactured goods. Following Confederation, the new country established trade protections to encourage domestic businesses. By the middle part of the twentieth century Canada had developed strong trade ties to the United States despite government efforts to broaden trade to other countries.

Today, the United States is still our most important trading partner, with over $150 billion worth of goods crossing the border each year. These goods range from unprocessed raw materials, such as coal and petroleum, to manufactured goods, of which automobiles are an example. Some people point out that Canada exports raw materials and imports finished goods. They argue that more processing and finishing should be done in Canada.

Throughout our history, Canadians have discussed the trading relationship we have with our neighbors. Trade protections and free trade are two alternative ways of organizing trade ties. When trade protections are used, the price of goods entering a country may be increased by a tariff. This makes the goods less able to compete against domestic products, and gives an advantage to local businesses. The example of the Canadian pork industry showed how tariffs worked.

Under a free trade policy, goods and services would move across the international border without tariffs or duties. Competition between businesses in both countries would occur. The North American automobile industry is a case where free trade has operated within limits. The problems of protecting local business from outside competition has meant that completely free trade has never occurred between Canada and the United States.

The attack on the Canadian softwood lumber industry by American firms illustrates the complexity of trade issues. These issues are linked to global patterns and cannot be solved by simple solutions. The following chapter expands some of these ideas through an examination of Canada's linkages to countries around the Pacific Ocean and in the Indian Sub-Continent.

REVIEW

Checking Back

1. Write one- or two-sentence definitions for each of these terms.

   tariff   countervailing duty
   free trade   stumpage fees
   Auto Pact   branch plant
   economies of scale   economies

2. Write a paragraph summarizing the attitudes of Canadians towards free trade since the early part of the nineteenth century. In writing your paragraph you should pay attention to the conflicts over this issue between different groups within Canada.

Using Your Knowledge

3. In a table format, compare completely free trade and sectoral free trade using these headings: Advantages, Disadvantages, Groups, Who Will Benefit Most, Groups in Opposition.

4. What are advantages and disadvantages of foreign ownership in Canada?

Chapter 14

Pacific Rim Trading Partners

Look closely at the map of the world shown on page 286. What is unusual or unfamiliar about this view of the world? How does it differ from the usual world maps you see hanging in your classrooms? This map reflects an important change that has taken place in the world over the past fifty years. A half century ago, the industrialized world was limited to a few countries located on the northern shores of the Atlantic Ocean, and economic and political power was concentrated in these countries. These nations had dominated the world since the sixteenth century when they had begun to explore and colonize vast areas of Asia, Africa and the Americas. The traditional map of the world on page 287, centred on the Prime Meridian, reflects the importance those nations once enjoyed.

Today, more than thirty independent nations have shorelines on the Pacific Ocean. Taken together, these Pacific Rim nations have a great diversity of cultures, languages, economies and political systems. Among the lands bordering on the Pacific are:

- the five most populous nations in the world,
- the three largest countries in terms of area,
- the three most powerful industrial economies, and
- the two strongest military superpowers on Earth.

The nations of the Pacific Rim account for 60 percent of total world trade. Particularly in Asia are found some of the most rapidly modernizing and industrializing countries on the globe–many of them colonies only a few decades ago. In the early 1980s, Canada's

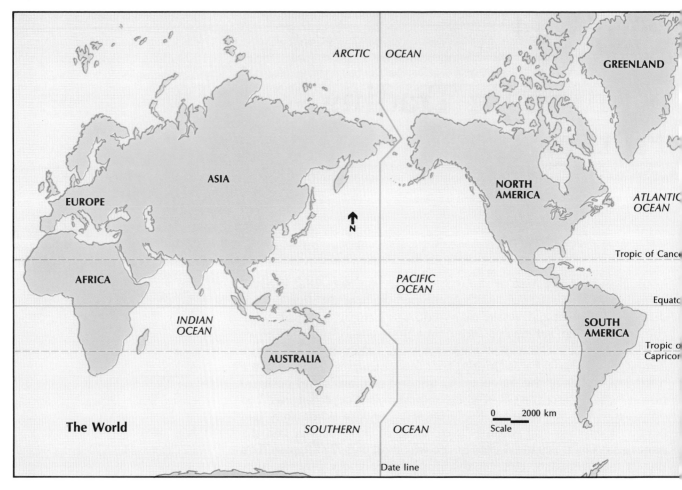

The World

What is the centre of this map of the world? What is the centre of most maps used in Canadian schools?

trade with Pacific Rim nations exceeded for the first time our trade with Europe, making the nations of this region our second most important trading partners after the United States.

Why has the centre of the industrialized world shifted from the Atlantic community to the Pacific Rim? Why have the Pacific Rim nations emerged as the world's leading economic partners in just a few short decades? What are the implications of these changes for Canada as a Pacific Rim nation? To properly examine these questions requires more information than could be presented in a single book, let alone one chapter. We will, however, begin to explore these very important topics in a series of brief snapshots of the Pacific Rim community of nations, focussing on Canada's place in that community as a trading partner.

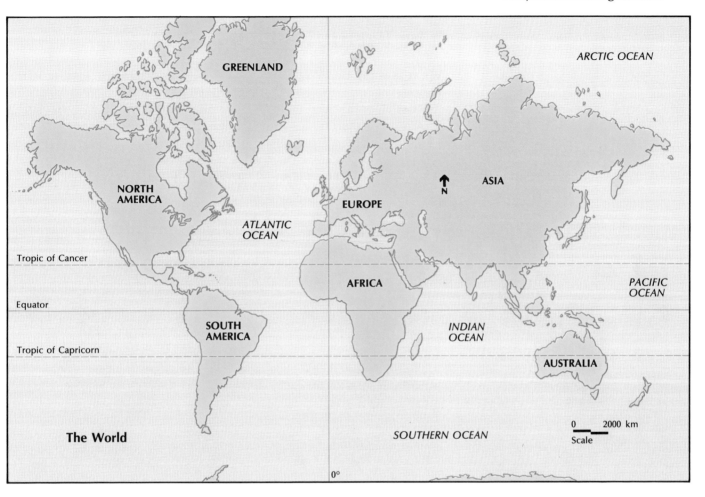

The World

As you read through this chapter, keep the following key questions in mind:

- What is a region? On what basis is the Pacific Rim defined as a region?
- Why has the centre of the industrial world shifted to the Pacific Rim region?
- What links does Canada have to this area of the world?
- How have Canadians benefited from economic growth in the Pacific Rim? How have Canadian industries been hurt by this new growth?
- What economic lessons can Canadians learn from participation in the Pacific Rim community?

The world map with which we are all familiar dates from the eighteenth century when Great Britain was the world's most powerful nation. The Royal Observatory at Greenwich, just outside London, became the point of reference on which all maps of the world were centred. The line passing through Greenwich and joining the two poles is the Prime Meridian (0° longitude).

The Pacific Rim Region

What is a region? What do we mean by the term the Pacific Rim region?

Most geographers will tell you that a region is an area with common characteristics and with boundaries that ensure the region is quite different from surrounding areas. Yet, among the diverse nations of the Pacific Rim, there are no cultural, economic, political or physical characteristics common to all. The only characteristic

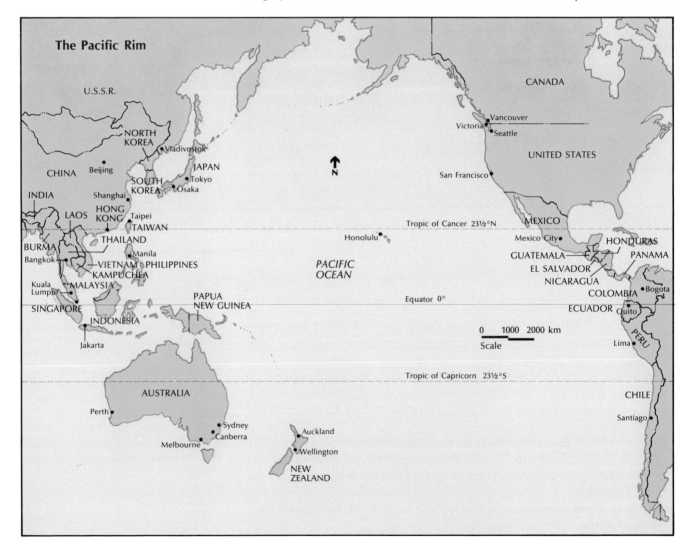

The Pacific Rim

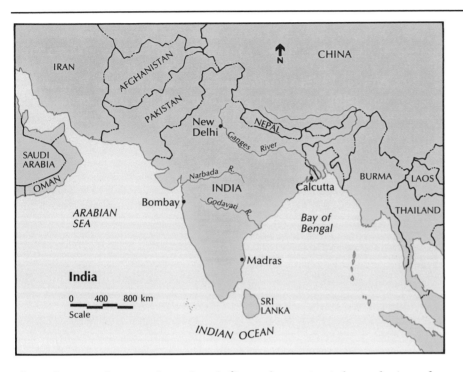

they share is the one that also defines the region's boundaries – the Pacific Ocean. This is not very useful as a defining characteristic for it only defines where the region's boundaries begin, not end. Are Atlantic Canada, Soviet Central Asia, the American Midwest or western China part of the Pacific Rim region?

The Pacific Rim may be divided into a number of subregions, which vary according to the criteria used to define them. Geographically, the largest and most cohesive of these subregions is East Asia which includes China, Japan, the Koreas, Taiwan and Hong Kong. The countries of this subregion share some cultural similarities as well as geographic proximity. Other important subregions of the Pacific Rim are: South East Asia (including Malaysia, Singapore and Indonesia), Oceania (Australia, New Zealand and Papua-New Guinea), the Pacific Islands, coastal South America (Chile, Ecuador and Colombia), Central America (of which Mexico is the largest country), and coastal North America. For this chapter we will also consider the Indian Sub-Continent to be part of the Pacific Rim even though it technically does not face the Pacific. It does, however, have strong ties to the Pacific Rim and so the countries of India, Pakistan, Bangladesh, Sri Lanka and Burma will be included as a subregion.

The subregions of the Pacific Rim are very diverse, yet one characteristic is emerging as a powerful unifying force–economic interdependence through trade. The nations of the Pacific Rim are finding mutual benefit in increasing and enhancing patterns of economic development and trade around the Pacific. The opportunities for the entire region appear limitless. This is the promise, and the challenge, of the Pacific Rim region.

Pacific Rim Casebook

Australia

Area	7 682 300 km²
Population (1983)	15 451 900
Major Cities (Population)	Sidney (3 332 600) Melbourne (2 864 600) Brisbane (1 138 400)
Gross Domestic Product	$166.2 billion (U.S.)
Unemployment	10%
Inflation rate	3.9%
Imports (1983-1984)	$24.1 billion (U.S.)
Exports (1983-1984)	$23.6 billion (U.S.)
Australia-Canada Trade	$826 million (Cdn.)

The Land
Australia is entirely surrounded by water. Much of the continent lies in tropical or semitropical latitudes, with only the extreme southern area lying in more temperate latitudes. The coastline of northern Australia is subject to tropical monsoons which produce wet summers and dry winters. In southern Australia, winter is the wet month, although in all areas rainfall drops off sharply the farther one moves away from the coast. Much of the vast interior region of the country is comprised of semi-arid or arid regions.

The People
The nation of Australia occupies the entire continent of Australia, along with the adjoining island of Tasmania. In 1985, the popula-

In Australia climates range from tropical to desert. In many parts of the continent hardy sheep are grazed on land too dry to support crops.

tion of Australia was approximately 16 million people. Of these, 62 percent live in two states–New South Wales and Victoria. Most Australians are descendants of immigrants who went to Australia when it was colonized by the British during the eighteenth century. The official language of Australia is English and the level of literacy is very high as Australians have an excellent public school system. Most Australians enjoy a standard of living and quality of life comparable to that of Canadians. The original peoples of Australia, the Aborigines, have undergone an experience that closely parallels that of Native peoples in Canada.

Government
Australia has a federal system of government similar to that of Canada. In addition to the central government, which makes laws for the whole nation, there are six state governments and two territorial governments. Australia differs from Canada in that governments serve for only three years. Its upper house of parliament, the Senate, is elected, and most state governments have both upper and lower houses.

The Economy
The Australian economy has changed greatly since 1960. These changes have been similar to those experienced by Canada and other

industrial nations. In 1956-1957, agriculture accounted for 14 percent of Australia's **Gross Domestic Product**, while manufacturing generated 29 percent, mining accounted for less than 2 percent and services 47 percent. Twenty-five years later, agriculture and manufacturing had declined to 7 percent and 19 percent respectively, while mining (5 percent) and the service sector (61 percent) had both increased significantly. These changes have resulted from important mineral discoveries and from the growing interdependence of Australia with other Pacific Rim economies.

Economic growth in Australia exceeded that of most industrialized countries up to the early 1980s, when the country's economy was severely affected by a worldwide recession. In recent years, a lowering of the value of the Australian dollar combined with aggressive marketing tactics have made Australia highly competitive as a supplier of coal, iron ore, grain and other raw materials to the other industrial nations of the Asian portion of the Pacific Rim region.

Five primary products accounted for 42 percent of all exports from Australia in 1984: coal, wheat, wool, iron ore and beef. Major imports included machinery and transportation equipment, petroleum-based fuels and lubricants and basic manufactured items. Japan is Australia's largest trading partner, accounting for about one-quarter of total trade, with the United States second and Great Britain third.

Canada-Australia Trade Relations

The economies of Canada and Australia are quite similar: both nations depend heavily on primary industries for export sales. As a result, Australian exports compete actively with some Canadian products, especially mineral and agricultural products from western Canada. On the other hand, Australia imports forest products, sulphur and fertilizers from Canada, with most of these products coming from British Columbia and Alberta. In the mid-1980s, trade analysts believed that Australia could be a potential market for Canadian technology and services, particularly in the mining and energy resource fields.

1. What percentage of Australia's population lives in the three largest cities? Locate these three cities in your atlas. Suggest why they are located where they are.
2. Use your atlas and the information in this casebook to sug-

Canadian Exports to Australia—1983	($000)
Lumber, softwood	43 804
Sulphur	37 878
Wood pulp	26 508
Fertilizers and fertilizer materials	21 930
Newsprint paper	20 406
Motor vehicle parts except engines	19 851
Telecommunications and related equipment	18 469
Office machines and equipment	15 624
Fish, canned	13 879
Other personal and household goods	11 311
Other	208 355
Totals	437 966

Source: B.C. Ministry of International Trade and Investment

Canadian Imports From Australia—1983	($000)
Misc. metals in ores, concentrates and scrap	82 217
Raw sugar	76 589
Aluminum ores, concentrates and scrap	56 153
Meat, fresh, chilled or frozen	46 790
Fruits, dried or dehydrated	23 112
Plate, sheet and strip steel	4 924
Other meat and meat preparations	4 783
Wool and fine animal hair	4 100
Other special transactions, trade	4 089
Other	50 016
Totals	357 487

Source: B.C. Ministry of International Trade and Investment

gest some reasons why 62 percent of all Australians live in New South Wales and Victoria.

3. Explain how increased imports from other Pacific Rim nations might have contributed to the declining role of manufacturing in the Australian economy.

4. What was Australia's balance of trade (difference between imports and exports) in 1984? Why would devaluation (lowering the value of the Australian dollar relative to other currencies) help that country increase its exports and reduce imports? How would this affect the balance of trade?

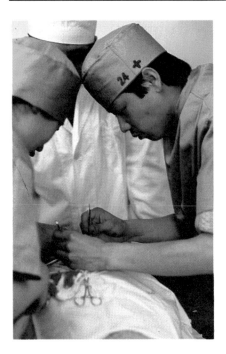

Delicate surgery at the Beijing Agricultural University in China.

The People's Republic of China

Area	9 561 000 km²
Population (1980)	1 032 000 000
Major Cities (Population)	Shanghai (12 000 000) Beijing (9 330 000) Tianjin (7 850 000)
Gross Domestic Product (1983)	$313.0 billion (U.S.)
Unemployment	2.6%
Inflation rate	2.1%
Imports (1983)	$21.5 billion (U.S.)
Exports (1983)	$22.4 billion (U.S.)
China-Canada Trade	$1.8 billion (Cdn.)

China-Canada Trade Relations

Trade between Canada and the People's Republic of China has expanded rapidly since the establishment of diplomatic relations between the two nations in 1970. The leading commodity exported to China is wheat from western Canada, but aluminum and wood pulp from British Columbia are also important exports. In return, Canada imports a wide variety of clothing, footware and other manufactured items from China.

Canada enjoys a very favorable trade balance with China: in 1982, we had a surplus of more than $1 billion. Yet, this surplus presents a barrier to increased Canada-China trade as the Chinese government prefers balanced trading arrangements. Opportunities are present, however, for increased sales of Canadian technology and equipment in a variety of industries, particularly forestry, mining, agriculture and energy resources. These are areas where China has a real need and Canada has the expertise to help them.

1. What percentage of China's gross domestic product is accounted for by imports and exports? How does this compare to Australia? What does this suggest about the nature of China's economy compared to that of Australia?
2. China has a socialist government, in which many aspects of the economy are controlled by the state. How might this fact

A street scene in China. As this nation develops economically, it will undoubtedly become a more important trading partner for Canada.

explain China's unemployment and inflation rates compared to those of Australia or Canada?

3. Use your atlas and other resource materials to prepare a summary description of China, similar to the one for Australia on pages 290-293, using the following headings: The Land; The People; Government; The Economy.
4. Suggest some reasons why the Chinese would prefer balanced trading relationships with countries such as Canada.

China's Major Trading Partners—1982		(U.S. $ million)
Country	Imports	Exports
U.S.A.	4 244	1 741
Japan	3 859	4 756
Hong Kong	1 297	5 117
Canada	1 229	204
Germany	955	763
Australia	903	221
All Others	6 212	8 865
Total	18 699	21 667

Source: International Monetary Fund

Canadian Exports to China—1982	($000)
Wheat	736 562
Aluminum, including alloys	190 224
Wood pulp	89 137
Synthetic rubber and plastic materials	49 982
Sulphur	41 449
Plate, sheet and strip steel	26 945
Zinc, including alloys	20 289
Other crude wood products	19 528
Newsprint paper	10 447
Lumber, softwood	9 116
Other	35 744
Total	1 229 453
B.C. Share of Total	173 200

Source: B.C. Ministry of International Trade and Investment

Canadian Imports from China—1982	($000)
Outerwear, except knitted	38 489
House furnishings	24 944
Other apparel and apparel accessories	16 009
Other vegetables and vegetable preparations	14 818
Broad woven fabrics, cotton	13 461
Outerwear, knitted	12 913
Broad woven fabrics, mixed fibres	11 268
Nuts, except oil nuts	10 609
Kitchen utensils, cutlery, tableware	7 006
Footwear	5 309
Other	48 828
Total	203 654

Source: B.C. Ministry of International Trade and Investment

India

India-Canada Trade Relations

Canada exported nearly $300 million worth of raw materials and goods to India in 1982, while importing less than $100 million worth of Indian products. This unequal pattern of trade between the two countries has persisted for a number of years. India imports

Area	3 300 000 km²
Population (1984)	746 000 000
Major Cities (Population)(1981)	Calcutta (9 100 000)
	Bombay (8 200 000)
	Delhi (5 700 000)
Gross Domestic Product (1983)	$150 billion (U.S.) est.
Unemployment	not available
Inflation rate	8.3%
Imports (1983)	$13.6 billion (U.S.)
Exports (1983)	$8.6 billion (U.S.)
India-Canada Trade (1983)	$363 million (Cdn.)

A large part of India is arid and the people rely on wells for water. Canadian programs have helped the people drill for deeper water sources.

raw materials needed to supply its rapidly expanding industrial sector, but does not yet produce sufficient consumer goods to sell to the Canadian market. Products imported to Canada from India have continued to be traditional items, such as food products, coffee, tea, clothing and handicraft items.

British Columbia Exports to India—1982	($000)
Metal bearing ores	1 246
Sulphur	5 500
Zinc blocks, pegs and slabs	8 702
Asbestos milled fibres	8 409
Lumber	84
Wood pulp	6 634
Aircraft equipment and parts	1 150
Telecommunications equipment	1 555
Other	2 098
Total	35 378
Canadian Total	292 481

Source: B.C. Ministry of International Trade and Investment

Indian Foreign Trade by Country—1982-1983			
Exports	(%)	Imports	(%)
USSR	17.6	USSR	10.5
United States	10.8	United States	9.5
Japan	9.0	Japan	7.4
United Kingdom	5.2	United Kingdom	6.2
West Germany	3.9	West Germany	5.5
Saudi Arabia	2.6	Iran	5.4
United Arab Emirates	2.5	Canada	1.7
Other	48.4	Other	53.8
Total	100 %	Total	100 %

Source: B.C. Ministry of International Trade and Investment

1. What percentage of India's gross domestic product is accounted for by imports and exports? How does this compare to China? to Australia? What does this suggest about the nature of India's economy compared to that of China?
2. More than 70 percent of India's labor force is engaged in peasant agriculture. How might this fact make it difficult to determine the level of unemployment in India?
3. Use your atlas and other resource materials to prepare a summary description of India similar to the one for Australia given on pages 290-293, using the following headings: The Land; The People; Government; The Economy.

Japan

Area	377 700 km²
Population (1984)	119 896 000
Major Cities (Population)	Tokyo (8 170 000) Yokohama (2 915 000) Osaka (2 534 000)
Gross Domestic Product (1983)	$1204 billion (U.S.)
Unemployment	2.7%
Inflation rate	4.0%
Imports (1983)	$126 billion (U.S.)
Exports (1983)	$146 billion (U.S.)
Japan-Canada Trade	$9.2 billion (Cdn.)

A well-known Japanese land-mark, Mount Fuji towers above the surrounding countryside.

Japan's Economic Miracle

There is a popular and widespread myth that Japan's highly successful economy developed miraculously in the years following World War II. The truth is that Japan became industrialized more than a century ago–the first non-western nation to do so. By the early decades of the twentieth century, Japan's industrial power rivalled some of the leading nations of Europe. The country's first exports were traditional products, such as silks and lacquered goods. The money earned from these export sales was reinvested in new factories and machinery to make cotton textiles and clothing for export. By World War I, Japan was equal to many European nations in such areas as iron and steel production, machine tool making, shipbuilding, electrical power and coal mining. During World War I, the European Allies purchased warships and other armaments from the Japanese.

By 1919, manufacturing had replaced agriculture as Japan's leading source of employment at a time when most Canadians still worked on farms. Yet few Westerners realized the extent of Japan's industrial strength until World War II. Even then, many Westerners dismissed the Japanese as a second-rate industrial nation after that country's defeat by the Allies. During the early postwar years, North Americans thought of "Made in Japan" as being synonymous with cheap, mass-produced, poor quality products. The Japanese, however, as they had in the late nineteenth century, once again used low-cost exports to acquire the capital needed to rebuild their war-shattered economy.

By the 1960s, "Made in Japan" had come to stand for an ever increasing range of high quality cameras, electronic products, home appliances and heavy industrial equipment. Since 1955, Japan has had the fastest growing economy of any of the major industrial nations. Its economic growth rate has averaged about 10 percent per year. Today, 90 percent of Japan's output is bought by Japanese consumers whose wages now are higher than those of many European workers.

The reasons for Japan's economic miracle are many. Japan is a small nation with few natural resources but a wealth of human abilities, and the will to make the most of those abilities. The Japanese have a long tradition of willingness to acquire the best ideas, technology and culture from other nations, and the inventive genius needed to improve upon these borrowings. Even more important, however, are the long-standing Japanese traditions of skilled craftspeople and excellence in the arts as well as in business.

A steel mill in Japan. The Japanese are world leaders in steel production in spite of their limited natural resources.

The Japanese people have learned the benefits of co-operation in the pursuit of common goals, goals which are pursued with a vigor most Westerners find difficult to understand. In Japanese factories, for example, worker loyalty is encouraged through company songs, uniforms and daily rituals. The result is a work force that puts loyalty to the company ahead of all else, except family and nation. Workers will willingly work six days a week, fifty weeks a year, and feel deprived if they cannot. In return, the firms have a loyalty to the workers, ensuring them lifelong employment. As well, Japanese companies often provide their workers with low-cost housing, excellent recreational facilities and other "cradle-to-grave" benefits.

INSIDE A JAPANESE SCHOOL

Consider the schedule of typical Japanese students. They go to school five and a half days a week, including Saturday mornings. After school, they receive another three hours or so of private tutoring. They have daily homework (and have had since Grade 1). They have fewer holidays than Canadian students–just a little over one month during the summer and a week-long break around the beginning of the year.

The Japanese are among the most highly educated people in the world. They consider education the key to Japan's technological development and economic success. In Japanese society, people's status is often determined by their educational background. Students who do well and graduate from the top high schools and universities are almost guaranteed good jobs for life in major companies or the government. Education is so impor-

tant that families sacrifice in other areas to pay for extra tutoring for their children.

There is a great deal of pressure on children to perform well in school, particularly on entrance examinations. The first set of entrance examinations are written at the end of Grade 9 to determine which upper secondary school the students will attend. Competition is fierce, since students from the best high schools are more likely to get into the best universities. University-bound students write another set of entrance examinations at the end of Grade 12.

Japanese students study similar subjects to those found in Canadian schools. If there is a difference between teaching styles in the two countries it is that the Japanese put more emphasis on rote learning (learning by repetition) and less emphasis on developing individual creativity.

British Columbia's Exports to Japan—(1982)	(c$ millions)
Coal	564.6
Lumber	384.5
Wood pulp	290.3
Copper concentrates	230.8
Fish products	159.7
Aluminum ingots	148.3
Gold and silver in ores and concentrates	58.3
Molybdenum concentrates	50.2
Logs	45.9
Pulpwood chips	41.0
Other	158.0
Total	2131.6
Canadian Total	4571.2

Source: B.C. Ministry of International Trade and Investment

Canadian Imports from Japan—(1982)	(c$ millions)
Passenger automobiles and chassis	829.9
Telecommunication and related equipment	397.3
Other motor vehicles	212.8
Trucks, truck tractors and chassis	180.7
Photographic goods	142.1
Television, radios and phonographs	114.7
Pipes and tubes, iron and steel	107.8
Motor vehicle parts, except engines	106.4
Miscellaneous equipment and tools	80.4
Other transportation equipment	75.7
Other	1279.3
Total	3527.1

Source: B.C. Ministry of International Trade and Investment

1. What percentage of Japan's gross domestic product is accounted for by imports and exports? How does this compare to China? to Australia? to India?
2. Some American industries have complained that Japan's highly industrialized economy has been built on exports and that consumers in the United States and other nations have played a major part in that country's success story. Does the percentage of GDP represented by exports indicate that

Japan's economy is highly export-oriented? Explain your answer.

3. Officials of many firms in Canada have argued that Canadian workers put loyalty to the company well down their list, after loyalty to their friends, unions, church, and so on. This, the officials point out, is very different than the highly successful Japanese approach. Do you agree with this opinion? Explain your answer. What are the consequences if this is correct?

4. Canada is a country with many natural resources, while Japan has surprisingly few. In a few sentences, summarize the characteristics that have allowed the Japanese economy to develop as one of the world's strongest.

THE NEW JAPANS

Nations such as South Korea, Singapore and Taiwan have come to be known as the "new Japans." During the 1970s, these countries had economic growth rates of from 9-10 percent (the global average was 4 percent). Many of the manufactured goods Canada bought from Japan a decade ago, such as textiles, television sets and electronic equipment, now come from these newly industrialized countries. They have followed the Japanese lead in industrializing, basing their economies on low-cost exports to pay for new factories and production facilities.

Can the Japanese model work for developing nations in other parts of the Pacific Rim, such as Central and South America? Increasingly, Japanese economists, technicians and corporations are becoming involved in economic development projects in nations around the world, both through direct investment and through foreign aid programs.

Mexico

Area	1 949 706 km²
Population (1984)	77 659 000
Major Cities (Population)	Mexico City (12 900 000 est.) Guadalajara (3 000 000) Monterrey (2 700 000)
Gross Domestic Product (1983)	$168.0 billion (U.S.)
Unemployment	25% (est.)
Inflation rate (1984)	65.4%
Imports (1983)	$7.7 billion (U.S.)
Exports (1983)	$21.4 billion (U.S.)
Mexico-Canada Trade	$1.4 billion (Cdn.)

303

Above: An outdoor market in Guadalajara.

Above right: Mexico earns a large proportion of its income from catering to American and Canadian tourists. This pottery is for sale in Acapulco, an important tourist Mecca facing onto the Pacific Ocean.

Mexico-Canada Trade Relations

Mexico enjoys a highly favorable balance of trade with Canada, with exports to Canada in 1983 totalling $1079 million while Canadian goods sent to Mexico in that year had a value of only $382 million. Canadians import large amounts of fresh fruits and vegetables from Mexico, especially during the winter months. Each year, large numbers of Canadian tourists visit Mexico, significantly influencing the balance of trade with that country.

1. What percentage of Mexico's population lives in Mexico City? Locate Mexico City in your atlas. Suggest why it is located where it is. What problems would having such a high percentage of its population living in a single city create for the country's economy and political system?
2. Calculate the GDP/capita for Mexico. How does it compare with those of Australia, Japan and Korea?
3. Use your atlas and other resource materials to prepare a summary description of Mexico similar to the one for Australia on pages 290-293, using the following headings: The Land; The People; Government; The Economy.

4. There is an old Mexican saying that goes "Poor Mexico. So far from Heaven and so close to the United States." What problems, in your opinion, might a developing nation such as Mexico face having a highly industrialized nation such as the United States for a neighbor? What benefits does it receive from its proximity to the U.S.? How is Mexico's situation similar to that of Canada? How does it differ?

5. Why, in your opinion, would a nation such as Mexico that has difficulty feeding all of its fast-growing population export food products to countries such as Canada and the United States?

WHAT DO THEY THINK OF CANADIANS?

Canada is respected on both sides of the Pacific for its performance in the areas of international diplomacy, immigration and foreign aid. But how do people in the Pacific Rim region see Canada as a trading partner?

Perhaps the first thing to realize is that Canadian trade is not a very significant part of the total trade of most Pacific Rim countries. Although Japan is Canada's second largest trading partner, Canada is only Japan's sixth largest trading partner.

When business people in Pacific Rim countries think of Canada, they see it as a source of raw materials. Like a vast mine and farm, Canada produces minerals, timber and cereals needed by factories in the United States and Asia. Canada has not normally been seen as a source of manufactured goods, expertise or technology. Increasingly, however, nations in both Latin America and Asia have turned to Canada for technological assistance in such areas as mining, forestry, the pulp and paper industry, transportation and port development. These efforts are often linked to our foreign aid program.

The general impression among some Asian countries of Canada's economic performance is not flattering. Canada is seen by these people as a huge country with a small population, most of which lives in a series of communities strung out along the United States border like beads on a necklace. They see people living in the different regions of Canada as spending a great deal of time in arguments with each other, instead of working together toward national goals. As one Hong Kong journalist sees it, Canadians squabble "over language, the Constitution, the ownership of energy resources and provincial differences." With eleven different governments (provincial and federal) having their say, Canada does not speak on trade issues with one clear voice.

When it comes to the workplace, Canadians are not viewed as very productive or hard working. Compared to workers in a country such as South Korea, Canadians seem lazy and overpaid, with a poor work ethic. The number of days lost by Canadian workers through absenteeism or labor conflicts is very high. Canada also has relatively high unemployment. In Japan, it is considered better to "underemploy" workers at low-paying jobs than to pay them when they are not working.

Links Around the Pacific

British Columbia is linked to the Pacific Rim through strong transportation and communication linkages.

The links between Canada and the Pacific Rim region are many and varied. This section first provides a sampling of these links. It will then examine, in turn, three activities where ties between Canada and Pacific Rim regions are especially important: immigration, foreign aid and trade.

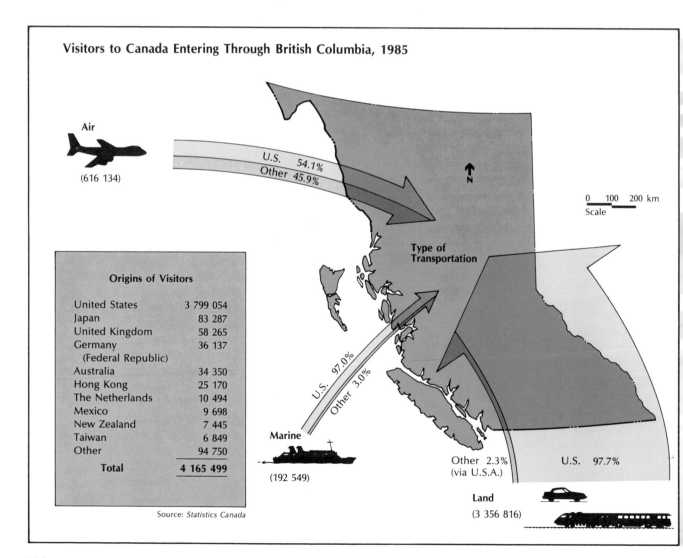

Visitors to Canada Entering Through British Columbia, 1985

Air
(616 134)

U.S. 54.1%
Other 45.9%

Type of Transportation

0   100   200 km
Scale

Origins of Visitors	
United States	3 799 054
Japan	83 287
United Kingdom	58 265
Germany (Federal Republic)	36 137
Australia	34 350
Hong Kong	25 170
The Netherlands	10 494
Mexico	9 698
New Zealand	7 445
Taiwan	6 849
Other	94 750
Total	**4 165 499**

Source: *Statistics Canada*

U.S. 97.0%
Other 3.0%

Marine
(192 549)

Other 2.3% (via U.S.A.)   U.S. 97.7%

Land
(3 356 816)

Immigration

Immigration is an important link between Canada and the Pacific Rim, one that has left a vibrant cosmopolitan stamp on Vancouver and other Canadian centres. New Canadians from Pacific Rim nations have made many significant contributions to the economic and cultural life of Canada ever since the days of the building of the CPR (see pages 193-202). In 1983, Asia replaced Europe and Britain as our major source of immigrants. Thirty-four thousand Asians emigrated to Canada that year. Although Asians have been coming to Canada since the 1800s, their numbers increased dramatically after 1967 when new immigration laws were passed. These laws removed immigration restrictions based on the country of origin of the immigrants. During the 1970s, large numbers of people arrived from the Indian Sub-Continent. Today there are about 250 000 Canadians of East Indian origin. In 1973, Prime Minister Trudeau visited China and announced a family reunification plan. It allowed over 20 000 Chinese to emigrate to Canada to join relatives from whom they had been long-separated. Today there are over 300 000 Canadian citizens of Chinese descent. Canada has also opened its doors to waves of refugees from other countries in the region, including more than 70 000 Vietnamese in the period 1979-1981.

VANCOUVER'S MULTICULTURAL SCHOOL POPULATION

In Vancouver's school population, more than 50 percent of the students have a language other than English as their mother tongue. Many of these students come from Latin America, Asia and the Indian Sub-Continent. During the past decade in particular, these numbers have soared.

To accommodate this influx, Vancouver schools have implemented a number of programs. There are "English as a Second Language" classes for students not fluent in English. Home-school workers speaking different languages have been hired to help the school staff communicate with parents. For instance, they translate report cards and other school materials before the students take them home. Race relations programs implemented by the schools help students get along with students from different backgrounds.

Teachers, too, need training to understand students who may have very different cultural values and traditions. For example, the Christmas concert is traditionally an important event in Canadian schools, but many Vancouver students come from cultures that do not celebrate Christmas. So in Vancouver's schools today, you might also find classes celebrating events such as the Chinese New Year or Baisakhi Day, the Sikh new year.

These immigrants have brought their languages and customs with them, allowing other Canadians to become more familiar with other cultures. They have also helped stimulate tourism and business contacts between Canada and other Pacific Rim countries. Canada has not always treated its immigrants well, and even today there is prejudice directed towards some ethnic groups. Generally, however, Canada is respected in the eyes of people in Pacific Rim countries for its generosity in opening doors to immigrants.

Foreign Aid

Canadian aid has provided another important link between Canada and developing nations of the Pacific Rim region. The Canadian International Development Agency (CIDA) is the channel for most of Canada's foreign aid. Founded in 1968, CIDA helps poorer nations get their economies off the ground and cope better with social problems. Canada's aid program began in Asia and the area currently receives over $300 million annually. Canada concentrates on eight nations that are home to 90 percent of the poorest people in the world: Bangladesh, India, China, Pakistan, Sri Lanka, Thailand, Indonesia and Nepal. Canadian aid programs are also underway among the underdeveloped nations of Central and South America.

Projects funded by the Canadian International Development Agency have helped workers acquire the skills the country will need as it develops. This welder is in Bangladesh.

Many of CIDA's projects focus on improving basic health and food production. Other projects develop other aspects of the countries' economies. Here are a few of the projects CIDA was involved in in 1983. In Pakistan, CIDA vaccinated more than 15 million children under the age of five against polio. In Bangladesh, it established farming co-operatives to help some of the country's 40 million poor produce food. CIDA worked with India on research to improve crop yields on the three-quarters of India's farmland that is not irrigated. In Thailand, CIDA helped establish a Forest Tree Seed centre for reforestation projects. In China, Canadian forestry knowledge helped the Chinese control forest fires.

While CIDA's major goal is to help poorer countries, it also boosts sales of Canadian goods and services in the various countries in which it operates. With this foothold in the door, Canada hopes to be a step ahead of its competitors when it comes to future sales. As their economies grow, the newly developed and developing Pacific Rim countries will need to purchase more and more goods and services to serve the needs of their enormous populations. This may open up opportunities for Canadian suppliers.

Trade

Trade between Canada's west coast and other Pacific Rim nations has been carried on since the days of the Maritime fur trade (see pages 128-133) during the nineteenth century. In the late 1800s, lumber became the basis of our export trade with the Pacific Rim region. The arrival of the Canadian Pacific Railway in 1887 made Vancouver a key port of entry for goods such as tea destined for Toronto and Montreal and silks bound for Europe.

Pacific trade became much more important during the second half of this century. Grain shipments dominated our exports to the region during the mid-1950s and remain important exports to China and the Soviet Union. The first shipments of coal, now Canada's major export to the region, were sent to Japan. During the 1970s, while the value of Canadian exports as a whole grew by nearly four and a half times, exports to Pacific Rim countries grew by nearly six times.

Examine the figures below illustrating the value of Canada's trade (exports and imports) with Asian countries of the Pacific Rim in 1984. Which country in the region is by far our largest trading partner? How does the value of imports from South Korea, Taiwan,

Hong Kong and Singapore compare with imports from the other Asian nations?

Value of Canadian exports and imports to and from the Asia Pacific region—1984		
($ millions)	Exports	Imports
Japan	5628.6	5710.8
China	1272.1	333.5
South Korea	712.6	1152.4
Taiwan	400.6	1223.8
Hong Kong	214.8	966.2
Singapore	143.0	214.3
Indonesia	290.5	71.9
Malaysia	187.7	168.0
Philippines	56.8	117.3
Thailand	116.8	103.4
India	468.2	147.1
Pakistan	90.3	54.2
Bangladesh	102.8	14.7
Sri Lanka	44.6	33.9
Source: Statistics Canada and Canada-Japan Trade Council		

1. Prepare a similar chart for the remaining nations of the Pacific Rim, using the *Canada Yearbook* and other resources.
2. Using the most recent *Canada Yearbook*, calculate changes in Canada's trading relationships with these Pacific Rim nations since 1984. Which nations have had the greatest increase in imports from Canada? exports to Canada? Suggest some reasons for this pattern.

Trade Issues

Canada's total trade with the Pacific Rim region, in comparison to that with the United States, may be just a drop in the bucket. Yet trade between Canada and the other Pacific Rim countries is growing rapidly. Below, you will first look at some of the issues involved in our trading relationship with the region. You will then observe some of the challenges that arise from that same relationship.

For Canada, the emergence of the Pacific Rim economies can be seen as a threat or an opportunity. The threat is that Canadian manufacturers will not be able to compete against inexpensive, well-made products pouring into Canada from Pacific Rim countries. The opportunity lies in the sales Canada might be able to make to this expanding market, one that contains half the world's population.

In the chapter on Canada and the United States, you read about the debate over trade protection versus free trade. The same debate applies to our trading relationship with the Pacific Rim countries. The Canadian government has taken some measures to protect Canadian industries against competition from Pacific Rim nations. Canada has defensive tariffs on imports of clothing and footwear from these countries. It has persuaded Japan to agree to a voluntary quota on the number of Japanese cars entering Canada. Most of the pressure to maintain these protectionist measures comes from the manufacturing belt of central Canada, especially Ontario, where most of the automobile, textile and footwear factories in Canada are located.

Trade was an important subject during discussions between Japan's Prime Minister Yasuhiro Nakasone and Prime Minister Brian Mulroney in January 1986.

The pressure to reduce tariffs and quotas comes largely from western Canada which stands to gain most by increased trade with the Pacific Rim region. Western Canada has natural resources needed by Japan and the newly industrialized countries. For instance, coal from British Columbia and Alberta helps fuel Japan's automobile industry. Naturally, Canadian coal producers are not keen on import quotas on Japanese cars that might slow down that industry. In general terms, Canadians pushing for freer trade ask how we can expect Pacific Rim countries to buy from us unless we are willing to buy from them. They ask why we should, for example, hold trade fairs to promote sales of Canadian products in countries such as Hong Kong, while at the same time we extend the quotas on footwear we import from that country.

Opponents of quotas cite examples such as the following to show the problems they cause. In 1984, a Canadian company negotiated a multimillion dollar deal to sell steam generating boilers to Indonesia. At the same time, the Canadian government decided to limit imports of Indonesian clothing into Canada. The Indonesian government reacted with threats to withdraw the boiler contract. These threats forced the Canadian government to reconsider its quota on clothing.

Canada is not the only country taking measures to protect its industries. Pacific Rim countries also have tariffs and quotas preventing us from free access to their markets. For instance, Japan has tariffs on plywood and some lumber products. More importantly, quality control standards and other non-tariff barriers effectively keep most foreign goods out of Japan.

Hyundai car sales skyrocketed in the mid 1980s. To counter critics of Korea-Canada trade, Hyundai located a new automobile assembly plant in Quebec.

Another trade issue involves the Pacific Rim region's demand for raw materials rather than processed goods. Canada could create more jobs at home if it processed and manufactured more of its resource products before it exported them. To counter Canadian fears that jobs in manufacturing are being sacrificed, some larger Pacific Rim countries have invested in manufacturing plants here in Canada. Japanese and Korean car manufacturers have set up factories to manufacture automobile parts in several Canadian provinces. Pacific Rim companies are also ensuring access to Canadian resources by investing in resource industries in western Canada. They are partners in several British Columbia pulp mills and coal mines, and in some of Alberta's oil fields. Nipponkokan, a major Japanese steel company, is a partner in the Quintette coal mine near Tumbler Ridge. Recently, Crown Zellerbach Canada was purchased by a forest company from New Zealand.

On one point in the trade debate all sides agree: we cannot afford to ignore what is happening in the Pacific Rim region. Already Pacific Rim countries are starting to dominate fields of technology on the "cutting edge" of the future. For example, automation is becoming increasingly important and Japan leads the world in the use of robots in automated factories. Telecommunications is another important area. Japan is a leader in designing complicated switching devices used to connect computers with communications lines (so that, for instance, computers can send information to other computers). Ironically, Canada has had some success in selling our advanced telecommunications technology to Japanese industries.

The Pacific Rim markets are the markets of the twenty-first century. As a country dependent on trade, Canada cannot afford to ignore this fact. Since the region contains more than half of the world's population, there are strong prospects for increased trade.

1. In your own words, explain why some Canadians want tariff protection against Asian imports, while others want tariffs reduced or dropped. Which side of the argument do you support? Why?

Summary

The countries of the Pacific Rim region vary greatly. Most of them, however, have very large populations that are continuing to grow. Since 1970, the economy of the region has been the fastest growing in the world, although not all nations share in this growth. Japan has been the economic leader of the region. The newly industrialized countries are following in Japan's footsteps as highly productive exporters of manufactured goods.

The culture and society of the East Asian subregion of the Pacific Rim are key factors in their economic success. While wages in those countries are rising, they are still, on the average, less than in North America. Lower labor rates allow these countries to produce goods less expensively than Canada or the United States does. People in the Pacific Rim countries often feel a strong sense of loyalty to their employers and their nations; to North Americans, they appear very diligent and hard-working, and seem to value group decisions over individual wishes.

Canada has had many links with Pacific Rim countries. Immigration, foreign aid and especially trade are the main links. Our trade with the region is a controversial issue. Some Canadians feel that we should reduce tariffs on goods from the region, while others feel that we need tariffs to protect our industries against competition from the region.

In order to make effective use of our opportunities for trade with the Pacific Rim countries, Canadians must learn to appreciate the differences between their cultures and ours. To do so, will require changes in attitudes and hard work on behalf of our governments, business leaders, workers and the general public. The challenges of the Pacific Rim are indeed great, but so are the opportunities.

REVIEW

Checking Back

1. In a paragraph, explain what is meant by "Japan's Economic Miracle."

2. Suggest two or three problems Canada would have to overcome to improve our trading relationship with the Pacific Rim. How might Canada overcome each of these problems?

Using Your Knowledge

3. How do nations use foreign aid as a means of improving trade?

4. In your own words, explain how Canada's immigration policies can influence our trade relations with other nations.

5. Draw a graph that shows the value of trade (import and export) between Canada and any six nations of the Pacific Rim, using the figures on page 310 of the text.

6. As a foreign manufacturer wishing to establish a plant in British Columbia, what will your needs be? What could governments do to meet these needs? (Consider the advantages the plant would bring to the province in relation to the costs of your proposals.)

UNIT 4

BRITISH COLUMBIA MAKES A LIVING

Chapter 15

The British Columbia Economy

Canada's early economy was based on harvesting natural resources for foreign markets. Canada's present economy has a service orientation. Now, much of our economic activity results in goods and services destined for markets in other parts of the world. Chapters 13 and 14 gave details about our trading relationships with the United States, our largest trading partner, and the Pacific Rim and Indian Sub-Continent. In this unit of *Our Land: Building the West* the focus will be on British Columbia's economy and its ties to the rest of Canada and the world. This chapter provides a brief overview: the following six chapters examine parts of the British Columbia economy in more detail.

Our overview will begin with a tour through the province to see where various economic activities are located. Then, we will discuss the problems of an economy that depends heavily on the extraction and export of natural resources. As you read through this chapter, keep these questions in mind:

- How has the physical geography of the province been an advantage? a disadvantage?
- What are the province's economic regions, and how are they different?

How and Where British Columbians Make a Living

The graph on page 317 compares the market value of goods and services of British Columbia's major industries. Which industry adds the greatest amount to the provincial economy? Which industry was largely unaffected by the difficult economic times of the early 1980s? Which industries have experienced relatively little growth?

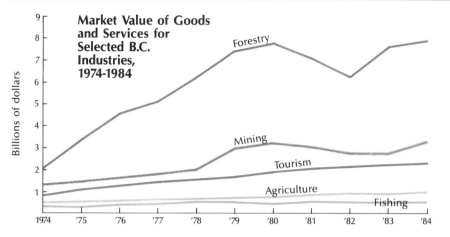

Market Value of Goods and Services for Selected B.C. Industries, 1974-1984

Forestry

Mining

Tourism

Agriculture

Fishing

Billions of dollars

To see where these industries are located, we will take a tour through the province. The map on pages 318-319 shows the province divided into nine economic regions. As you read about the economy of each region, consider how the physical geography has influenced the industries in the region. We will start the tour at the southeast corner of the province, and move in a clockwise direction.

A Resource-Based Economy

British Columbians are fortunate to have rich natural resources. But an economy based on such resources is a "narrow" one. Instead of having many different ways to make the money we need (a "broad" economy) we tend to depend on just a few major resource industries. When our resource industries do well, the province prospers. When they do poorly, the province is hard hit because it has no alternate sources of income.

Since most of our resource products are exported to foreign markets, we are limited in what we can do to prevent these industry downturns. We cannot control either the worldwide demand for our products or the price customers are willing to pay for them. The market for resource products tends to be cyclical, with frequent ups and downs. Only by indirect means can these markets be influenced. Producers can promote their products hoping to create an interest in the marketplace and they can try to cut costs and lower their prices. But these measures cannot guarantee sales and so British Columbia is forced to ride a roller coaster of good times and bad times, booms and busts. The following chapters of this unit will provide examples of such booms and busts.

1. East Kootenay Region
In the mountainous Fernie area, coal mining is the dominant activity. The Cranbrook-Kimberley area has a broader economic base including tourism, farming, logging and sawmilling. There is a pulpmill at Skookumchuck and a large mine and fertilizer complex at Kimberley. In the north, near Invermere, logging, sawmilling, ranching and tourism are important industries.

2. Central Kootenay Region
Forestry is the major industry in this mountainous region; a pulpmill is located at Castlegar. Farming is concentrated on the only flat areas near Creston and Salmon Arm. Salmon Arm also benefits from tourism. The region has a history of mining, and several small mines are still operating near Nelson.

3. Okanagan Boundary Region
A huge smelter dominates the local economy at Trail. Elsewhere in the region, agriculture and forestry are the main industries. Orchards and vineyards grow in the Okanagan, where tourism is also important. Copper mining provides jobs in Princeton, Peachland and Hedley.

4. Lillooet-Thompson Region
The bulk of this region is prime cattle ranching country. However, forestry and mining are now more important than agriculture. There is a pulpmill at Kamloops. Southwest of Kamloops, in the Highland Valley area, is the greatest concentration of copper-molybdenum mines in the province.

5. Lower Mainland Region
This region, dominated by a deep sea port, contains only about 3 percent of the province's land area, but a little over 50 percent of its population. It is the financial, educational, manufacturing, tourism, transportation and cultural centre of the province. It is also the leading centre for all the major industrial activities in British Columbia except mining.

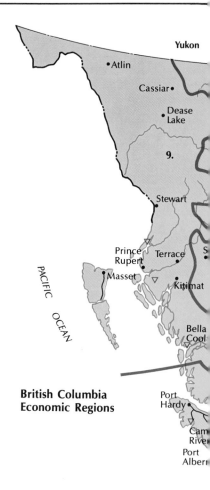

British Columbia Economic Regions

The impact of these cyclical ups and downs is less severe on a province-wide scale than on a local or community scale. Provincially, a downturn in the mining industry may be offset by a good year for the forest industry. However, many communities in British Columbia are "single industry towns," almost entirely dependent on a single resource. They are true narrow economies. When the

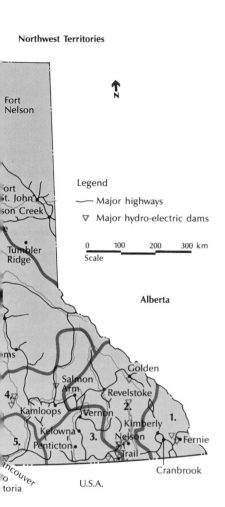

6. Vancouver Island and Coast Region

This region is second only to the Lower Mainland in terms of population and economic activity. More than half the population of this region lives in the area of Victoria, a major tourism and trade centre as well as the province's capital city. Elsewhere, forestry is the main primary industry. There are six pulp and paper mills on Vancouver Island. Farming, fishing, mining and tourism are also important in this region.

7. Cariboo-Fort George Region

This region is primarily high, rolling plateau. The southern portion is the centre of cattle ranching in the province. Forestry provides the economic base of the region. Pulp mills are clustered at Prince George, Quesnel and Mackenzie. Large open-pit mines are located near Williams Lake, Fraser Lake, Houston and Granisle.

8. Peace River-Liard Region

Farming of grain, forage crops and cattle is important in the triangle formed by Chetwynd, Dawson Creek and Fort St. John. In the past three decades, forestry and drilling for oil and natural gas have provided most of the economic growth in this region. In the 1980s, coal mines were developed at Tumbler Ridge.

9. Skeena-Stikine Region

This is the largest region, covering 28 percent of the province's land area but containing barely 2.5 percent of its population. The economy is diverse. Coastal communities rely heavily on the fishing industry. The forestry industry is important in the southern half of the region. There are pulp mills at Prince Rupert and Kitimat. Mining supports the communities of Cassiar, Atlin, Dease Lake and Kitsault. Kitimat was established in the 1950s to support an aluminum smelter there.

price of copper falls on the world market, the effect on a town like Logan Lake, where most of the workers are employed by a copper mine, can be disastrous.

Another problem faced by resource-based economies is that the resources can be exhausted. Non-renewable resources are eventually used up. Even forests and fish, renewable resources, can be depleted if they are overharvested. In the past, the resources of the province were so bountiful it seemed they would never run out. Today British Columbians know otherwise. We have to replant forests, restock fish runs, and replenish farmland so that our resource industries can continue to operate.

Most of British Columbia's resources are sold in an unprocessed or semiprocessed state. Some British Columbians would like to see secondary industries developed that would process our resources more before shipping them off to other countries. For instance, instead of selling pulp to the United States so people there can make paper towels, we could make the paper towels here and sell them to the Americans. This extra processing adds value to the products being sold, while the manufacturing process creates jobs for British Columbians. Those jobs are valuable to the province.

A counterargument to this proposal is that other countries do not necessarily want to buy our processed resources. They might rather provide jobs for their own people by processing our raw resources in their own countries. The province may be faced with the choice of either selling its resources in an unprocessed state, or not selling them at all.

Even without this additional processing, resource industries have traditionally provided the jobs in British Columbia. But automation is reducing labor requirements on farms and in sawmills, mines, fish canneries, and other industrial plants. While our resources may continue to generate great wealth for the province, we cannot rely on them for future employment.

The economy is not just something we read about in newspapers. It has a bearing on our day-to-day lives. Changes in the province's economy affect all of us who live in British Columbia. That is why it is important that we understand this economy.

The next five chapters take a closer look at five key industries in British Columbia. The first four are the traditional resource industries that have fuelled the development of the province: forestry, mining, fishing and agriculture. The fifth, tourism, has emerged as an important industry for the future. For each, we will trace the industry's history, its importance and impact on the provincial economy today, and some of the problems and issues it faces. The final chapter will examine the city of Vancouver, and its role in the provincial economy.

1. The foresters and miners of British Columbia obviously depend on the province's natural resources. Suggest reasons

why the people who are employed by manufacturing and service industries also depend on natural resources for their livelihood.
2. List British Columbia's nine economic regions. Beside each one write an example of how the region makes use of its physical geography.

SOME FIGURES ON BRITISH COLUMBIA'S MAJOR INDUSTRIES

This table allows you to compare five of British Columbia's major industries. It shows the value of all goods produced by each industry, the value of each industry's exports, and the number of people each industry employs.

While this table provides a useful comparison, you should treat the actual figures with caution, as you should treat most sets of statistics. Here are some reasons the figures presented here are only approximate:

• Industries have good and bad years. This table uses information from 1984. Figures from another year might be quite different. For instance, 1984 was a good year for the mining industry. In 1983, by contrast, the value of goods produced by the industry was only about $2.9 billion.

• Depending on where you look, you can find a variety of different statistics for each industry's performance in 1984. These differences

exist because some sources include different jobs under each industry. For instance, the fishing industry figures in this graph include people who work in fish processing plants, freezing and canning the fish. Some fishing industry figures include only those workers actually involved in catching the fish. Another example is in the tourism industry. Accurate figures for employment are difficult to obtain because many people working in restaurants or gas stations serve regular customers as well as tourists. Should they be included? Also, many more people work during the busy tourist season (approximately 126 000 in all) than at other times. So the figure given here is an average for the year.

• Some figures are not available. You will notice that there is no figure given for agricultural exports. Statistics are available that show the value of agricultural goods shipped from British Columbia to other countries. However, these figures include food grown in other provinces and shipped from British Columbia ports, such as wheat from the Prairies.

	Value of Goods Produced ($)	Exports ($)	Employment (#)
Forestry industry	7.8 billion	6.0 billion	73 000
Mining industry	3.2 billion	1.9 billion	16 300
Fishing industry	460 million	365 million	20 000
Agricultural industry	971 million	not available	62 000
Tourism industry	2.3 billion	665 million	103 000

(Industry figures normally include processing [e.g. paper mills, smelters, fish canneries].)

Chapter 16

The Forest Industry

Forestry is British Columbia's most important industry. The province's economy rests on its vast forests: this industry still generates more wealth than any other economic activity in British Columbia. Because of this, the strength of the province's economy and the well-being of its residents are closely tied to the health of its forest industry.

British Columbia's forests, however, have changed greatly since the time when Native peoples of the Pacific coast cut the tall cedars to build their longhouses and ocean-going canoes. Changing technology has greatly increased the loggers' ability to cut trees, even in the most remote and inaccessible areas of the province. Nearly all first-growth forest in the province has fallen to the axes and saws of the loggers over the past century. These changes have left a lasting mark on both the landscape and the economy of British Columbia. They have also led the government and people of British Columbia, particularly those closely connected with the forests, to ask some important questions about the future of the forest industry. This chapter will explore these questions and their significance to British Columbia's economy. As you go through this chapter, you will examine the history of the British Columbia forest industry, its importance to British Columbia's economy today, and some issues and problems facing the industry as it looks to the future. Among the questions you will examine are:

- How have ways of cutting and using British Columbia's forests changed over the past 200 years? What impact have these changes had on British Columbia's forests?
- Will there always be a forest industry in British Columbia? Are trees always growing up to replace the ones cut by British Columbia's loggers?

Introduction: British Columbia's #1 Industry

Let us briefly examine the resource on which the province's #1 industry is based—the forest. Over 60 percent of the province is covered with forest, but only half of that forest is commercially valuable. Almost all British Columbia forests are coniferous evergreens rather than deciduous trees.

Variations in climate and soil result in different forest types. The biggest, tallest trees are found on the coast, where the forests consist of western hemlock, Douglas fir and cedar. Trees in interior forests tend to be smaller and to grow more slowly. Interior forests are also more diverse, containing lodgepole, ponderosa and white pine, spruce, larch, interior Douglas fir and true firs. This diversity decreases as you go northward, where the growing season is shorter and the climate is more severe. In much of northern British Columbia, only low elevation forest land is productive enough to grow **commercial timber.**

The different terrain and tree species found on the coast and in the interior have resulted in two separate forest industries in British Columbia. The giant trees and rough terrain of the coast are logged by a large work force using chain saws. Here, the loggers face significant challenges in transporting the fallen trees to the sawmills. Logging on the coast is expensive, both in terms of labor costs and the investment in equipment used to haul logs out of the woods. However, the size and quality of the trees makes them very valuable for a wide variety of uses.

In the interior the trees are smaller and more widely separated, and the terrain is flatter. Automated fallers can be used to cut and transport the logs, so fewer workers are required.

Processing methods vary too. On the coast, larger logs require a sawing technique that can give each log individual attention. A **sawyer** can produce several types of lumber, some of it high quality, from one coastal log. The smaller logs that feed interior mills are often used for "construction" grade lumber. However, the mills can be fully automated to produce great volumes of this lumber at high speed.

Today, most of the giant trees of the coastal forests have gone. If you want to see what they look like, you will probably have to go to a park where the forest has been preserved. Over the years, these **old growth** forests have been logged, burned or cleared to make room

Harvesting the coastal forest

Harvesting the interior forest

for cities, roads, powerline and pipeline right of ways, farms or hydro dam reservoirs. Now there is less forested land in British Columbia, and most of it consists of **second growth** timber which has grown up in the past century. Second growth trees are younger and smaller than the towering old growth.

1. Why are trees in coastal forests harvested and processed differently from those in interior forests?

History: From Muscles to Management

British Columbia's forests were an important resource for the Native peoples who lived here before the first Europeans arrived. The peoples of the Pacific coast, in particular, developed a culture that made great use of the red cedar. Tall and straight-grained, it was strong, yet easy to work. It split easily to make planks for building large longhouses or making storage boxes. It could be carved into household utensils, pleasing shapes to decorate homes, or ceremonial objects. It could also be worked with stone tools and fire to create the large and graceful ocean-going canoes used by the Natives for whaling and fishing. Even the bark of the cedar was used to make clothing, fish nets, ropes and baby cradles. Much of what the peoples of the Pacific coast used was made of cedar.

British Columbia's commercial forest industry began with the coming of European settlers in the mid-1800s. The biggest trees grew on the south coast and the easiest way to transport a two-tonne log from the forest to the mill was by water. An early logger described the industry this way:

> In those days good timber was plentiful–good timber, on seacoast slopes, that could be felled and shot right down to water–hand-logger's timber. The country bristled with opportunities for loggers–opportunities that were the making of men who had the spirit to venture out and seize them.

Logging history is full of colorful stories about the men who pitted muscle and axe against British Columbia's towering trees. However, there was another side to the early forest industry. W.R. Ross, Minister of Lands in the 1910 provincial government, described these early days of lumbering as "an epoch of reckless devastation of the natural resources with which we, the people of this fair young Province, have been endowed by Providence."

Because it took so much work to fell and haul even one tree, it is not surprising that the early loggers wanted only the biggest and best trees. From our perspective today, they were extremely wasteful. They cut just the high-grade timber and left behind a mass of tall stumps and broken, smaller logs. No regulations existed to prevent them from doing so.

1. What characteristics of cedar made it a useful resource for Native peoples?
2. What conditions promoted a "reckless devastation" of the forests in the early days of the forest industry?

325

Changing Markets for Forest Products

Without markets for its logs and sawn lumber, the forest industry would never have gotten off the ground. One early market was the forts and settlements of nearby Vancouver Island. Then the discovery of gold along the Fraser River in the 1850s (see pages 167-169) opened up a major new market. As thousands of fortune seekers flooded into the Cariboo region of the interior, lumber was required to build the mining towns that housed them. Because it was the jumping-off point for the gold seekers arriving by sea, the residents of Victoria needed lumber to build more saloons and plank sidewalks. Mining booms continued to provide a market for the forest industry through the rest of the nineteenth century.

The construction of the Canadian Pacific Railway during the 1880s gave the young industry a further boost. Wood was needed to make ties and trestles for the track and to build bunkhouses for the railway workers. When the completed railway brought new settlers to the Prairies, they needed wood for homes and fences. To serve this Prairie market, sawmills were built and communities sprang up in the interior of British Columbia, particularly in the East Kootenay area.

The biggest market for British Columbia lumber, however, was not at home but overseas. British Columbia had a reputation for the longest, toughest and most durable spars and masts used on sailing ships. From the early 1850s, a time when the population of British Columbia numbered only a few hundred, spars, masts and lumber were loaded onto sailing ships bound for San Francisco, South America, Australia and the Orient. In 1884, timber from what is now Vancouver's West End was shipped to China to become the huge beams of the Imperial Palace. Although the market for spars and masts disappeared when ships switched from sails to steam power, lumber in varying shapes and sizes continued to be the province's major forest export. Today, most of the province's lumber is still exported, with 25 percent of the lumber used to build new homes in the United States being supplied by British Columbia's forests.

British Columbia also became an important producer of pulp and paper products. The first major pulp mills were built after 1910 in coastal locations, such as Swanson's Bay near Prince Rupert, close to the necessary sources of wood, electrical power and fresh water. By 1950, with demand on the wood supplies increasing, it became more economical to locate pulp mills where they could run on wood chips left over from sawmills.

In 1961, all but one of the province's pulp mills were still located on the coast. However, the following decade saw a dramatic increase in pulp and paper manufacturing near sawmills in the interior of the province. By 1971 there were nine pulp mills in the interior, three in Prince George alone. The first paper mills produced mostly newsprint, but the newer mills catered to the growing market for stronger paper used in cartons and packaging. During the 1980s, British Columbia's pulp and paper industry has continued to be export oriented, with 50 percent of its newsprint production going to the western United States.

British Columbia is also the country's largest producer of plywood. The plywood industry started on the coast in the 1930s, after the invention of an effective waterproof glue. It developed rapidly after 1950, soon spreading to the interior of the province. Plywood panels are made by peeling very thin sheets of wood veneer from a spinning log, then pressing them together with glue into a multilayered sandwich. British Columbia has large diameter, straight-grained Douglas fir trees that make excellent "peeler" logs.

The market for plywood is mostly in Canada rather than in the United States or overseas. Demand for wood-veneer plywood has been dropping since 1979, as customers switch to the newer, less expensive particleboard made from compressed waste wood products such as chips. Some plywood mills have closed, while others are adapting their product for new uses. For instance, specially coated plywood panels are used to make the forms into which concrete is poured.

1. How did the 1850s' gold rush on the Fraser River affect the market for British Columbia's lumber? How did the building of the CPR affect it?

2. (a) List the major markets, both past and present, for British Columbia's forest products.
   (b) Explain why British Columbia's forest products are able to do well in these markets, but less well in other markets, such as Europe.

3. What is plywood? Why is British Columbia the country's largest producer of this product?

Shorter Hours and Better Pay, Boys!: The Rise of Unions

And we're going to find a way, boys,
For shorter hours and better pay, boys,
And we're going to win the day, boys,
Where the Fraser River flows.
[Early union song]

Before World War I, working conditions in the camps and mills were rough. Hours were long, the food was poor and the bunkhouses were crowded and filthy. The workers even had to provide their own bedding, and tools as well. They were not protected by safety regulations, health care provisions, pension plans, unemployment insurance or any of the benefits that are standard for workers today.

The struggle to organize unions began after World War I. Some employers refused to let union organizers into their camps to talk to the workers and fired workers who joined the unions. There were several union-organized strikes during the Depression of the early 1930s when forest companies, faced with low lumber prices, reduced pay rates and allowed working conditions to become less safe.

In 1937, various unions combined into a new union, the International Woodworkers of America (I.W.A.), representing workers in

These are striking loggers on a march to establish picket lines at Port Alberni during the general lumber strike in 1934.

both Canada and the United States. Also in 1937, the British Columbia government granted workers the legal right to form unions. The following year, unions were given the right to represent the employees of a company in collective bargaining (negotiating working contracts with an employer). In the 1960s, separate, Canadian based unions, were created representing many pulp and paper workers.

Today, most of the British Columbia forest industry is unionized. The unions have made British Columbia's forest workers among the best paid in the province. However, the unions are not just concerned with wages and working conditions. They also deal with issues such as the effects of new technology on employment, reforestation, environmental protection and Native rights.

Changes in Forest Management

Until the early part of this century, British Columbia's timber supply seemed inexhaustible. Rather than limiting the amount of timber that companies could cut on public land, the government gave out permits and encouraged more logging activity. It was hard to imagine the day when there would not be more good logging just over the next hill.

Eventually, the government of the province began to tighten its control over the province's forests. The Forest Act of 1912 laid the groundwork for future management of the resource. In return for cutting rights, companies now had to pay the government a fee called "stumpage," based on the value of the timber.

As loggers moved farther northward and inland in search of new forests, concern mounted: could loggers continue to harvest more and more trees without in time running out of good timber? In his 1945 Commission of Inquiry into Forest Policy, Chief Justice Gordon Sloan answered this concern. He recommended a new kind of forest management program called **sustained yield.**

Under the sustained yield program, the forest was to be managed as a renewable resource, one that should continue to supply wood forever. In theory, no more wood was to be cut in a year than the forest could replace by new growth. Government forest managers would survey the timber growing in each area of the province and set an Allowable Annual Cut for that area.

The sustained yield policy did not entirely live up to expectations. The forests continued to fall faster than they could grow back. To speed up natural growth, reforestation programs were introduced.

By the 1970s, government forest managers were worrying about

EXCERPTS FROM THE FOREST ACT, 1979

The Forest Act states that the Ministry of Forests shall:

...manage, protect and conserve forest and range resources having regard to immediate and long-term economic and social benefits that may confer on the province...

and

...plan the use of the forests and range resources of the Crown so that the production of timber and forage, the harvesting of timber, the grazing of livestock and the realization of fisheries, wildlife, water, outdoor recreation and other natural resource values are coordinated and integrated in consultation and co-operation with other Ministries or agencies of the Crown and with the private sector.

1. What are the differences between immediate benefits and long-term benefits?
2. Who is the "Crown"? For whose benefit should Crown lands be managed?

more than just the timber supply. They had to answer a growing public concern that the fish, wildlife, fresh water and recreational opportunities of the forest lands be protected. The government brought in regulations to reduce the environmental damage caused by logging operations. The Forest Act of 1979 emphasized the need for forest managers to consider all resources, not just wood.

Over the past 150 years, British Columbia's forest industry has grown from a few logging camps to a multibillion dollar industry. As the province's largest, and most important industry, forestry is closely tied to all aspects of economic life in British Columbia today, affecting the well-being of everybody. In the next section, we will take a closer look at the impact and importance of this key industry.

1. In your own words, describe what is meant by "sustained yield."

A Province Fuelled by its Forests: The Importance and Impact of the Forest Industry

Although British Columbia has only one-fifth of the forest land in Canada, the province's annual forest harvest is nearly one-half of Canada's total. In the early 1980s, the British Columbia industry alone each year, on average, produced goods worth over $7 billion, two-thirds of which were exported. These exports accounted for 60 percent of British Columbia's total export shipments.

To make its products, the industry cuts over 70 million cubic metres of wood annually. The industry employs about 80 000 to 95 000 people, approximately 8 percent of working British Columbians. It generates indirect employment for another 15 percent. The industry and its employees pay over $500 million to the British Columbia government in taxes, stumpage fees and other payments. This contribution represents from 10-20 percent of all money that the government receives.

Yet employees of the forest industry are not the only people who benefit from it. The taxes and stumpage fees paid by the industry help pay for public services such as roads, railways, power plants, schools and hospitals. If the industry were to shut down tomorrow, British Columbians would definitely feel the effects.

The following graphs and charts summarize various aspects of the industry's economic impact and importance.

Automation is beginning to reduce the number of workers required by the industry. As both cutting and milling operations upgrade their technology, fewer and fewer workers may be needed. This graph shows the trend over a recent five year period.

1. What year was wood production at its lowest? What is the relationship between wood production levels and employment levels between 1979 and 1982? after 1982?
2. (a) What impact on the British Columbia economy as a whole might this shift to increased use of technology rather than human resources have?
   (b) How would the province's economy be affected if the machinery used was manufactured outside of British Columbia?

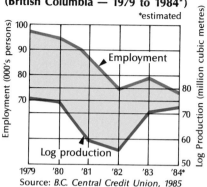

Wood Production & Employment in Forest Industry
(British Columbia — 1979 to 1984*)
*estimated

Source: B.C. Central Credit Union, 1985

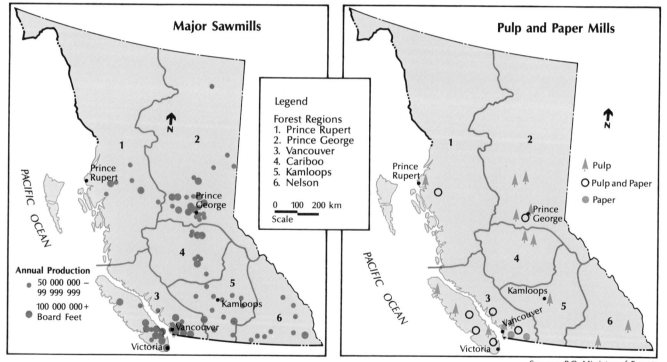

Source: B.C. Ministry of Forests

1. Name three major sawmilling regions in British Columbia.
2. Compare the two maps. From what you have read in this chapter, explain why pulp mills and sawmills would be located in the same areas.
3. What region of the province has few major sawmills or pulp mills? Explain why.

Major Customers of B.C. Wood Products — 1985

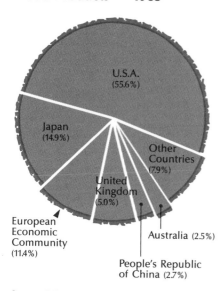

U.S.A. (55.6%)

Japan (14.9%)

Other Countries (7.9%)

United Kingdom (5.0%)

European Economic Community (11.4%)

Australia (2.5%)

People's Republic of China (2.7%)

Source: *B.C. Ministry of Finance*

1. What country or area is the major customer of British Columbia lumber? of British Columbia pulp?
2. Explain how and why a slowdown in housing construction in the United States would affect the people of British Columbia.

Problems and Issues in the Forest Industry

With the end of the old growth forests in sight, the forest industry will soon be entirely dependent on second growth forests to supply its mills. During the old growth era, trees that had been growing undisturbed for hundreds of years were available for the taking. They were mined, just as gold might be mined from the ground. There was no thought of replacing the resource. In the future, forests will have to be farmed rather than mined. Foresters will have to grow a crop before they can harvest it.

As the forest industry moves into the era of second growth, it faces a number of problems. Some are related to timber supply; others to competition from wood-exporters outside of British Columbia. There is concern about the impact of forest industry booms and busts on communities. There is also concern about the industry's impact on the environment. Finally, there are problems that have to do with conflicting views of how the forest should be used. We will look at each of these five problem areas in turn.

The Problem of Timber Supply: Will the Bounty End?

Although mills may still have sufficient wood for their present needs, future shortages will occur in many areas. Several factors have contributed to the timber supply problem.

One such factor is the shrinking of forest lands available for harvesting. This process is known as **forest-land alienation.** Some areas once covered by forest are now covered by railroads, highways, right of ways for powerlines and pipelines, farms, or cities. Other areas have been flooded by reservoirs, the lakes formed when rivers are dammed for hydro-electric generating stations. Some forests are protected in parks where logging is not permitted.

Forest fires, pests and disease make up a second factor in the increasing timber shortage. Fires consume roughly 80 000 ha of forest land in an average year. Pests and diseases destroy about five times that volume, amounting to approximately one-third of the annual harvest, enough wood to build one million homes. Scientists are working on techniques to control pests and diseases, but the research is costly and time-consuming. The industry has used chemical pesticides, but questions about the safety and effectiveness of these pesticides has forced it to look for other solutions.

MOUNTAIN PINE BEETLE ATTACK

If you fly over lodgepole pine forests in some areas of the British Columbia interior, you will see nothing but red needles for kilometres. The culprit is the mountain pine beetle, just one of the several kinds of bark beetle that destroy vast areas of valuable timber each year.

Bark beetles bore through the bark of the tree and chew out galleries in which to lay their eggs. The following year, the new beetles bore their way out and fly on to attack new trees. Affected trees become cracked and the inner wood is stained blue from a fungus carried by the beetle.

In the past, insect attacks were controlled by naturally occurring forest fires that would burn the dead stands and prepare the ground for new forest growth. Because we have now reduced the number of such fires, our forests are more susceptible to the unchecked spread of insects.

To combat the insects, foresters use various techniques. For instance, they can harvest stands before they are eighty years old, which is when the thicknesses of the bark will make the trees susceptible to attack. They can also lure the beetles to specially felled "trap trees" to prevent them from spreading throughout the forest.

Mountain Pine Beetles

A third factor affecting timber supply is "the fall-down effect." Fall-down, as foresters call it, refers to the decreased volume of wood available to the forest industry from second growth forests, whose trees are smaller than those of the first growth. Foresters believe that the impact of fall-down could be significantly reduced by using silvicultural techniques to increase the amount of wood in these second growth forests.

Silviculture, the science of growing trees, is the basis of modern forestry. Silvicultural activities can improve all stages of forest growth, from developing better seedlings for planting to thinning overcrowded stands while they grow. Forest land receiving the complete range of silviculture treatments can produce twice the normal yield. Research in silviculture is being carried out by the government, universities and major forest companies. A 1984 partnership agreement between the province and the forest industry saw the beginning of major silviculture initiatives in British Columbia.

The factor that has probably contributed most to the timber supply problem is our failure to replace forests cut or burned long ago. Roughly 25 percent of the land that could be growing valuable timber is now covered in brush or non-valuable tree species. Not only have we failed to replace the forests cut many years ago; we are not even adequately replanting forests that we log today. Some experts estimate that British Columbia is spending only a fifth of what it needs to spend just in order to maintain the present rate of harvest. But who will pay for reforestation? Perhaps an even more important question is "Can we afford not to reforest?"

Since 94 percent of British Columbia's forests grow on provincially owned land, the forests are largely the responsibility of the provincial government. Elected government representatives decide how much public money should be invested in our forests. However, money spent on forests will not show a return for many years. Governments always have other pressing or more immediate demands on public funds. At present, only about five cents of every dollar the province receives from the forest industry is put back into the resource.

Experts predict that worldwide demand for wood will increase 82 percent by the year 2000, and 234 percent by 2025. But unless people in British Columbia take action now to solve their potential wood supply problems, they will not be able to take advantage of these market opportunities in the future.

1. In a sentence or two, describe what is meant by "forest-land alienation."
2. Suggest reasons why forest pests and diseases have been difficult to control. What are some methods that have been tried in an effort to control pests and diseases?
3. Name some activities that are included under the term "silviculture."

The Industry's Impact on the Environment

Logging operations unavoidably damage or interfere with the natural environment. Removing large numbers of trees upsets the balance of the watersheds and **ecosystems** in which the forest plays a key role. The cutting of trees also changes the visual quality of the landscape, affecting recreation and tourism.

Trees play an important part in controlling the movement of both water and soil. Much of the rain that falls on the coastal mountains is returned to the air by the trees after carrying nutrients from the soil to the leaves. Tree roots also help to stabilize the soil, preventing erosion by the run-off of surface water. When the trees are removed, run-off is greatly increased, and soil is washed away. Erosion removes soil and nutrients needed to ensure adequate reforestation of logged-off areas. The increase in run-off can also cause severe flooding downstream, possibly washing out rail lines, highways or bridges. The increased silt carried by the streams may affect fresh water supplies to nearby communities, clog irrigation canals and damage salmon spawning grounds. Silt deposited on the spawning beds covers salmon eggs, cutting off the supply of oxygen, and killing them.

In addition to causing increased run-off, logging operations disturb the soil on the forest floor. Heavy equipment such as skidders and bulldozers loosen the soil in some places, and compact it in others. Soil compaction increases run-off, while loose soil is easily eroded by the surface water.

Pulp and paper operations also affect water quality. A producing pulp mill uses a quantity of water equivalent to that used by a city the size of Victoria. Unless it is treated, the water that is discharged after the washing of the pulp carries chemicals dangerous to fish.

The disposal of pulp mill industrial wastes is strictly regulated by both the provincial and federal governments and the mills do remove the toxic chemicals from their waste water. However, accidents such as ruptured pipes occasionally lead to major fish kills.

While habitat damage is still a problem, the situation today is much better than it was in the past. Then, logs were floated down rivers and no environmental regulations existed. Today, a section of the federal Fisheries Act states: "No person engaging in logging, lumbering, land clearing or other operations, shall knowingly permit any slash, stumps, or other debris into any water frequented by

Conflicts over the use of forests can be minimized through good planning. Some areas may need to be preserved from cutting while other areas can accommodate both the forest industry and recreational uses.

fish or that flows into such water." Well managed logging operations now leave a protective strip of trees along creek banks rather than felling trees right to the water.

British Columbia's forests have important recreational uses for both visitors and tourists. The tourist industry relies heavily on the scenic appeal of the province's landscape. Until they "green up," clearcuts detract from this appeal. Some people enjoy visiting forests to go hiking, skiing or camping, and logging operations detract from their enjoyment. Logging and recreation are not always incompatible, however. Forest companies may leave protective strips of forest along the sides of trails and around campsites. Instead of logging large clearcuts, they may selectively log an area, taking out only some trees and leaving the rest. Snowmobilers and skiers are often grateful to have access to logging roads. Even after an area has been logged, campers and hikers can enjoy the second growth forest.

However, some people enjoy visiting areas that are still undisturbed. After more than a century of logging in British Columbia, there is less and less undisturbed first growth forest, particularly within easy reach of the cities. There is conflict between those who want to log these last remaining wilderness areas and those who want them preserved as parks. Both sides in the debate mount strong lobbies to persuade the provincial government to see their point of view.

The worst environmental abuses of logging occurred in the past. At that time, there was far less planning and control over what took place in the forest. However many people today are still concerned that we are not adequately protecting our forest environment. They feel we are still mining our forests for short-term profit.

1. In what ways do trees help to control the movement of water in an ecosystem?

2. (a) Explain how the forest industry causes damage to each of these aspects of the environment: soils, water quality, wildlife habitats, visual quality.
   (b) Why is damage to the environment by the forest industry unavoidable?

3. Conflicts over use of the forests often deal with recreational use versus industrial use. What actions have the forest industries taken to reduce the impact logging has on the recreational environment?

Conflicting Views on How the Forest Should be Used

Forests have more different values tied to them than probably any other resource. Some values, such as those of the forest to a logging company, can be measured in dollars. Other values, such as those that nature lovers might give to a hike through the forest, are more difficult to measure. Logging is just one use of the forest, and it can often be in conflict with other uses. As the amount of forested land in the province diminishes, there is more pressure on that remaining land.

Some areas of forest can be managed on a "multiple use" basis. Logging operations are carefully planned so that they do not prevent the forest from being used for other purposes. Logging takes place in the Capilano River watershed that supplies the city of Vancouver with its water, for instance.

We have been logging for well over a century now. Yet only recently have we started to reforest and practice silviculture. We have to consider the consequences of this shabby treatment of the resource over the long term. As one forester asks, "Have we starved the goose that lays the golden eggs?"

To renourish the goose and ensure the continued health of British Columbia's major industry, people in British Columbia must be prepared to invest in their forests, not just take from them.

1. Explain what the forester meant when he asked "Have we starved the goose that lays the golden eggs?"

Case Study: The Decision to Adopt New Technology

George Killy is the owner of Lakeland Sawmills in Prince George, British Columbia. His pride and joy is the company's new mill, built in 1980. According to forest experts, it represents a major technological improvement in British Columbia's forest industry.

The new mill has answered Killy's concern over the inefficiency of an older mill. The old mill would leave a great deal of waste material: bark, sawdust and wood chips. For a while, this wastage presented no problem. The bark and some of the sawdust could be used as fuel for the mill's burners. The rest of the sawdust plus the wood chips could be sold to pulp and paper mills. But when a slump occurred in the pulp and paper market in the mid-1970s, Lakeland Sawmills was left with huge quantities of wood chips that it could not sell. The mill's burners could not handle the wood chips, so they could not be used as fuel either. Unable either to sell or to use the wood chips, the company saw its profits drop. It was forced to reduce its shifts and lay off workers.

The problem Killy faced was how to reduce the wastage of wood chips. The first attempt to deal with this problem was a search for better burning equipment that would handle the chips. But, says Killy, "After a year of study, looking at what other people were doing, we realized that the best decision we could make was to minimize the waste. We realized that we were producing too much waste because we were inefficient in turning round logs into square timber." Killy and his staff began looking for new technology that would allow them to make those improvements. They soon realized that it would be cheaper and easier to build an all-new sawmill than to up-grade the older, less efficient operation.

After six months of detailed engineering studies, construction of the new mill was begun in July, 1979. Lakeland had to co-ordinate the efforts of five different Canadian and American suppliers to purchase and set up the new equipment. One company supplied the log grading and separating equipment; another, the lumber handling equipment, while a third supplied the cutting centre. A fourth company supplied the computers used to co-ordinate the various machines. Yet another company was employed to develop and produce the computer software needed to control the whole operation.

Eighteen months later Lakewood Sawmills ran the first logs through the new mill, using equipment designed by company engineers. Killy explains that the construction schedule was longer than normally required when building a new sawmill. "We couldn't buy much of the equipment we put in the new mill off-the-shelf. As we went along, we were developing brand new concepts in the use of equipment. Instead of just buying saws and putting them in the mill, we installed a series of machines designed to improve the yield from each log." Lakeland's new mill cost $15 million to design and build. Was the investment worth it? Killy is emphatic. "We are getting 40 percent more salable product of a log using this new technology."

The computer is the nerve centre of the entire operation. None of the sawmilling operations is directly controlled by a human worker.

"The operator cannot overrule the computer," Killy says. "He simply monitors it to ensure that it is running properly and safely. In front of him is a stop button he presses if something goes wrong."

Killy points out that his company's search for greater productivity starts with the cutting-down of the trees that will be sawn in the new mill.

Lakeland does not do its own timber cutting. "We have contractors who log for us, but they log using methods we approve of," says Killy. Those methods must ensure that, during cutting, each tree yields as much lumber as possible while suffering as little damage as possible.

When the logs first arrive at the new mill, they are graded and separated so that the best use can be made of each one. Photo-optical and laser scanners help position each log as it approaches the sawing centre. Computers are used to read the measurements, make the calculations and adjust the flitches as they approach the saw blades. (Flitches are logs which have been squared off on two sides.) Says Killy: "It's that marriage of computer technology with very sophisticated measuring devices and very positive, high speed positioning devices that has allowed us to improve the lumber yield."

This diagram shows the number of pieces of lumber possible from a large log.

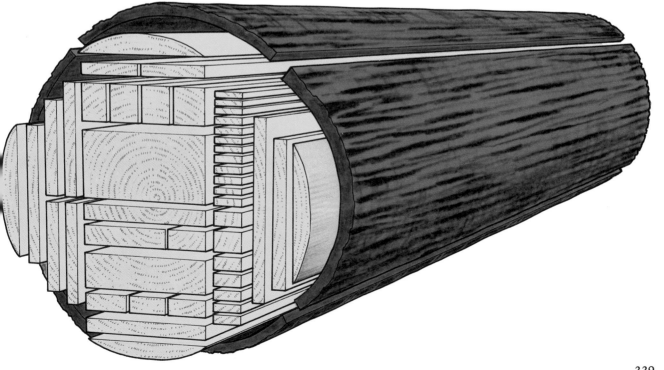

The new Lakeland mill produces a limited range of products. Most of the timber is turned into standard length construction materials for Canadian and American housing markets. There is still wood waste: sawdust, bark and wood chips. But the amount of sawdust is much less than before, as the new mill uses sawblades one-third as thick as those in other, older operations. The sawdust and bark are used as fuel sources for the kilns that dry the newly sawn lumber.

Killy insists that efficiency is more than just reducing waste. It also involves finding new and imaginative uses for sawmill by-products. For example, Lakeland produces frames for an American mattress manufacturer, using leftover pieces of wood that are too thin for construction materials. As Killy notes, "If I have a choice of making wood chips to sell to a pulp mill or a piece of lumber to sell to a mattress company, there is four times more value in a cubic foot of wood sold as lumber."

As a result of its new technology, the new Lakeland sawmill is as efficient as the best mills in Sweden or the United States. Killy is surprised that, five years after the new mill had opened, no other British Columbia sawmill had followed Lakeland's model. He has read studies indicating that there is a ten to twelve year lag before Canadian companies tend to adopt technological advances made in European or American lumber production.

Lakeland's new operations have helped make the company highly competitive in the lucrative United States housing market. In 1986, Killy expressed his concern about efforts by American lumber producers to have the United States government impose duties on imports of Canadian lumber (see pages 280-283). Nonetheless, he remains convinced that more efficient sawmills will mean a greater competitiveness for British Columbia's forest industry in the world marketplace.

1. Summarize the reasons why Lakeland decided to build a new sawmill in 1979. In what ways does Lakeland represent a major technological improvement in British Columbia's forest industry?

2. What does George Killy see as the best way for a sawmill operation to become more efficient? Why?

3. What effect has computerization had on the workers in the Lakeland mill?

REVIEW

Checking Back

1. Markets for B.C. forest products have changed over time. Compare the markets for two time periods: the mid- and late 1800s, and the post World War II era. Use a chart to organize the information you find, using the headings: Locations of Markets, Products, Uses for the Products. Write a short paragraph summarizing the information you have put in your chart.

2. Make a flow chart to illustrate the steps in going from a tree through to a finished piece of lumber for sale in a lumberyard.

3. Describe the changes that have taken place in the working conditions for forestry workers. What role have unions played in getting these changes?

Using Your Knowledge

4. If you were the owner of a sawmill, what qualities, skills, and experience would you look for when hiring new workers?

5. Explain the effect of sustained yield policies on timber supply.

6. Suppose you were placed in charge of managing a large forest in the province. Make a list of considerations you would want to take into account before deciding which uses will be approved for the forest.

7. British Columbia only reinvests about 5 percent of revenue from the forest industry back into this resource. What are the implications of this level of investment? Research how this compares with other countries.

8. Suggest some ways communities based on the forest industry could reduce the impact of a slumping economy and the loss of jobs.

Chapter 17

The Mining Industry

Mining is a treasure hunt. It requires skill, perseverance and, even today, no small amount of luck. Even with today's highly sophisticated equipment and techniques, finding a mineral deposit worth mining can take years. Once a deposit is found and a mine opened, there are still financial risks to the mine's owners. Mineral prices fluctuate wildly, and mines that began as profitable ventures often wind up in bankrupt failure.

To most British Columbians, mining is an almost invisible industry. Yet it has played a leading role in the development of the British Columbia economy.

This chapter begins with a brief survey of the mineral resource itself. You will then look at the history of the mining industry in British Columbia, its importance and impact, and some of the problems and issues it faces. In reading the chapter, think about these key questions:

- Why is mining an invisible industry to many British Columbians?
- What makes mining such a risky business?
- What are some of the advantages and disadvantages of living in a province heavily dependent on the mining industry?
- Why is most of British Columbia's mineral production exported?

The Mineral Resource: Hidden Treasure

The geological processes that formed mineral deposits are many and complex. For millions of years, the earth's crust has been constantly, though gradually, changing. As it buckles and twists, fractures are formed. From deep inside the earth, molten material containing minerals rises up through these fractures. Rivers carry sand and mud downstream and deposit them, layer on layer, in lakes and oceans. Buried plant matter slowly changes to coal. Tiny organisms decay to form oil and gas. By understanding these processes, prospectors can choose areas that are likely to contain valuable mineral deposits.

The minerals found in British Columbia include **precious metals** such as gold and silver; **base metals** such as copper, molybdenum, lead and zinc; plus **fossil fuels** such as coal, natural gas and petroleum. In addition, **industrial minerals** such as asbestos and **structural materials** such as limestone (used to make cement) and gravel are mined. No two deposits are exactly alike. For instance, some copper deposits may contain 20 percent copper, while others contain only 0.5 percent copper. Often, several metals are found together, such as lead-zinc-silver deposits or copper-molybdenum deposits.

When the deposit contains a high enough concentration of valuable metals to be worth mining, the rock is called ore. Depending on how deep the deposit is, the ore is extracted either from a large open pit on the surface or through underground shafts and tunnels.

Deep underground, the operator in the photo on the left is drilling three blast holes with a jumbo drill. The photo on the right shows the ore benches of an open pit mine.

**Oil Deposits in
Rock Formation**

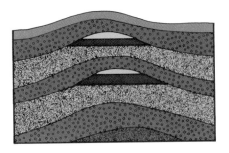

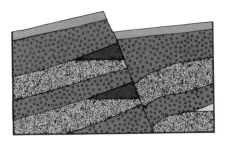

Legend

Gas

Non-porous rock

Oil

Water

*Oil is trapped by non-porous
rock layers either through fold-
ing or faulting of the layers.
What clues will guide geologists
towards the oil traps?*

After the ore is blasted out of the deposit, the valuable minerals must be separated from the waste rock. This process starts in the mill. There, the chunks of ore are crushed and ground. Various chemical solutions are used to separate out the desired metals. Further processing may take place at a smelter or refinery, where heat or chemicals are used to increase the purity of the extracted minerals.

Petroleum and natural gas pools are found deep underground, trapped within porous rock such as sandstone, which is in turn bounded by layers of less porous rock such as shale. To find oil and gas fields, geologists need an understanding of subterranean rock structures. When exploratory wells are dug, these structures some-times yield nothing more than dry holes.

1. Give two examples of each of the following British Columbia products:
   precious metals   fossil fuels
   base metals   industrial metals.

2. In your own words, briefly describe the processes involved in digging up and refining metals.

The History of the Mining Industry

During the past century and a half, the spotlight of mining activity in British Columbia has shifted from one area of the province to another and from one mineral to another. As these changes took place, the mining industry had considerable effects on the development of transportation, communication, commerce and government in the province. This section will look first at this shifting pattern of development, and then at the industry's effects upon these other aspects of the province's history.

The Development of the Industry: From Gold to Copper

In the history of the province's mining industry, the minerals that have taken star billing at various times are gold, coal, silver, lead-zinc, and copper.

In Chapter 10 you learned that the first of several gold strikes in

Small communities, often only rough shacks, were built to service the miners working nearby claims. Many of the towns died as quickly as they grew.

British Columbia took place in 1858 on the lower Fraser River near Yale. When news of the strike reached California, fortune-seeking adventurers boarded ships bound for Victoria. In the summer of that year alone, 25 000 people passed through Victoria on their way to the gold fields. These prospectors then faced a 300 km journey up the Fraser River and its canyon before they could start digging or panning for gold. No roads went through the mountains, and few canoes or barges crossed the dangerous rivers.

In 1860, gold fever swept north from the lower Fraser River into the Cariboo. News of gold strikes in Williams Creek spread quickly. By 1862, two thousand fortune seekers had arrived there from eastern Canada, the United States and Britain.

The Cariboo gold rush was followed by others around the province. Steam shovels and dredges soon replaced the pans. But by the latter decades of the century, many of the surface diggings were exhausted. The excitement subsided. The once-noisy saloons of the instant mining towns became deserted. By the turn of the century, the focus of British Columbia's mining activity had switched to coal and base metals.

The discovery of coal on Vancouver Island, while less glamorous than the gold rushes, marked the true beginnings of British Columbia's mining industry. In 1836, Hudson's Bay Company men discovered coal at the northern end of Vancouver Island while conducting

LABOR STRIFE IN THE EARLY DAYS OF COAL MINING

Working conditions in coal mines were difficult and dangerous. Miners worked as many as ten or eleven hours a day for wages considerably lower than those paid in the gold fields, and they were concerned about the lack of safety standards in the mines. Finally, they formed a workingman's association, or union, and went on strike at Robert Dunsmuir's Wellington mine to back their demands for higher wages, an eight hour day and safer working conditions. Dunsmuir responded by calling in the militia to put down the strike, then fired the strikers, replacing them with Chinese workers. Because mine owners like Dunsmuir often employed Chinese strikebreakers, the early mine workers' unions of British Columbia sought to have restrictions imposed on Oriental immigration to Canada.

a survey of the Island's resources. Appropriately, the survey was carried out using the HBC vessel, *Beaver*, the first steamship on the coast of British Columbia. Steam power would create the market for Vancouver Island coal, first for ships and later for the railways.

More coal was discovered in the Nanaimo area in 1852. The Hudson's Bay Company created its own mining company, the Nanaimo Coal Company, and ran Nanaimo as a company town. Later, as more and more coal deposits were found around Nanaimo and nearby Wellington, British and local entrepreneurs started mining companies to compete with the Hudson's Bay Company. One of these mine owners, Robert Dunsmuir, would later become the richest man in British Columbia and an influential political leader.

Work in the early coal fields was not only dirty and poorly paid but also dangerous. Underground gas explosions and fires were common. In the decade from 1893-1903, over four hundred men died in British Columbia mines. The working conditions helped the rise of miners' unions and triggered several major strikes.

Silver, lead and zinc mining were particularly important in the East and West Kootenay areas of British Columbia. Large-scale mining of these ores became possible during the 1890s with the arrival of the railroads in that mountainous terrain. In a process known as rawhiding, strings of packhorses and mules dragged the heavy ores on cow hides down the steep mountainsides to the lakeshores. Sternwheelers steamed along the lakes, connecting the pack trails with railway spur lines. The first railroads in the area followed the north-south lying valleys to smelters south of the border. The completion of the Canadian Pacific Railway's Crowsnest Pass line at the turn of the century finally provided an all-Canadian route out of the Kootenays.

Second in value only to gold, silver was a metal highly prized by prospectors. Lead and zinc mining, however, became very important after a technological breakthrough in the 1920s. This process, invented at the Sullivan mine near Kimberley, made it possible to separate lead, zinc and iron concentrates from the rest of the rock. The Sullivan mine became the world's largest producer of lead and zinc. Ores from the Sullivan mine were transported to the Cominco plant at Trail for smelting and refining. Cominco is a giant mining company owned by Canadian Pacific. Its Trail smelter became the largest lead-zinc smelter in the world. During the 1950s and 1960s, the value of lead and zinc production was more than that of any other metal in British Columbia.

Today, the king of metals in British Columbia is copper. It is found in many areas of the province, often in combination with other metals, especially molybdenum. A soft metal with a high melting point, molybdenum is used primarily as an ingredient in the manufacture of steel.

Most copper is now mined from huge open pits. These pits contain a lower concentration of copper than vein deposits, but the deposits themselves are vast. One tonne of ore may contain only about 3.7 kg (or 0.37 percent) copper. The Highland Valley area near Kamloops is the focus of most copper mining today.

Because of new technological advances in exploration and mining, better transportation, new foreign markets and increased government incentives, the mining industry has expanded enormously over the past two decades. The following graph shows how dramatic this increase has been for British Columbia's two most valuable minerals, coal and copper.

During the early 1980s, however, the mining industry went through several years of unprecedented losses. Prices for metals were down, many metals mines were losing money or had closed, and the industry was operating at well below capacity.

In the early 1980s, coal and copper were the leading money producers in British Columbia, followed by natural gas and petroleum, silver, gold and molybdenum. Zinc, lead, asbestos and iron provided smaller revenues. Even by the time you read this information, this ranking may have changed. As the demand and market price of minerals rise and fall, so does the relative importance of various minerals. As you will see later in this chapter, these fluctuations are a major problem for the industry.

The industry is changing in other ways. It takes more than one prospector with a pick and a shovel to start up a mining operation today. Most of the mineral deposits that lie at or near the surface have already been found. Today's prospectors search for deposits lying well below the earth's surface. A modern mineral search involves trained exploration crews, skilled scientists, aircraft such as helicopters, sophisticated mineral-hunting equipment and computers. Since mineral searches are so expensive, they are usually financed by large corporations that can afford them. Even if minerals are found, a great deal of further exploring is required before it is known whether the deposit is rich and large enough to support a mine. Only one in every 1000 exploration prospects actually becomes a producing mine.

It takes a great deal of money to open a mine, extract the ore, process it, and ship it to markets. To raise the money to cover these

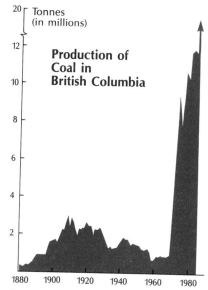

Source: B.C. Ministry of Mines

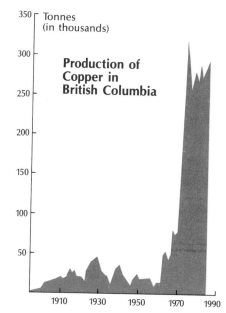

Source: B.C. Ministry of Mines, annual reports; Statistics Canada

How stable have the markets for coal and copper been over the past decades?

costs, mine owners often issue shares in the company, which are bought and sold through the stock exchange. By selling the shares, or stocks, to investors, the owners reduce the financial risks they face while giving the investors a chance to share in the profits. These investors in business suits may not look much like the early fortune seekers with their packsacks and picks; their goal, however, is the same; they hope to reap riches from treasures hidden beneath the ground.

1. Draw a chart to show where and when these minerals have been important in the British Columbia industry.

   gold   lead   copper
   coal   zinc

2. How did the discovery of ore deposits and the development of mines lead to the establishment and growth of communities in British Columbia?

3. What changes in transportation were encouraged by mining activity? How were mining activities influenced by improvements in transportation?

A Province Built on Mining

More than any other industry, mining has affected the early development of transportation, communication, commerce and government in the province.

Most of the early gold prospectors were drifters who disappeared once the gold ran out. Yet they left behind a network of trails, wagon roads, and steamships. One example is the Cariboo Wagon Road up the Fraser Canyon, an extraordinary engineering feat for its time. Originally built to service the gold fields, it is now the route of the Trans-Canada Highway.

The mining industry is responsible for the establishment of many communities in British Columbia. Yale and Atlin owe their origins to gold mining; Nelson to silver mining; Kimberley to lead-zinc mining; Trail to smelting; Greenwood and Britannia to copper mining; Endako to molybdenum mining; and Nanaimo, Comox and Cumberland to coal mining.

Mining activity is shifting and unpredictable. Minerals are a **nonrenewable resource**. Once a mineral deposit is depleted, mining companies are forced to uproot their operations and move on.

Once-thriving communities such as Barkerville, Pioneer and Sandon are now ghost towns. The Vancouver Island mines that were a major source of coal in the 1800s are now depleted. Most British Columbia coal today comes from the East Kootenays. Recently, new coal mines in northeastern British Columbia have started operations, resulting in the new town of Tumbler Ridge.

The mining industry is unstable not only because ore bodies become exhausted, but also because the demand for specific minerals goes up and down. This changing demand is sometimes related to technological advances that create a need for different mineral products.

For instance, coal was in great demand during the railroad boom around 1910, but slumped when the railroads switched from coal to diesel fuel in the 1950s. In the late 1960s and 1970s, however, coal became increasingly important in the steel industry of Japan, and British Columbia's coal once again had a market. More recently, world demand for coal has dropped at a time when British Columbia has excess production capacity.

Copper, now the most important metal mined in British Columbia, only became important with the invention of electric power. Copper is used in transmission lines, generators and batteries. However, copper prices have fluctuated from year to year, depending on the demand for the metal.

1. Minerals are a non-renewable resource. How has this fact affected the communities built around the mines?
2. Explain how changes in transportation technology have influenced the mining industry in British Columbia.

The Importance and Impact of the Mining Industry

The mining industry is "Number Two" in the province. It is second only to forestry in its contribution to the British Columbia economy. During the early 1980s, generally poor years for mining in British Columbia, the industry still produced almost three billion dollars of minerals annually. In a poor year such as 1983, despite losses of $62 million, the mining industry still contributed $350 million in taxes and other payments to the government.

Value of Mineral Production in British Columbia
(in millions of dollars)

	1980	1981	1982	1983
Metals				
Copper	670.6	611.3	495.0	548.7
Gold—placer and lode	170.1	136.0	118.3	140.9
Zinc	49.4	67.0	63.6	89.3
Lead	66.1	61.5	43.0	46.9
Molybdenum	288.9	198.2	155.0	91.9
Silver	156.5	152.4	158.3	186.9
Others	27.4	20.3	24.4	16.8
Total Metals	1429.0	1246.7	1057.5	1121.3
Industrial Minerals				
Asbestos	81.7	76.8	57.0	79.7
Sulphur	21.7	33.3	29.1	21.7
Others	12.5	12.4	9.5	10.7
Total Industrial Minerals	115.9	122.5	95.6	112.2
Structural Materials				
Sand and gravel	98.7	87.6	65.6	72.9
Cement	90.1	82.4	69.3	66.5
Others	53.5	30.8	29.2	29.1
Total Structural Materials	242.3	200.8	164.2	168.6
Fuels				
Coal sold or used	461.5	554.3	566.9	560.7
Crude oil	189.6	236.2	333.4	402.3
Natural gas to pipeline	612.5	616.8	542.7	448.6
Others	26.2	31.6	36.3	45.9
Total Fuels	1289.8	1438.9	1479.3	1457.5
Grand Total	3077.0	3008.7	2797.1	2859.6

Source: *Ministry of Energy, Mines and Petroleum Resources.*

1. Look at the 1983 column. Which was the most important mineral by value mined in that year? Which was second most important? How do petroleum and natural gas rank?
2. Examine the value of metals produced since 1980. In general, has the value of most metals produced in British Columbia

risen or fallen? Has the value of coal production risen or fallen?

3. In 1980, molybdenum was the second most important metal after copper. In 1982, a dramatic fall in the price of molybdenum forced some mines to close. What can you say about the relative importance of molybdenum in 1983?

There are mines dotted throughout British Columbia. Many communities depend on mining for their economic existence.

1. Determine the number of mines in British Columbia in 1984.
2. Write the minerals that are included in the legend in your notebook. For each one, count the number of mines in the province that recover that mineral. (You will need to read the symbols carefully.) Which mineral is recovered at the greatest number of mines?
3. Consider the locations of the mines. Is there an apparent pattern in the mine locations?

**Taxes and Other Payments
by the B.C. Mineral Industry
to Governments**

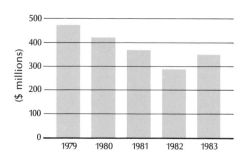

Distribution of 1983 Taxes

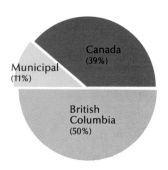

1. Notice how the amount that mining contributes to the government has fluctuated from year to year. In what year did the industry contribute $474 million? Approximately how much did it contribute in 1982?
2. Examine the graph showing the distribution of 1983 taxes. Which level of government receives the greatest protion of industry taxes?
3. Name one government service provided by each level of government with tax revenue.

Problems and Issues

I'm here today to tell you in blunt language that, although the mining industry in B.C. is facing some very serious problems, we have no intention of fading quietly into the sunset.
[1984 speech by the President of the Mining Association of British Columbia.]

Miners are optimists. They have to be in order to survive in a business with such ups and downs. Mining faces some challenges now and in the years ahead. This section looks at the international market and environmental issues.

The International Marketplace: Falling Prices

Over 80 percent of British Columbia's mineral production is exported to other countries. These exports allow us, in return, to buy products from foreign countries. Yet we have little control over the foreign market for British Columbia minerals. If our customers cut back on steel production, they buy less of our coal and molybdenum. If they build fewer houses, they buy less of our copper. If they manufacture fewer automobiles, they buy less of our lead and zinc. When the demand for British Columbia minerals drops, these minerals have to be sold at lower prices, if they can be sold at all. In this situation, some British Columbia mines can no longer make a profit on their operations. They are consequently forced to close.

Advances in technology initiated outside Canada are reducing the amount of minerals needed to make some standard products. For example, plastic is replacing some of the metal used in automobiles. A new kind of photographic film uses significantly less silver per roll. Computer designers are experimenting with machines operated by light rather than electronics. New steel-making techniques promise to reduce requirements for coking coal.

Some developing countries are now discovering and developing rich mineral deposits. This is happening while the British Columbia industry is being forced to switch to lower grade ores because the richest deposits have been mined out. Mining companies in developing countries frequently pay lower wages to their workers than British Columbia operations do. Therefore, these countries can still afford to mine even when prices are low. In some cases they will sell their minerals at very low prices because they are eager to buy foreign goods in exchange.

It is difficult to predict when or even if the next upswing in international mineral prices will occur. During the decade from 1973 to 1983 fifteen new mines were built in British Columbia. Yet in 1984, metal prices were so low that eleven of the thirty-three mines in the province were shut. Poor prices is the major problem facing the mining industry today.

1. Give two examples of how changing technology influenced the demand for British Columbia's minerals.
2. Why does British Columbia have little control over its markets for minerals?

Environmental Issues

Mining operations affect the environment in a variety of ways, both directly and indirectly. These effects include scarred landscapes left by open pit mines, tailing piles or smelter wastes; damage to streams and rivers caused by mining operations; and disruption to animal

World Lead Price

(U.S. cents/lb.)

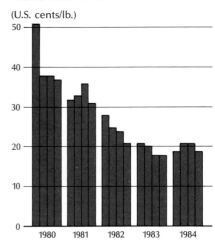

World Copper Price

(U.S. cents/lb.)

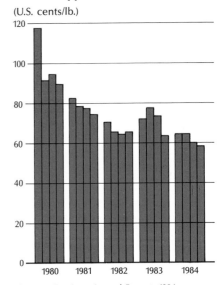

Source: *Cominco Annual Report, 1984*

During these five years, a world-wide economic recession pulled most mineral prices down to unprecedented levels. How would falling metal prices affect British Columbia miners? How would they affect towns that depend on the mining industry?

habitats. Other effects may include downstream problems arising from stream diversion; air pollution problems resulting from smelter smokestacks; and soil or water pollution caused by tailing piles or chemicals used in refining processes. As well, mining operations may conflict with other possible uses of the environment, particularly in parks or recreational areas.

Recently scientists became concerned that sulphur dioxide emissions from smelter smokestacks might be a potential source of acid rain in British Columbia. Acid rain can kill fish in lakes and streams and may affect the growth of forests and farm crops. The impact of smelter emissions on vegetation was dramatically evident in the Trail area where air pollution from the lead-zinc refinery had turned surrounding hillsides into barren wastelands. Even after the introduction of controls on the Trail smelter in the 1930s, it took several decades for the hillsides to become green again.

In the past, little was done to control or repair the damage done to the environment by mining and smelting activities in British Columbia. However, in recent years, all levels of government have responded to public and scientific concerns by carefully monitoring the environmental impact of this industry. Nevertheless, there is still considerable potential for harm to the environment from mining activities; our knowledge of the full impact on natural systems is far from complete.

Case Study: Life in a One-Industry Town

Tumbler Ridge, British Columbia, is a brand new one-industry town (there are about 800 towns in Canada identified as one-industry towns). Located 112 km south of Dawson Creek in northeastern British Columbia (see map on page 351), the town would not exist if it were not for the major coal mining operations nearby.

In 1982, the provincial government created Tumbler Ridge as part of the $3 billion North-East Coal Project. This project was developed in order to bring economic growth and development to this frontier region, and spur growth throughout the whole province. In the mid-1980s, however, the demand for coal for Japan's steel mills dropped, casting doubt on the future of the project. It also cast doubt on the future of British Columbia's newest town. In Tumbler Ridge there are frequent, worried discussions among residents like

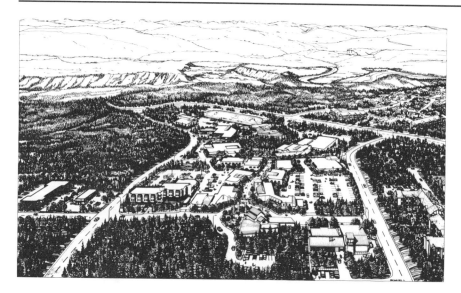

A sketch showing the layout of the town centre of Tumbler Ridge.

Mike and Esther Wallensky. [The Wallenskys are a fictional couple based on actual people living in Tumbler Ridge.] Before his move to Tumbler Ridge, Mike was unemployed for two and a half years. The last mine at which he had worked closed down because of declining sales. Mike was pleased to go to Tumbler Ridge and to begin working again. The wages here were better than those earned by most other workers in British Columbia. Tumbler Ridge has one of the highest per capita incomes in the province.

The Wallenskys and their two young children live in a house rented from the Quintette Coal Company. Nearly all of the homes and apartments in Tumbler Ridge are owned by Quintette or one of the two companies with mines nearby. The Wallenskys like their house, which is new, and they believe the rent is fair.

Mike Wallensky has watched Tumbler Ridge evolve from a few camp trailers surrounded by a sea of mud and stumps to a modern, planned community. He came here in 1982 as a heavy equipment operator, taking part in development of both the townsite and the huge mine nearby. Esther and the children joined him later that year. The town was quickly taking shape, with houses and apartment buildings going up. A shopping centre and commercial buildings soon provided most of the goods and services available in larger urban centres, at prices about the same as those in Dawson Creek. A large recreational complex offers more facilities than other towns the size of Tumbler Ridge. Today, the town also has a modern medical centre and dental clinic.

Heavy equipment can be used to haul the minerals out of open pit mines. How do the working conditions of open pit mines compare to those of underground mines?

The Wallensky's children, Chris and Sarah, first attended school in a cluster of portable classrooms. Now they get their education in a modern elementary school, one of two in the town. There is also a new secondary school for the older students. While the children are in school, Esther works part-time in the drug store.

Mike drives one of the giant Wabco haul trucks that carry the coal from the open pit mine to the stock piles. The Wabco stands ten metres high, weighs 170 t and can carry 168 m³ of coal. Mike describes the coal mining and loading operation as "highly co-ordinated teamwork."

The process begins with the hydraulic shovel operators, whose giant machines eat away at the rocky overburden to reveal the seams of coal below. A pit geologist checks out the seam to see if it is worth mining. If it is less than half a metre thick, the coal is treated as waste rock and stripped away.

When a workable seam is located, the blasting crew goes to work. They use a twelve metre high drill to bore up to 300 holes into the sandstone and the coal seam. Each hole is filled with explosive and linked with primacord (a special kind of wire). The primacord is connected to a detonator. When the blaster plunges the detonator, a series of explosions will break up 2500 to 3500 m³ of coal and rock.

After the dust and smoke from the explosion clears, bright green Demag bull clam shovels move out to load the Wabcos. Twelve scoops later, the Demag has filled Mike's giant haul truck. He drives off, carrying a load of coal to the stock pile. Another Wabco immediately pulls up to take his place, ready to be loaded. Coal is taken from the stock pile to the processing plant where it is cleaned and dried, and separated from any worthless rock.

From Tumbler Ridge, the coal is carried by train along a rail line built especially to serve the North-East coal mines. Joining the CNR main line, the trains haul the coal to Prince Rupert. There, in a modern terminal built specially to handle North-East coal, it is loaded onto ships and carried to Japan. It will be used in the plants which make steel for the automobiles Canadians import from Japan.

Esther Wallensky says of Tumbler Ridge, "It's a good place to raise kids. We've got all of the facilities of a larger town without the problems." She says that the mining companies have emphasized the hiring of men and women with families. "That's why the town of Tumbler Ridge was built. The companies wanted to make sure they had a workforce that was stable. They've seen what has happened in other mining operations where the men stay in camps, just bunkhouses and mess halls really. Nobody stays very long, and it costs the companies a lot of money to train people to run machines like Mike's. Even here, the single guys have problems. There's nothing much for them to do after work."

When Esther first went to Tumbler Ridge, there were few women there. That has all changed now. Says Esther, "The town's grown very rapidly. Every day we see new changes. We like to boast that it's B.C.'s fastest growing community." In 1985, the town had a baby boom, experiencing the highest per capita birth rate in the province. In five years, the town's population had gone from 0 to more than 5000. The population is expected to level off at about 6000 people. "That is," says Esther, "if the demand for our coal holds up. Everybody up here knows that instant towns can fold as quickly as they were built if the mines shut down."

1. What problems might arise when a company owns all or most of the housing in a single resource town? Why would a company want to make the housing as comfortable as possible?

2. The companies and the province of British Columbia went to great lengths to develop Tumbler Ridge as a carefully planned community in order to avoid social problems often found in frontier resource towns. In your opinion, what might some of these problems be? How could establishing a community

357

complete with shops, recreation centres, schools, etc., help prevent these problems?

3. Throughout this chapter and case study you have learned about factors that influence the mining industry. List six factors that might influence the future of a town like Tumbler Ridge. Try to identify equal numbers of positive and negative factors.

REVIEW

Checking Back

1. Draw a time line to show events in the history of mining in British Columbia. The following dates should be marked on the time line, along with the events which occurred at that time.

   1836   1860
   1852   1890s
   1858   1920s

2. Record three or four pieces of evidence in this chapter that supports each of the following statements.
   (a) Technological improvements have been important in the development of mineral resources of the interior of the province.
   (b) Mining in British Columbia is influenced by forces and events outside of the province and the country.

Using Your Knowledge

3. Suppose you were asked by a visitor to British Columbia to explain the problems faced by the mining industry. Write a two- or three-paragraph summary in which you discuss the nature of the problems and the attempts that have been made to overcome them.

4. Identify three reasons why a mine might be shut down. For each reason, suggest some ways to soften the blow of the closure on the miners employed there.

5. Suppose you were a miner looking for work in British Columbia. A job has been offered to you in a remote part of the province in a mine which has just been opened. Think about the living and working conditions in the community. Make up a list of questions you would want information about before deciding to move. What would be the most important thing you would consider? Explain why you chose this aspect.

6. Compare the problems of the forest industry with the problems of the mining industry. How are the problems alike? How are they different? Write two general statements about resource industries based on your findings.

Chapter 18

The Fishing Industry

Visitors and local residents alike enjoy fishing in the ocean waters off the coast of British Columbia. Imagine yourself in a small boat, fishing for salmon. With your lines out over the side of the boat, you troll slowly through the water. All around you are other small boats carrying people like yourself. Further off, toward the horizon, you watch larger commercial fishing boats heading out to sea. Occasionally, you see a very large fishing boat, rusted and battered from months at sea, coming in to take on supplies, the flag of Poland, Japan or some other far-off nation flying from its stern.

As you wait for the fish to bite, you think about the licence you had to buy and the catch limits it imposes on you. You wonder if you will catch even one fish, let alone your limit. You wonder why there are fewer fish in British Columbia waters than there were just a generation ago. As well, you think about the effect this decline in fish stocks has had on the lives of people who make their living by fishing. Many others, in government, in the fishing industry, and those who fish for sport, have been concerned about the same problems too. Once among British Columbia's most important economic activities, the fishing industry appears to have fallen on hard times in recent years.

In this chapter you will examine these issues as you explore the changing nature of British Columbia's fishing industry over the past 150 years. You will learn about the important, if somewhat reduced, role that fishing plays in the economy of British Columbia today. And, you will examine some of the serious problems and issues facing the industry. Among the key questions examined in this chapter are:

- How has technological change affected British Columbia's fishing industry?
- Who owns the fish that live in the waters along Canada's west coast?

- Who regulates the fishing industry? Why are these regulations necessary?
- How has depletion of the fish stock affected this industry and the people who work in it?

History: An Industry Expands

Long before the first Europeans arrived, the salmon harvest and other fishing activities were very important sources of food for British Columbia's Native peoples. They ate more fish per capita than British Columbians do today. However, because their population was relatively small and the fisheries so vast, they had little impact on the resource base. Using nets, spears, hooks and fish traps they caught and consumed large amounts of fish and other seafoods. When the fish were running, families moved from their permanent villages to camps on their traditional fishing grounds. Much of the fish they caught was dried and smoked for the winter.

Compared to the east coast of Canada, the continental shelf on the west coast is narrow. Nevertheless, it yields a varied harvest of fish.

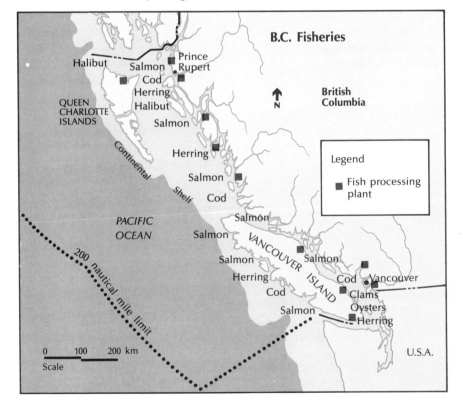

Salmon also played an important role in the feasts, ceremonies, legends and art of the Native peoples.

European fur traders and explorers first began to acquire dried and smoked fish from the Native peoples of British Columbia during the late 1700s. In the early nineteenth century, the traders began shipping salt-cured salmon to Hawaii and Asia. However, real growth in the salmon fishing industry did not occur until the introduction of canning as a means of preserving the fish. Canning ensured the freshness of British Columbia salmon sold in far-off export markets. Canned fish was also tastier and more attractive to consumers than salt-cured fish.

To see how the commercial fishing industry has evolved, we will look in turn at the canneries, the boats, the workers and the management of the fisheries.

The Canneries

Today, all that remains of many fish canneries is a few rotten pilings protruding from the water of the bay, or an old boiler rusting on the beach. Most of the canneries that once dotted the British Columbia coast are now closed, but people who used to work in them remember them well.

I was fourteen when I started working in the cannery, but the records show I was two years older. Tips [heads] and tails. I used to work all day to fill two bins that they paid $2.50 for. Two fifty a day. It was fun though, and in those days $2.50 was a lot of money. It got us quite far. You had to fill the bin with tips and tails and you had tickets on your back that they punched every time you filled a bin.
[Hazel Stewart, cannery worker.]

The first cannery in British Columbia was built in 1870. By 1911, salmon canning had become well established, with most of the canneries located near the mouths of the Fraser and Skeena rivers. By 1928, there were canneries near the mouth of every major salmon river. Fleets of rowboats and small sailboats with gillnets supplied each cannery with fish. Workers washed, cut and packed the fish into cans that were then steamed, sealed and exported to America and Europe.

After its expansion, the cannery industry began a period of consolidation. In 1919, there were ninety-seven canneries on the coast employing more than 9000 people. Fifty years later, there were only fifteen canneries, all but three in the Fraser and Skeena river areas, employing about 3700 workers. By the mid 1980s, only a half dozen major canneries remained, all located near the mouths of the Skeena and Fraser rivers.

Technological changes in both the fishing fleet and the canning industry played a major role in this change. Canneries were no longer needed at every river mouth when fishboats had motors and could travel faster and further with their catch. Later, improved on-board cold storage and freezing facilities meant the boats could travel for several days with their loads of fish.

On land, other technological changes meant that a large cannery with the latest machinery could process more salmon using fewer workers. The small, isolated canneries became uneconomical to operate compared to the larger, centrally located processing plants. A few large companies gradually bought up most of their smaller competitors and closed those uneconomical canneries. Today, the four largest British Columbia salmon canning firms account for over 80 percent of the total output.

Canning today also faces competition from other means of preserving and marketing fish. Improved transportation systems allow a greater portion of the British Columbia catch to be sold fresh

Canneries such as this supplied employment for cannery workers and fishermen. What forces led to a reduction of the cannery industry into just a handful of locations?

in both domestic and export markets. Fish and other sea food products, both whole and processed, are increasingly being frozen rather than canned before being shipped to market.

The Changing Technology of the Boats

Everybody used the sailboats then, no gas boats. We sleep in there and when the boat turns, water comes in. It was lots of fun. We were always wet. When I was about ten years, I started fishing with my dad for Rupert Cannery, about six miles up Tucks Inlet.

[Frank Alexcee, early Skeena River fisherman.]

At first, the canneries owned most of the boats, painting them in company colors and renting them out to fishermen. The small sail-powered gillnetters could not hold a catch for more than a few hours without it spoiling, so they did not venture far from the cannery. Company steam tugs sometimes towed the boats out to the river mouth. There, each fisherman would pay out the gillnet while his "puller" rowed the boat. The boats would then drift for a period of minutes or hours, depending on the run. Then, the fisherman would haul in the net by hand while the puller backed up the boat.

Two other types of fishing vessels, trollers and purse seiners, appeared on the British Columbia coast in the early 1900s. The first trollermen usually worked alone, trailing handlines from an open rowboat or skiff and catching the salmon on hooks. The seiners used large, fine-meshed nets. Up to sixteen workers were needed to haul in the seine nets laden with thousands of salmon or herring. Wind, tides and swells made pulling the seine net alongside the boat a dangerous job.

Technological advances during the early twentieth century resulted in gasoline motors replacing oars, sail and steam in the British Columbia fishing industry. Gasoline-powered gillnetters, popularly known as the "mosquito fleet," could now travel much farther and faster with their catches. On the purse seiners, winches powered by gasoline engines allowed workers to set and haul in their nets in half the time, using fewer people. Following World War II, other technological changes led to the construction of larger fishboats that could carry greater amounts of fuel and larger catches. These boats could remain at sea for long periods of time, allowing more fish to be caught.

FISHING VESSELS IN THE PACIFIC COAST FISHERY

The gillnetters used today are larger than the early cannery boats and use mechanized nethandling equipment. Yet the basic technique of gillnetting has not changed. Needing crews of no more than two people, the gillnetters fish in sheltered water near river mouths. As the fish migrate to the spawning grounds, they are caught in nets that have been strung across their path of travel.

The purse seiners are larger and more expensive vessels with elaborate gear for fish detection and net handling. When the crew locates a school of fish, the boat is steered in a circular path while the net is paid out. Once the school is encircled, the base of the net is drawn tight, or "pursed," to entrap the catch.

Trollers are smaller but sturdy vessels that fish farther out at sea. They catch fish using lures attached to lines mounted from four long poles and towed behind the boat.

In general, these technological changes have made fishing boats safer and more efficient. Today, most are equipped with powerful diesel engines and sophisticated fishing gear. Electronic equipment, such as sonar, autopilots and radios, is used for fish-finding, navigation, and communication. These changes have resulted in boats that can harvest large numbers of fish with very small crews. Such boats, however, are very expensive to own and operate. In the early 1980s, rising interest rates and increased fuel costs, combined with declining catches, caused many fishermen to face severe financial hardships.

1. Technological change brought a sharp reduction in the number of canneries. The number of fish boats has also dropped but not nearly as sharply. Suggest why this might be so.
2. In what ways have technological changes benefited fishermen? In what ways have they caused problems for fishermen?

A Way of Life for the Workers

In the founding years of the fishing industry, Native people made up the bulk of the seasonal work force. Women and younger children worked in the canneries while the men fished. The Chinese were also vital to the early canneries. Chinese contractors were hired to provide all the cans and round up a crew of Native, Chinese and Japanese workers. The workers were paid on a piecework basis, so much per can. The contractor would pay their transportation to the cannery, supply their meals, and settle accounts at the end of the season.

Once the gold rush fever cooled, European settlers joined the ranks of the fishermen. These settlers included Norwegians, Scots, Finns, Germans, French, Irish, Greeks, Yugoslavs and Portuguese.

Japanese fishermen began settling along the coast in the late 1800s. As their numbers increased, other fishermen resented their skill and willingness to work steadily for low wages. Some groups of fishermen persuaded the federal government to pass laws intended to eliminate the Japanese from the commercial fishery.

The biggest setback for Japanese-Canadian fishermen occurred during World War II. The Canadian government feared that some Japanese Canadians might actively aid the Japanese war effort. Even though there was little evidence to support their fears, the government relocated thousands of Japanese Canadians away from the coast for the duration of the war. The government also confiscated over 1300 vessels belonging to Japanese-Canadian fishermen. After the war, many of these fishermen drifted back to the industry to start all over again, but most felt the government had failed to adequately compensate them for their seized property. The issue of compensation for the losses suffered by the Japanese Canadians remains contentious more than forty years after the war's end. Spokespeople for human rights groups still claim the relocation was brought on by racist attitudes and not concerns about national security.

NATIVE PEOPLE IN THE FISHING INDUSTRY

Native people found it easier to adjust to the fishing industry than to most other industries. One Indian group explains why:

> Participation in the fishing industry allowed us to remain living by the sea with our own people. And it was a kind of work that was more compatible with our way of life than other kinds of work in the white man's economy. It was, if nothing else, at least the lesser of two evils. It did not require us to give up our communities and our culture altogether.
>
> [From a submission to the 1982 Commission on Pacific Fisheries Policy]

Native people were particularly affected by developments in the commercial fishery. Of all the various populations that made their living from the sea, the Native peoples have probably relied on it the most. Commercial fishing was always a precarious source of income, but it was often the only one for Indian communities on the coast.

During the 1920s and 1930s, Native peoples began to be squeezed out of the commercial fishery. Those who fished could not afford the newer, more powerful and expensive boats. Those who worked in the small coastal canneries lost their jobs as the canneries closed. Between the early 1950s and the 1970s, the number of Native people employed in fishing or processing dropped by half. Despite government programs such as support for a Native fish processing co-op and a boat buy-back scheme, this loss of jobs is still devastating to dozens of Native communities.

1. Suggest why the quotation above describes commercial fishery as the "lesser of two evils" for Native people in British Columbia.

Many different fishermen's organizations have been created in British Columbia. Some represent ethnic groups, others the different types of fishing methods. Fishermen first began organizing to push for better fish prices from the canneries. During the 1900 Fraser River sockeye strike, fishermen demanded twenty-five cents per sockeye instead of the going cannery rate of twenty cents. This marked the beginning of determined, unionized activity in the industry. Later, many splinter fishermen's groups united to deal with issues that affected all of them, such as the reduction in jobs due to automation in the canneries, and the wage and price cuts made by the canneries during the Depression. The United Fishermen and Allied Workers Union, formed in 1945, today represents a major portion of the fishermen and the majority of the shoreworkers in the industry. The Native brotherhood represents Native workers in the fishing industry.

In the past, as today, an important part of the appeal of being a fisherman is the lifestyle. For those who love the sea, it offers challenging, physically vigorous work far from the world of time clocks and three-piece suits. Most fishermen own their own boats today. For many, the job is a way of life they do not want to give up in spite of the uncertainty and financial hardships. However, as we shall see, the commercial fishery has played a major role in reducing fish stocks to their present levels. As the resource is now at risk, the traditional lifestyle of the fisherman is also threatened.

1. Two groups of workers, people of Japanese ancestry and Native people, have found long-term employment in the fishing industry difficult to maintain. Outline the issues that have aggravated this problem.
2. What are the goals of fishery workers in using collective action?

Importance and Impact of the Fishing Industry

No painting of a British Columbia coastal scene would be complete without a fishboat chugging off into the distance. The fishing industry is part of our province's character and culture. It provides employment for thousands of British Columbians, both directly through jobs on the boats and in fish processing plants, and indirectly to the people who provide goods and services to the industry and the people who work in it. But the industry's economic importance to the province has declined steadily since the 1950s.

The tables in this section provide an economic overview of the fishing industry. However, you should remember that the industry is important to the people of British Columbia in a variety of ways. It is the mainstay of many coastal communities that would otherwise disappear. For some fishermen, commercial fishing is a preferred way of life as much as a job. Sport fishermen benefit from improved fish stocks, as do Native people fishing for food.

Wholesale Value of British Columbia Fish Landings
(in millions of dollars)

Species	1982	1983	1984
Salmon	315.3	284.3	276.2
Herring	86.4	111.1	99.0
Halibut[1]	7.9	11.2	13.8
Grey Cod	7.6	7.5	7.0
Sablefish	7.1	7.4	8.8
Geoducks	5.2	4.2	5.6
Sole	4.7	4.1	4.9
Hake	3.8	5.0	5.3
Lingcod	3.7	3.8	3.9
Shrimp and Prawns	3.4	3.6	5.1
Crabs	3.3	3.9	5.6
Other Species	18.4	25.7	31.7
Total	466.8	471.8	466.9

Source: Ministry of Environment, Fisheries Production Statistics of British Columbia
[1]*Includes landings by Canadian Fishermen at U.S. ports.*

1. The dominance of salmon is evident from this table. What percentage of the total value of fish landings does salmon make up?

British Columbia Exports of Fish and Marine Products
(millions of dollars)

Market Area	1982	1983	1984
Japan	159.7	135.7	144.6
European Economic Community[1]	74.8	68.8	74.9
United States	49.3	55.0	66.1
United Kingdom	43.6	68.5	44.1
Australia and New Zealand	18.5	17.3	27.2
Others	19.7	15.6	13.7
Total	365.6	361.1	370.6

Source: Ministry of Industry and Small Business Development, Estimates of B.C. Product Exports
[1]*Excluding United Kingdom*

1. What country provides our biggest market for fish exports?
2. The United States is our closest neighbor. Suggest reasons why our sales to them are not higher.

367

Problems and Issues: How to Turn the Tide

"We begin with a paradox," wrote Peter Pearse at the start of his 1982 report on the Pacific fisheries, "Turning the Tide." This paradox (a self-contradictory or seemingly absurd statement), as outlined by Pearse, is as follows. On the one hand, British Columbia has some of the world's most valuable fish resources. On the other hand, many commercial fishermen and fishing companies are near bankruptcy, there are fewer fish available to sport and Native fishermen, and the fisheries are a heavy burden on Canadian taxpayers.

What has happened to Canada's Pacific fishery? From what you have read about the history of the fishing industry, you may already be able to come up with some answers to this. An equally important question is: What can be done to improve the situation? In his report for the federal government Pearse emphasized the need for major changes that, he claimed, could "turn what is now a bleak and problematical picture into an exceedingly bright one."

In this section, we will look at aspects of this "bleak and problematical picture."

Fish Habitat: The Basis for Survival

All fish depend on their habitat. Salmon, which spawn and rear in freshwater streams and lakes, are particularly vulnerable to habitat disruption. An ideal salmon spawning site will have clean gravel and water that is well-oxygenated, cool and of constant temperature. A good rearing habitat will have an adequate food supply and cover (between boulders, under overhangs or in weeds) for protection from predators.

When spawning and rearing habitats are disrupted, salmon stocks cannot reproduce. Some damage to fish habitat arises from natural causes, such as landslides that block the streams. Most habitat damage, however, arises from the activities of people. Hydro dams and poorly designed stream crossings block upstream migration. Logging and related activities such as road building can have a major impact on salmon habitat. Early logging practices were particularly destructive (see page 335). Waste minerals and toxic chemicals from mines were sometimes dumped into the stream beds. Soil can erode into the streams during construction of nearby highways, pipelines

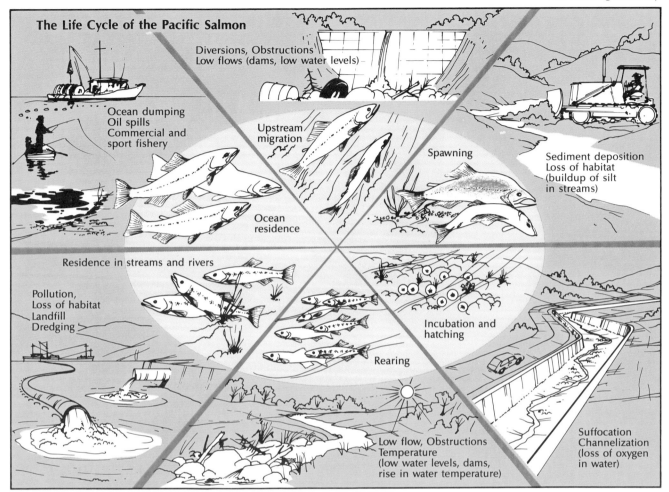

The Life Cycle of the Pacific Salmon

Diversions, Obstructions
Low flows (dams, low water levels)

Ocean dumping
Oil spills
Commercial and
sport fishery

Upstream
migration

Spawning

Sediment deposition
Loss of habitat
(buildup of silt
in streams)

Ocean
residence

Residence in streams and rivers

Pollution,
Loss of habitat
Landfill
Dredging

Incubation and
hatching

Rearing

Low flow, Obstructions
Temperature
(low water levels, dams,
rise in water temperature)

Suffocation
Channelization
(loss of oxygen
in water)

and housing developments. Pollution of the ocean by sewage, oil spills and various chemical discharges can also affect the fisheries.

Today, environmental regulations protecting salmon habitat are much stricter than in the past. Developers are now required to replace any habitat they destroy with an equivalent amount of new habitat, so there is no net loss overall. They may be required to build artificial spawning channels or to replace gravel beds and vegetation in and along existing streams.

In some cases, careful planning can prevent damage to salmon runs. In other cases, conflict is inevitable; for example, whether to preserve a salmon run or to dam the river to generate hydro-electricity. A fisherman will have a different answer from someone who needs the electricity.

This diagram shows threats to the Pacific salmon during its life cycle. Which problems could be improved?

Spawning channels, such as this one for sockeye salmon on the Fulton River, have been built to improve the chances of eggs hatching and the young fish surviving their first few weeks.

Faced with deteriorating fish habitat, fisheries managers can approach the problem from two angles. They can set stricter regulations to protect the remaining natural sites from further destruction or they can also improve or enhance potential sites, finding ways to produce additional fish to compensate for those lost due to deteriorating fish habitat.

Increased salmonid production remains the major goal of the Salmonid Enhancement Program initiated by the federal and provincial governments in 1977. SEP has experimented with a wide range of techniques to increase salmonid stocks. They include removing log jams and other obstructions from stream beds, building fishways to help fish migrate past dams and other immovable obstructions, and building spawning channels that duplicate the best conditions for egg laying. One of the most successful projects has been aerial fertilization of lakes, which creates more food in the lakes for young salmon. However, fish hatcheries are still the main means of increasing fish stocks.

In a hatchery, eggs are stripped from an adult salmon and raised under controlled conditions. The small fish, called fingerlings, are then released into the stream. Those that are not caught, eaten or killed for some other reason, eventually return to the hatchery. However, since eggs spawned in hatcheries have a much higher survival rate than those hatched in the wild, very few returning fish are needed to ensure the continuation of the run. Thus, a much greater proportion of hatchery fish can be harvested without depleting the fish stocks.

For several reasons, hatcheries are not necessarily the cure-all for deteriorating fish stocks. Hatchery fish can be more susceptible to disease than wild fish. Hatchery stocks may compete with weak wild salmon runs for food. The presence of hatchery fish may also lead to overfishing of wild stocks when the two populations are mixed together. This is because wild stocks cannot sustain the same high rate of harvest as hatchery stocks.

1. What steps have been taken to protect salmon spawning habitats in British Columbia? Why?

WHEN WILD AND HATCHERY STOCKS MIX

When wild stocks of fish mingle with hatchery stocks, the wild stocks are susceptible to overfishing. Here is how this could happen.

Suppose 200 wild adult coho return to a particular salmon stream. Of those 200 fish, 100 may be females. Although each female coho lays about 2500 eggs, few survive to return as spawning adults. In fact, from the eggs laid by the original 200 adult coho, 450 adults may return to the stream three years later. How many of these spawners can be harvested without reducing the run?

If 250 fish (approximately 55 percent) are harvested, there will still be 200 left (approximately 45 percent) to migrate to the spawning grounds and lay eggs for the next generation. Therefore, 55 percent is the maximum number of fish you would want to harvest to sustain the run. If more than 55 percent are harvested, fewer and fewer fish will be left to spawn. The run will weaken.

Now let us look at the hatchery run. Suppose a hatchery has a return of 2000 adult fish. Hatchery stocks can bear much greater rates of harvest, because in the carefully controlled conditions of the hatchery only eggs from a few spawners are required to sustain the run. Even if 80 percent of the returning fish were harvested there would be enough left to keep the hatchery well supplied.

What happens if those 2000 hatchery coho are mixed with the 200 wild coho on the same run, resulting in some 2200 fish migrating upstream? Suppose the catch rate for those returning adults is set at 80 percent. If the wild fish are evenly mixed with the hatchery fish, what percentage of the wild stocks would be harvested? Can the wild stocks support that rate of harvest? What would be the eventual result of mixing these hatchery and wild stocks?

Overfishing

Too many boats are chasing too few fish. In recent years, the government has attempted to deal with this problem by regulating the number of licensed vessels allowed to fish, the type of fishing gear used, the length of the fishing season, the areas where fishing may take place, and the minimum fish size. Because of these measures, herring, halibut and most groundfish stocks are in good condition or are recovering from past overfishing.

This is not the case for salmon stocks, however. Chinook salmon stocks appear to be close to collapse, wild coho stocks are declining rapidly, and most wild chum stocks are below what they should be. While large runs in 1985 hold out hopes that these stocks may be improving, it is likely that pink and sockeye will be the mainstays of the salmon fishing industry in the near future.

A major factor contributing to this overfishing is the huge capacity of the commercial fishing fleet. Although the number of fishing

FISHERIES MANAGEMENT

Fisheries management is a difficult and complex science. Its goal is to control the harvest in order to conserve fish stocks.

The first step is to measure existing stocks. Biologists count the number of spawning salmon in a run, and estimate how many fish are likely to survive from those eggs. With this information they attempt to predict the size of the run which will return to the stream in perhaps four years' time. The next step is to decide how many fish can be caught by commercial fishermen without harming the run (still allowing enough spawners to return to the stream). This figure must be adjusted to take into account fish that will be taken by the sport fishery, the Native food fishery, or foreign fishing fleets. Once the harvest limit is determined, fisheries managers can announce a series of

openings for commercial fishing in specified areas. During the openings, they keep track of the catch from each run so they can shorten or lengthen the allowed time if a run looks weaker or stronger than expected.

It is not as simple a process as it may sound. For one thing, salmon runs are erratic in size and timing so it is impossible to make entirely reliable forecasts of future runs. For another, fish from many different stocks may mingle in the same area, making it impossible to know whether the harvested fish come from one run or another. Controlling the harvest means taking into account several different commercial fishing fleets. Each fleet uses different gear and catches the fish at different points along their migration path. What is more, fish cross international boundaries, so Americans catch Canadian fish while Canadians catch American fish. In those instances, fisheries management must be an international concern.

boats has dropped over the past decade, the remaining vessels are larger and have much better fish-finding and harvesting equipment. The modern fleet is so effective that it can fill its storage holds in a few hours or days of fishing. However, while the capacity of the fleet has increased, the number of fish in the water has not. To prevent overfishing, the federal government sets limited "openings" during which time commercial fishing may take place. Sometimes the openings are only a day or two long depending on the size of the run.

Despite these restrictions, fishermen continue to acquire bigger boats and better equipment, each hoping to net a greater share of the catch during these openings. Since 1975, British Columbia's commercial fishermen have invested $500 million to upgrade the fleet without any increase in the total harvest.

Competition for the Fish

Competition has increased among the different groups scrambling for dwindling fish stocks. These groups include commercial fishermen, recreational fishermen (in both saltwater and freshwater), and Native people fishing to obtain food for their families.

In the commercial fishery alone, gillnetters, seiners and trollers compete among themselves for the salmon catch. Sport fishing has grown to the point where there is as much money invested in the charter vessels and private boats of the sport fishing fleet as there is in the commercial fishing fleet. Sport fishermen particularly favor chinook and coho, and in the Strait of Georgia they take more of these two species than commercial fishermen.

While workers in the commercial fishing industry may resent fish taken by recreational users, sport fishermen answer that recreational fishing is an important attraction for the tourist industry. Recreational fishermen spend money on boats, tackle, moorage and other services.

A Different Future?

Some people suggest that the good old days of the fishing industry are gone. They say it is no longer realistic for fishermen to scramble among the fishing areas competing for the available fish and gambling on the occasional big catch. One alternative would be to give fishermen quotas—to guarantee them harvest rights to a certain number of fish but not allow them to catch more than their quotas.

However, such a quota system would be very difficult to set up. Another alternative would be to catch all salmon stocks with traps or nets at the mouths of the more productive streams. Fish managers could then ensure the required number of fish were allowed upstream before letting fishermen harvest the rest. Weak runs could be protected altogether. Fishermen would not need all their expensive technology and gear. However, such a plan is unlikely to appeal to most of today's commercial fishermen, to whom fishing the sea is a way of life.

Another alternative would have fishermen switch from being hunters to being ranchers or farmers of the sea. Ocean ranching is already practiced in areas of the United States. It involves rearing

Thousands of salmon fry can be kept in a very small space until they are ready to be released into larger tanks. The survival rate of salmon in fish farming operations is as high as 85 percent.

young salmon in a hatchery, letting the fish range in the ocean for several years, then harvesting the adults when they return. Ocean ranching is not currently being practiced on a commercial basis in British Columbia.

Ocean farming (or mariculture) differs from ocean ranching in that the fish raised are never set loose to mingle with wild stocks. When the fish are ready for saltwater life, they are put into huge net pens in a sheltered bay or cove. There, they are fed and pampered until they are large enough to be marketed. An advantage is that they can be harvested year round, ensuring a reliable supply for restaurants and other customers.

In other parts of the world salmon farming is well-established. Norwegians have been farming Atlantic salmon for more than twenty years. Their harvest now exceeds British Columbia's entire commercial salmon catch. British Columbia, like Norway, has ideal conditions for salmon farming–sheltered inlets and bays along with cool, nutrient-rich waters. Recently, there was a surge of interest in salmon farming in British Columbia. By 1984, thirty salmon farms were in operation along the British Columbia coast, most raising chinook and coho. The fish farmers included Native bands, former commercial fishermen and other private entrepreneurs. Salmon farming remains a risky business, because much remains to be learned about fish diet and diseases. However, some fishing industry analysts feel it has more potential, in the long run, than harvesting wild fish.

Change is inevitable if the Pacific fishery is to survive. Fisheries managers must take strong measures to prevent overfishing, to stem further damage to fish habitat, and to restore runs that have suffered from past misuse. For the fishing industry, as well as other users of the resource, this may mean painful losses and adjustments. It may mean new regulations, reduced incomes, and changes to traditional lifestyles.

Such changes are necessary to bring back the bountiful harvests of the past. Only then will the people of British Columbia benefit from the full potential of one of the world's most valuable fish resources.

1. What are the potential benefits of fish farming? What risks would a would-be fish farmer face?
2. Who, in your opinion, should pay for the costs of managing and protecting British Columbia's fisheries? the Federal government? the provincial government? the commercial and sports fishermen themselves? Why?

Case Study: On Board a Purse Seiner

Four metre swells in the Strait of Juan de Fuca pitch and roll Bobby Sam's fourteen metre purse seiner like a rodeo cowboy's horse. But experienced fishermen like Bobby Sam, his sons Tom and Charlie, and his nephew Ray Alphonse do not seem worried as they move slowly through the churning waters. (These are fictional characters, based on real fishermen.) Behind Bobby, attached to the aluminum bulkhead of the fishboat, is a small, carved cedar model of a North West Coast Native canoe. It is there as a reminder to Bobby that he is still making his living from the fishery, much as his ancestors did hundreds of years ago. But the methods have changed.

On the bridge of the purse seiner, Bobby is watching the radar closely. Dense fog has reduced visibility to near zero. He knows that there are fifteen to twenty other seiners out there. All are looking for the same thing, a "big set" (net load) of sockeye salmon. Out there, too, is the fisheries patrol vessel *Tanu*. It is monitoring the activities of the fishing fleet and checking on the size of the catch. The vessel's radio is on, tuned to the marine weather reports. These reports can mean life or death to Pacific coast fishermen.

The time is the summer of 1985. Bobby Sam and his crew are going after their share of the largest sockeye salmon run since 1913. The fishermen know that this year's run is much better than others

How does a purse seine net work?

in recent years. The Department of Fisheries and Oceans has been tracking the sockeye and other salmon species for many months.

Based on the data, Fisheries officials had set a quota of 9 million sockeye salmon as the maximum allowable catch for the commercial fishing fleet. Soon after the 1985 sockeye season opened, one big set after another was hauled aboard fishing vessels. Fisheries officials soon realized that the salmon supply for 1985 was going to be much larger than they had expected. Therefore, they increased the quota to 13 million, the largest in seventy-two years. Bobby is hoping that he will soon come across one of the "big sets." Yesterday, the sets were disappointing, averaging fewer than 100 fish each time the huge net was drawn in. Over the radio, he and his crew have been hearing of boats hauling in as many as 2000 sockeye in a single set.

A good catch this year is very important to Bobby Sam and his family. They need a good catch in order to pay off some of the money they owe on the boat. Even with a good down payment, the Sams had to borrow nearly half of the $175 000 purchase price. Over the past two years, they have barely been able to cover their operating costs and pay the interest on their loan. Fuel costs have been high, but the Sams are happy that the rate of interest on their loan has remained relatively stable.

Ray Alphonse is sitting in a small aluminum skiff, bobbing up and down in the churning sea alongside his uncle's boat. Tom and Charlie Sam are working to play out the seine net from the huge drum mounted on the afterdeck of the fishboat. Charlie passes one end of the net to Ray, who then revs up the outboard on the skiff and heads out to sea pulling the net. Ray follows a circular course just over 100 metres in diameter, returning the end of the net to Charlie and Tom. A tight pull of the line closes the bottom of the huge, hanging, nylon net, as if drawing the strings of a purse.

Electric winches slowly turn the drum, winding in the net. As the three crewmen guide the heavy, wet net onto the drum, they hear the winches straining against the resistance of their heavy load. The crew eagerly watch as the net rolls in. Is this the big set they have been waiting for?

Thirty minutes later, Bobby Sam and his crew have their answer. Hundreds of shining silver sockeye have been slapped down onto the aluminum decks of the seiner. Quickly, the crew sends their catch sliding down into icy sea water in the vessel's storage holds. The set is a large one. More than one thousand sockeye are hauled in. Bobby and the crew share a quick coffee in the wheelhouse, then get ready to run out the net again. Depending on the weather and the size of the sets, Bobby's crew will repeat this procedure from eight to twelve times each day during the period the sockeye run is open.

Bobby hopes each set will be as large or larger than today's first one. At approximately five dollars a fish, it will take many sets this size just to pay for the net, which costs between forty and fifty thousand dollars. The net may not even last a season. Bobby also has to pay for licence fees, diesel fuel, maintenance repairs and other operating costs of a modern fishing boat. After all of these costs have been met, and payments have been made on the bank loan, Bobby shares the profits of the sockeye run with his sons and nephew. They have to support themselves and their families for the whole year with these profits. Unemployment Insurance helps in years when the catch is poor, but the fishermen would rather earn their living from the sea. Today, with a good set already on board, Bobby feels confident that this will be a profitable season. Next year, however, may be a different story.

1. If Bobby Sam's interest payments are $2000 a month, his operating costs for the fishing season $5000 and his annual repair and maintenance costs $50 000, how many sockeye (at $5 each) would he and his crew have to catch in order to break even?

REVIEW

Checking Back

1. Compare the Native fishery and the fishery of modern times. Organize your findings in a table form with these headings: Fish Types Caught, Methods Used, Preservation Methods.

2. Of the 20 000 people employed by the fishing industry, 17 000 work on the boats and 3000 work in processing. In addition to these direct jobs, what are some of the indirect, spin-off jobs that are generated by the fishing industry?

Using Your Knowledge

3. Describe how each of these improvements has benefited the fishing industry.
   (a) refrigeration units on board boats
   (b) mechanization of nethandling equipment
   (c) electronic equipment such as sonars and radios

4. Summarize the roles of the federal and provincial governments in the fishery.

5. "Fish are a difficult resource to protect."
   (a) Give examples of problems that make it difficult to manage the fish stocks.
   (b) Suggest some methods that could be tried to protect the fish resource.

Chapter 19

The Agricultural Industry

When you eat a hamburger, do you think about where the meat comes from? the cheese? the bun? When you have fresh fruit with your lunch, do you know who grew it and where it was grown? When you have a glass of milk, a piece of cheese or a dish of ice cream, do you stop to think about the source of these dairy products?

Even though we cannot live without food, most Canadians tend to take it for granted. We enjoy a wide choice of things to eat, buying our food from supermarkets, grocery stores, restaurants and fast-food outlets. If we stop to think about food at all, we are likely to think about where we get it and, perhaps, the price or quality of the food we get there. Few of us think about the source of that food–the farm–and the things that affect the price or quality of food we consume in Canada.

Our lack of knowledge about farming is not surprising. Less than 3 percent of Canada's population live on farms. A century ago, things were very different. Many Canadians lived on farms, growing food for themselves and for the people who lived in the few urban centres of that time. The farms provided city dwellers with fresh meat, dairy products, grain, vegetables and fruit. Much of the food was bought directly from the farmers on market day.

Changes in agricultural technology, in transportation systems and in settlement patterns have dramatically changed Canada's agricultural industry since the days of the early pioneer farmers. In this chapter, we will look at the changing role of agriculture in British Columbia since the first European settlers arrived in the 1800s. Then, we will examine the importance and impact of farming in the province's economy today. As well, we will study some of the current issues and problems facing British Columbia's agricultural industry. As you read through this chapter, keep the following questions in mind:

- Who were British Columbia's first farmers? Where were their farms located?
- How did changing transportation and settlement patterns affect the distribution of agriculture in British Columbia?
- How do government regulations affect farming in British Columbia?

About what percentage of the province is suitable for farming?

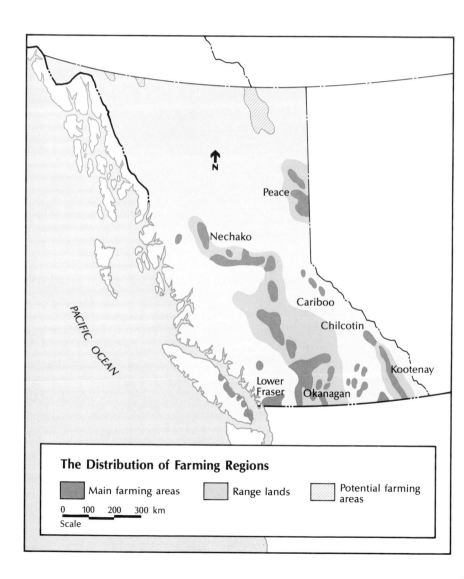

The Distribution of Farming Regions

Main farming areas   Range lands   Potential farming areas

0   100   200   300 km
Scale

The History of Agriculture in British Columbia

Farming in British Columbia began with the arrival of the European fur traders in the early 1800s. The Native peoples of this part of Canada were not farmers. Instead, they hunted and gathered their food from the forests and waters of the area. At first, the fur traders brought their food with them or traded with the Natives for food supplies. However, the establishment of permanent trading posts at places such as Fort Langley and Fort Victoria was quickly followed by the clearing of land and the planting of crops.

As you learned in Chapter 9, the policy of the Hudson's Bay Company discouraged farming activities in the lands where it traded for furs. However, the Company itself ran small farms near its forts to supply the traders. The amount of land under cultivation increased as traders retired from the Company and settled in the area, establishing farms of their own. Other settlers joined the former Hudson's Bay Company men. Most settled in the Fraser Valley near Fort Langley, attracted both by the rich soil and the market created by the gold miners. Still others cleared land and established their farms on the fertile Saanich Peninsula, north of Victoria.

Clearing the land for farming was a formidable task. An area was first burned-over to clear branches and undergrowth. Then the trunks of trees were cut down and the stumps blown out with dynamite.

381

Agriculture was slow to develop in British Columbia for several reasons. The permanent population was small, and export markets were limited. Areas of good agricultural land were few and often isolated so transportation was a problem. The costs of clearing and maintaining farms were higher than in other regions of Canada. When agricultural activity was finally established in British Columbia, the province's farmers faced stiff competition from already productive agricultural areas of Canada and the United States.

The gold rush of the mid-1800s gave the farming industry its first real boost. As miners flooded into the interior of the province, cattle ranches were established in the Thompson, Okanagan and Nicola valleys. At first, transportation from the interior to the coast was poor. Cattle were driven along narrow dirt trails from Lillooet to the head of Harrison Lake, then shipped by boat to New Westminster. Wagon roads constructed during the 1880s and 1890s connecting isolated areas of the interior to the CPR and the Cariboo Wagon Road helped the industry flourish.

The completion of the transcontinental railway spurred agriculture by attracting more people and industry to the province. Further railroad construction in the 1920s opened up the Peace River country, the last major agricultural region in British Columbia. At the same time, new rail links encouraged pioneer settlement in the Bulkley and Nechako valleys west of Prince George.

Improvements in transportation were not entirely beneficial as they increased the competition British Columbia farmers faced from the Prairies and from south of the border. By 1905, despite the increasing number of orchards in the Okanagan and the growing number of dairy and vegetable farms in the Fraser Valley and Saanich Peninsula regions, British Columbia was still a net importer of agricultural products.

To try to improve their output and to minimize competition, British Columbia growers have adopted **specialized farming.** Rather than raising a variety of crops and animals they concentrate on one or two products best suited to the particular region.

In many cases, farming has become more **intensive,** so that each unit of land produces in greater and greater abundance. Vegetables, fruit, eggs and poultry are examples of products farmed intensively. Irrigation, fertilizers and new growing techniques have been used to increase the yield obtained from each hectare of land. This intensive use of the land has been encouraged by high land prices, particularly in the Lower Mainland and Okanagan areas. **Extensive farming,** using large areas of land, is still practised in the cattle

High yields from small areas are possible with the proper techniques. The land needs to be heavily fertilized to avoid loss of fertility. Strawberries are farmed intensively in the Fraser Valley.

Ranching is an example of extensive farming. This photograph was taken in the Kamloops area.

grazing areas of the Cariboo and the grain producing plateaus of the Peace River country.

As a result of the changes in farming, it is difficult for new farmers to set up an operation with a limited amount of money. Instead farming has become "agri-business," an occupation in which people need a lot of money to get started. Here is how one early farmer sums up the changes:

This big machinery, big farms, and big operations, this means that the small man has not a chance in the wide world to ever get into business himself. If he does, he's either got to go head and ears into debt so far that he can make an awful amount of money one year, or he goes broke. Way back years ago, people would have one, two horses, a couple of cows, a couple of sheep, and a sow and a few hens, and that would be the full stock they'd have to start off on a farm. And you could go and work for a couple of years and you could own it. But now you couldn't start, if you worked out for twenty years, you couldn't earn enough to start farming.

[Excerpt from *Remembering the Farm* by Allan Anderson.]

Farming has also become more complex and scientific. Farmers use chemicals to control pests, nutrients to fertilize the soil and nourish livestock, and sophisticated machinery to do work formerly done by hand. While they have to know a lot themselves, they sometimes have to rely on veterinarians to cure sick animals, on skilled mechanics to repair machinery and on accountants to prepare income tax returns.

Modern farmers still encounter emergencies such as hailstorms, early frosts and insects. Farming has not become a secure occupation with a guaranteed income, even if there are now programs such as crop insurance to tide farmers over the worst disasters. For many farmers, however, farming is still a way of life they would never trade for a nine-to-five job.

It is a mistake to think of farming as a relaxed way of life. It is a highly competitive industry that makes a significant contribution to the British Columbia economy. In the next section we will take a closer look at the industry's importance and impact on British Columbia today.

1. In two or three sentences, describe the role played by Hudson's Bay Company workers in starting agriculture in British Columbia.
2. By giving examples from the early days of British Columbia, show how farming followed settlement rather than preceded it.
3. Compare "intensive" and "extensive" agriculture using these headings: amount of land used, crops produced, equipment needed, problems.
4. In several sentences compare agribusiness to the traditional family farm operation.

Importance and Impact of Agriculture

"Farming–it's everybody's bread and butter." That slogan is used by the British Columbia agriculture industry to stress the importance of agriculture in our daily lives. Although the industry is ranked fourth in the province in terms of revenue (after forestry, mining and tourism), its importance cannot be adequately measured just in dollars and cents. We simply could not live without food.

Fifty-five percent of the food consumed in British Columbia is produced in the province. Eighty-five percent of eggs, 46 percent of red meat and 40 percent of the vegetables eaten by residents are produced by residents. Much of the tree fruits, berries, milk, poultry and honey that the people of British Columbia consume comes from the province's farms.

Below is a quick summary of the agricultural scene in each of the five agricultural areas of British Columbia.

South Coastal Agricultural Area

- This area has a warm coastal climate and extremely fertile soil along the Fraser Valley. It is close to processing facilities and large markets such as Vancouver and Victoria.
- This is the most productive and intensive agricultural area of British Columbia.
- Farming activity, in order of importance, is dairy, poultry, vegetable and berry crops, and beef production.
- The average farm size is small–only fifteen hectares (provincial average is 126 ha).

  1. Why would farms in this area be smaller than the provincial average?
  2. Why does this area have the largest dairy herd in the province?

Picking raspberries

Okanagan-Kootenay Agricultural Area

- Farming takes place in the river valleys of this mountainous area.
- The major sources of farm income in the area are fruit and vegetable farming (45 percent), dairy farming (26 percent), and cattle (12 percent).
- The Okanagan is the largest fruit-growing region in Canada and produces 96 percent of British Columbia's tree fruits. It also produces 99 percent of the province's grapes, most of them used to make wine.
- The Kootenay region to the east is primarily cattle country.
- The area has the second largest dairy herd in the province after the lower mainland.
- Irrigation is vital to farming in this area. It is needed to grow winter feed for cattle in the Kootenays, and has allowed the Okanagan to be more intensively farmed than before.

  1. Explain why the lakes in the Okanagan Valley are important to the agricultural industry.
  2. The population is growing rapidly in the Okanagan region. How might this affect farming in the region? Name at least one advantage and one disadvantage.

Grape vines in the fall

A cattle drive

Thompson-Cariboo Agricultural Area

- This is a region of mountain ranges and rolling plateaus cut by deep river valleys.
- Cattle ranching is the main form of agriculture. Seventy percent of the area's farm income comes from cattle sales. Forage crops (winter feed for cattle) are grown in meadows and on irrigated land in the valley bottoms.
- In the Cariboo, agricultural researchers have developed a variety of potato that is resistant to disease. It should yield a bigger crop.

1. Why is the average farm size in this area 504 ha, four times the provincial average?
2. Farming in this area is partly limited by the distance to large markets. Explain how this distance would affect farming.

Combines in the Peace River area

Peace River Agricultural Area

- The terrain in this area ranges from rugged mountain slopes in the west to prairie grasslands in the east. Most of the farming takes place south of Fort St. John between the Rocky Mountain foothills and the Alberta border.
- The area produces more than 86 percent of the province's grain. It also produces more forage, canola (used for cooking oil) and honey than any other area in British Columbia.
- There is a growing market for honey from the Peace River area. This demand is expected to double in the next twenty years.
- The average farm size in the area is three times the provincial average.

1. Explain how a severe climate and high transportation costs hinder agricultural growth in this area.
2. Despite the large size of farms in this area, farmers spend less than average on maintaining the productivity of their land. Suggest reasons for this.

Central Agricultural Area

- This area is largely mountainous, and contains a variety of climatic conditions.
- It is the largest of the five areas, but its agricultural income is only 5 percent of the British Columbia total.

- Major sources of farm income are beef cattle (44 percent), and dairy products (28 percent).
- More than 80 percent of farmers are involved in beef production in some way. Many of these beef producers run small operations.

   1. Suggest some of the obstacles facing the agricultural industry in this area.
   2. Poultry and egg production account for 5 percent of farm income in this area. All these poultry and eggs are sold within the area. Explain why they would not be transported for sale to other parts of the province.

Mowing alfalfa

Problems and Issues

Shoppers at the check-out counter may groan when their final bill is rung up. But the fact is that Canadians spend a smaller proportion of their incomes on food than people in any other country except the United States. Canadians also spend less now (16-18 percent) than they did thirty years ago (approximately 25 percent). Due to higher production and transportation costs, British Columbia prices are slightly above the Canadian average. Yet for most British Columbia residents, food is relatively plentiful and cheap. This food is, however, neither easy nor cheap to produce, even though the public may be misled by the attractive and abundant displays on the supermarket shelves. All is not peaceful and bountiful out on the farm.

British Columbia farmers face two pressing problems. One is the difficulty of earning a reasonable return on their labor and investment. The other is the loss of farmland to other uses such as urban development. In this section, we will take a closer look at these and other problems that challenge the province's farming community today.

No Way to Get Rich

Today's farms are efficient, and have to be. They are also very expensive to set up, requiring expensive land and a great deal of machinery and equipment. The money required to purchase or start a farm is called capital, and modern farming is "capital-intensive." To raise sufficient capital, most farmers must borrow large sums from banks or other lending institutions. They hope to pay this money back through farm earnings.

Consider the following example. Suppose your family wants to take up farming. A family vegetable farm in the Fraser Valley might cost about $400 000. Perhaps your family has $100 000 to put towards this farm. You will then have to borrow the remaining $300 000 and pay interest on that debt each year. If interest rates are 10 percent (and often they rise much higher), your family will be paying $30 000 in interest charges each year. This amount does not even begin paying off the original $300 000 loan.

In addition to paying these interest charges, your family will have heavy operating costs to pay, including expenses such as fertilizer, labor, fuel and machinery repairs. You may find you need to take out another loan to meet these operating expenses. Obviously, your farm will have to be very productive and profitable to carry such an enormous debt load.

Your farm will likely have good years and poor years. Factors such as weather and diseases will vary the yield you can expect from your farm. The cost of fuel or feed will also vary, affecting your operating costs. Market prices will go up and down according to customer demand and competition from other growers. The return you can expect for your produce will go up and down accordingly. Some farming operations are extremely profitable, but many farmers are deeply in debt. They are hard pressed to get enough return from their farms to pay the interest charges. When interest rates rise, the problem becomes even more acute.

Various programs are in place to assist farmers financially. Crop insurance covers production costs in the event of major crop failures, but it does not cover all the income that the crop would have produced. Provincial government programs compensate farmers in years when market prices drop drastically. Farmers themselves have established marketing boards to regulate the marketing of certain products such as eggs and poultry. Some boards negotiate prices for the farmers, getting a better deal than individual farmers could get on their own. Some boards manage the supply of a product. They set quotas on the amount of goods each farmer may produce, making sure prices do not drop because of surplus production. In general, marketing boards try to give farmers a better, more stable price for their goods. While at first glance consumers seem to pay higher prices for food than they would in a free market situation, they do not have to subsidize products that are supported by marketing boards. They are also assured of a supply at relatively stable prices.

These and other programs help farmers, perhaps easing them

In spite of the most advanced technology and real effort, agriculture is still a risky business. Good yields and high quality crops cannot be absolutely guaranteed.

through the worst years. Still, the fact remains that farming is no easy way to earn a living.

1. Identify three factors outside the farmer's control that can affect his/her income.
2. Discuss the merits of marketing boards. Should farmers have to be more competitive in the marketplace?

Creeping Concrete

In mountainous British Columbia, less than 5 percent of the land is suitable for agriculture. Yet that arable land is also in great demand for housing, highways, railroads, pipeline rights of way, tree farms, airports, and any number of other uses. Some of it lies in valley bottoms that could be flooded by hydro-electric projects. Before 1972, British Columbia was losing 4000-6000 ha of farmland to other uses each year. Most of it was in the lower Fraser and Okanagan valleys, areas with particularly rich agricultural land. At this time, British Columbia was importing 65 percent of its food needs.

What messages does this cartoon give to the reader?

"...so, you are the new shepherd!..."

In 1972, the provincial government established the Agricultural Land Reserve (ALR) to control the takeover of British Columbia's fertile valleys by urban uses of the land. The most productive, or potentially productive, agricultural land was identified and included in the ALR, and could not easily be converted to other uses. Nevertheless, there is still great pressure on existing farmland, particularly land adjacent to urban centres.

Here is how a parcel of farmland not in the land reserve might be lost to urban sprawl. Suppose a city is located, as most of our cities are, in the middle of a prime agricultural area. Over time, the city gradually extends its boundaries. In addition, suburban communities spring up in the surrounding countryside. Where suburbia rubs shoulders with surrounding farms, conflicts may arise.

Suburban residents turn their noses up at manure smells wafting into their neighborhood, complain about farm noise, and object to the use of chemical fertilizers and pesticides. For their part, farmers must cope with rising land prices, vandalism, trespassing and people stealing produce from the fields. The suburban dwellers want improved street lighting or sewers. The farmers are forced to pay through taxes their share of these new services they really do not always need or want. The farm supply depot, where the farmer buys feed and fertilizer, is replaced by a shopping mall serving the increased suburban population. At this stage, farmers may sell their land to a real estate developer. They have already discovered they can get more money by selling their land than by farming it.

1. What does a community gain when farmland is converted to urban uses? What does it lose?
2. How does the loss of farmland affect the quality of life in a community or society?

Other Problems and Issues

Another issue concerning the public is the use of chemical pesticides to protect crops. The pesticides kill the insects that blemish produce, reduce yields or even cause total crop failures. When chemical pesticides and fertilizers were developed after World War II, they were considered a major technological breakthrough. Later, people began to worry about the effects of these chemicals.

Once hailed as the solution to global insect problems, the chemical pesticide DDT was banned in Canada in 1971. Today, government regulations restrict and control the use of potentially danger-ous pesticides. Also, these petroleum-based pesticides have become more expensive. As a result, alternative techniques of pest control are being developed. Biological controls use non-harmful predators to keep the harmful pests in check. To control mites, for instance, Okanagan orchard growers have encouraged the activities of another non-harmful mite that eats the harmful one. Physical con-trols include rotating crops from one field to another in successive years. Insects that attack only specific crops then have no chance to become established.

Many agricultural researchers today are promoting a technique called integrated pest management. This technique uses a variety of biological, physical and chemical controls. For instance, a plant called knapweed is a problem throughout large areas of British Columbia's rangeland. It competes with grass yet is not a useful food source for animals. A chemical spray called Tordon can be used to control knapweed. However, Tordon is too expensive to use throughout the entire area. Regulations restrict its use near streams and in other sensitive areas, so ranchers use a biological control as well. They release a species of fly that can reduce the growth of knapweed by up to 95 percent. The flies lay eggs in the grassland and the hatching larvae eat the knapweed seeds. They do not damage grass. By using these flies, ranchers can reduce the amount of Tordon they need.

Control of pests is a major con-cern for farmers. Our society has come to expect high quality pro-ducts, and these can only be pro-duced through the control of insects and diseases.

For the present the agricultural industry still relies on chemical fertilizers and pesticides to produce its goods. But the trend is to minimize their use and treat them with more caution. Even if it acknowledges the need for safety controls, the industry feels frus-trated that some pesticides have been banned while new ones take a long time to be approved for use in Canada. On the other hand, the public is becoming increasingly alarmed by possible health hazards associated with these chemicals. The debate for and against chemi-cal pesticides is bound to continue.

A further problem confronting some farmers involves pests of a larger variety: ducks and geese destroy cauliflower crops, deer nibble on tender fruit buds, elk feed on haystacks and rangeland, wolves and coyotes harass or kill cattle and sheep. The industry estimates that damage due to wildlife costs farmers as much as $2 million per year. In some instances, wildlife has actually been introduced into an agricultural area, or received protection to boost their numbers. In the Fraser Valley, for instance, large wetland areas adjacent to farmland have been set aside as waterfowl habitat. The

The Okanagan Valley

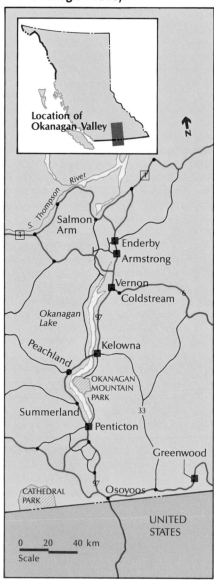

Communities in the Okanagan area.

needs of farmers often run contrary to the objectives of wildlife enthusiasts.

1. In what ways has the chemical industry helped farmers deal with some of their problems?
2. Suggest reasons why integrated pest management techniques would be more beneficial than other methods of pest control.

Case Study: An Apple Orchard in the Okanagan

Sandra Thompson (a fictitious person) owns and operates a small apple orchard near Oliver, a small town south of Penticton. Sandra is in her mid-forties, with two children. She has been growing apples for just ten years. Sandra used to live in Vancouver and was the manager of an insurance agency when she decided to leave the city and try farming.

Why did Sandra choose to take up farming? "I wanted a change of pace," she says. "I was getting tired of the rat race in the city. My job was a well-paid one, but I had to put up with a lot of stress and frustration to earn my pay cheque. My working world was defined by the four walls of the office. I sat at my desk all day. The only exercise I got was a short walk to the photocopier."

Being a single parent played a part in Sandra's decision to try farming. "My children rarely saw me. They spent most of the day in school or daycare. In the evenings and on the weekends I was too tired to spend much time with them. And, I was worried about the problems they might face growing up in the city."

One day, Sandra decided to move from Vancouver to the Okanagan Valley. "I was sitting at my desk, under a flickering fluorescent light, breathing in second-hand smoke, when I said 'that's it!'. I want to live and work in fresh air and sunshine." At first, Sandra considered taking an office job in Kelowna or Penticton but decided that really would not be much of a change. She decided to try farming.

"I was really naive, ten years ago," laughs Sandra. "I figured that all I had to do was to buy an orchard, make sure that the trees were getting enough water, pick the apples and sell them." When she started looking into the purchase of an orchard, Sandra soon realized that farming would demand that she use all of her business skills, and more.

Working through a real estate agent, Sandra located an apple orchard near Oliver. She and the children visited the farm, and fell in love with the peace and beauty of the location. She decided to buy the orchard. The price agreed upon was $150 000. Sandra had $25 000 in savings; she could get another $50 000 from the sale of her house in Vancouver. The rest of the money would have to be borrowed from the bank.

Sandra quickly discovered that getting a mortgage for a farm was not as simple as it had been when she bought her house. The bank manager in Penticton required her to prepare a comprehensive business plan for the orchard operation. With the help of the local Agriculture Canada offices, Sandra learned about the costs of running an orchard. She soon realized that while the apples grow by themselves, they require a great deal of human help.

Her business plan slowly took shape as she calculated the costs of the machinery, pesticides, labor and new tree stocks she would need to use over the coming year. Sandra also had to show that she was able to get a quota from the Tree Fruit Marketing Board, permitting her to sell enough fruit to meet her operating costs. Finally, the bank required an assessment of the orchard by an agronomist (an agricultural scientist) to ensure that the trees were healthy, the soil of good quality and the water supply adequate. Once it was confirmed that the orchard met all of these requirements, the bank approved the loan. Sandra and her family moved to the Okanagan, ready to begin a new life as apple orchardists.

Just ten hectares in size, Sandra's orchard has 1250 trees. Half the trees produce the popular red B.C. Delicious apple. The rest are divided between McIntoshes and Newtons. Most are sold through the B.C. Tree Fruits Co-Operative, ending up in supermarkets all across North America. Some are sold by Sandra's children at the fruit stand they operate on the road in front of the family's orchard. Naturally, some end up in Sandra's pantry, freezers, cold storage and cider jugs for the family's own use.

Sandra quickly found out that apple-growing is hard work, with tasks to be done at all seasons of the year. The trees require careful tending and must be pruned each year to ensure the fullest possible production of apples from each tree. Insects and other pests can attack the fruit or even the trees themselves. Says Sandra, "I had to learn how to deal with mice, moles and dozens of different insects. Fortunately, I was able to hire a retired fruit farmer to help me on a part-time basis. I've learned a lot from him about the industry and how it's changed since he started in the 1940s. In those days, they

Apples growing in the Okanagan Valley.

lost a lot of apples to pests, frosts and windstorms. Now, we can use chemical sprays and scientific cultivation techniques to protect the crop. Still, the weather can cause problems that technology can't overcome. I've watched the effect that a severe spring frost or an unusually dry winter can have on the crops."

Variations in market demand are also beyond Sandra's control. "Some years I can sell all the apples I can grow; other years the demand is low and so are the prices paid to the growers. I've lost money some years and done well in others. On balance, I'm lucky. I don't owe the banks too much money and I'm still in business."

Sandra has been fortunate. She bought the orchard at a time when interest rates were relatively low and demand for apples strong. By 1980, she had been able to pay off $50 000 of her loan. When an adjoining orchard came up for sale, she seriously considered buying it. After careful consideration, she decided not to. The purchase would mean borrowing more money from the bank. It was a wise decision. Two years later, interest rates skyrocketed, demand for apples dropped, and it was all Sandra could do to make the payments on her original loan. Another neighbor, who had bought the adjoining orchard, had to declare bankruptcy and lost both orchards.

Has Sandra's move to the country from the city been worthwhile? She seems to think so. "It's hard work–the kids and I haven't had a real vacation since we started ten years ago, just a few long weekends down at the coast. I'm not rich, but I'm my own boss–if you ignore the marketing board, that is. I feel a lot better for working outside, happier and healthier. My family has benefited from the change, too. We are much closer and I feel that my kids are more responsible than they would be growing up in the city. Farming for me is now more than a job, it's a way of life."

1. What steps did Sandra have to go through before the bank would lend her money for the purchase of her orchard? In what way did these steps help to protect the bank? How did they help protect Sandra?
2. What skills must a modern farmer have?
3. In your own words, explain what Sandra meant when she said "farming for me is now more than a job, it's a way of life."
4. Explain why many Canadian farmers would rather go deeply into debt and risk bankruptcy than sell the farm and move to the city.

REVIEW

Checking Back
1. Develop a table to compare the five agricultural areas of British Columbia. The names of the regions should be listed down the left-hand side of your page, and the following headings across the top: Climate Characteristics, Principal Crops, Average Farm Size.

2. Agriculture was slow to develop in British Columbia for the following reasons.
   • the permanent population was small
   • good agricultural land was limited
   • the land was difficult to clear
   • competition with other areas was stiff
   • transportation facilities were poor
   For each factor, explain how it helped to restrict development of a strong agricultural industry.

3. In a few sentences, describe the important physical factors that affect agriculture in each part of British Columbia.

Using Your Knowledge
4. Operating a farm is much the same as running a business. Identify three or four ways in which this is so.

5. On page 389, a cartoon shows the Agricultural Land Reserve as a shepherd protecting its flock (agricultural land) from hungry wolves (developers). Draw another cartoon, this time from the perspective of the land developers. How do you think they view the ALR? What is their attitude towards land controls?

Chapter 20

The Tourist Industry

When you and your family or friends plan a holiday trip, what do you consider when choosing a place to visit? Do you look for beautiful scenery, warm sandy beaches, deep powder snow, untouched wilderness, historic sites, museums and art galleries, or lively entertainment? All of these features are attractions that draw tourists to a place.

Do you take into consideration the kinds of transportation available, or the hotels, restaurants and facilities you will find there? These services are important considerations for most tourists choosing a vacation spot.

Often there are several equally tempting places that provide both the attractions and the services you need to make your holiday a success. What other things help you to decide? Do things like cost, security, language or the attitudes of the people play a role in your decision?

Since the 1880s, British Columbia has been a popular tourist destination. Beginning with the arrival of the CPR, tourists from all over the world have found a wide variety of attractions in British Columbia. In response, British Columbians have built a major tourist service industry, one of the province's most important economic activities.

The tourist industry has grown dramatically in importance over the past few decades, and has the potential to develop even more if it is able to attract and serve additional visitors. In this chapter, we will look at the history of this industry, its present importance to the province's economy and some of the problems and issues it faces as it looks to the future. As you read this chapter, put yourself in the place of someone who might be planning a trip to British Columbia. Consider the following key questions:

- What things attracted early tourists to British Columbia?
- What attractions draw tourists to British Columbia today? What kinds of services are made available to them?
- What competition does British Columbia face? What can British Columbians do to compete effectively for tourists?

History of Tourism in British Columbia

The history of the tourist industry in British Columbia can be divided into three periods: the railway years, the automobile age and the modern tourist era. Each is characterized by specific attractions and by the development of new or improved services to meet the needs of tourists.

The Railway Years

Tourism, as an organized industry in British Columbia, began in 1885 with the arrival of the Canadian Pacific Railway. Railway officials began a very effective campaign to attract tourists to western Canada, particularly the Rocky Mountains. They saw this as a way of increasing the number of people using their rail service. Through attractive brochures and testimonials from famous and important people, the railway promoted the great natural beauty of this region. Soon, British Columbia was world famous for its rugged and dramatic mountains and glaciers, its spectacular waterfalls and powerful rivers, its placid lakes and its everchanging coastline.

From the start, William Van Horne, president of the CPR, realized that suitable services would have to be provided for tourists. While the main line through the Rockies was being built, he ordered the construction of a series of hotels and lodges along the rail line. Some, such as the Banff Springs Hotel, the Chateau Lake Louise and Mt. Stephen House, near Field, were luxurious hotels, rivaling the best in Europe. Here, wealthy tourists found not only fine food and lodging, but also hunting and fishing guides to lead trail rides. These services, combined with the striking scenery, were intended to ensure that these early tourists would enjoy their stay, perhaps return in the future, and certainly tell others of the adventures to be had in the "Canadian Pacific Rockies."

CPR officials were quick to realize that the mountains were not the only tourist attractions in British Columbia. The province's location on the Pacific made it an ideal jumping-off point for tourists wanting to visit the Orient. Canadian Pacific luxury liners were soon connecting with the trains, picking up and letting tourists off in ports such as Vancouver and Victoria. In those cities, the CPR also built first-class hotels to serve the tourist trade.

Completion of a second transcontinental railway, the Grand Trunk Western (now the Canadian National Railway), in 1915, gave

The CPR's advertising campaign for tourism in the West was aimed at wealthy people, particularly in Britain. With its fleet of ocean liners and transcontinental rail system, the CPR offered "an all-British route around the world."

rail-borne tourists access to central British Columbia. Visitors could travel to Prince Rupert by rail, then take steamships north along the coast to Alaska or south to Vancouver and Victoria.

1. What two things must be present for a tourist industry to develop? In your own words, explain the importance of each.
2. How did the CPR promote tourism? Why did they do this?

CANADA'S FIRST NATIONAL PARKS

With the building of the CPR, news of the tourist potential of the Rocky Mountains quickly spread to eastern Canada. Several entrepreneurs tried to establish claims to the Banff-Lake Louise area. The government decided not to grant private title to these lands, but instead, to preserve them for the benefit of all Canadians. Canada's first national park was established in 1887. Other mountain wilderness areas along the rail line through British Columbia, including Yoho, Kootenay, Glacier and Mount Revelstoke, were reserved for future national park development during the period of 1887-1895. By 1920, all of these reserves had been turned into national parks.

National Parks located in British Columbia.

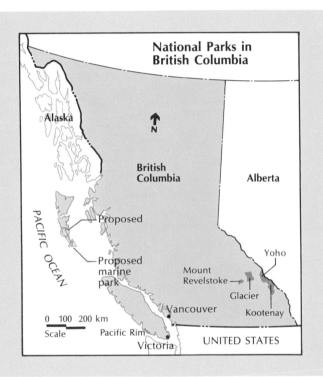

National Parks in British Columbia

The Age of the Automobile

The automobile greatly expanded British Columbia's tourist industry. Motor cars made it possible for almost everyone, not just the wealthy, to explore the province's scenic beauty. Also, tourists could now visit a far greater range of attractions than those served by the railways. These mobile visitors required a new and widespread system of services for themselves and their vehicles.

During this period, the provincial government began to play an increasingly active role in tourism. Expansion of the tourist industry was one of the driving forces behind the growth in the highway system through the province. By the early 1960s, a network of highways, many of them paved, linked all of the regions of British Columbia. This system of highways was connected to the rapidly expanding interstate highway network in the United States and to the Trans-Canada Highway, officially opened in 1962.

In many communities along the highways, motels (MOtor hoTELS), restaurants and automobile repair facilities developed. Car and recreational vehicle rental agencies were established in every major city to serve visitors from overseas who wanted to tour British Columbia by road.

The provincial park system was also expanded and new attractions such as the Bowron Lakes canoe circuit developed. Campgrounds, picnic areas and scenic view points were established along the highways.

BRITISH COLUMBIA'S PROVINCIAL PARKS

British Columbia was the first western province to establish provincial parks. Strathcona Provincial Park, a mountain and lake area on Vancouver Island, was created in 1911. Three other major parks, Mount Robson, Mount Assiniboine and Kokanee Glacier, were set up in the Rocky Mountains along or near the rail lines between 1913 and 1922. The largest of British Columbia's provincial parks, Tweedsmuir in the Coast Range, was set up in 1938. However, the greatest number of provincial parks, campsites and recreation areas have been created since World War II with the expansion of the highway network. Today, British Columbia has more than 45 000 km² of provincial parks (an area just slightly smaller than the province of Nova Scotia), serving more than 12 million visitors each year.

Source: *B.C. Ministry of Tourism*

Some provincial parks in British Columbia.

The early 1970s were boom tourism years. Easier travel and higher incomes contributed to this boom, but society was changing, too. The "work-oriented" society of the post-World War II years was giving way to a more leisure-oriented society. People began to search for a richer, more fulfilling life, often in the form of travel.

With its scenery and fine camping areas, British Columbia benefited from this trend. The rise in gasoline prices that began in 1973 only modestly slowed the growth in tourism. But by the late 1970s, the industry was having problems. Visitors loved the scenery but were complaining about the accommodation, food and prices. They were demanding more in the way of services and facilities. To meet these demands, the province's tourist facilities needed to change.

1. How did the tourist industry respond to changes in transportation technology?
2. Explain why efficient road connections to the United States and eastern Canada are important to British Columbia's tourist industry.

The Modern Era

The provincial government not only continued to promote the industry but also began to plan, fund, and develop new tourist facilities. In 1978, the federal and provincial governments together launched a five year, $50 million program to upgrade tourism in British Columbia. This program, known as the Travel Industry Development Subsidiary Agreement, made funds available to develop tourist facilities such as ski lifts at Whistler and Mount Washington. The federal and provincial governments have also stimulated the industry through projects such as the 1986 world's fair and the Canada Place convention and cruise ship facility in Vancouver.

Most visitors still use cars or recreational vehicles to tour British Columbia. However, in recent years the tourist industry has seen increased demand for packaged tours to specific destinations. These packaged tours are very popular with overseas visitors, but also attract many North American tourists. Among these packages are: helicopter skiing, allowing skiers access to the powder snow conditions high above the tree line; float plane fishing expeditions to remote lakes; and white water river rafting excursions.

Package programs, combined with an increased range of services and high-profile international advertising campaigns, have made

British Columbia's tourist industry very competitive in the world tourism marketplace. In recent years, the declining value of the Canadian dollar relative to other major currencies has increased the tourist industry's ability to compete. So, too, has the increase in political terrorism in other parts of the world which are popular tourist areas, the Mediterranean area in particular. Some economists predict that if these conditions persist, and British Columbians continue to effectively develop their tourist industry, tourism could overtake forestry as the most important producer of wealth in the province. In the next section, we will examine the importance of tourism in the British Columbia economy today.

1. Tourism in the age of the railways was largely limited to the very wealthy. Today, visitors to British Columbia come from all socio-economic groups. What changes since 1885 might account for the increased ability of all Canadians to enjoy tourism?
2. Examine the tourism advertisement. In two or three sentences, summarize the message that is being presented.

Importance and Impact of Tourism

The tourist industry is British Columbia's third-largest revenue producer, exceeded only by the forest and mining industries. In some parts of the province, such as the Okanagan and the city of Victoria, tourism is the major source of revenue.

The industry consists of over 10 000 individual businesses that cater to visitors: from luxury hotels to fishing camps and from transcontinental airlines to taxi companies. It employs about 86 000 people full-time, though during the summer months, its peak season, this figure rises to about 126 000 people in full- or part-time positions.

Because of its seasonal nature, the tourist industry is by itself usually not enough to support a community. However, it provides important extra income in towns dependent on forestry, mining or fishing. The mining town of Fernie in the East Kootenays and forest-based Chemainus on Vancouver Island are two such communities.

Almost 12 million tourists took trips in British Columbia in 1983. Most were vacationers, but some were people attending conventions. The figure also includes the growing number of film crews who have come to British Columbia to shoot television and movie productions.

Effective advertising is the key to promoting tourism.

Tourism Revenues, 1976-1984

1. Assuming the rate of growth stays constant, estimate the revenues for the tourist industry in 1990 and 1995.
2. What factors would account for minor variations in the growth rate, such as the small decline in revenues in 1982?

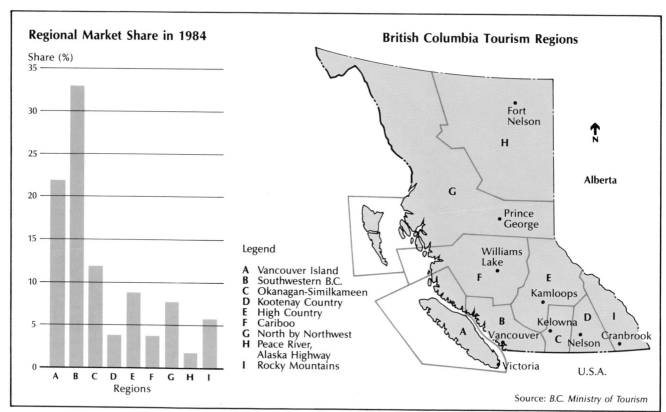

Regional Market Share in 1984

Share (%)

British Columbia Tourism Regions

Legend

A Vancouver Island
B Southwestern B.C.
C Okanagan-Similkameen
D Kootenay Country
E High Country
F Cariboo
G North by Northwest
H Peace River, Alaska Highway
I Rocky Mountains

Source: *B.C. Ministry of Tourism*

1. Two regions account for over half the tourist revenue generated in the province. Which are they? Suggest some reasons why these two regions might account for such high levels of revenue.
2. Which region generates the least tourism revenue? Why might this be? Suggest some ways in which tourism revenue might be increased for this region.
3. In 1984, tourists visiting British Columbia spent an average of $38.00 per day. However, tourists visiting Vancouver Island and Southwestern British Columbia spent more per day than tourists visiting other regions. Give at least two possible reasons why they might spend more in these regions.

---

1. The graph on the right breaks down tourist expenditures into six broad categories. List three tourist businesses that would fall under each of these categories.
2. Many tourists come to British Columbia to stay with friends or relatives. How would that affect the money earned by tourist services?

Where Do Tourists Spend Their Money?

Total Expenditure 1984 — 2.3 Billion Dollars

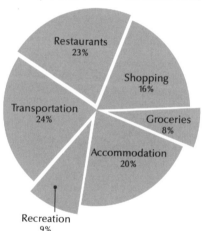

Source: *B.C. Ministry of Tourism*

Problems and Issues

While other British Columbia industries have experienced booms and busts, the tourist industry has seen continuous growth. However, the industry is not without problems or future challenges. Below, you will look at four such challenges: co-ordinated planning and promotion, social and environmental impacts, conflicts with other resource users, and international competition.

Co-ordinated Planning and Promotion

From his roadside ice cream stand in the Okanagan, Joe Thiessen does a roaring business with the hot, thirsty tourists travelling that route during the summer. At a service station on the Alaska Highway, Jenny Mossop pumps gas as she gives tourists advice about the road ahead. On kayak trips off the coast of Vancouver Island, David Yuen acts as a naturalist and guide. At the counter in the main lobby of a large Vancouver hotel, Marion Moriarty checks guests in and out.

The tourist industry is made up of many different people and activities such as these. They form the backbone of the industry, serving the needs of tourists who are enjoying British Columbia's attractions. Although these services are independent operations, each one contributes to or detracts from the overall prosperity of the others. For instance, a new ski development may increase restaurant and motel business in the area. On the other hand, a disappointing camping trip may cause a family to decide not to return to British Columbia the following summer. The restaurant that served the family its meals will not get the return business.

Because so many different services contribute to the tourist industry, it is difficult for them to co-ordinate their planning and promotion. Yet such co-ordination is crucial. For example, government and hotel operators might work together to build a convention centre or to organize an annual festival. These co-operative efforts could attract more visitors in the off-season. Tourist bureaus in different parts of the province might act together in order to divert visitors away from overcrowded areas towards lesser used tourist facilities. By co-ordination of their advertising campaigns, several businesses can target more potential tourists than a single business could do on its own. Different operators along the same scenic route might put out common promotional materials. The resulting business will be shared by all the operators.

1. Explain why it is difficult to co-ordinate tourist activities. What role can the government play in helping the members of the tourist industry work together?

The Social and Environmental Impact

Although tourism brings economic benefits to an area, it has social and environmental liabilities. Imagine this scenario. You like to spend weekends camping and fishing at a lake near your home. Recognizing the potential of this lake, businesses in your community get together to promote the area as a tourist destination. At first you welcome the tourists because they increase business in town. You even get a part-time job pumping gas at a service station. But as the number of tourists increases, you find it impossible to get a weekend camping spot at the lake. More people mean more noise and garbage. You begin to resent the tourists.

As this example shows, tourism can put a strain on the local community. Residents may find themselves in competition with visitors for restaurant tables, tennis courts or service at the post office. This is particularly true of areas of limited space or restricted resources, such as the Gulf Islands and southern Vancouver Island.

The kind of tourist development that takes place in an area is as important as the number of tourists that visit it. These developments sometimes do and sometimes do not respect local traditions. As an example, consider tourist attractions that focus on the cultures of Native peoples. The restored village at 'Ksan, near Hazelton, respects and revives the culture. On the other hand, plans to build a health spa and motel at Spotted Lake in the south Okanagan outraged Native peoples to whom the site is sacred.

The environmental impact of tourism was described as early as 1909 in a guidebook to the Lake Louise area of the Rockies.

Trees are ruthlessly cut down and destroyed by campfires, branches are hacked off for firewood and bedding, the bark is blazed from trees and replaced by a multitude of names of those seeking a misguided notoriety, while the green carpet of grass and beautiful Alpine flowers is changed into a waste of empty cans and broken glass.

[Wilcox, Walter: *A Guidebook to the Lake Louise Region*]

If tourism is not carefully managed, tourists may destroy the very resources they have come to see. They leave garbage or fail to put out their campfires. They disturb wildlife breeding and feeding habits; for example, they sometimes encourage bears to find their food in garbage cans rather than in the wild. Because of their ever increasing numbers, even environmentally sensitive backpackers harm fragile alpine wilderness areas with their trails. An influx of tourists may contribute to overfishing of lakes or depletion of wild game.

When it leads to preservation or rejuvenation of scenic or recreational areas, tourism can have a beneficial effect on the natural environment. An early example is Canada's first national park, Banff, which was set aside in 1885 "to develop the hot springs area and attract visitors to the Canadian West." While Banff is in Alberta, the adjoining areas of British Columbia were subsequently included in the expanded Rocky Mountain Park of Canada, formed in 1887.

However, as outdoor pursuits become more and more popular, park and land-use managers are forced to take protective measures. They must balance the promotion of tourist access to these areas with their preservation from overuse or misuse.

Alpine meadows are fragile environments. They are sensitive to overuse and will quickly become disturbed by thoughtless tourists.

1. Make a list of groups or individuals who should be consulted before a major new tourist development goes ahead.

2. Make two lists, one showing positive aspects of tourism, the other showing harmful effects. Suggest ways the harmful effects can be overcome.

Conflicts with Other Resource Users

The tourist industry competes and sometimes conflicts with other resource users. The industry relies on British Columbia's natural resources to attract visitors to the province, but other resource industries depend just as heavily on these resources. Logging, mining and hydro-electric developments can mar scenic highway views and unspoiled recreation areas. Commercial fishermen compete with recreational anglers. Ski facilities are built in watershed areas and new highways cut through wildlife habitat.

While improving its facilities and services, the tourist industry cannot afford to forget its dependence on British Columbia's natural resources. It is ultimately up to the government to decide how these resources will be used. But in some instances, compromises are possible. For instance, the forest industry has been trying to reduce the unsightly effects of logging in particularly scenic areas.

Landscaping techniques have been used on the forested hillsides along the highway leading to Rogers Pass.

International Competition

In the late 1880s, the president of the Canadian Pacific Railway, William Van Horne, declared, "Since we can't export the scenery, we shall have to import the tourists." British Columbia's tourist industry is still in the business of importing tourists, a business that is becoming increasingly competitive. More than ever, the British Columbia industry must now understand the needs of potential visitors and provide facilities and services to meet those needs.

To identify who these visitors are and will be, tourism researchers first look at population trends and social patterns. In the early 1990s, nearly half the Canadian population will be between twenty-five and forty-four years of age, the prime age for travelling. There will be an increase in the number of retired people over sixty-five years of age, and these retirees will be more active than those of today. Families will tend to be smaller, to have more money, and to spend more time on recreational pursuits. In general, travellers will be more educated and more environmentally aware. Researchers suggest that British Columbia will attract about the same number of tourists from the United States as it does today. However, the province will be attracting more tourists from countries such as Japan, West Germany, Australia and the United Kingdom.

Market researchers suggest that these tourists will want shorter, more active and more meaningful package tour vacations. Rather than just drive through spectacular countryside, these visitors will want to go to a specific destination for a specific purpose. They may go whale watching off the Queen Charlotte Islands or river rafting in the interior of the province. They may fly in for a five-day ski package, or take a two-week cruise from Vancouver to Alaska.

British Columbia has to cater to these special interests in order to maintain or improve its share of the international tourism market. The province's tourist industry must upgrade its infrastructure and improve its marketing strategies. It must develop better products and do a better job of selling them. It must remind itself that while British Columbia's scenery is spectacular, there are other places in the world tourists also find worth visiting.

1. Suggest ways to make British Columbia more attractive for tourists from Europe, Australia and the Asia Pacific region.

Case Study: Marketing B.C.

A Canadian Pacific Airlines flight from Tokyo has just landed at Vancouver International Airport. Among the more than 350 passengers disembarking from the Boeing 747 are four large parties of Japanese tourists. Inside the terminal, each group of fifty or so tourists waits patiently by the baggage carousels for their luggage. Outside, four large tour buses wait for the Japanese visitors. They will use these buses for two days of sightseeing in Vancouver, then travel in them for a ten-day tour of the Rocky Mountains.

As the Japanese tourists watch for their luggage, so does another visitor from Japan. Saiko Uyeyama glances at the tour groups, checking them out with an expert's eye. She has been to Vancouver many times before with similar groups of Japanese tourists on their way to the Canadian Rockies. As well, she has conducted tour groups to many other places, including Europe, Hawaii and California. This time, however, Saiko is in Vancouver on her own. She is here to address a tourism convention and will be giving a talk on effective ways to promote British Columbia as a destination for Japanese travellers.

The next day, Saiko conducts a workshop for advertising executives, government officials and others involved in the promotion of tourism in British Columbia. She begins by telling her audience that Japan's economic growth over the past thirty years has made the Japanese world travellers. Each year, millions of Japanese tourists visit scenic or historic places all over the globe. Of this number, she tells her audience, just over 80 000 came to British Columbia in 1985. The Japanese were the second largest group of overseas visitors to the province in that year. But, it is a small number compared to the hundreds of thousands of Japanese who visit Hawaii and California each year.

"British Columbia could attract many more Japanese visitors," says Saiko, "but you have to sell yourselves better." The province has many sites with great potential for Japanese tourism, she explains, but few of them are well-known in Japan. As a result, Vancouver is for many Japanese visitors little more than a port of entry. From there, they hurry across the province to well-known attractions such as Banff and Jasper in the Rocky Mountains.

Vancouver is a world-class city, states Saiko. "It has many features that make it attractive to Japanese visitors. Vancouver is safe, clean and comfortable. The people and the scenery here make Japanese

Tourists at one of Vancouver's landmarks. Suggest one or two ways of making British Columbia more attractive for tourists from abroad.

visitors feel very much at home." Vancouver has first-class hotels and restaurants, good shops and excellent recreation facilities. All of these things are very appealing to Japanese visitors. So too is the presence of Japanese-speaking employees in many of the major shops and hotels, she explains.

Unfortunately, not enough people in Japan know these things, the Japanese travel expert claims. The problem, she feels, lies in the way that Canada and British Columbia are promoted as tourist destinations. "Your advertising materials often leave an impression that the country is little more than Niagara Falls, the Rocky Mountains and pretty sunsets," Saiko tells her audience. Instead, she recommends that promotional campaigns should focus more on specific places like Vancouver, Victoria or Whistler.

"Take Whistler, for example," she says. "I went there last year with a group of Japanese travel agents. They loved it. The Japanese are great sports and outdoor enthusiasts. Many are avid golfers or skiers. Whistler with its world-class ski slopes, its golf facilities and its spectacular mountain setting has something to offer Japanese tourists all year 'round. And, it has the high quality accommodations we demand when we travel. Yet almost none of those travel specialists had ever heard of Whistler before that visit. To get Japanese tourists there, you'll have to actively promote Whistler itself and what it has to offer, not just lump it in with the rest of the province."

Saiko tells the British Columbians that Japanese are highly desirable tourists. Most are affluent, either young newlyweds on their honeymoons or over the age of fifty. "Japanese tourists in British Columbia tend to stay longer and spend more money here than the average North American visitor," she emphasizes. Many travel in organized groups like the ones that got off the plane with Saiko.

Most Japanese live in crowded cities, she points out. When they travel abroad, they do so in search of open space and scenic beauty. It is this quality that makes British Columbia a potentially attractive destination for Japanese tourists, Saiko explains. "However, there are many other scenic places in the world. Hawaii, Scandinavia, Switzerland and California are all being marketed strongly in Japan right now, and that's where our tourists are going. British Columbia's tourist industry must compete with those places, if it wants to attract more Japanese visitors."

Saiko's address ends with a statement that Expo 86 will be an important event in drawing Japanese visitors to British Columbia in general and to Vancouver in particular. Again, she emphasizes the need to actively promote Expo 86 and what it will have to offer Japanese visitors. In her concluding remarks, Saiko again stresses how much British Columbia has to offer visitors from Japan. "You're sitting on a gold mine," she tells the audience, "but you can't get at the gold unless you start digging."

1. Summarize the qualities which Saiko feels make British Columbia an attractive destination for Japanese tourists. Are they the same qualities that would attract Canadian or American tourists to this province?
2. (a) What are the advantages when a provincial government or tourist bureau promotes specific destinations such as Vancouver, Whistler or Banff?
   (b) What problems might arise from such promotion?
   (c) Which do you think would be more effective, promotion of the province as a whole or promotion of specific destinations?
3. In your opinion, what kinds of tourists should British Columbia seek to attract, and what kinds of attractions should it promote? Should it try to attract more visitors from Japan and other overseas markets, or should it concentrate on promoting the province's tourist attractions to its traditional North American markets? Give your reasons.

REVIEW

Checking Back
1. Develop a time line to show the history of the tourist industry. These events should be included on your diagram.
   • completion of the CPR
   • establishment of the first national park
   • opening of the Trans-Canada Highway
   • 1986 World's Fair
   What other dates and events can you add? Make your time line as complete as possible.

Using Your Knowledge
2. Two promotion advertisements for tourism appear in this chapter. One was used in the late 1800s (page 397) and the second in 1986 (page 401). Compare these two ads by identifying
   (a) the target audience.
   (b) the natural features being promoted.
   (c) the tourist facilities suggested.
   (d) the "message" of the advertisement.

3. Make up a list of twenty jobs that are directly tied to the tourist industry. Organize your list into these groups: transportation-related, food services, accommodation-related, promotion-related, other. Which group do you think likely generates the most income for the province?

Chapter 21

Vancouver: Port City

Vancouver is British Columbia's largest city and the centre of the province's economic, social and cultural life. One of the largest port cities on the Pacific, many people and products enter or leave Canada via Vancouver each year. Connected to the rest of the country by sea, road, rail and air routes, and to all parts of the world by sea and air, Vancouver is truly a "gateway" city.

Since its founding in 1886, Vancouver has been a point of connection between Canada and the nations of the Pacific Rim. With the completion of the Canadian Pacific Railway to the excellent harbor at Vancouver, trains immediately began carrying goods and passengers to and from freighters and liners which served the Pacific Rim. Since then, Vancouver has grown steadily in size and importance to become one of the world's best known and busiest ports.

In this chapter, you will focus on Vancouver's role as a port city and point of connection between Canada and the Pacific Rim. You will consider briefly the history of the Port of Vancouver and examine the importance of the Port of Vancouver to the economies of British Columbia and Canada today. As well, you will look at some of the key issues facing the Port of Vancouver as it enters its second century as Canada's gateway to the Pacific.

Keep the following questions in mind as you work through this chapter:

- What advantages did Burrard Inlet have that led to the building of the western terminus of the Canadian Pacific Railway there in 1886?
- What role has Vancouver played in trade between Canada and the nations of the Pacific Rim?
- How have changes in transportation technology over the past century affected Vancouver's role as a port of entry?

History of the Port of Vancouver

The history of Vancouver as a port city may be divided into four major periods: the pioneer days, the early days of transpacific trade, the expansion years and the establishment of modern, specialized port facilities. Each of these stages in Vancouver's development has shaped the economy of the city, its urban structure and its population patterns.

The Pioneer Days: 1858-1885

At the time of the British Columbia gold rush of 1858, the only settlements on the shores of Burrard Inlet were scattered Native villages. The thick stands of tall Douglas firs and red cedars ringing the inlet soon attracted the attention of settlers in the new colony. These forests contained some of the finest timber to be found anywhere in the world. In 1863, a sawmill was built on the north shore of the inlet. Trees were cut within 100 m of the mill and dragged there by teams of oxen. The following year, Captain Edward Stamp selected a site just east of present-day downtown Vancouver for a major logging and milling operation. Stamp's mill, which went into production in 1867, marked the beginning of large-scale timber exports from Burrard Inlet.

Shipments of Timber from Burrard Inlet	
Year	Number of Shiploads of Timber
1864	1
1865	4
1866	5
1867	15
1868	33
1869	45

By 1869, there were three small settlements on the shores of Burrard Inlet: Moodyville on the North Shore, Granville or "Gastown" clustered around Stamp's mill (also known as Hastings' mill), and, New Brighton, a resort for New Westminster's wealthier citizens. These frontier communities clung close to the water's edge, barely visible against the towering forests behind. Buildings were placed randomly on the landscape and joined by muddy paths. Their residents were a diverse lot: sailors, loggers and merchants

drawn from the United States, Great Britain, and the Canadas. They shared a common goal though: to exploit the rich stands of timber of what was then one of the most remote frontier regions in the world.

Most of the residents did not expect to stay long on the shores of Burrard Inlet. All along the Pacific coast of North America logging settlements would be created, then abandoned when the logs were gone. The loggers would move on to the next inlet where the trees crowded the water's edge, build another settlement, and the cycle would repeat itself. It is likely that this would have been the case at Burrard Inlet before the end of the nineteenth century had not the CPR chosen this great harbor as its western terminus.

1. List the advantages of Burrard Inlet that encouraged the development of a permanent community at that location.

A photo of Gastown, circa 1884. What building materials are most evident? Is this a part of town for the wealthy or working people of the city?

Pioneer Port Community: 1886-1914

In 1886, the CPR main line was extended twenty-five kilometres westward from Port Moody to Burrard Inlet. Here the waters were deeper, permitting larger ships to dock alongside the railway tracks. Even before the extension was completed, the area south of the Inlet was being surveyed and a new city planned. A fire which destroyed much of the city in 1886 made it possible to rebuild along a rigidly surveyed gridwork of streets.

The lumber industry remained the main economic activity in the new city of Vancouver. In the early 1880s, the area's economy had grown by supplying lumber to the railroad builders. After the CPR was completed, the mills found a strong market in the timber-poor Prairies, then undergoing rapid settlement. The fast-growing city of Vancouver itself also provided a market for sawn lumber products. Vancouver's sawmills were able to keep operating despite the depleted state of the local timber resource as steam tugs were used to haul logs down the coast to the mills. New mills were built along the Fraser at Marpole and Fraser Mills and on the shores of False Creek.

Transpacific liner service was established in 1887 and new docks and railyards were built. However, as most of the passengers, mail and imported cargoes of tea, silk and porcelain passed through the port on their way to other parts of North America, lumber remained the principal export commodity throughout the period 1886-1914. During this period, much of the port's growth was caused by increasing coastal shipping.

Vancouver prided itself on being a modern city right from the start: the first electric lights were installed in 1886, the year the city was incorporated. In 1890, an electric streetcar system linked Vancouver to New Westminster, and nearly every store, hotel and many private homes had telephones. By then, Vancouver had an opera house, a roller skating rink and an imposing new railway station for passenger service. Substantial stone and brick commercial and government buildings were being built along streets like Main and Hastings, the heart of Vancouver at this time. In Vancouver's early years, these streets were sometimes paved with planks or wooden blocks; more often than not they were muddy much of the year and dusty when dry. The first asphalt pavement was laid along Cordova Street in 1891 and soon paved streets, sewer systems and water lines were being installed throughout Vancouver.

The first automobile was seen on Vancouver streets in 1899. Vancouver's first gas station was established in 1908 and from that time on motor vehicles played a steadily increasing role in the transportation of goods and services in the port city.

Vancouver's population began to increase significantly after 1905, with 100 000 people coming to the city and surrounding area over the next seven years. Large amounts of available land, combined with effective streetcar and road systems, prevented the city from taking on the crowded appearance of older eastern centres.

New subdivisions were opened up all around the urban core. The expanding city was clearly divided by social class. Vancouver's elite lived in Shaughnessy, a subdivision developed by the CPR, to the south of the city centre. To the east of downtown, working-class

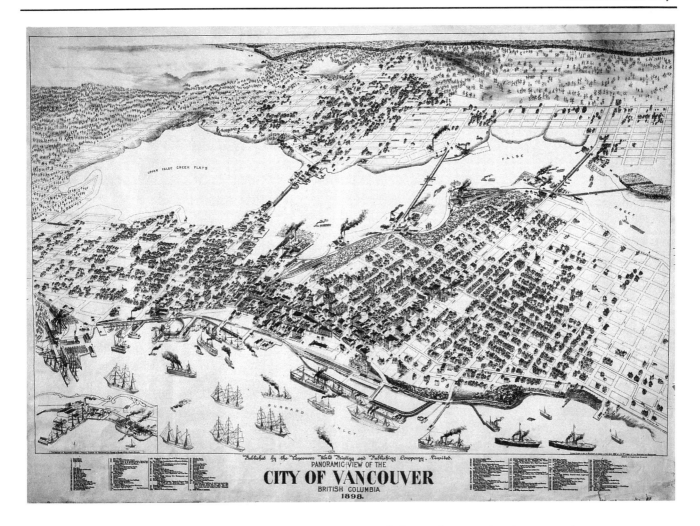

Published by the Vancouver World Printing and Publishing Company, Limited.

PANORAMIC VIEW OF THE

CITY OF VANCOUVER

BRITISH COLUMBIA
1898.

families were able to buy land and build their homes, while to the west, middle-class families occupied homes in such areas as Point Grey, Kerrisdale and Kitsilano. Only the very poor, or transients like loggers and sailors, made their homes in the centre of the city near the docks, warehouses and railway tracks.

What features of Vancouver in 1898 did the artist of this panoramic view emphasize? Describe the pattern shown by the transportation routes in Vancouver. What forces would help create this pattern?

1. What role did technological change play in Vancouver's early development as an industrial seaport?

2. Suggest why only the very poor or transient population of pioneer Vancouver lived near the centre of the city.

Rapid Expansion of the Port: 1915-1945

When the railway came to Burrard Inlet in 1886, investors and speculators saw trade with Asia being the basis for the city's development and growth. Ironically, that growth would occur not as a result of trade with Pacific Rim nations, but because of trade with places on the Atlantic: the opening of the Panama Canal in 1914 created new markets for British Columbia lumber in the eastern United States and Europe. As well, the canal made it cheaper to ship Prairie grain to Europe by sea through the Port of Vancouver than to send it to eastern ports. The first grain elevator in Vancouver was built in 1916, and a decade later, there were seven large grain elevators on the Vancouver waterfront. The Crow's Nest Pass Agreement of 1927 further improved Vancouver's situation by reducing freight rates on westward shipments of grain. The volume of grain shipments through Vancouver elevators was significantly increased as a result. At this time, two-thirds of the grain shipped was destined for European consumers, with only one-third being shipped across the Pacific to Asian markets.

Trading activity in the Port of Vancouver also increased greatly during this period. Ships arriving at Vancouver to pick up loads of grain or lumber would discharge cargoes of goods from Europe and the Pacific Rim. New general cargo piers, warehouses and railyards were constructed during the late 1920s and early 1930s to handle this increase in traffic. As well, the Fraser River was dredged to allow large ocean-going vessels access to the new general cargo dock at New Westminster.

This was also the time when the luxury liners of the CPR's Empress fleet carried large numbers of passengers across the Pacific. Regular service between China, Japan and Vancouver was a featured part of the CPR's comprehensive worldwide travel service. Before World War II, CPR boxcars carried the slogan "Spans the World" on their sides: the Port of Vancouver as a rail and sea transportation centre was a key point in that worldwide system.

1. Use a globe or atlas to determine the shortest distance from Vancouver to each of the following places.
   (a) before the Panama Canal was opened in 1914
   (b) using the Panama Canal route:
   - New York
   - Liverpool
   - Naples
   - Tokyo

2. Was "Spans the World" an appropriate slogan for the CPR during this period? What role did Vancouver play in that transportation system?

Specialization and Diversification: 1945 to the Present

The Port of Vancouver has grown tremendously since the end of World War II, with much of that expansion coming in the form of highly specialized dock operations. Bulk cargo handling is now the major activity of the port. (Commodities shipped in bulk are unfinished or semifinished products such as coal, grain, wood chips and other raw materials.) These facilities usually include storage areas and specialized loading docks, permitting very large vessels to be loaded or unloaded quickly. The coal-loading systems at Neptune Terminals, for example, can handle more than 4000 t per hour. Because of this need for specialized facilities, most bulk cargo terminals handle one commodity exclusively. Only three of the bulk cargo facilities in the Port of Vancouver are designed to handle a variety of commodities.

Examine this map showing the facilities of the Port of Vancouver. What are some problems that are likely to be encountered as a result of this development?

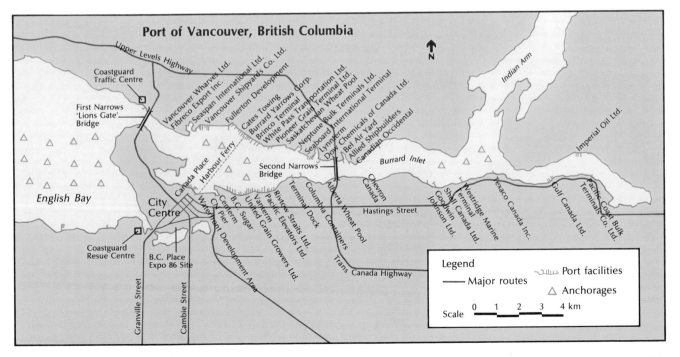

Port of Vancouver, British Columbia

Why is a large storage area necessary for handling a bulk cargo such as sulphur shown here?

The table shows the principal bulk cargoes handled by port facilities. Which products have shown the greatest growth over the time period?

Principal Commodities Moving Through the Port of Vancouver (Thousands of tonnes)

EXPORTS	1980	1981	1982	1983	1984
Grain	7 960	9 093	10 023	10 897	10 887
Coal and Coke	15 002	15 622	15 702	15 717	19 804
Sulphur	5 112	5 515	4 972	4 485	5 558
Lumber	2 467	1 984	2 027	2 074	1 939
Wood Pulp	815	756	796	877	824
Potash	3 448	2 955	2 558	3 206	4 065
Copper Ores	653	718	729	678	720
Fodder and Feed	460	499	523	644	742
IMPORTS					
Raw Sugar	126	80	120	105	100
Phosphate Rock	952	835	725	688	989
Common Salt	401	327	352	290	279
Iron, Steel, Metals	110	171	90	70	75

Source: B.C. Ministry of International Trade and Investment

General cargo facilities handle a wide range of products and commodities, from agricultural products to large industrial machines being imported into and exported from the Port of Vancouver. General cargo facilities such as Centennial and Ballantyne piers have large, covered warehouses where freight can be stored before being loaded onto ships, rail cars or trucks. Cranes and hoists are used to move cargo in slings on and off the ships. Gangs of longshoremen handle the freight, moving it to and from the warehouses with forklift trucks. Railway cars and semitrailer trucks line up at dockside and in the loading areas alongside the warehouse.

In recent years general cargo has increasingly been shipped in containers, large metal boxes that can be loaded onto rail cars or truck trailers directly from ships. Containers have several advantages over older ways of handling general cargo. A large retail store can have a shipment of television sets or other goods loaded directly into a container in Japan and have the container stay locked and sealed until it is unloaded at the store's warehouse. This reduces handling costs, minimizes damage en route, protects the cargo from theft, and greatly speeds up the shipping time.

Vancouver's major container facility is Vanterm. Here, huge lift cranes are used to load and unload the container ships which arrive from around the world. The containers are stacked on the 20 ha site like large multicolored building blocks.

Vancouver is the major port of entry for automobiles imported from Japan and Korea. When the first Japanese automobiles arrived

This is the container facility at Vanterm. What are the advantages of using a container instead of traditional methods when shipping general cargo?

419

in Canada in the 1960s, they were unloaded from freighters by crane at Vancouver's general cargo docks. Today, the number of cars being imported is so great that the Asian car makers own and operate their own specialized **roll-on roll-off** (ro-ro) vessels capable of carrying more than 1000 cars. These vessels require specialized docking facilities and large storage areas for the cars they unload. Some automobiles are unloaded at Vanterm, but most are landed along the Fraser River at facilities such as those located on Annacis Island.

Vancouver has become the hub of the west coast cruise ship service. Before commercial aviation dominated international travel, ocean liners carried passengers to and from Vancouver and ports all around the Pacific Ocean. Today, few people travel by ship, but many people enjoy taking their vacations on luxury cruise ships. These vessels are like floating hotels from which passengers can view the spectacular scenery of the British Columbia coastline. Most of the cruise ship passengers fly into Vancouver, then board their ships for the trip up the coast to Alaska. In the mid-1980s, cruise ship tourists spent an estimated $50 million a year in Vancouver.

1. How have changing patterns of trade between Canada and other parts of the world affected the Port of Vancouver since 1945?
2. What advantages result from the specialization of cargo-handling facilities in a port such as Vancouver? What disadvantages might there be to such specialization?
3. The Port of Vancouver has many direct and indirect benefits for the economy of Greater Vancouver. Make a list of possible indirect benefits such as jobs or services that may arise from port activities.

The Port of Vancouver: Issues

The future looks bright for the Port of Vancouver, especially if Canada is able to maintain its traditional trading patterns while developing stronger trading ties to nations around the Pacific Rim. Improved wharf facilities and new cargo-handling technologies have increased both the capacity and efficiency of the port. As a result, the amount of cargo handled by Vancouver's port facilities should grow despite fluctuations in the Canadian and world economies. Several issues, however, will affect the Port of Vancouver's ability to remain competitive in the years to come.

External Forces Affecting the Port of Vancouver

The role of the Port of Vancouver in British Columbia's economy, like most other aspects of our import-export based economy, will continue to be shaped to a large extent by the world economy. When global industrial output and demand are high, the volume of cargo handled by the Port of Vancouver increases. When grain crops in the Soviet Union or China fall short of those nations' needs, Vancouver's harbor and grain elevators are busy. However, during a worldwide economic recession, or when demand for Canadian grain drops, the volume of business in the Port of Vancouver also declines.

Environmental and Safety Concerns

Port facilities, and the nearby industrial activities they serve, give rise to a variety of environmental and safety concerns. Some of these concerns are largely aesthetic, pitting the beauty and natural features of Vancouver's harbor against the sights, sounds and smells of the industrial activities. Other concerns arise from possible damage to the environment and to the residents of the city by pollution and dangerous cargoes in the port. Many residents of

This area was once a smoky and polluted industrial area of Vancouver's waterfront. Who benefits from the kinds of changes that have taken place here? What social, political or environmental costs arise when industries are relocated away from the heart of the city?

421

Vancouver, particularly those who live near the harbor or along the rail lines leading to the docks, are fearful of the possible results should a cargo of highly toxic or flammable substances be released into the environment. While the transportation industry and various levels of government have developed strict guidelines for the handling of hazardous materials, there are those who feel these cargoes should be handled well away from populated areas.

Much of the future expansion of cargo-handling facilities is likely to take place in the outlying areas because of land costs and related problems. As the City of Vancouver and surrounding suburbs have grown up over the past century, the amount of land available for development has decreased. This may create environmental problems for those areas that have previously experienced little or no industrialization.

1. For the two issues identified in this section, give your opinion on the appropriate role of the federal and provincial governments. Back up your opinion with supporting arguments.

Summary

From its beginnings as a sawmilling and lumber exporting centre, Vancouver has developed into one of the most modern and highly specialized ports on the Pacific. With the completion of the CPR main line in 1886, it became a key link in British Columbia's economic ties to the rest of Canada and to other parts of the world. The opening of the Panama Canal in 1914 also played a key part in the growth of the Port of Vancouver, giving it sea access to the markets of Europe and eastern North America.

Today, Vancouver remains a largely export-oriented port. Its cargo-handling facilities specialize in bulk commodities shipped from the mines, forests and farms of western Canada to consumers all over the world. Japan and the other nations of the Asia-Pacific region also supply many of the imports that enter Canada through this port. Should Canada's trade with the Pacific region continue to grow, the Port of Vancouver will grow with it.

The port facilities of Vancouver dominate the shoreline of the city. These facilities, and the transportation systems that link them to other parts of British Columbia and Canada, have given rise to a number of safety and environmental issues. Other problems with which the port must deal include competition from other west coast ports, such as Seattle; labor and land-use problems resulting from technological change; and problems that arise from increased specialization in cargo handling.

Still, the Port of Vancouver remains a vital transportation hub with the promise of a bright and prosperous future.

REVIEW

Checking Back

1. In this book, the history of the Port of Vancouver has been divided into four periods: 1858-1885, 1886-1914, 1915-1945 and 1945 to the present. Organize the information into a table with these headings: Description of the Community; Important Developments; Exports; Major Markets. In which period of time did the port grow the fastest?

2. Make a table showing advantages and disadvantages of using containers to ship general cargo.

Using Your Knowledge

3. At one time the CPR used the slogan "Spans the World" to get people's attention. In the tourism chapter we see that British Columbia has used "Super, Natural" as its slogan. Make up three slogans that the Port of Vancouver might use to promote itself. What image or features would the port want to highlight in a slogan?

4. Four methods of handling cargo are described in this chapter and are shown as headings in the following table. Make this table in your notes and add twenty more commodities to the list. For each commodity, put a check mark in the column of that transportation method which would likely be least expensive. What types of products are not suitable for shipment by water transportation?

Commodities	Bulk Cargo	General Cargo	Containers	Ro-ro
Raw sugar				
Bicycles				
Light trucks				
Farm machinery				
Social studies textbooks				
..				
..				
..				

5. Many industries benefit from being located on the waterfront of a port. Often, people in a port city want to be located near the waterfront because of its scenic value. Problems arise when these two land uses conflict with each other. Suggest some ways that both industrial and residential uses could use the Port of Vancouver with a minimum of conflict.

Glossary

annexation: to be joined or added to another state.

aristocracy: a titled class of people within a society that inherits both wealth and status.

assimilate: to adopt the customs, values and behavior of another society.

Auto Pact: an automobile trade agreement between Canada and the United States.

autonomy: the right to political freedom.

auxiliary kingdom: the proposal by the leaders of the Great Coalition that the colonies be granted limited independence.

base metals: any of the non-precious metals, such as lead, zinc, and iron.

bilateral: between two nations.

cabinet: an advisory body, appointed by the prime minister. Members are from the majority party and usually have been elected.

Canadian Shield: Canada's largest geographic region. It is made up of ancient weathered rock.

capital: the amount of money or property used to operate a business.

capitalist: a person who invests money or property into a business to make a profit.

Château Clique: the oligarchy that controlled the government of Lower Canada.

chief factor: a manager of a Hudson's Bay Company post.

civil law: the body of law that deals with property and the rights of the individual.

Clergy Reserves: lands, set aside to meet the cost of maintaining a protestant clergy.

commercial timber: stands of trees of value to the forest industry.

Conservatives: members of a political party that opposes radical change and tends to support existing institutions.

constituency: an area represented by an elected member to a legislative body.

constitutional monarchy: a monarchy whose powers are limited by the laws of a state.

consumption: using goods or services to meet needs.

content restrictions: controls that force the consumer to buy goods produced in their home country.

countervailing duty: the use of a tariff to counterbalance an unfair trading relationship.

criminal law: the body of law that deals with crimes against the community.

Crown reserves: one-seventh of all public lands set aside to meet the cost of government.

currency rate: the value, at any given time, of the Canadian dollar as compared to the U.S. dollar.

double majority: the need in the Canadas for the government to have support from Canada West and Canada East, in order to gain a majority in the Assembly.

economic region: an area where communities share common economic activities.

economies of scale: savings in cost that arise from an increase in the rates of production.

ecosystem: the system formed by the interaction of all the living things of a particular environment with one another and with their habitat.

entrepreneur: a person who organizes, manages and accepts the financial risks of a business.

exchange: the trading of goods and services.

executive: the body of government that has the duty and power to put laws into effect.

Executive Council: originally an advisory council appointed by a colony's governor. Under responsible government, the council became responsible to the legislative body.

export: to take out of a country.

extensive farming: the use of a small amount of labor, machinery and fertilizer to farm a relatively large area of land.

Family Compact: name given to the oligarchy that controlled the government of Upper Canada.

federal union: the joining of separate states (or colonies) to form a single nation.

finished product: a product which is ready for consumption.

forest-land alienation: the shrinking of forest lands available for harvesting.

fossil fuels: fuel derived from deposits of ancient plant and animal life.

free port: a port where no taxes or duties are paid.

free trade: the exchange of goods between countries, without payment of duties.

governor: an appointed representative of the Crown sent to oversee a colony.

Great Coalition: the sharing of leadership by Brown, Macdonald, Cartier and Galt in order to break the political deadlock in the Canadas.

Great Plains: a vast area of low, flat or rolling land.

Gross Domestic Product: the total market value of all goods and services produced within a nation over a given time period (usually one year).

import: to bring into a country.

industrial minerals: minerals used in industry.

intensive farming: the use of a great deal of labor, machinery and fertilizer to farm a relatively small area of land.

intermontane plateau: a high and usually level area of land found between mountains.

judiciary: the body of government that has the duty and power to enforce laws.

laissez faire: a system in which business is allowed to operate without government controls.

legislative: the body of government that has the duty and power to make laws.

Legislative Council: the upper chamber in a colonial government.

Liberals: members of a political party that supports moderate progress and reforms.

lieutenant-governor: the crown's representative in Upper Canada. Modern-day official head of a provincial government.

loose fish: elected representatives who are not members of a political party.

martial law: the use of the military to enforce law during a time of emergency.

mechanization: the use of machines, rather than human labor, to complete a task.

mercantilism: an economic system in which a nation depends on its colonies to supply raw materials and markets for manufactured goods.

"middle" class: people between the aristocracy or the very wealthy and the working class.

multilateral: between two or more nations.

muskeg: a boggy area in northern forests.

natural resources: natural materials that are useful or necessary to people.

navvy: a laborer who works on railways, roads, etc.

non-confidence: vote taken in the legislative body that indicates the majority have lost faith in the government's ability to rule.

non-renewable resource: any resource that once depleted cannot be regrown.

non-tariff barriers: methods of controlling imports, without the use of tariffs.

old growth: the vegetation in forest regions that have never been cut for timber.

precious metals: valuable metals, such as gold, silver or platinum.

primary activities: economic activities involved in the harvesting of raw materials.

process: a series of steps in manufacturing.

production: the manufacturing of goods.

provisional government: a temporary government usually established to rule until an officially recognized government can be established.

quota: the limit placed on the amount (of trade).

Radicals: name given to those reformers in Upper and Lower Canada who wanted to establish a republican form of government.

raw materials: all the resources needed to manufacture a product.

reciprocity: a trade agreement based on mutual benefits.

Reformer: a supporter of the movement to bring responsible government to the colonies.

regional disparities: the difference in economic performance between Canada's regions.

representation by population: the use of population figures as a base to determine the number of representatives elected to a legislative body.

republic: a democratic system of government, whose head of state is usually a president.

residual powers: those legislative powers not recorded in the Constitution Act, 1867.

responsible government: a system of government in which the executive must have the confidence of the legislative body.

riding: an area represented by an elected member of either a federal or provincial legislative body.

roll-on roll-off vessels: ships capable of carrying more than 1000 cars.

sawyer: a person whose work is sawing timber.

scrip: a certificate issued to the Métis entitling them to a land grant.

second growth: the vegetation that grows in a region after the forests have been harvested.

secondary activities: economic activities involved in the manufacturing of goods.

sectoral free trade: when some sectors of the economy enjoy free trade, while other sectors do not.

Seigneurs: landowners of New France.

semifinished products: products that are not yet ready for consumption.

service industries: businesses which offer a service to their customers, rather than a product.

silviculture: the science of growing trees.

specialization: concentration on a particular product or activity.

specialized farming: concentrating on one or two agricultural products.

speculator: a person who buys something in the hopes of selling it later at a higher price.

structural material: materials used in construction.

stumpage fees: the costs producers must pay to harvest timber from publicly owned land.

subsidy: a grant or contribution of money.

sustained yield: the management of the forests to ensure that no more wood is cut in a year than can be replaced by new growth.

tariff: duties to be paid on import or export goods.

tertiary activities: economic activities involved in providing services.

Tories: name given to members of Britain's Conservative party. Also used in Canada.

treason: the act of betraying your country.

Whigs: name given to members of Britain's Liberal party. Also used in Canada.

Index

Acknowledgments

Apple and the Apple logo are registered trademarks of Apple Computer, Inc., 273; Australian Tourist Commission, 291; Bob Bierman, 389; Vivien Bowers, 374; Information Services, Media Production Center, British Columbia Ministry of Agriculture and Food, 382, 383, 385, 385, 386, 386, 387, 388, 391, 394; British Columbia Ministry of Energy, Mines and Petroleum Resources, 356; British Columbia Ministry of Forests Photograph, 281; Courtesy of British Columbia and Yukon Chamber of Mines, 343, 343; Excerpts from *Skeena: A River Remembered* by Joan Skogan. Used by permission of British Columbia Packers Limited—1983, 361, 363; Burger King Canada Inc., 273; Excerpt from *The North West Company* by Marjorie Wilkins Campbell, Macmillan, Toronto, 1957, and Douglas & McIntyre, Vancouver, 1983, 124; Canadian Forestry Service, 324, 333; Canadian Pacific Corporate Archives Collection, 200, 397; Canapress Photo Service, 272, 280; Excerpts from *The Life and Times of Sir Alexander Tilloch Galt* by O.D. Skelton. Used by permission of Carleton University Press, 95; Chrysler Canada Limited, 273; CIDA, 308; CIDA/Gary Chapman, 294; CIDA/Dilip Mehta, 297; Coca-Cola Ltd., 273; Commonwealth Holiday Inns of Canada Limited, 273; Excerpts from *Maintain the Right* by Ronald Atkin. Used by permission of Curtis Brown Group Ltd., 190, 205; Department of Fisheries and Oceans/D. Harvey, 370; Department of Fisheries and Oceans/Pacific Region, 376; Department of Regional Industrial Expansion Photo, 408; Excerpts from *Forty Years in Canada, Reminiscenses of the Great North-West* by Sam Steele. Used by permission of Dodd, Mead and Co., 191, 192, 202; Graham Draper, 421; Excerpt from *David Thompson* by James K. Smith. Used by permission of Fitzhenry & Whiteside, 127; Excerpt from *Canada: Growth of a Nation* by Garrod, McFadden and Neering. Used by permission of Fitzhenry & Whiteside, 210; Excerpt from *The Last Best West* by Jean Bruce. Used by permission of Fitzhenry & Whiteside, 214; Glenbow Archives, Calgary, Alberta, 121, 152, 155; Courtesy of Glenbow Museum, Calgary, Alberta, "Dickering with the Factor" by Frank E. Schoonover, 126, "Treaty No. 7" by A.B. Stapleton, 192; Al Harvey/Masterfile, 113; Tim Hendrie, 336; Hudson's Bay Company, 140, 141; Hyundai Auto Canada Inc., 312; Excerpt from *The Firebrand William Lyon Mackenzie Almanac,* used by permission of Irwin Publishing Inc., 35; Courtesy of the Embassy of Japan, 299, 300; Levi Strauss Canada. 273; Library of Congress, 10; Excerpts from *A Source Book of Canadian History,* 3rd ed., by Reid, McNaught and Crowe. Used by permission of Longman's Canada, 56-59, 61, 74; Excerpt from *Remembering the Farm* by Allan Anderson. Copyright © 1977 by Allan Anderson. Used by permission of Macmillan of Canada (A Division of Canada Publishing Corporation), 383; Foote Collection, Manitoba Archives, 244; The Mansell Collection, "Over London by Rail," by Gustave Doré, 24; Excerpt from *Roughing it in the Bush* by Susanna Moodie. Used by permission of The Canadian Publishers, McClelland and Stewart Limited, Toronto, 46; Excerpt from *Woodsmen of the West* by Allerdale Grainger. Used by permission of The Canadian Publishers, McClelland and Stewart Limited, Toronto, 325; Metropolitan Toronto Library (T 16969) 33, (T 16286) 34, (T 15591) 69; Mexican National Tourist Council, 304; Mexico Ministry of Tourism, 304; Excerpt from *Turning the Tide: A New Policy for Canada's Pacific Fisheries*—Cat. #FS23-18/1982E. Reproduced with permission of the Ministry of Supply and Services Canada, 365; The National Gallery of Canada, Ottawa, "Old Parliament Buildings, Ottawa" by Otto R. Jacobi, 83; National Museums of Canada (J-6249) 217; Courtesy New Brunswick Museum, 93 (bottom); Office of the Prime Minister, 311; Excerpt from *John Strachan* by George Spragge. Courtesy of The Ontario Historical Society, 33; Manfred Petz, 109, 406; Port of Vancouver, 251, 418, 419; The Province of British Columbia, 324; Province of British Columbia, Ministry of Tourism, 401; Provincial Archives of British Columbia (2652) 161, (44361) 165, (766) 168, (24288) 170, (4059) 172, (28730) 177, (3579) 180, (70525) 328, (1379) 345, (92108) 362, (29782) 381, (A-1009) 413; Provincial Archives of Manitoba N5730, 148; Picture Division, Public Archives of Canada, Ottawa, (C-12248) "The Death of General Wolfe," by Benjamin West, 4, (C-276) "The Battle of Queenston" by James Dennis, 17, (C-11229) "Quebec Settlers 1848" by Cornelius Krieghoff, 38, (C-18737) "Battle of Ridgeway," 96, (C-85854) "Western Canada—The New Eldorado," 213, (C-518) "Entrance of the Rideau Canal, Bytown, Upper Canada, 1839" by Henry Francis Ainslie, 234; Public Archives Canada (A-197) 6, (C 73435) 27, (C 3305) 32, (A 694) 35, (C 73725) 39, (C 8279) 42, (C 7043) 46, (C 5456) 53, (C 5962) 54, (C 92198) 59, (C 52187) 60, (C 10231) 62, (C 22744) 63, (PA 25465) 64, (C 22325) 75, (C4752) 76, (C 733) 89, (C 6165) 92, (PA 26375) 92, (C 26745) 93, (C 33615) 111, (C-1346) 136, (C-73663) 138, (PA 25397) 174, (C 8549) 199, (C 17430) 208, (C1875) 209, (PA 31489) 242, Public Archives of Canada, National Map Collection, (C 26258) 415; W.J. Topley/Public Archives Canada (C 21290) 84; The Quaker Oats Company of Canada Limited, 271; RCMP Photo, 188; Saskatchewan Tourism and Small Business, 110; SSC—Photocentre—Photo by Harold Clark—75, 270; Stelco Inc., 236; Reprinted with permission—The Toronto Star Syndicate, 265, 277; Toyota Canada Inc., 257; TransCanada Pipelines, 266; Norma Trypis, 295; Courtesy Tumbler Ridge, B.C., 355; Robert Waldock, 239.